Glasgow's Secret Geometry

THE WORLD OF HARRY BELL

Western Geomancy

GLASGOW'S SECRET GEOMETRY

▢ ▢ ▢   LEYLINE PUBLICATIONS, EAST KILBRIDE

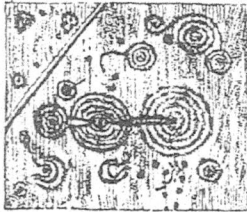

If you're interested at all in the city's past,
why not check out the wonder of the New
Age — the Glasgow Network of Aligned Sites?
It was still in use in St. Mungo's time, but
nowadays millions of people walk over it
unaware of its existence.

It's a miracle it survived. Centuries of housing and industrial
development obliterated surface traces of Glasgow's first settlements; but special sites in this area 4,000 years ago had been
placed in alignment with the surrounding hills. Though these
sites were later built over, we
have been left with a network of
invisible lines that ran between
the sites and can still be
traced through ruined castles,
churchyards and ancient sites in the hidden corners of the
city...it's weird! Once you know the invisible pattern you'll
never see Glasgow the same way again!

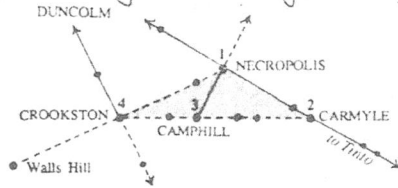

Do you know the wee Travel Centre building in St. Enoch
Square? It's built over one of the sites — in Medieval times
there was a sanctuary and curative well there. Going back
even further, a dugout canoe and a jade axe from the Neolithic
era were found on the site when the subway was being built.

Places like Govan Old Parish Church, Crookston Castle, Provan
Hall and the ruins of Cathcart Castle are all linked to the
Network. Not that these buildings themselves are of any great
antiquity — it's the sites they occupy that are important.

At present there are 19 known sites on the Network inside
the city and over 40 others within a
15-mile radius in East Kilbride,
Paisley, Hamilton, Kilsyth, Renfrew,
Inchinnan, etc. Take your pick — you
can puzzle your skull with
wonders at Saint Conval's Chariot,

admire the view from the Craw Stane, or go walkabout between the Deil's Plantin and the Fort of the Dove. On the map at the back of 'Glasgow's Secret Geometry' there is a gazetter with grid references given to help you find the sites. Grid references are also handy for computer experts who want to run a probabilities check on the Network. Though the Network is invisible, it is also very real.

For confirmation, ask the ley-line buffs who snapped up the first and second editions of 'Glasgow's Secret Geometry.' You often see them walking round the Necropolis and the highest part of Queen's Park with their dowsing rods and pendulums.

To trace the Network yourself, take this leaflet home and draw a line from point 'A' to point 'B' on the map beneath.

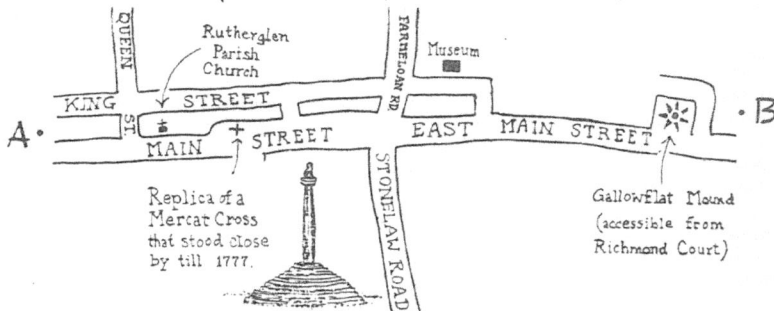

QUEEN
Rutherglen Parish Church
RUTHERGLEN RD
Museum
KING   STREET
A•
MAIN   STREET   EAST   MAIN   STREET   •B
Replica of a Mercat Cross that stood close by till 1777.
STONELAW ROAD
Gallowflat Mound (accessible from Richmond Court)

The line you've just drawn is part of the baseline of the Glasgow Triangle. Did you notice how closely the oldest street in Rutherglen follows it? You'll find three sites on your map but there are many more.... How did they get there? It's all part of the mystery! The unanswered questions are: Who designed the network and what is its purpose? Will we ever find out?

The guide for those who would carry on the quest is 'Glasgow's Secret Geometry' and the 1993 (revised) edition is now on sale for £5.95 at John Smiths and other bookshops~ you'll like it!

Previous pages: A hand-crafted flyer by Harry for the third edition of Glasgow's Secret Geometry.

Front cover: Camphill Ringwork, Glasgow. Photo: Grahame Gardner.

Glasgow's Secret Geometry

THE WORLD OF

Harry Bell

A compilation of Harry Bell's works, including *Forgotten Footsteps*, *Glasgow's Secret Geometry*, his website *Leyline Quest*, plus articles and letters. With additional commentaries and analysis by Kenneth Brophy, May Miles Thomas and Grahame Gardner.

EDITED AND ANNOTATED BY

Grahame Gardner

ADDITIONAL MATERIAL BY

May Miles Thomas

Kenneth Brophy

Grahame Gardner

Foreword by John Billingsley

Forgotten Footsteps originally published 1977
Glasgow's Secret Geometry originally published 1984
© Harry Bell — Leyline Publications, East Kilbride

Glasgow's Secret Geometry — The World of Harry Bell
Published 2024 by Western Geomancy
Glasgow, Scotland
westerngeomancy.org

ISBN: 978-1-8380461-5-6

Contents

For Harry

Foreword

John Billingsley

Harry Bell was one of the unsung heroes of the earth mysteries movement. By the time I heard of, and from, him in the mid-1990s, he had privately published several small engagingly constructed books and papers related to mysterious landscapes around his native Scotland and Glasgow. Sadly, though circulating among friends and colleagues north of the border, his investigations only came to the notice of the (largely English) earth mysteries community when he sent a review copy of *Glasgow's Secret Geometry* to my magazine, Northern Earth – NE being the nearest earth mysteries or neo-antiquarian journal to his stamping ground. I only wish he'd found us, or we'd found him, sooner; and sadly I never had the opportunity to meet Harry personally. Just how much of a cause for regret that is becomes clear with this collection of Harry's writings and memorates and annotations from fellow travellers. Harry would have made great company, that's for sure; that much shines clearly through his writing, which is still a pleasure to read today.

Having said that, much of the content is 'of its time', especially with regard to leys — whoops, 'prehistoric site alignments', the more diplomatic term Harry employed for the purposes of certification from Glasgow University as a Field Archaeologist. From the time of Alfred Watkins in the 1920s, but particularly from the days of John Michell's kickstarter *The View Over Atlantis* in the 1970s, the alternative antiquarian field has been a fast-moving palimpsest of discoveries, perspectives and weird fancies, continually teetering on a pin-head between empirical objectivity and precarious (unfortunately often erroneous) insights. The debate over leys as energy lines, for instance, has grown no clearer since the 1970s, and a lack of theoretical definition and empirical confirmation has led many in the field to dismiss energy lines as an unprovable red herring in ley research; many argue that we need to return to the land itself and its folklore to glean a better understanding of Watkins' concept, and that hence a phenomenological approach will prove more rewarding. But that is hindsight — in Harry's day, such an approach in these contexts was yet unknown.

To move forward, we sometimes have to take steps backward to see how we got to where we are, and perhaps see where we took a wrong step; and then to move on with a new map. The goal of earth mysteries was always to ask questions of received thinking, and it remains so now, when we have built up our own banks of dodgy orthodoxy that must equally be questioned lest we get caught up in our own comfortable mindsets. If Harry were still with us, I am sure he would have embraced and investigated the new paradigms of 21st century alternative archaeology with enthusiasm. Like the bulls of St Kentigern, Harry was one of those who "came by a straight road along where there was no path". In this book we get a strong sense of the vitality of those debates and, thanks to Harry's vigorous enquiry, of the ongoing value of learning directly from the landscapes around us.

It's perhaps a too-familiar quote from TS Eliot's poem 'Little Gidding' to close this foreword – but I think it bears repeating when we honour Harry Bell's memory and thank the editors for their efforts in bringing his work back to attention in this valuable publication.

We shall not cease from exploration
And the end of all our exploring
Will be to arrive where we started
And know the place for the first time.

John Billingsley was co-founder of the Northern Earth Mysteries Group in 1979 and is the editor of Northern Earth magazine, the world's longest-established journal of alternative antiquarianism.

WHAT IS THE GLASGOW NETWORK OF ALIGNED SITES?

I t is a tapestry woven through space and across time, linking the past to the present. Like some crazed '70s black velvet pinboard-and-thread picture, its alignments snake back and forth across the landscape, each thread linking power points of different eras — Medieval castles sit atop Bronze Age hillforts, Roman fortifications overlie Druid groves, Victorian churches subsume Neolithic burial grounds. Every string of the network is woven from several strands, each carrying a story about its past, and sometimes too, its present. Look up at the hills around the Clyde valley and ponder how you could use them to navigate in ancient times, and you will begin to see the invisible lines connecting them. Myths and legends are jumbled higgledy-piggledy with historical tales to generate their own 'mythtory'. Viking warriors and Celtic saints march out their trajectories alongside Roman legions and Pictish tribes, all of them reaching across the centuries to make their voices heard. All we must do is learn to listen, and we can hear their stories echoing along these psychogeographic songlines of the Glasgow Network of Aligned Sites that Harry Bell revealed.

Introduction

Grahame Gardner

> *What really matters ... is whether it is a human-*
> *designed fact, or an accidental coincidence ... that*
> *mounds, moats, beacons and mark stones fall into*
> *straight lines throughout Britain, with fragmentary*
> *evidence of trackways on the alignments.*
>
> — *Alfred Watkins, The Old Straight Track*[*]

My induction into Harry's world transpired when I stumbled across his 1977 book, *Forgotten Footsteps*. I still have my well-thumbed copy of the second edition, although it is in a rather sorry state these days. The book was a portal to the mysterious, the numinous, the liminal world of earth mysteries in Scotland — the first to describe (and map) ley-lines across the country, from Glasgow to Edinburgh and as far north as Dundee. To enhance its popularity, Harry clearly targeted the book at the alternative 'new age' community. It was the 1970s, and Alfred Watkins' concept of leys as archaic trackways had been embellished with ideas of dowsable lines of energy, spirit walkways, UFO flight paths and other equally outré theories. As Harry's book contained plenty of references to ley-lines, ghostly hauntings, landscape zodiacs, spirit paths and UFOs — even likening tumuli and barrows to earthly replicas of flying saucers — it easily meshed into that paradigm. An exquisitely-drawn fold-out map at the back of the book showed positions of the sites yet

---

[*] Watkins, Alfred, The Old Straight Track, (original preface) p.vi

invited the readers to draw in the alignments themselves in join-the-dots fashion — a guaranteed way to engage them in the realm of ley hunting. Pretty soon my Ordnance Survey one-inch sheet 64 map of Glasgow was sprouting circles around any sites marked with Gothic text, with a mass of pencil lines connecting them — a favourite pastime that I still observe to this day whenever I buy a new OS map.

Harry's second book, *A Guide to the Haunted Castles of Scotland*, was published in 1981. Although clearly inspired by his research trips for the earlier book, which contained many castles on his alignments, *Haunted Castles* was an attempt to attract a more conventional reader base and undoubtedly enhanced the tourist trade for those castles lucky enough to be mentioned. It also laid the groundwork for further research, as he discovered that most of the castles he visited appeared to be constructed on much older sites. "Even if the structure occupying a site is Medieval, the site itself can be very much older", he wrote. The same rule can be applied to pre-Reformation churches, which were often deliberately constructed on former 'pagan' sites to re-sanctify them into the new Christian religion.[*]

Harry followed up with his masterwork, *Glasgow's Secret Geometry* in 1984, although it was the third 1993 edition that crossed my path. Harry was now a fully-qualified Field Archaeologist, having taken evening classes with the Archaeology Department at Glasgow University, and he downplayed the ley-line aspects of the network (much as his hero Alfred Watkins had done in later years) in favour of the less contentious term 'Prehistoric Site Alignments' (PSAs), which he hoped would be more acceptable to the archaeological community. This volume, like its predecessors, was self-published (Harry was a printer

---

[*] wikipedia.org/wiki/Christianity_and_paganism#Christianization_during_the_European_Middle_Ages

to trade), with a highly unusual binding on the right-hand side of the folded pages that made it challenging to read. This time the map came as a separate entity, tucked into a corner pocket of the front cover for easy field reference. Not only were the alignments pre-drawn on this one, but the rear of the map comprised a gazetteer listing all the sites, complete with basic map references and short descriptions.

Although I never met Harry, I can honestly credit him as being a primary motivator in my own interest in ancient sites, alignments, and archaeology in general. Both books were frequently referred to before field trips — notes were taken, maps annotated, compass bearings logged. I taught myself to dowse with a pair of home-made L-rods, constructed from two wire coat-hangers and a couple of old Biro pen cases, at Bar Hill Roman fort on the Antonine Wall, one of Harry's sites. Looking back at the books now, I am frequently surprised by how many nuggets of Harry's wisdom I have absorbed into my own geomantic worldview and working practice without being consciously aware of their origin. I often feel that Harry has been walking beside me all these years, gently guiding my path in the right direction.

After leaving school at 14 with no qualifications, Harry's good-humoured and gregarious nature quickly led him into many adventures. He began a printing apprenticeship with Nautical Press learning the skills that would later stand him in good stead when it came to self-publishing his books. However, his printing career was interrupted when he was called up to join the Black Watch regiment for his National Service. On finding out that the Parachute Regiment would be training in Cyprus, and knowing that it had a better climate, he quickly volunteered and was accepted into the 'Paras'. This was the time of the Cyprus Emergency, when Cypriot nationalist forces were fighting for an end to British colonial rule, demanding a transfer of power to Greece. Harry's lifelong friend Ian Marshall tells of an incident that Harry described as typical of the "bloody incompetence" and downright inanity of the British Army. They had received intelligence about the location of a high-ranking guerrilla leader (probably George Grivas) and were planning a midnight raid to capture him. The plan was to load the men into trucks and drive round the roads surrounding the village, dropping men off at regular intervals to form an encircling perimeter, who would then sneak towards the target, closing the net as they got closer. This all sounded fine, except that the troops, being paras, were expected to jump off the rear of the trucks as they were moving, as hearing them stopping and starting again would arouse suspicion. The trucks were driving quite fast, and the first man to jump out fell badly and broke his leg. His screams raised the alarm in the village, and by the time they had reached it, their target was long gone.

It was several years later that Harry was to return to Cyprus with the Association of Certificated Field Archaeologists (ACFA) — of which more in the ACFA section. But that wasn't his only experience in the Middle East, as his regiment was also involved in the 1956 Suez Crisis, tasked with seizing control of the canal zone. According to Harry's friend Gerry Hearns, they were not parachuted in due to insufficient training at that time, but were landed on the beach in old WWII landing craft. Harry was quite confident that the paras could have taken control of the whole area in a few days, except politics intervened. Nasser, the Egyptian president, had proclaimed the conflict "a people's war", and ordered Egyptian troops to wear civilian clothes, while guns were freely distributed to civilians. As a result, the Allied forces, unable to tell friend from foe, were presented with an unsolvable dilemma. If they killed innocent civilians, they faced global opprobrium; but if they reacted more cautiously it provided opportunities for Egyptian soldiers to get closer by 'hiding in plain sight' amongst civilians. So, until this impasse was resolved, the British forces were ordered to dig in where they were, maintain control of their own area, and not to shoot at anything unless they were fired upon first.

It was during the subsequent few weeks that Harry managed to acquire a 'prisoner' — a young Coptic Christian who was quite happy to befriend the Brits as he felt rather detached from Nasser's Islamist leanings and plans for Egypt. He became a sort of unofficial manservant to Harry and the men, cooking meals, carrying things and generally helping out where he could. From time to time, the Egyptians would unleash a burst of gunfire towards the Brits, more as an act of bravado than with any hope of hitting anything. Harry's young Copt friend was completely blasé about this and continued walking around as though nothing was amiss; after all, he was Egyptian, he thought nobody was his enemy. Until, that is, he was killed by a burst of gunfire, right beside Harry. If Harry had been standing up at the time, he would have been killed too. "I just couldn't train this guy as a soldier", said Harry. "He just didn't understand that you had to keep your head down all the time."

That incident traumatised Harry, and even recounting the story to Gerry later caused him a great deal of anxiety. It was one of those wartime things that many veterans would simply refuse to talk about. Yet it may have prompted some change in outlook. On finishing his National Service, Harry embarked on a trip to India with the intention of following the Ganges in search of the site of the Bodhi tree where Buddha gained enlightenment. Gerry is unsure whether he completed the trip, but thinks that Harry made the pilgrimage in honour of his Coptic friend. More travel adventures followed, such as the famous 1959 Israel trip with his friend Mike Lang, where they managed a three-month trip on a budget of £30 by working in a kibbutz, a railway station, and even selling tablecloths at one point.

Back home, Harry found employment as a printer on a Glasgow newspaper. He often worked night shifts producing the morning editions, which didn't bother him as he was used to sleeping at odd times in the military, and the extra overtime payments were very welcome. The print office was in the basement, but had street level windows, and some nights they would see the legs of 'ladies of the night' walking up and down waiting for a car to stop and pick them up. Gerry Hearns, who knew Harry at that time, relates that the ladies would often come into the print shop on cold nights to warm up and have a cup of tea, or perhaps escape from a hostile client, because they felt safe in the company of Harry and the other printers. Harry would befriend them, as he loved to hear their stories. Many of them were from well-to-do circles but, having fallen on hard times, had taken to the streets as a necessity to make ends meet. Harry heard tales of transatlantic crossings, excursions on cruise ships, performing in the theatre and other adventures. "He loved people with a story to tell", said Gerry.

According to Harry's son Colin, it was during this period that he met people like Bobbie Gillespie, who went on to front the band Primal Scream, and a young aspiring actor called Billy Boyd, who later found fame in *The Lord of the Rings* films. Both were working as bookbinders. Gerry thought that Harry's Indian adventure may have inspired one of Bobbie's songs.

Harry also invested £1,500 of his overtime money into buying his own printing press, which was installed with due honours in the garage at home and later used to produce the first edition of *Forgotten Footsteps*. And the rest, as they say, is history.

In the late 90s, Colin Bell flexed his nascent web-writing skills by producing *The Glasgow Network of Aligned Sites* (GNAS) website, based on his father's book *Glasgow's Secret Geometry*. Then in 2000, Colin collaborated with his father to launch another website called *Leyline Quest* detailing his earlier research. Both websites were dependent on free hosting providers, and sadly vanished into the internet ether when their hosts were discontinued.

Meanwhile, the first decade of the new millennium introduced the novel technology of Google Earth, which allowed me to attempt to plot Harry's alignments as .kml placemark files. At the time this was a monumental task due to the poor satellite imagery available, resulting in several incorrectly placed sites and alignments. I basically had to locate the sites on OS maps using Harry's (often rudimentary) grid references, then try to visually locate them in Google Earth. Just as Harry had noted about the alignments in his first book *Forgotten Footsteps*, some of the longer leys refused to connect all the sites in a nice straight line, which meant that I had to break alignments into shorter sections on the map to get things to work. Inevitably, there had to be some compromises and adjustments. However, working in Google Earth allowed creation of pop-up boxes for each site containing map references, some descriptions from the books with links to further information, even a picture in many cases. Over the years the Google imagery has improved dramatically, and I've continued to update the placemark files, adjusting alignments and adding additional discoveries to the network. It is simplicity itself to

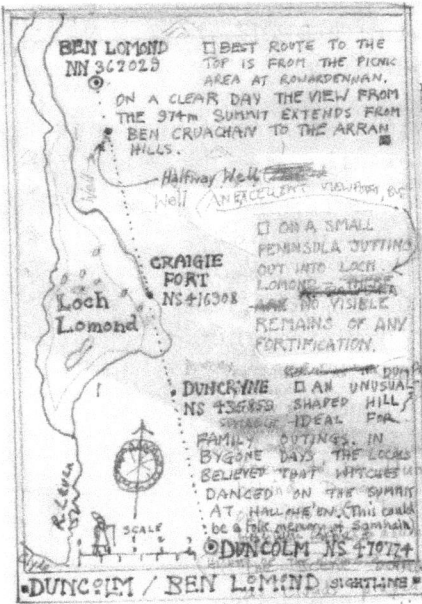

BEN LOMOND NN 367029

☐ BEST ROUTE TO THE TOP IS FROM THE PICNIC AREA AT ROWARDENNAN.
• ON A CLEAR DAY THE VIEW FROM THE 974m SUMMIT EXTENDS FROM BEN CRUACHAN TO THE ARRAN HILLS.

– Halfway Well ☐ AN EXCELLENT VIEWING PT

CRAIGIE FORT NS 416908
☐ ON A SMALL PENINSULA JUTTING OUT INTO LOCH LOMOND – RATHER ~~ARE~~ NO VISIBLE REMAINS OF ANY FORTIFICATION.

Loch Lomond

DUNCRYNE NS 436853
☐ AN UNUSUAL SHAPED HILL ~~SUITABLE~~ IDEAL FOR FAMILY OUTINGS. IN BYGONE DAYS THE LOCALS BELIEVED THAT WITCHES DANCED ON THE SUMMIT AT HALLOWE'EN. This could be a folk memory of Samhain.

SCALE

◉ **DUNCOLM** NS 47074

• **DUNCOLM / BEN LOMOND** SIGHTLINE •

---

en the weather was fine and the for the hill. Although it's only ten st confess I had never heard of ring alignments. I knew men who Annapurna, but no-one who had the highest of the Kilpatrick Hills range some 401m above sea level three miles from Erskine Bridge. rt of the dove' or 'fort of Columba,'

could certainly have made it a veller, but when I finally reached a for tangible evidence of such a to be found; no cairns, no So I looked for a place where my ave rested, and I sat there in a wind, eating cheese and pickle ie view, I could see the islands in t hill in the middle distance that I

cryne. Across the water a small peninsula jutted t Balmaha pier, and was the Ben itself.

me changed constantly hide and seek with the sun, casting huge moving shadows over the landscape, I was at peace with the world. Though I had found nothing of archaeological interest, I still felt that in some inexplicable way the presence of the early folk still lingered on Duncolm.

☐ I sat gazing at the mountains vignetted into the mist on the far side of the loch, an infinite space where earth and sky dissolved ... greens ▓▓▓ and blues changing to gray in overlapping planes of perspective like an old-time Oriental scroll painting —— the Ben, the peninsula, and the hill of Duncryne —— all in visual alignment...

☐ Slowly it dawned on me that I had found another sightline.

☐ But had it ever actually been used as such? There was no way of knowing this, although the surrounding area had certainly been settled in prehistoric times. Dotted about the Kilpatrick Hills are tombs dating back to early in the Neolithic era, a period that lasted roughly from 3500 B.C. to 1800 B.C. Neolithic peoples were the founders of our civilisation. They introduced pottery to Britain, grew crops, raised cattle and changed the economy of the country from hunting and food gathering to Agriculture. Nobody knows what form their roads or paths took, but it is believed they followed rivers and mountain ridges. Duncolm and Ben Lomond could have been very useful landmarks to a Neolithic community.

☐ These thoughts were much in my mind as I tramped back down the braes of Cochno, steering a rough course in the general direction of Glasgow. This time my route marker was a distant hilltop showing blue-grey against the horizon almost 40 miles away. Unless I was mistaken, this landmark was Tinto Hill, a hill associated with the Druids from time immemorial.

One of Harry's original galleys for the second edition of Glasgow's Secret Geometry. This is what real 'cut-and-paste' looks like!

draw connecting lines between locations on Google Earth without resorting to the complex calculations needed to accurately transfer alignments across sheets of Ordnance Survey maps as Harry had to do. I have no doubt that this technology would have transformed Harry's research, but unfortunately, he passed away in 2001, just as his work was gaining popularity.

One early beneficiary of my Google Earth file was film-maker May Miles Thomas, who, in 2007, received a Scottish Arts Council's Creative Scotland award to produce what became a BAFTA award-winning interactive website and iPhone app called *The Devil's Plantation* based on Harry's network. May undertook her own voyage of discovery and has probably covered more of the network on the ground than anybody since Harry in her quest to film as many of the locations as possible. She subsequently produced a highly evocative film of the same name, narrated by Kate Dickie and Gary Lewis, and May has been a staunch advocate of Harry's work ever since. The iPhone app is still available, and you can rent the film from her website for a modest sum.*

Harry's books attracted a diverse audience including ley hunters, dowsers, psychogeography aficionados, local history buffs, UFO hunters, witches, druids and followers of other fringe disciplines. Yet, despite his efforts to integrate, Harry never achieved the recognition from the mainstream archaeological community that he so desired. Although his close friends in ACFA loved him for his affable nature and sense of humour, and were (mostly) sympathetic to his ideas about Glasgow alignments, there were others who regarded his concept of PSAs as fantasy, refusing to take them seriously, pointing out the lack of reliable archaeological dating evidence at many of his sites that prevented them being recorded as truly prehistoric. There are clearly some sites on the

---

* https://www.devilsplantation.co.uk/

Network with no ancient provenance that Harry added to bolster the validity of an alignment.

But are we looking at this the wrong way? Does it matter if some sites on a PSA, or even the entire alignment, are not as ancient as the archaeologists would like? Surely the alignment is the thing, not the sites along it? Harry's argument was that sites would be subject to serial re-use and that a lack of evidence did not mean that they couldn't be older than they appeared. This argument was also used by Alfred Watkins, who noted that (e.g.) churches were frequently built on top of older sites. Later peoples may have been aware of an alignment and deliberately constructed their site to be on it. Does that make the alignment invalid? There are obvious alignments with no ancient past, such as the Victorian church ley of Great Western Road that I discuss later in this volume, and several examples around the country where church locations appear to be in some alignment or pattern, often hidden until revealed by later researchers. The London pentagram of Nicholas Hawksmoor churches centred on St Paul's Cathedral discovered by psychogeographer Iain Sinclair springs to mind here, but there are other instances where the alignment itself is the thing, not the sites along it.

Of course, it is easy to get sucked into this apophenia when studying a map, as sceptics have claimed by producing alignments of Greggs, or pentagrams of Woolworth's stores. But arguably, this very action creates informational connections between the sites, the very thing they are trying to discredit. Dowsers refer to these alignments as 'lines of intention' and categorise them as a type of ley. This lies at the very heart of psychogeography, where meaning is extracted from seemingly random connections between places. I think that is the best spirit in which to approach Harry's work, and it's one I have adopted myself in updating the network by adding locations of interest where some archaeological find was discovered, such as a Roman coin or a cist burial, even though the location is not a conventional sightline centre. Harry was guilty of this himself to an extent in his attempt to enhance the viability of some of his PSAs. It all adds to the colour and flavour of the alignment and, at some subliminal psychological or psychic level, creates a connection with our consciousness. And maybe that's okay.

Over twenty years have elapsed since Harry's death. It's time for a reappraisal of his work. 2024 marks the 40th-anniversary of the original publication of *Glasgow's Secret Geometry*. With the full permission and blessings of Harry's family and the assistance of his friends, I embarked on this mission to collate and republish as much of his material as possible. Initially, I recreated the old web pages, with the addition of my interactive Google map, at glasgowsecretgeometry.uk. There is an associated YouTube playlist where I document my own explorations.* Harry's printed works relating to his alignment research have been collected and expanded into this volume, to become what we might call a 'compendium and field guide' to Glasgow's Secret Geometry and the world of Harry Bell. His second book, *Guide to the Haunted Castles of Scotland* has not been included in this volume as it's not really germane to his alignment research, although some of the sites and the leys that Harry mentions in that book have been included in the Gazetteer and in the interactive online map.

I'll leave you with this thought — unbeknown to us at the time, all three of the extra contributors to this volume (including myself) were either born on and/or grew up on one of Harry's PSAs. Still think there's nothing in this leyline stuff?

---

* youtube.com/playlist?list=PLMrSdbmW6J7k4_Od9WrZnUKsMdwfnp3hl

*Harry examining the cup-and-ring marked stone
at Tealing Souterrain.*

Acknowledgements

I am grateful to everyone who has helped and given encouragement on this project, in particular May Miles Thomas; Kenneth Brophy, senior archaeology lecturer at Glasgow University; Helen Maxwell, Ian Marshall and Gerry Hearns, friends of Harry's and fellow ACFA members (with extra Brownie points to Ian and Helen for sharing their photos and archive material).

Thanks also to Janie Munro of ACFA, who provided some ACFA historical background and photos; John Billingsley of Northern Earth for support and tirelessly delving into their archive to locate a couple of Harry's articles; and of course, Harry's family, Colin and Sheila, for graciously sharing their father's archive material and photographs, and giving me their blessing to proceed with this project.

A few photos have been scanned from the original books. In *Glasgow's Secret Geometry*, photos are credited to 'Harry Bell and Jim Cairney', but are not individually identified. The quality of some pictures was too poor to use in this volume. Where possible, alternatives have been used. In *Forgotten Footsteps*, all the original photographs have been replaced. Some photos are used under the appropriate Creative Common licence or are public domain. See: https://creativecommons.org/licenses/ for details.

Map data is © OpenStreetMap contributors under a Creative Commons CC BY-SA 2.0 licence. See: https://www.openstreetmap.org/copyright for details.

All other photos used are credited appropriately. Most of the line drawings are by TCF Brotchie, sourced from various books.

LIFELINES

May Miles Thomas

On a sub-zero winter's day in January 2001, I walked with my brother, Ross from our parent's flat to the end of Linthaugh Road, Pollok, the scheme in a south-west corner of Glasgow where we were raised. Our destination lay at the end of our road – an abandoned part of Leverndale Psychiatric Hospital, that, Ross assured me, could be accessed through a loosely-boarded entrance.

Built for the Govan District Lunacy Board, Leverndale, originally named Hawkhead Asylum, was designed by Malcolm Stark in the Renaissance Revival style and was opened in 1895. To the children of Pollok, it was less a building than a mythical construct built from whispers, the kind of place that furnished childhood tales of a fugitive maniac from 'Hawkheid' who lurked in the woods behind McGill Primary School from where he watched over us with malign intent.

In the gloom of Leverndale's corridors and wards, I felt the presence of the departed. Most of the rooms were intact, as if suddenly vacated. Here stood institutional bed frames, lockers and chairs. Files, clothing and other personal effects littered the floors. Judging by the ripped cables, graffiti and fire-scorched walls, we were not the hospital's only recent visitors. Here was an aura of both anger and melancholy; the remanence of past occupants.

In one ward, a single curtain hung limply against the pale winter daylight. From the floor I peeled a damp greetings card. Addressed to Marjory and signed by Auntie Jean, it read *Happy Easter*, evoking a resurrection of sorts. How did the patients come to be here? How long did they stay? And what was their fate after decades of institutional living? On leaving, I noticed a red plastic ring binder with a Dymo-printed label: *Visits After Discharge*. I took it with me, unaware of its contents and how eventually it would find a place alongside Harry Bell's story.

Following this foray into urban exploration, while trawling the web for information about Leverndale's history, I chanced on GNAS — *The Glasgow Network of Aligned Sites*. Not only was it my introduction to the writings of Harry Bell, it would also have an influence on my work as a writer and filmmaker. I sought out his self-published, *Glasgow's Secret Geometry: The City's Oldest Mystery*, disappointed to find it out of print. Rare second-hand copies, particularly the 1984 first edition, were unaffordable. Amazon currently has one for sale at $195.

Thanks to the writer and historian, Dr Ronnie Scott, I obtained a photocopy of Harry's book. From my first reading, I was enchanted by his humanity and warmth, his audacity and determination and most of all, his faith — faith in his apparently cockamamie theories of PSAs — Prehistoric Site Alignments — he believed spanned the city.

Delving deeper, I embraced its premise: that Glasgow was built to an ancient and occult pattern. Rejecting the term leyline as too new-agey for his liking, Bell's theory departed from Alfred Watkins 1925 publication, *The Old Straight Track* while adhering to the rule: that three aligned sites do not a leyline make, since the rule insisted on four at a minimum. I knew nothing about Harry Bell, but instantly felt an affinity with him and his quest: to make a series of field studies to determine whether these alignments and sites, like Watkins' leylines, existed in Scotland.

Unlike Bell, however, my own interest in Glasgow and landscape was rooted less in archaeology and artefacts than in the nebulous terrain of psychogeography and its intersection of place, memory and spiritual residuum that, as I write, has fewer exponents and writers in this country than in England. To me, this dearth of interest in psy-geo north of the border is, arguably, symptomatic of the cultural predominance of its southern neighbour, being in such thrall to metrocentric institutions. That, and London-based publishing and media cartels. Indeed, Scotland remains a fertile ground for those seeking greater meaning from their environment.

My own awareness of leylines began in the 1970s. Having won a scholarship to the then 'selective' Hillhead High School, each day I travelled to the city's affluent north-west. True to the Zeitgeist, in that heady era of hippydom and psychotropics, I learned how the churches lining the Great Western Road were said to be in alignment. True or not, the seed was sown. Captured by the idea of an occult connection between places, I developed a fascination for Ordnance Survey maps, poring over contours, placenames, roads and rivers, thrilled on seeing the words, 'Ancient Monument,' 'Mound' or 'Tumulus,' printed in Germanic Blackletter, as if to embellish their mystery.

Shortly after reading Harry's work, three things occurred. First, after proposing a project inspired by *Glasgow's Secret Geometry*, in 2007 I won the Scottish Arts Council's Creative Scotland Award. Second, I was contacted by the geomancer and dowser, Grahame Gardner, who kindly shared his Google Earth plotting of Bell's Network of Aligned Sites, a useful resource in my research. Third and last, I was ecstatic to find on Harry's Necropolis-Crookston Castle PSA the line passed through both my childhood homes in Kinning Park and Pollok.

This frisson of connection and coincidence propelled me. In 2004, on the day I left the Garnethill flat I had called home for 25 years to live in Edinburgh, I remarked to my husband how one day I hoped to make a film about Glasgow and how this task might be enhanced if I returned in the guise of a tourist. I summoned Walter Benjamin's quote:

> *The superficial inducement, the exotic, the picturesque has an effect only on the foreigner. To portray a city, a native must have other, deeper motives - motives of one who travels into the past instead of into the distance.*

Benjamin's words could well have been written for Harry Bell, whose death in 2001 would forever keep his deepest motives secret. Certainly he was drawn to ancient sites and archaeology, local history and its artefacts, just as he was driven to venture on field trips to unlikely corners of the country in an attempt to prove his thesis. In a sense, Bell was a completist whom, by discovering and visiting each site aligned on his PSAs, was a pilgrim on a journey of faith, faith in the land, in nature and in human endeavour; he had found his life's purpose.

My project, *The Devil's Plantation* was named after Bell's starting point, an ancient burial tumulus also known as The Deil's Plantin or Bonnyton Mound, situated roughly seven miles south-east of Glasgow, a site he claimed was haunted. In October 2007, I set out from Edinburgh on the 800 bus to Glasgow, my first trip to the city in three years. To keep me company, I brought along my trusty Ordnance Survey maps: the Landranger 64 and the Explorer 342.

Alighting at Buchanan Street Bus Station, however, I soon got lost, not so much geographically than psychically. How could I know at that point my journey would take six years and thousands of miles? As if to rehearse my bearings, my first three trips to Glasgow led me to the places of my childhood. Travelling on the Outer Circle of the city's subway, I visited West Street, Shields Road, and points between to Govan Cross where, inspired by Benjamin's instruction, I became a tourist.

In Glasgow's southside I wandered the streets, revisiting past haunts: the Albion Way in Wine Alley, aka Broomloan Road, Govan, my first 'official' visit to a pub, aged 14 and chaperoned by my grandmother, Lizzie, recalling earlier episodes, of the 5-year-old me hustling in the bars of Kinning Park on payday, pretending to look for my father and extorting the odd sixpence or shilling for my effort.

Drifting down Scotland Street, I paused to photograph Howden's Engineering Works, long disused, where both my mother and grandmother catered for the workforce in the canteen's kitchen. Today it is still standing, its purpose long forgotten.

At one of Harry's favoured sites, Govan Old Parish Church, I met Tony, a steeplejack by trade, who regaled me with stories of his life in high places. He was one of many people I met along the way. My sonsie face and high-spec camera seemed to attract all comers, because on my first three visits I was approached by a homeless man, an ex-soldier, a fantasist, a bottle collector, a film student and a plasterer. How could I explain to them the purpose of my expedition?

Sooner or later, I knew I had to get to work and follow in Harry's footsteps. First, there was the prosaic matter of access to overcome, since the 800 bus was impractical. Having learned to drive late in life, I had inherited my late mother-in-law's battered azure Nissan Micra and so, driven more by fear of failing than collision, I packed my camera kit, plus a flask and sandwiches before steering nervously onto the M8 heading west, determined to reach my destination: Bonnyton Mound.

Having checked the forecast in advance, on a bright autumn Sunday I arrived at Harry Bell's first viable site, situated on a quiet back road close to a pylon and a broken traffic sign that, once repaired, indicated a roundabout with two horns sprouting from a black circle, resembling the De'il himself. Later it would become a motif for the project.

To access the mound, I scaled a barbed wire fence on the other side of which a small herd of Friesians paced in a stand of beeches placidly chewing the cud. They paid me little mind as I set up my camera between two indents on its shallow summit. Pointing my lens north-west toward a range of hills some twelve miles away, I wondered, what was I looking at?

Then, as described in the *Secret Geometry*, it emerged from its surrounding slacks: the squat profile of Duncolm, the highest point of the Kilpatrick Hills. At that instant I grasped the connection, of how Harry once stood on this spot, surveying this same horizon as it dawned on him a De'il's Plantin-Mearns Castle-Crookston Castle alignment held promise, a promise fulfilled when joined by Renfrew Old Parish Church to form a leyline, or PSA.

From that day forward I was captured. My project, to make a website, a type of interactive gazetteer listing Harry's sites, together with a series of embedded short films, was scheduled to take two years. Not for the want of effort, *The Devil's Plantation* took from 2007 until its completion in 2013.

Fate, like God, will laugh as soon as you reveal your plans. By 2007, with my husband working in Glasgow and with me travelling to Harry's sites, I longed for an easier life. By spring 2008, the Edinburgh house was sold, and another — a fixer-upper in southside Glasgow — was bought and the move was made.

Returning to Glasgow, all seemed positive until I learned the tragic news that, a stone's throw from our new home, a 40-year-old woman, Moira Jones was brutally murdered in Queen's Park, her naked corpse found close to one of Harry's most significant sites: the Camphill Earthwork. Immediately the park was closed to the public for two weeks while a fingertip search was made of its 148 acres.

When it reopened, one day I was caught unawares by two police officers while shooting at the very site visited by Harry, accompanied by a American psychic, Marsha. He wrote:

*'There's really three circles here, not just one,'
she said, hopping off the rampart and walking
towards the stones in the middle of the ringwork.
'I feel three circles over lapping - there's a bit in
the center that's common to all three.'*

Once the noise of helicopters had subsided and police were no longer hiding in the shrubbery, I spent a lot of time communing with the Camphill stones. One glorious summer morning, while shooting the patterns of dappled sunlight on the trees, I was alerted by the sound of footfalls in the undergrowth as a startled female jogger appeared in my viewfinder. Realising we were safe, we were able to breathe again, laughing with relief.

This episode and the hundreds, even thousands of encounters shaped my project. None more so than when, during my house move, while packing our worldly goods, I found the red plastic ring binder marked *Visits after Discharge*. Debating whether or not to toss it, I opened it for the first time.

On these pages, written in blue cursive script by an unnamed hand, I learned about the lives of the patients discharged from Leverndale. Listed among them was a woman, Mary Ross whom, aged 17 in 1959, gave birth out of wedlock and as was customary for the illegitimate at the time, the infant was put up for adoption. Her parents, unable to cope with their daughter's post-partum psychosis, had her admitted to the then Hawkhead Mental Hospital (it became Leverndale in 1964, named for the Levern Waters). Unlike the case notes of her fellow ex-patients, Mary's file reported unauthorised absences, a habit continuing long after her discharge. Among the places she visited were several sites mentioned by Harry. Could it be a coincidence?

Touched by Mary's story, I realised that while Harry's quest was based on a plausible theory with a rational structure, Mary's walks were random, unplanned and chaotic; frequently she got lost. She did, however, admit she was searching for her lost child, a daughter. Was she still alive, I wondered? My enquiries proved fruitless. Both the hospital and the social work department were, understandably, unforthcoming.

On a chill January day in 2009, while revisiting the recent conversion of Leverndale to apartments, by chance I met an elderly woman walking her dog. To this day, her words still have the power to stun me:

You're the spit of your mother, you know that?

I had never met this woman in my life but as we spoke it became clear she knew my late mother, a hairdresser by trade. She told me her late husband also knew my father and together they would walk their dogs by the White Cart Water. She was retired, she said, and lived with her daughter in one of the new apartments, adding how odd it was to live where she once worked as a psychiatric nurse. Naturally I was compelled to ask — did she know Mary? Her reply sparked yet another uncanny coincidence.

Not only did she know her, she also knew Mary was living in a flat within walking distance of the hospital, close to my childhood home from where I had set out with my brother eight years earlier. In a letter to Mary I asked if she would be willing to meet. Two months later, as I was about to give up, she replied in tiny handwriting on the back of a Christmas card. Having agreed to my request, on our first meeting at her modest first-floor flat, she seemed nonplussed. Indeed, Mary struck me as someone who lived in the moment and not much given to nostalgia.

Over the next 18 months or so, we met several times where I bartered packets of biscuits for her reminiscence. My guess is she simply longed for company. Over time, I also got to know her neighbours who often expressed concern for her welfare. At times it seemed I had stepped into a small soap opera.

Gradually I learned from Mary of her perambulations in the city and beyond — Paisley and Renfrew were regular haunts, as were Faifley, close to the Cochno Stone, Carmyle, Rutherglen, Duncolm and even as far as Carron Ford, the place where Harry hoped to locate the 'straight road along which there was no path.'

Mary Ross had never heard of Harry Bell. Even so, it occurred to me how the pair were tourists travelling in time and place in their separate ways and at different times. While Harry reached back to the Neolithic Age, Mary seemed destined to dwell forever in the 1950s and 60s. Intuitively I decided to include her in my project for no other reason than her story mattered to me. With both parents deceased, and with no other known relatives, Mary deserved to live on, even if only in a stranger's consciousness. She died in 2011 of a respiratory disease.

The Devil's Plantation was completed twice. Once, in 2009 as a website and later as an app. In 2010 it won a BAFTA Scotland Award in the Best Interactive category. In 2013, I compiled 66 short films and the text I'd written from the website/app into a feature-length film. It is narrated by two of my favourite actors, Kate Dickie and Gary Lewis. The film, completed the night before it screened, premiered at the Glasgow Film Festival to a sell-out audience and was later nominated for a BAFTA Scotland Audience Award.

With this republication of Harry's work, I'm delighted to be one of several devotees who, for the last 40 years, have held the torch that keeps his flame alive. Through his writings, Harry gifted me the inspiration and a novel principle that serves my own work: how the experiential, the journey one takes, is as important as the endpoint. More importantly, I've discovered new ways of telling stories on screen. That, and finally — to always keep an eye on the weather.

A native Glaswegian, for years I lived under the delusion that I knew the city and its environs, so I'm grateful to Harry who taught me to look beyond the streets to the surrounding hills, to recognise their shapes and names. He also taught me to look more closely at man-made artefacts, ancient and modern. Those yet to read Harry's works are about to embark on an adventure without having to leave home. That said, I would urge the reader, as I did, to get out and explore the place where you live. To borrow the line Harry borrowed from Lao Tzu:

A journey of a thousand miles begins with a single step.

May Miles Thomas is a writer and film director. Her blog devilsplantation.co.uk — is still live. The film version and app of The Devil's Plantation is available in the Apple App store and as a video-on-demand from her website.

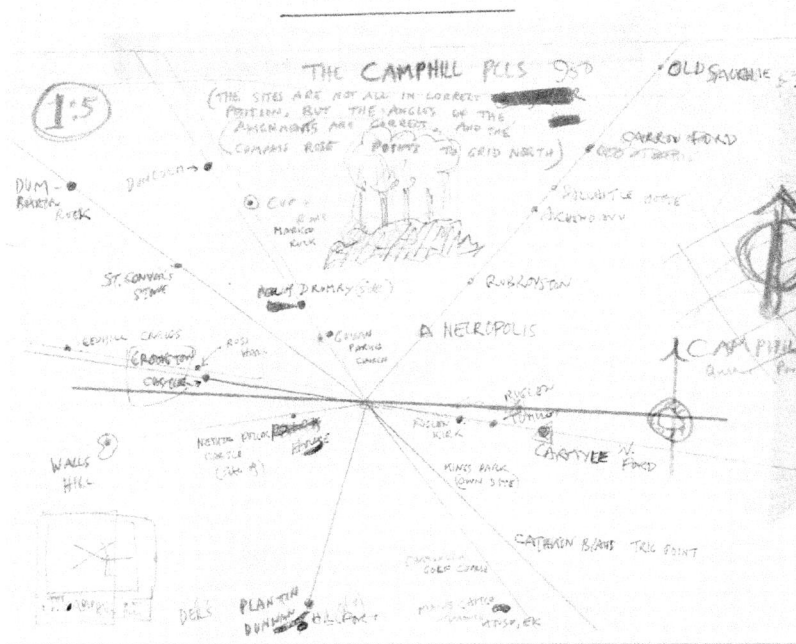

An early sketch by Harry of the alignments from Camphill.

THE LEY OF THE LAND

A SHORT HISTORY OF LEYS RESEARCH

Grahame Gardner

> *"Ley," Jane snapped. "Alfred Watkins called them leys. Ley lines — that's just a term that's been adopted in almost a disparaging way by so-called experts who say they don't exist."*
>
> — *Phil Rickman,* **The Remains of an Altar**

Most people today are familiar with the idea of aligned sites proposed by Alfred Watkins in his 1925 book *The Old Straight Track*. Watkins thought of his leys as 'archaic trackways', picturing them as trade routes between settlements. He found that certain placenames appeared with a high frequency along some lines. Names with White, Red or Black seemed the most common, but he also noted Cold or Cole, Dod, Merry and Ley — the last appearing so frequently that he used it to name his alignments (he always called them 'leys' and never used the term 'leyline'). He suggested that certain trackways were known by those traders who most travelled them. So, for example, 'White' names picked out routes used by salt traders, e.g. 'Whitley',

'Whitelee' etc. 'Red' denoted those used by potters, 'Black' those favoured by iron merchants, and so on. He also included the 'Knap' prefix for flint traders.

Of course, Watkins wasn't the first researcher to note alignments in the landscape, and he was well aware of others' work, in particular citing Sir Norman Lockyer's Stonehenge alignments (Lockyer, 1906), saying: "...the sunrise alignments of Lockyer are identical to long-distance leys" (Watkins, 1925, 106). Other early researchers include the antiquarian, physician and Anglican clergyman William Stukeley, who in the mid-18th Century pioneered the scholarly investigation of Stonehenge and Avebury, noticing that the axis of Stonehenge and the Avenue leading from it were oriented to the north-east, "whereabouts the sun rises when the days are longest." (Stukeley,1740, 81) A century later, the Rev. William Henry Black, an archivist at the British Museum and an early member of the British Archaeological Association, pronounced at their 1870 Congress that "Monuments exist marking grand geometrical lines, lines which cover the whole of the west of Europe, extending beyond Britain to Ireland, the Hebrides, the Shetlands, the Orkneys, right up to the Arctic circle. These lines are all carried out upon a principle which I have had the happiness of detecting." (Black, 1871)

Closer to home, a contemporary of Watkins, who we shall become more familiar with later in this book, was Glasgow's own Ludovic McLellan Mann, an insurance broker to trade and part-time archaeologist with his own unorthodox ideas about ancient metrology and landscape geometry. Mann was active mainly in the 1920s and 30s, yet as early as 1914, in his paper *Archaic Sculpturings in Dumfries and Galloway*, he wrote.

> *The apparently isolated cairns, the groups of standing stones far distant from each other, and*

the detached sets of rock carvings well removed
from each other, may all form part of one widely
spread design ... A scrutiny with the aid of Ordnance
Survey charts of certain sacred areas, covering
great stretches of ground both in Scotland and
Ireland ... demonstrates that locations marked by
the erection of cairns and standing stones and by
rock scribings and by prominent topographical
features or points (often later chosen for the site
of forts) are arranged in an exact geometrical
relationship. (Mann, 1915, 133)

Mann was in general agreement with previous researchers regarding the astronomical alignments of Stonehenge, but he went a step further, claiming that the entire landscape around Stonehenge was a giant map of the heavens, with groups of tumuli representing constellations (Mann/a) — a concept that he later developed into his theory that cup and ring marked stones represented star maps of their area. This idea culminated in his 1937 painting of a multicoloured grid on the Cochno Stone outside Glasgow and his prediction of a solar eclipse in the area around 3,000BCE based on the cup and ring marks thereon.

However, it was Watkins' vision of a network of lines laid across the landscape 'like a string of fairy lights' connecting high points and ancient sites that was to inspire the popular zeitgeist:

Imagine a fairy chain stretched from mountain
peak to mountain peak, as far as the eye could
reach, and paid out until it touched the 'high
places' of the earth at a number of ridges, banks,
and knowls. Then visualise a mound, circular
earthwork, or clump of trees, planted on these
high points, and in low points in the valley other
mounds ringed round with water to be seen from a
distance. Then great standing stones brought to
mark the way at intervals, and on a bank leading
up to a mountain ridge or down to a ford the track
cut deep so as to form a guiding notch on the
skyline as you come up... (Watkins,1925, 218)

Watkins' original classifications for ley mark points included ancient mounds such as tumuli, cairns, barrows, tumps and alignments of same; ancient unworked stones, e.g., standing stones and mark stones; moats, islands in ponds and lochans; traditional or holy wells; beacon points, which he noted often marked the start of a ley; crossroads, especially named ones; ancient crosses and fords; churches of ancient foundation and hermitages; ancient castle sites and old 'castle' placenames; and straight roads aligned between other points. Curiously, Watkins made no mention of stone circles or henges. These were a later addition during Paul Devereux's time as editor of *The Ley Hunter* magazine in 1975. Paul Screeton (author of *Quicksilver Heritage*) also suggested including the additional landscape features mentioned by Watkins in his previous book *Early British Trackways*, such as barrows, dolmens, earthworks and hillforts, hill figures, and significant trees, particularly Scots Pines. This latter recommendation was based on a mention by Watkins that "The Scotch Fir or Pine is the tree which seems most characteristic of a ley, for a group of them are almost always (I notice) signs of a sighting point."(Watkins, 1922, 17). It is well-known that cattle drovers bringing their herds to market would seed clumps of Scots Pines at high points and path junctions along their route to aid future navigation, giving credence to Watkins' theory that leys were archaic trackways.[*]

The 1970s led to an explosion of interest in Watkins' work. The New Age was upon us. Dowsers had been finding water associated with ancient sites since at least the 1930s but were now busy exploring the energetic dimensions of leys. An increase in UFO sightings led to claims that leys were flight paths for inter-dimensional craft, an idea promoted by journalist Arthur Shuttlewood in his book *The Warminster Mystery* and eagerly taken up by Tony Wedd, an ex-RAF pilot and early member of The Ley

[*] www.localdroveroads.co.uk/scots-pines/

Hunter's Club. The idea of leys having some sort of psycho-spiritual energy attached to them was gaining popularity and the term 'ley line' was entering common usage (Tony Wedd was probably the first person to use the term).* Books by John Michell, such as *The Flying Saucer Vision* and his masterwork *The View Over Atlantis*, published in 1969, were a major influence here (Michell also avoided the term 'ley line'), leading to a profusion of works such as Paul Screeton's *Quicksilver Heritage* and Janet & Colin Bord's *Mysterious Britain*, all birthing an area of popular research that became known as 'Earth Mysteries', with John Michell presiding as its affable grandfather.

Meanwhile, in North America, Terry Ross, then President of the American Society of Dowsers, wrote in 1974 about dowsing 'ley lines' in Vermont, stating that they are lines of subtle energy that "range from 4.5 - 6.5 feet in width" and that they are "marked in ways analogous to the European lines ... and were known to the early inhabitants of the continent". (Ross, 1974, 86)

Later, Ross reinforced his belief that these energy lines are the same as Watkins' leys:

> In researching the ley-line, it may be helpful to start with a map. In connecting, for example, Paleo-Indian or pre-historic sites of mound-builders in North America, or the pre-Colombian temples of Mexico, one may discover that he has also plotted the path of a ley-line. The alignments must be perfectly straight. (1974, 88)

This conflation of energy lines with visual alignments introduced a level of confusion that is still prevalent on both sides of the pond today. Matters were not helped after American dowser Sig Lonegren, who had trained with Terry, immigrated to the UK and started using the term 'leys' to describe the dowsable

---

* westerngeomancy.org/leys-not-ley-lines/

straight lines of energy that he was finding. To clarify things, John Michell advised Sig to start calling these lines 'energy leys' to distinguish them from Watkins-style visual alignments.* However, the damage was done, and as a result today many people, including dowsers, freely use 'leyline' as a generic label. (From a dowsing perspective, energy leys *may* coincide with a visual ley but can also be found independently. They are quite different beasts.)

This 'New Age' aggregation of leys with UFO sightings, dowsing and intangible 'earth energies' was a step too far for more serious researchers like Paul Devereux who, like several others, tried to distance himself from such heresies. Harry Bell was no exception. Although his earlier book *Forgotten Footsteps* was clearly aimed at the 'new age' end of the market, e.g. likening the concrete dome of Cairnpapple Hill to a grounded UFO, by the time he came to write *Glasgow's Secret Geometry*, he was a Certificated Field Archaeologist and unsurprisingly, took a more measured approach:

> From what I had read in The Ley Hunter magazine and elsewhere, it seemed that most English researchers now believed their ley-lines followed invisible 'lines of force' across the country. As the only lines I had found were simple overland alignments of hilltops and ancient man-made features detected without recourse to dowsing or astronomy, I felt I could hardly call them ley-lines. (Bell, 1984, 25)

Thus, Harry's alignments are leys in the strict original sense as described by Alfred Watkins. They are purely visual alignments between significant points on the landscape that can be used as aids to navigation.

---

* geomancy.org/index.php/geomancers-i-have-gnown/michael

How wide is a ley?

One of the criticisms levelled at Watkins' leys was that, in many cases, his leys appear to run straight up near-vertical hills that would be impossible to ascend, or over bogs, bodies of water or other inhospitable terrain that would be unfeasible to traverse. This is largely a result of Watkins' insistence that leys were early trackways; indeed, he stopped calling them leys after a few years and referred to them solely as 'archaic trackways'. This was an unfortunate name and didn't do him any favours in academic circles as it gave people the wrong idea about visual leys.

Harry was aware of this misconception, which may explain why he ended up calling his alignments 'Prehistoric Site Alignments'(PSAs) — an ambiguously clever phrase when spoken that could equally well mean Prehistoric *Sight* Alignments. Because that is the true definition of a visual ley, it's simply an alignment between sighting points in the landscape. *It's as wide as it needs to be.* That doesn't mean that you must maintain a straight track between each point; provided that you position yourself between two points in alignment, one ahead and one behind, you know that you are located on that ley. In the case of travellers coming along the Clyde valley from the south-east, if they put Tinto Hill at their back, they could see the alignment to Duncolm ahead of them and know that if they kept to that heading, they would eventually arrive at the main settlement on the hill that we know as the Necropolis in Glasgow. Due to the topography of the landscape around the Glasgow basin, this is the most obvious approach for the prehistoric traveller on foot, as David Daiches explains in his 1982 book, *Glasgow*:

> To reach the hollow otherwise than by sea from the west or across the low watershed that divides it from the Forth Valley (a route apparently not favoured in prehistoric times) the earliest settlers in the region would have had to seek out the

> *passes, of which the most obvious was the Biggar Gap, a natural route from the North Sea coast between the Tweed and Clyde Valleys... (Daiches, 1977, 3)*

This particular route ended up being one of the longer alignments in Harry's Glasgow Network, and it's easy to see why, with the prominent hills of Tinto and Duncolm at either end, both allowing good sighting points. On the map for Glasgow's Secret Geometry, Harry wrote:

> *It is difficult to assess the width of a PSA. It can be as narrow as a path between two stones, or as broad as the line of sight to a distant hillfort. It all depends on the viewpoint of the observer. (Bell, 1984 — map)*

Considered in this way, a ley can be as narrow as your thumb (if you're using that to sight with), or as wide as you need it to be to get to the next site on the alignment. It doesn't matter if you must divert a little to climb a hill, avoid an obstacle, detour round a swamp or cross a river, you can soon get yourself back onto the correct line by aligning yourself with sighting points behind you and ahead of you.

I'll give Harry the last word on this. In a later paper for the Association of Certificated Field Archaeologists (ACFA), he wrote:

> *PSAs were not tracks or pathways. They were a means of finding your bearings using skyline markers. There was no need to follow them all the way up to the hilltops. Those who use stars for navigation don't have to fly to the heavens to get where they are going either, but they use the same principle. (Bell, 2000, 3)*

When is a ley not a ley?

Alfred Watkins specified that a ley should contain at least four or more sites within roughly five miles. This increases the probability of it being a genuine alignment. It is easy to connect three random sites on a map, but much harder to link five; and finding seven sites in alignment practically eliminates any chance alignments. Harry was aware of this stipulation, saying, "Alfred had written 'three points alone do not prove a ley, four being the minimum'" (1984, 3); and yet he subsequently decided to include three-point leys in his network provided that at least one of the three sites intersected another PSA. This approach results in some alignments of questionable validity in my opinion. For example, consider the three PSAs emanating from Walls Hill fort — to Craignethan Castle, Camphill and the Necropolis. The one to Craignethan Castle passes through Lickprivick Tumulus and just grazes Duncarnock hillfort, but only Lickprivick intersects another PSA. I have managed to add three other possible sites to bolster this lengthy alignment — Cowdon Hall, Neil's Stone and Double Dykes fort — but it still leaves a ten-mile section with no sites. Of course there may be other visual clues along the way that would help to reinforce the route — skyline notches, clutches of Scots Pines and so on — that could be identified through additional fieldwork.

The Walls Hill to Camphill alignment has only one connecting intermediate site, Nether Pollok Castle, along its length. The one to the Necropolis at least has St Enoch Sanctuary and Crookston Castle on it, the latter connecting to several other PSAs, but the section between Walls Hill and Crookston has nothing apart from two standing stones on Glenniffer Braes that I've managed to add.

In the first edition of *Glasgow's Secret Geometry*, Harry postulated another alignment running from

[1] I'm using the
'official' name
here. Harry always
called it
'Dumdruff'.

Walls Hill to Drumduff[1] Hill, passing through Myres Cairn and Dunwan Hillfort. However, on subsequent investigation, he decided that Myres Cairn was not that close to the line and, with no other sites to support it, he omitted that PSA from the second edition.

Another site that I regard as questionable is Seedhill Craigs (also known as The Hammills) in Paisley, beside the White Cart at its high-water mark, which Harry claims is the site of St Mirin's original settlement. He bases this on a statement he found in Margaret McCarthy's *A Social Geography of Paisley*, where she says that the site was believed to have been occupied in prehistoric times, long before the arrival of the saint. Yet of the two PSAs emanating from here, only one has any credibility in Watkinsian terms. The alignment to Camphill has just a single intermediate site — an 'underground cell' on Minard Road that was excavated by Ludovic McLellan Mann. This cannot be said to fit the recognised pattern of a true 'Watkins' ley.

Of the longer alignment that runs through the Necropolis to Woodend Loch, the section to the Necropolis is almost seven and a half miles in length, and even Harry himself says, "Five miles without a site seemed too long"(1984, 7). One possible site that may be added to that alignment is the graveyard of Ramshorn Kirk, one of the oldest burial grounds in the city, but that's only because I added that at the suggestion of Kenny Brophy.

Beyond the Necropolis, the alignment from Seedhill Craigs continues through Provan Hall, before ending at another low point in the landscape at Woodend Loch, a known Mesolithic settlement with no distinguishing features other than a couple of boulders on the bank that Harry thought were of interest. Both origin and terminus of this PSA are relatively low points in the landscape so can hardly be considered good sighting centres. Consequently, it is difficult to see how the alignment could have been surveyed as Harry describes. A better choice of origin for this PSA would be Paisley Abbey, which Harry used in *Forgotten Footsteps*; although if we are basing our choices on high points in the landscape, an even better sighting centre would be Oakshaw Trinity church, located at the top of Church Hill and prominent on the skyline from a distance. There is evidence that it was once the site of an Iron Age hillfort. It's also situated on another one of Harry's alignments, between Paisley Abbey and Duchal Castle, yet he doesn't mention it at all.

The only other possibly Mesolithic site acknowledged by Harry is Barrack Street, just a couple hundred metres south of the Necropolis, where a midden of oyster shells was unearthed during building work in 1982. Harry mentions this site as it is located on his Cochno Stone-Tinto Hill alignment, although there are few other sites to justify this as a proper ley, and it is overshadowed by the nearby Duncolm-Tinto alignment, some few hundred metres to the east of the Cochno Stone.

Mapping the Glasgow Network

A former paratrooper, Harry was trained in military navigation and reconnaissance techniques. For accuracy in gunnery sighting, calculations are made using mils, which are units of angular measurement equivalent to 1/6,400 of a circle. Mils provide greater accuracy than degrees and minutes of arc and allow easier calculation. Harry used his military protractor, calibrated in mils, when transferring his compass bearings to maps. He could calculate the azimuth of an alignment on OS maps from any two grid references, which circumvented the inaccuracies that tend to creep in when drawing a line that traverses two map sheets.

Nowadays, with Google Earth, it is simplicity itself to draw accurate alignments on screen without having to visit a site to take compass bearings. This is a luxury for which I am ever grateful as it enabled me to reproduce the Glasgow Network without all that tedious visiting of sites and noting compass bearings. One problem I had initially was trying to find the optimum point in the Necropolis for the sightline centre. Harry mentions 'the north side' for an alignment to Crookston Castle and Walls Hillfort that coincided with an alignment written about by Ludovic Mann that passed through St Enoch Square. This would suggest the high point of the Necropolis by the John Knox statue. However, I was unable to resolve all the alignments from this point; instead, a locus to the south of the statue on the flat shoulder of the hill nearer the Monteath Mausoleum gave the best fit for a majority of alignments. This would have been the inhabited part of the hill in prehistory and seems a more natural location for the sightline centre. If I had drawn the lines perfectly straight from end to end, some of them would no doubt have passed through the higher part of the hill, but the map would have been a mess of overlapping lines with no obvious locus so, for neatness, I divided many of them into shorter sections to keep things tidy.

At the other end of the scale, the low point of Carmyle Fords proved troublesome even for Harry to find a definite mark point. Harry mentions two fords; the 'King's Ford', also called the 'Thief's Ford', is where the Clydeford Bridge is now, just beside the mouth of the Kirk Burn; the other ford he places around 300m upstream where there was once a ferry crossing, leading him to postulate a hypothetical settlement somewhere "on the banks of the Clyde between the fords" (1984, 49). Given that his own schema postulates sight lines between high points in the landscape, it is difficult to see how this location could figure in the network, yet so many alignments seem to pass through the area that it became the easternmost point in what Harry calls his 'Glasgow Triangle' of sites   (the other points being the Necropolis at the apex and Camphill and Crookston Castle along the base line). For travellers navigating up the Clyde valley along the Tinto-Duncolm PSA, it is a natural place to ford the river, so perhaps it's not unreasonable to consider it a mark point on the way.

Some of the alignments that Harry surveyed are not as bullet straight as you might think. When plotting them in Google Earth, I was forced to break some of the longer ones into shorter sections, resulting in some slightly dog-legged lines on the map. There are some positively egregious examples in *Forgotten Footsteps*, such as the Cairnpapple/ Plean Tower/ Stirling Castle/ Doune Castle/ Doune Cross ley, which can align with either Doune Castle or Doune Cross, but not both. Or take Houston Cross, which is supposed to be on the ley between Paisley Abbey and The Motte near Duchal House according to the map in *Forgotten Footsteps*, yet is almost 200m off the alignment, and anyway was long ago moved from its original position by the parish church, which was even farther away.

> Don't take the results too seriously. Some of the alignments stand up to analysis, others don't. I followed Watkins' instructions as best as I could, but the Scottish landscape refused to conform.
> — Harry Bell*

I have managed to add a few additional sites from my own research to bolster the validity of many of Harry's PSAs, but had I been doing the original research, I don't think it likely that I would have included all these alignments, particularly Walls Hill fort. It may be the third-largest hillfort in Scotland, enclosing an area of 7.5 hectares, and the likely oppidum of the Damnoni tribe, yet from the north of the city, it is not particularly noteworthy as a skyline feature compared with other sites like Neilston Pad,

---

* glasgowsecretgeometry.uk/leyline-quest/#nap

which Harry completely ignores despite the presence of ancient earthworks on its top. But perhaps this reflects the fact that Harry, who lived in East Kilbride, was better acquainted with the north side landmarks as he was looking in that direction, whereas I've always lived in the north-west of the city and looked southwards.

In updating and expanding Harry's network, I have tried to adhere to Watkins principles for the most part when adding new sites. Although, like Harry, I am not averse to including a three-site alignment providing at least one of the sites intersects another alignment. I also include items of general historical or psychogeographic interest if they happen to fall on an alignment. So, on the interactive website map, you will find things that are not sightline centres, such as cist burials, Roman coin deposits, holy wells, haunted buildings etc. For fun, I've even included the 'Victorian Church Ley' that is Great Western Road, and there are some other as-yet unconnected sites that may yet end up being part of the network.

Despite its quirkiness, the viability of the PSAs linking the basic core Glasgow Network sites of Necropolis, Camphill, Crookston and the Devil's Plantation is, in my opinion, beyond random chance. There is no denying that such sightlines exist within the city and could be used to navigate across the Clyde valley without getting lost, although whether they were utilised by early travellers in this way remains a matter of conjecture. Subsequent additions and extensions to the network have overlaid additional layers of complexity and meaning, each pathway leading deeper into the psychogeography of the city, whose secrets can only be revealed as you explore the Glasgow Network of Aligned Sites.

Dowsing the Glasgow Network

Speaking as a professional dowser and geomancer (and a past President of the British Society of Dowsers), I feel that a brief overview of the current dowsing scene might be beneficial for non-dowser readers.

Although not dismissing the idea out of hand, Harry retained a healthy scepticism of dowsing following a couple of experiments, firstly with his friend Jim Cairney and subsequently with a group of dowsers from the Scottish Dowsing Association. He says that over the years he had watched "at least 40" dowsers at work.[2] However, as far as I know, he did not have any formal dowsing training himself. On the latter outing, he noted that the dowsers seemed to find lines spaced about 30m apart, but they did not seem to bear much connection to his own alignments:

> ...*whatever they were finding, it had absolutely no demonstrable connection with Prehistoric Site Alignments. (Leyline Quest)*

Dowsing can be a very subjective activity, and when a group of dowsers work together, it can be difficult to keep everyone 'on the same page'. Mental focus is key when dowsing for anything, even more so when the target is something intangible like a ley, and it is essential to hold a clear picture of the object of your search in your mind as you dowse if you want to have any success at it. Without a common frame of reference, it is perfectly possible for different dowsers to interpret their findings differently in such situations, rather like the parable about the blind men trying to describe an elephant.[*]

Things have moved on considerably since Harry's day. There are any number of subtle earth energies that may be picked up with dowsing rods. These include the previously-mentioned energy leys

---

* wikipedia.org/wiki/Blind_men_and_an_elephant

(generally 3-4m wide or greater, sometimes they coincide with visual leys but can also be found independently), a bewildering variety of earth grids, undulating serpentine currents, dragon lines, spirals, vortices and so on (it is likely that the dowsers picking up lines "about 30m apart" that Harry mentions were dowsing some form of earth grid).[*]

Some of Harry's PSAs *may* coincide with one of these earth energy manifestations, in which case they could probably be classed as an energy ley,[3] but most are purely visual Watkinsian leys, which are more akin to the 'lines of intention' mentioned in the Introduction. The fallacy that every ley must contain some sort of spiritual or etheric energy is now so well-entrenched in common consciousness that it's almost impossible to escape, but it is perfectly possible to have a visual ley with zero detectable earth energy. Most of Harry's PSAs are of this type. It is possible to dowse for these, but it's really more of an intellectual exercise and, in my experience, requires prior knowledge of their presence at a site to be able to accurately locate them.

But this story is not about dowsing Harry's lines — that would be a book in itself. I recommend that you put such thoughts of mystical energy out of your head and, like Harry, approach the Glasgow Network with an open heart and an open mind, keeping your eyes on the horizon ahead.

[3] For an example, see 'The Ghost Ley of Paisley' in the Afterthoughts & Addenda section (page 218).

---

[*] For interested readers, a helpful glossary may be found at: britishdowsing.net/glossary-of-dowsing-terms/

References

Bell, Harry, *The Alternative Archaeology Project, ACFA Occasional Paper No. 2*, Dec. 2000
— *Glasgow's Secret Geometry*, Leyline Publications, 1984

Daiches, David, *Glasgow*, Granada, 1977

Black, William Henry, Address to British Archaeological Association Congress, September 1870. Cited in *BAA Journal* No. 27, 1871. Referenced at: www.cantab.net/users/michael. behrend/repubs/bg_pioneers/pages/black_bl.html

Lockyer, Sir Norman, Stonehenge and other British Stone Monuments Astronomically Considered, 1906. Referenced at www.gutenberg.org/files/62342/62342-h/62342-h.htm

Mann, Ludovic McLellan, 1915. Archaic Sculpturings in Dumfries and Galloway, *Transactions of* Dumfriesshire *and Galloway Natural History & Antiquarian Society*, Third Series Vol. 3. Referenced at: dgnhas.org.uk/sites/default/files/transactions/3003.pdf

Mann/a, *Salisbury Plain, an Astronomical Blackboard*. Referenced at: www.cantab.net/users/michael.behrend/repubs/mann_afr/pages/sal_plain.html

Ross, T Edwards, *The Ley Line in North America*, ASD Journal Vol. 14, No. 3 August 1974

Stukeley, William, *Stonehenge, A Temple Restor'd to the British Druids,* Innys & Manby, London, 1740

Watkins, Alfred, *Early British Trackways*, 1922.
—*The Old Straight Track*, 1925.

FORGOTTEN FOOTSTEPS

A baffling new dimension in Scottish history, charted for the first time in 4,000 years.

Harry Bell

Edited & annotated by

Grahame Gardner

Scotland has always been a land of mystery and strange happenings.

We have a monster in Loch Ness, a fairy flag at Dunvegan and a community in Findhorn who converse with the spirits of nature and produce forty-pound cabbages and eight-foot delphiniums.

We also have ley-lines...

'The Old Straight Track'.

...*a network of invisible lines stretching across Scotland from the Isle of Druids to Arthur's Seat, secretly signposted by standing stones, faery mounds and cairns, linked to sites in Glasgow, Edinburgh, Dundee, Paisley, Stirling, etc.*

You can follow them yourself — as straight as a laser beam through ancient forts, sacred Druid groves, haunted castles and extinct volcanoes. Ghosts have been seen along the way and phantom voices heard at dead of night — somewhere in an unknown time dimension the presence of the early folk still lingers...

Photo: Grahame Gardner

Doune Mercat Cross. In 1745, Prince Charlie's Highlanders rested from their march and supped brose on its steps.

Bonnyton Mound, aka The De'il's Plantin.

Introduction

You can call them leys, ley-lines, or the Prehistoric System of Aligned Sites. For over 4,000 years they've formed an invisible network of straight lines that run through Britain linking hundreds of ancient and sacred sites.

They were re-discovered in 1920 when Alfred Watkins, an amateur archaeologist from Hereford, noticed that the castles, fords, churches, crossroads and prehistoric mounds in his part of the country were joined together in an interlocking pattern of unseen lines. He called them 'leys' after the old Anglo-Saxon word for a forest clearing.

After five years of research on the subject, Watkins wrote *The Old Straight Track* which outlined his theories. Orthodox archaeologists of the day did not take kindly to discoveries by anyone outside their learned circle and the book was heavily criticised. For nearly fifty years *The Old Straight Track* went out of print, but not out of mind. The theories it expounded were never forgotten.

Interest was renewed at the time of the flying saucer sightings of the 1960s. The busiest place in Britain for Unidentified Flying Object sightings proved to be Warminster in Wiltshire, and when someone remembered that thirteen ley-lines ran through Warminster the theory was put forward that UFOs used ley-lines for navigation. Was it possible that some ancient power still flowed along the leys on a different wavelength from that perceived by the basic senses?

It was recalled how folk-myths and legends follow ley-lines throughout Britain with tales of haunted castles, water-sprites at the fords, ghostly music from ruined churches, phantom highwaymen at the crossroads, fairy forts — and now flying saucers! The type of phenomenon had changed with the times but it still clung tenaciously to the Old Straight Track. UFOs were seen over ley-lines from Kent to Yorkshire and controversy raged — until the sightings tailed off — by that time ley-lines were back in the news for a different reason.

In 1966, Professor Gerald Hawkins wrote *Stonehenge Decoded* and shocked the world of archaeology by announcing that the megaliths of Stonehenge had provided him with astronomical data so complex that he needed a computer to decipher it.

Again ley-lines were the link between past and future. Stonehenge is one of the oldest ley sites in the country and stands at the intersection of several long-distance alignments mentioned in *The Old Straight Track*. It was inevitable that after *Stonehenge Decoded* was written, the main areas of ley-line research would be stone circles and standing stone alignments.

Once again, strange things happened. People began to realise that some of Britain's ancient stones were 'live'.

[1] Tom Lethbridge was also a well-known dowser who developed his own 'long pendulum' system to determine the 'rate' of an object according to the length of string it reacted to.

At the Merry Maidens circle in Cornwall the Cambridge archaeologist TC Lethbridge[1] received a sensation like an electric shock from one of the stones. The same thing happened to observers at Harold's Stones in Monmouthshire and to Paul

Screeton (author of *Quicksilver Heritage*) at the Mark Stone, Hart, County Durham.[2]

[2] Other dowsers have reported similar reactions.

Quartz is an important constituent of many of those stones. Strangely enough, wafer-thin slices of quartz are used to control the frequencies of radio transmitters. Could the early Britons have known more about those things than was ever suspected?

Serious researchers began to wonder if stone circles had been some sort of neolithic cathedrals where the ancients had gathered to send waves of mental energy along the leys. Standing stones could have acted as boosters or transformers of such energy. It would tie in with ley-line legends of wishing stones, healing stones and fertility stones; different types of stone but each one leading to an altered state of consciousness.

The unseen power of the leys could be a natural phenomenon or some strange form of telekinesis that has lingered in the atmosphere since prehistoric times. The question remains — did the ancient Britons discover it or did they create it?

The possibility exists that the early Britons had psychic powers that have atrophied in modern man. Consider the fact that from the 15th to the 18th century thousands of psychics were burned at the stake, drowned in ducking stools or rolled downhill in barrels pierced with nails. Many young women who were executed for witchcraft had not lived long enough to bear the children that would normally have inherited their powers. If Stone-Age psychics were spared such persecution it is a reasonable supposition that there was a higher incidence of extrasensory perception in the neolithic population than there is today. The legends of lost knowledge could have a basis in fact after all.

Stirling Castle. Like many other sites along The Old Straight Track, the castle is said to be haunted. Ghostly footsteps have been heard pacing a disused sentry beat and the misty figure of the Green Lady, reputed to be an attendant of Mary Queen of Scots, has been seen walking the corridors many times.

Looking along the alignment from the ramparts of Stirling Castle towards Abbey Craig fort (which houses the Wallace Monument), Castle Law hillfort and Dumyat (this is not one of Harry's alignments —Ed.).

Photo: Stock via Pexels

Tracing ley-lines is one of Scotland's fastest-growing hobbies — a modern pastime that originated away back in the Stone Age. With the help of the chart at the back of the book, a newly-discovered network of leys can now be followed across the country through ruined palaces, ancient keeps, village kirkyards and strange UFO-shaped mounds. Ben Lomond, Edinburgh Castle, Dundee Law and many other well-known landmarks are linked to the network; a castle in a Glasgow housing scheme turns out to be the site of a prehistoric crossroads, a heap of stones in a town park becomes an ancient route marker — on ley-lines anything can happen!

Photo: Grahame Gardner

'The ship that never sailed' — Looking along the ley from the beach at Abercorn towards Blackness Castle (top right). The castle's pointed shape jutting into the Forth gives it the appearance of a grounded ship. Over the years it has mostly functioned as a garrison and prison, but in modern times it has featured in several film and television productions —Ed.

Cairnpapple Hill, sanctuary and burial cairns. The oldest site on your chart; constructed in five phases from 2,500 BC onwards. Access to the burial chamber is obtained through the roof of the mound. Ufologists claim that structures like Cairnpapple are primitive replicas of spacecraft built by the ancient Britons on sites where astronauts landed in prehistoric times.

Doune Castle. Built on a mound that must be thousands of years older than previously suspected. The castle is in direct alignment with the great basalt rock of Stirling, the buried Roman fort at Mumrills, and the Stone-Age sanctuary at Cairnpapple.

The New Stone Age

Until the 1960s, the common image of the ancient Briton was a man dressed in animal skins, carrying a club and dragging a woman by the hair. Stonehenge and other ancient structures were supposedly the work of Greek or Egyptian architects assisted by gangs of British labourers. Since the recent recalibration of the carbon-14 dating process all this has been proved false. It is now known that some of our megalithic monuments are actually older than the buildings from which they were supposedly copied.

Glasgow-born Professor Alexander Thom visited more than 500 megalithic sites from the Outer Hebrides to Brittany and came to the conclusion that many of them had once been used as lunar observatories. Throughout their construction a standard measurement of 2.72 ft. had been used; Professor Thom called it the megalithic yard.

The men who built those monuments lived in the Neolithic or New Stone Age, between 3500 BC and 1800 BC. Neolithic peoples were the founders of our civilisation. They introduced pottery to Britain, grew crops, raised cattle and changed the economy of the country from hunting and food-gathering to agriculture. They wove ropes with vegetable fibres and manufactured stone tools from easily flaked rock such as flint or basalt. Their homes were rough log cabins with pitched thatch roofs and mud-sealed walls; their dead were buried carefully in stone-walled communal graves covered by mounds of earth.

What did they look like, those architects of the Prehistoric System of Aligned Sites? 'Dark they were, and golden-eyed', whisper the legends linking them with lost continents, forgotten tribes and the like.

Down-to-earth archaeology is understandably reticent about golden eyes but tells us of a race of Mediterranean origin whose average height was 5'2" (1.53m) for a man and 4'11" (1.47m) for a woman. Grooved bones found in their graves point to the attachment of powerful muscles, so they must have been a short, stocky people. Their cranial capacity was much the same as our own, and their intelligence has been proved beyond doubt.

With stone axes, deer antler picks and shovels made from the shoulder blades of oxen, they built complex lunar observatories in stone, using geometric theorems that were forgotten till the days of Pythagoras over a thousand years later.

They were a peaceful people. They had no wars and left no evidence that their stone weapons were ever used for anything but skinning animals or other domestic purposes. Although they lived in mud huts they built monuments to an unknown deity that have lasted till the present day; they seem to have contented themselves searching for spiritual enlightenment rather than material gain.[3]

[3] Modern osteo-archaeological research suggests that the opposite may be true, There is considerable evidence of weapon-inflicted skull injuries and projectile wounds on excavated bones of the period.

Part of their search may have led to the evolution of a network of invisible lines linking the sites where they practised their religion. Like the Mayas of Mexico, the early Britons could have considered their roads to be holy and travellers on them to be under divine protection. No-one can say, but for some strange reason, from the New Stone Age onwards, people have been drawn to ley-lines without ever knowing why.

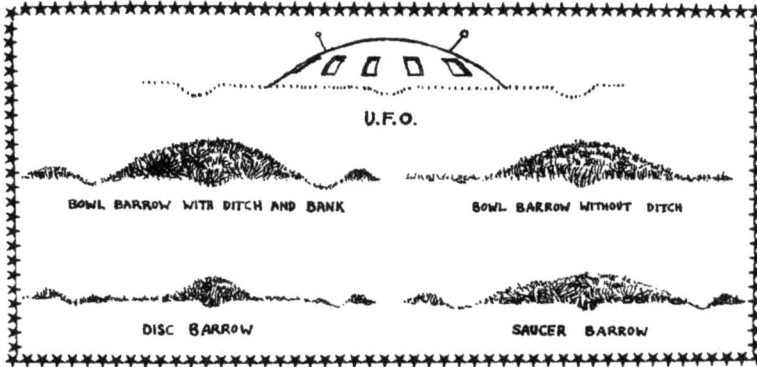

U.F.O.

BOWL BARROW WITH DITCH AND BANK

BOWL BARROW WITHOUT DITCH

DISC BARROW

SAUCER BARROW

Ley-line Mysteries

The most common type of prehistoric monument in Britain is the Bronze-Age barrow. Barrows are the mounds of earth that cover prehistoric burial areas; over 15,000 are still in existence, varying in diameter from 5 to 50 metres.

Ufologists (UFO-ologists) believe that barrows are crude earthen replicas of spacecraft, built to worship astronauts who visited the earth thousands of years ago. To support this theory they point to the close resemblance between barrows and the various types of UFOs reported over Britain.

Saucer, disc and bowl are categories of round barrow; they also appear to be categories of spacecraft. Flying saucer; disc-shaped object; inverted bowl — these are all terms that have been used in recent eye-witness accounts of UFO sightings.

The cigar-shaped neolithic long barrow could also have its counterpart in the skies; cigar-shaped craft were reported at Winchester in 1976 and at Broadhaven, Wales in February 1977.

Ufologists maintain that sightings occur on ley-lines because spacecraft made their first contact with earth-dwellers there.

Anyone particularly interested in a flying-saucer shaped mound can see one from the roadway on ley 292, near Kilmacolm, Renfrewshire. Though marked on the map as a Norman motte, it may well have earlier origins.

Cup and ring marks are another enigma of the Bronze Age. Averaging around 18 inches in diameter, they've been found on stones and outcrops of rock in many parts of Britain.

Their purpose is still unknown. They could be anything from charts that explain the motion of planets round fixed stars, to a sign that gold, copper or an underground spring can be found in the vicinity.

Scandinavian rock carvings, as illustrated above, often show cup and ring marks in conjunction with ships and stick figures. Since the pictures often overlap earlier ones, it has been suggested that they were carved for religious reasons — a new picture being made at every gathering.

In Tibet, pilgrims once carved single cup marks along the route of their holy wanderings. Nearer home, ley-line pilgrims can find a cup and ring mark carved on a rock 40 metres east of the seat overlooking Douglas Terrace on ley 628 in the King's Park, Stirling.[4]

[4] Harry's numbering system for leys remains a mystery.

In the Early Iron Age, giant outdoor drawings or hill figures began to appear on hillsides in the south of England. Formed by removing turf and exposing white chalky soil underneath, they were often constructed near ley-line forts or enclosures.

The 365ft. long Uffington White Horse on the Berkshire Downs is believed to represent Epona the Horse Goddess. Hill figures like this are visible for miles. Because the best viewpoint is from overhead, ufologists maintain that hill figures were intended to attract the attention of passing spacecraft.

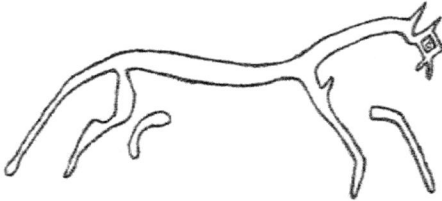

Around AD 100, a network of straight tracks was formed on a barren plateau above the Nazca valley in Peru.

The tracks, or *pistas* were made by a subtractive process similar to that once used to make hill-figures in Britain. Dark oxidised stones were lifted from the desert floor and sandy clay exposed beneath.

Some of the tracks look like six-mile long runways for jet aircraft, others radiate from mounds and piles of stones. Geometric figures, flowers and animal designs are laid out in the same way. One frequently recurring pattern is described as a 'target with seven circles'.[5]

Strangely enough, the largest cup and ring marks in Britain are also carved in this design. Cups with seven concentric rings can be seen three feet in diameter near Port William in Wigtownshire and on a ley-line at Achnabreck near Lochgilphead, Argyllshire. Both locations are near the sea.

Could ancient Britons have sailed the Atlantic?

Did their descendants attempt to start a ley system in South America?

[5] Ones with seven rings are frequently cited as early iterations of the seven-circuit Classical labyrinth pattern.

One of the strangest landmarks to appear on any ley-line is the Glastonbury Zodiac, also known as the Temple of the Stars.

It was first discovered in Elizabethan times when a scholar named Dr Dee found what he thought was the work of Merlin the magician in the unusual arrangement of prehistoric earthworks in the Glastonbury area. He drew a map of the area, noting that the stars that had been reproduced on the ground "lye onlie on the celestial path of the Sonne, moon and planets."

The Zodiac was rediscovered in 1929 by Mrs Katherine E Maltwood when she was researching the legends of King Arthur and the Holy Grail.

Outlined by rivers, footpaths and various natural features, the zodiacal figures are sprawled in a circle One of the strangest landmarks to appear on any ley-line is the Glastonbury Zodiac, also known as the Temple of the Stars.

An aerial photograph of the zodiac can be seen in Janet and Colin Bord's excellent book, *Mysterious Britain*. The figure of Leo appears to be the clearest of the group; the windings of the River Gary form the underside of the lion and footpaths form the head and back. The whole zodiac is best viewed from three miles overhead.

Did it appear by accident or was it part of a predestined plan that compelled people to use footpaths which eventually gave form to the figures? Because of the different origins of its features, the zodiac cannot be dated. The only fact that can be deduced with reasonable accuracy is that many of the footpaths inside the zodiac date back to the Iron Age — the days when Druids roamed the land.

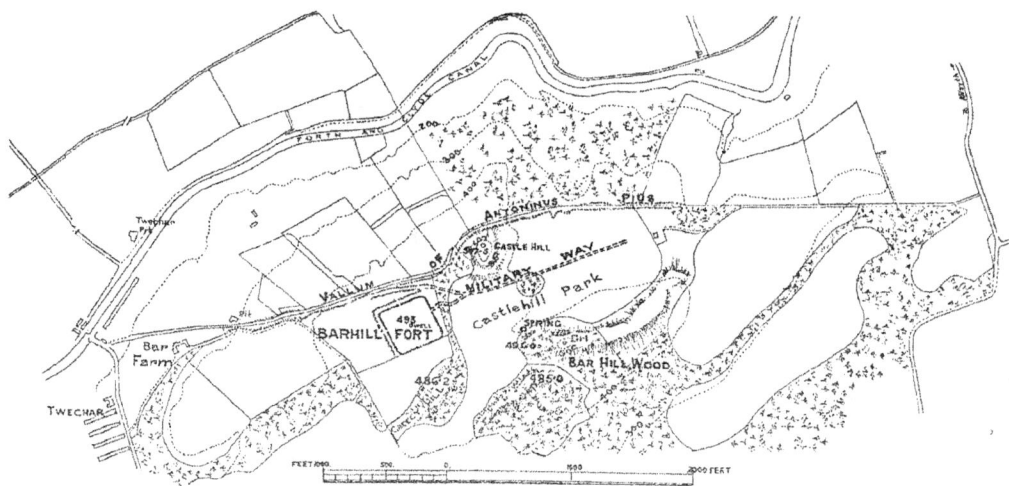

Medionemeton

One of the great unsolved mysteries of British archaeology is the whereabouts of the lost Druid sanctuary of Medionemeton. It was said by a Roman chronicler to be situated in that part of Scotland where the country is narrowest from sea to sea — obviously the isthmus between the rivers Forth and Clyde. At present the only sanctuary known in this area is Cairnpapple Hill, and because of this, archaeologists have occasionally suggested that Cairnpapple is, in fact, Medionemeton.

There is nothing that interests ley-line researchers more than a good unsolved mystery, but before we start to theorise, we should first examine the factors common to other Druid sanctuaries in existence at that time. According to Caesar, Druids in France met annually "in the centre of all Gaul, in the land of the Carnutes". Over in Ireland, Druidic assemblies were held at the Hill of Ushnagh in County Westmeath. This hill is so centrally situated that it is often called the

Navel of Ireland. Might not Medionemeton be in a similar location in Scotland?

The name Medionemeton is derived from two Gallo-Brittonic words: *medio* meaning 'middle', and *nemeton*, 'a sacred grove or sanctuary'. As Cairnpapple Hill is six miles from the Firth of Forth and over 30 miles from the Clyde estuary, it is difficult to see how it could have been the 'middle sanctuary'. There is also the fact that Druid sanctuaries were invariably set in forest clearings. As the photograph of Cairnpapple shows, it could hardly be called a forest clearing either.

At this point, the author will permit himself a little guesswork. It has long been one of my theories that if Medionemeton is ever found it will be somewhere in the vicinity of a ley-line crossroads. Stonehenge and Cairnpapple are on prehistoric intersections, so perhaps Medionemeton is, too. Ley-lines could be the missing link in the search for the lost sanctuary.

There is an old saying that all roads lead to Rome, and in this instance there might well be some truth in it. In my own, unsolicited opinion, the only logical site for Medionemeton is at Castle Hill, 200 metres north-east of Bar Hill Roman Fort. It is a natural forest clearing surrounded by trees and it overlooks an important ley-line crossroads; the Antonine Wall runs close by, and significantly, for an unknown reason at an unknown date, the Romans are believed to have destroyed the ramparts of Castle Hill and reduced them to terraces.

[6] Graham Robb, in his book *The Ancient Paths*, confirms this theory with the supporting evidence that Bar Hill Roman fort is positioned exactly halfway along the Antonine Wall.

Castle Hill is higher than Bar Hill and from its Summit both the Forth and the Clyde can be seen on a clear day. It is 14 miles from the Firth of Forth and 15 or less to the point where the Clyde met the sea in ancient times.[6]

If there was ever a middle sanctuary in Scotland, there could be no better site for it than Castle Hill, NS 709761.

Castle Hill is ten miles from Glasgow and easily reached by road or rail (Croy Station). The old map above may be of assistance to anyone who makes the pilgrimage.

Arthur's Seat in the King's Park, Edinburgh. A volcanic plug topped with the scarcely-visible remains of a prehistoric fort with an estimated area of 20 acres. In 1836 five boys hunting for rabbits found a set of 17 miniature coffins containing small wooden figures in a cave on the crags of Arthur's Seat. Their purpose has remained a mystery ever since —Ed.

Harry investigating a dolmen in Brittany.

Celts and Druids

Celtic peoples began to colonise Britain in the early Iron Age. Amongst the improvements they brought from Central Europe was the potter's wheel and an excellent iron plough that could crack through clay soils to produce crops on land previously considered useless. They were excellent craftsmen and brought many new tools and new skills to Britain. They also brought their priesthood, the Druids.

Today, the presence of the Druids still clings to The Old Straight Track in the hundreds of monuments that bear their name. Druid circles, Druid stones and Druid temples are found on ley-lines all over Britain.

It is now known that those monuments existed centuries before the Druids came to Britain. Druids possibly held ceremonies at those sites, but they never built them.

Much of what we know about the Druids comes down to us from the chronicles of Roman historians and the journals of early Christian monks. Because the Druids had enemies in both camps, unbiased accounts are difficult to find.

Druids are mentioned frequently in the old Irish tales and poems; in pre-Christian times the education of youth seems to have been left largely in their hands. All learning was committed to memory and school was held both indoors and outdoors. Most of the time, teaching was carried on as the master and his pupils travelled from place to place in a manner similar to the *seikan* or holy wanderings of Zen Buddhists.

According to Irish chronicles, the Druids were men of supernatural powers who were capable of astral travelling, reading omens and foreseeing the future. Their nirvana lay just below the horizon in *Tir na n-Og* the Land of Eternal Youth, wherein there is 'naught save truth, and where is neither age nor decay, sorrow nor gladness, nor envy nor jealousy, hatred nor haughtiness'.

There were four annual festivals in the Celtic ritual calendar, *Imbolc*, Feb 1st; *Beltane*, May 1st; *Lugnasadh*, Aug 1st and *Samhain*, Nov 1st. They still survive in Scotland, give or take a day, as Candlemas, May Day, Lammas and Hallowe'en. The last named has long been known as the night for "ghosties and ghoulies and long-legged beasties and things that go bump in the night".[7]

Ley sites have a reputation for extra activity at Hallowe'en, from singing stones in Wales to witches dancing at Duncryne on ley 374, near Loch Lomond.

Druids held their sacred rites in groves where 13 trees were planted for each of the lunar months. This could help to identify such places, but its doubtful if so many species of tree could still co-exist in such a small area centuries after the parent trees died off.

The great Druid sanctuary of Medionemeton in Southern Scotland has not yet been found, but if it ever is, it may well be on a ley-line like so many more of their haunts.[8]

[7] These are the cross-quarter days, when the sun's apparent rising position is midway between solstice and equinox (the quarter days) Together, these provide the eight-fold division of the Celtic year.

[8] See note #6 (page 64).

The Invaders

There is no mention of ley-lines in the chronicles of Britain's invaders. For those who can read between the lines of history there does not have to be, the ley-line story tells itself.

Britain was the last place on earth the Roman soldier wanted to see on his marching orders. It was Ultima Thule — the end of the world as far as the old sweats of the Roman Army were concerned.

It had a reputation as a land of ghosts and strange spirits; further discouragement came from the historian Tacitus in the form of the first recorded comment on British weather, "...unpleasant; though not cold it rains much".

Worst of all was the rumour that turned hardened veterans pale beneath their suntan — it was said that Britain was a land where grapes never grew. Even the dullest recruit knew that if there was no grapes there would be no wine!

Much of the ley system had fallen into decay long before the Roman invasion. Direct routes over the hills had been suitable for pedestrians, but wheeled traffic needed gentler gradients.

In flatter parts of the country the Old Straight Track was still in use, and to improve communications the Romans paved ley-lines for hundreds of miles, often joining them to new stretches of road they built themselves. It is unlikely they were aware of the vast network that once had existed.

Road building was an integral part of the Roman Army duties. The biggest rocks a man could lift were bedded into damp sand to form a foundation; hammers pounded gravel through the cracks and the crunching wheels of chariot traffic did the rest. It was rough and ready but it worked; 1,900 years later there are still 6,000 miles of Roman roads left in Britain. Much has been surfaced, but parts of the old Military Way still exist; neglected, forgotten, deeply rutted by the wheels of army supply chariots.

The ruts are 4' 8½" apart — amazingly enough, this measurement survived the centuries to re-appear at the time the first railways were constructed. The standard gauge of British railway lines today is the exact width of the old Roman chariots.[9]

[9] Fact-checking website snopes.com lists this as 'partly true'. (See note page 314)

The most impressive feat of Roman military engineering Britain is undoubtedly the stone wall built by Emperor Hadrian to keep out the "wild and unprofitable peoples" of the north. It runs from Tyne to Solway across 73 miles of rough moorland country and took about eight years to complete.

Further north is the Antonine Wall built across Scotland on narrow isthmus between the Forth and Clyde. This wall was built of turf and has largely disintegrated, but the ditch can be followed across Scotland for miles and most of the forts can still be seen.

According to orthodox archaeology, Bar Hill, highest of Antonine forts, stands on the site of a fort built during campaigns of Agricola around AD 80. It now seems likely that the site has even earlier origins. Ley 628 runs through Bar Hill on the way to Stirling Castle and ley 011 passes by on way to Arthur's Seat. Bar Hill was obviously a ley site long before it became a Roman fort. It is also the only Antonine fort detached from the wall; it stands about 40 metres south of the ramparts.

When the Romans left Britain in AD 410, many of the old Iron Age forts along the Old Straight Track were re-furbished and used again in the years that followed. One of those forts was Cadbury Castle.

It's a peaceful spot now, an 18-acre enclosure on a green Somerset hill guarded by steep banks and ditches. It is also home of one of Britain's most enduring legends because according to the Tudor historian John Leland, "at South Cadbury standeth Camelot."

The story of King Arthur and his court at Camelot has been known for centuries but only recently has it been seriously researched. Part of the legend has emerged as fact and today most historians agree that Arthur was the *Dux Bellorum* or battle chief of a highly mobile cavalry force that fought against Saxon invaders around AD 500. Victory at Badon (probably Bath) confined the Saxons to the east of Britain for another 50 years.

Arthur died of wounds after the battle of Camlann and was buried at the Isle of Avalon, now believed to be in the area encompassed by the Glastonbury Zodiac.

Legend has it that King Arthur is not dead but lies asleep beneath the hills, ready to rise again in his country's hour of need.[10]

[10] In more recent years, there has been an upsurge of interest in the idea that the Arthur mythos was based on Scottish tales. Hugh MacArthur and Stuart McHardy have written much about this theory.

The colonisation of England by the Anglo-Saxons was a slow and gradual process. Their involvement with ley-lines is more difficult to trace than most because so many of their buildings were impermanent structures made of wood. When they did build in stone, they built well. Their main contribution to ley-line history is Westminster Abbey.

In *The Old Straight Track* Alfred Watkins mentions an alignment running through the Abbey. This gives rise to the intriguing thought that for the past 900 years the kings and queens of England have been crowned on a ley-line.

The Scots settled in Britain in the middle of the 5th century. Sailing from Ulster, they occupied forts in Argyll and formed a buffer state between Strathclyde and the Picts.

At one time they owned a kingdom of Dalriada in Scotland and another of the same name in Ireland.

In AD 563, Colmcille (St Columba) sailed to the Scotic Dairiada in a wicker coracle and founded a monastery on the island of Iona. Before the time of Colmcille Iona was known to the Gaels as *Innis nan Druidhneach*, Isle of the Druids.

The last successful invaders of Britain were the Normans. They seem to have been attracted to ley-lines and built many of their timbered earthworks or mottes on cross-ley points. In Welsh border regions they sometimes fortified Bronze-Age barrows and used them as bases for cavalrymen and archers.

The Tower of London is a Norman castle built on the site of a wooden castle which in turn was built above a prehistoric mound.

True to the best ley-line traditions the Tower is said to be haunted. The execution of the Countess of Salisbury has been seen again on the anniversary of her death, and on one memorable occasion the appearance of a headless woman thought to be Anne Boleyn caused a guardsman to faint while on sentry duty.

It is easily seen how the Old Straight Track was modified by its many users through the ages. Different cultures built on the same site and obscured the origins of what had gone before. But for the fact that ley-lines are rigorously straight it would have been impossible to trace them and by now they would have been lost for ever.

'The Old Straight Track to Iona'

The Secret of Iona

When the Romans evacuated Britain they left behind a growing body of converts to the new Christian Church. Early Christians often accepted the new religion but were spiritually tied to the old places of worship. As a result, many Christian churches were built on prehistoric sites.

The most remote churches were often the safest from persecution, and in the Dark Ages many monasteries appeared on islands round the lesser-inhabited Celtic fringe areas of Britain.

One such island was Iona on the west coast of Scotland, known for centuries as 'the Blessed Isle'. Though only a mile broad and three miles long, Iona was held in such high esteem by the faithful that pilgrims came from all over Northern Europe to die there and lie till judgement day in its sacred soil.

St Oran's cemetery on Iona is the burial place of 7 Norwegian kings, 4 Irish kings, and 48 Scottish kings, including Duncan whose murder in 1040 became the subject of a Shakespearean play.

Today, the island is still a place of pilgrimage. Thousands of people go there year after year to walk in the footsteps of the men who kept the light of Christianity shining through the Dark Ages. They claim there is an atmosphere of sanctity on Iona that can be found nowhere else.

Modern pilgrims arrive by ferry from Fionnphort on the Isle of Mull and by steamer from Oban on the mainland — nobody goes the old way anymore.

The Old Straight Track to Iona starts on a huge basalt rock in the very heart of Scotland. Stirling Castle stands there today, but thousands of years ago the same rock was known to prehistoric man. The view must have been as breath-taking then as it is now. Highlands to the north, Ochil Hills to the north-east and the River Forth winding its way through the fertile plain below to a western skyline dominated by the graceful peak of Ben Lomond 26 miles away.

Stirling Castle, Ben Lomond and Iona: the names are legends in themselves.

Take a look at the map above, then draw a line from Stirling Castle westwards through Ben Lomond and on out to sea.

The line goes straight to the prehistoric fort of Dun I, the highest hill on Iona. At the foot of Dun I lies Iona Abbey, the most sacred place in Scotland.[11]

[11] Harry later said, *"The Old Straight Track to Iona that filled a vacant space in the top left-hand corner is a piece of New Age nonsense inspired by the 'geomantic corridors' and long-distance ley-lines in vogue at the time. It was once said of it 'only a crow or a holy man with a paraglider could travel that way'."* (see page 188).

Thus saith the Lord, stand ye in the ways and see, and ask for the old paths, where is the good way, and walk therein, and ye shall find rest for your souls.

— Jeremiah vi, 16.

Following the leys

There is an element of magic in ley-lines that has baffled archaeologists and computer experts alike. In spite of the fact that leys have been found in many parts of Britain, there is still no known way that a prehistoric society could have designed such an intricate network of alignments without maps and accurate surveying equipment.

At the end of this section of the book is a chart that will help you to appreciate the difficulties of this task. To complete the chart, follow the instructions and link the specified sites with a pencil and ruler. This is the first time your regional ley-lines have been charted like this in the 4,000 years of their existence, the results will surprise you.

You don't need to know anything about map reading to follow your ley-line chart. Just visit the main sites where the line surfaces and walk on from there. Most ley-lines are fairly well known locally and anyone will give you directions if you ask.

Naturally, things have changed since the Stone Age and it is difficult to follow ley-lines from end to end. The rights of private property owners must be considered and some sites will have to be passed by. There are still more than enough sites open to the public to make the venture well worthwhile.

The main things to look for are castles, fords, churches, crossroads and prehistoric monuments. There are no hard and fast rules, but to eliminate coincidence there should be at least four sites in alignment. The line must be exactly straight and only sites of pre-Roman origin can be considered genuine.

It is often difficult to determine this without historical knowledge of the area.

There's a mileage factor involved also; the sites should not be too far apart. For this reason, the Stirling Castle — Ben Lomond — Iona alignment has not been given a ley-line number yet. (To help in our research, Ley-line Publications have given index numbers to some of the leys north of Hadrian's Wall that we believe to be genuine).[12]

In the south of England, ley-hunters expect a site every two or three miles, churches and crossroads included. Scotland, Wales and hill districts of England have a smaller population and as a result churches and crossroads are thinner on the ground. In those areas any ley-line with an average of less than five miles between sites is worth investigating. Sites in this instance means those already marked on the Ordnance Survey map. A genuine ley-line followed on foot will soon reveal an amazing amount of unmarked sites.

Castles are sometimes 80 or 90 metres off the icy-line. Though prehistoric peoples stayed on the Old Straight Track, later generations often abandoned the original site and built defensive structures on the nearest high ground. In time, mansion houses were built on castle grounds, and though not exactly on the line, those places are still, in a sense, ley-sites.

In many cases the fords that prehistoric man used along the Old Straight Track have given way to bridges. Paradoxically, this can mean that a bright, new bridge stands on an ancient site while the old rustic bridge downstream does not. Again, a knowledge of local history is essential.

Churches included on ley-lines should be on sites that have been in continuous use for centuries. Modern churches in housing estates rarely qualify.

[12] Sadly, Harry's cataloguing system for numbering leys has not been passed on.

There is also some doubt about crossroads. Alfred Watkins' research in Hereford proved that although roads had changed direction, many crossroads remained in the same position. Because of recent escalation in road-building this is less than true nowadays. Without a market cross or other marker, the authenticity of crossroads as genuine ley-sites must now be questioned.

Prehistoric monuments can be barrows, cairns, stone circles,[13] dolmens, standing stones, forts or anything else constructed by the early Britons. Some of those sites are on private land and require permission to visit them. Leys cross rivers, lakes and sometimes the sea, without changing direction. The ancients often built crannogs (artificial islands) in the middle of a loch just to stay in line. When you consider the back-breaking labour involved, you can realise how important it was to them to stay on The Old Straight Track.

[13] As mentioned earlier, Alfred Watkins did not include stone circles in his original classification. These were added later by Paul Devereux.

Dumgoyach (aka Duntreath) stone row with Dumgoyne looming in the mist beyond.

The Map

(The following pages contain a facsimile of Harry's map, which was originally printed at a much larger scale on cartridge paper that was folded and glued inside the back cover of Forgotten Footsteps. *Sadly, that method proved to be impractical in this compendium volume. To maximise size, the map is printed across two pages. By carefully folding the right-hand page across, you will be able to match things up correctly. All the sites are listed in the master gazetteer later in the book. You can view all the alignments online at glasgowsecretgeometry.uk/ map — Ed.)*

There are 12 leys listed on the bottom right-hand corner of your chart. All ley-line termini are marked by a triangle and printed in capital letters; other sites are marked by a square and printed in smaller letters.

This is the first chart of Scottish ley-lines ever published. It was designed to prove existence of the invisible network of straight lines the run through churches, castles, and standing stones in Central Scotland. There is still no known way that a prehistoric society could have designed this network of alignments without maps and surveying equipment.

The ley-line story is 4,000 years old and by no means is this

The End

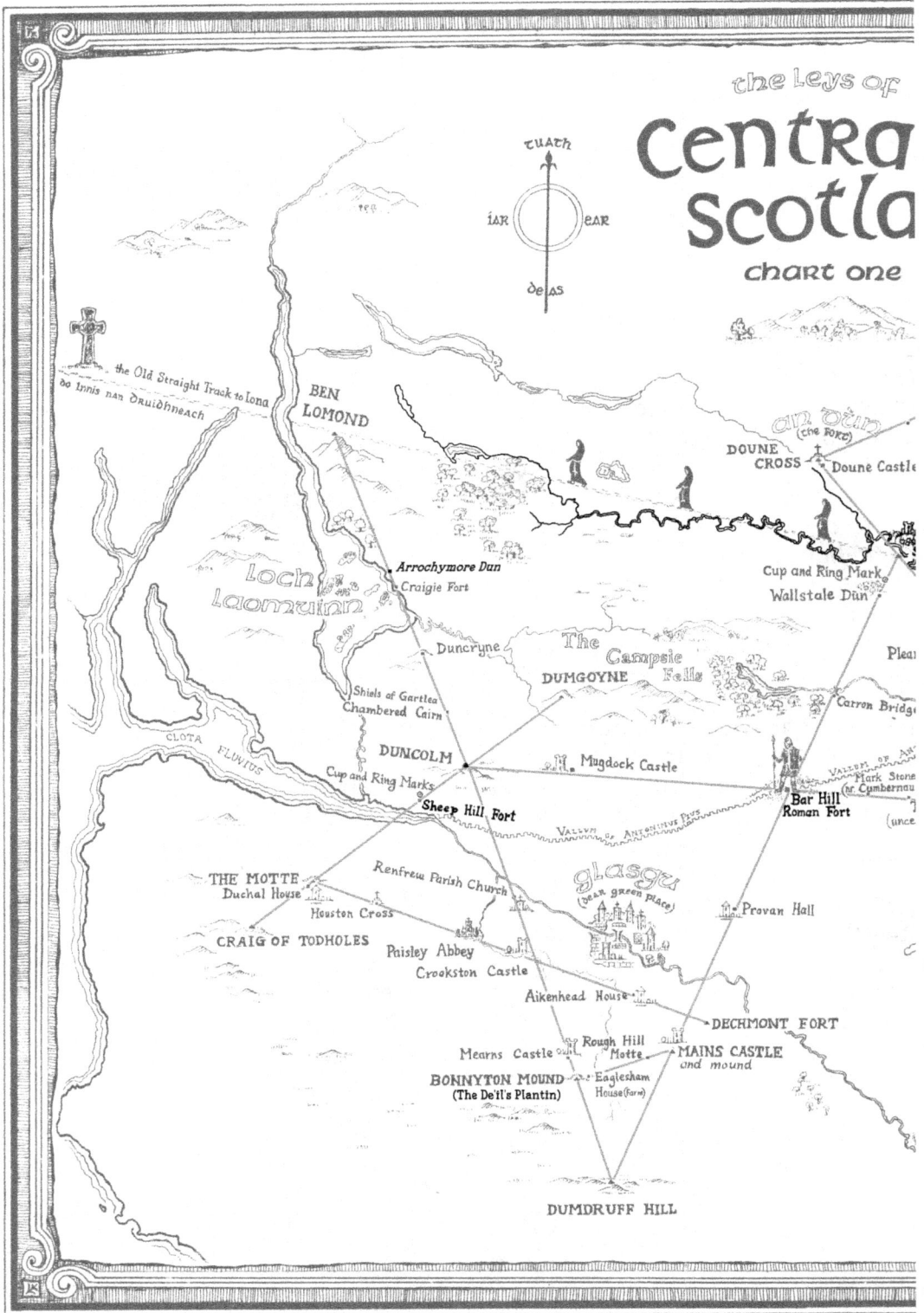

the Leys of

Centra
Scotla

chart one

τυατh

iar ● ear

deλs

the Old Straight Track to Iona
ao Innis nan Druidhneach

BEN
LOMOND

an oun
(the FORD)

DOUNE
CROSS — Doune Castle

Arrochymore Dun
Craigie Fort

Loch
Laomuinn

Cup and Ring Mark
Wallstale Dun

Duncryne

The Campsie Fells

DUMGOYNE

Plea

Shiels of Gartlea
Chambered Cairn

Carron Bridge

DUNCOLM

Mugdock Castle

VALLUM OF A

Mark Stone
(nr. Cumbernau

CLOTA FLUVIUS

Cup and Ring Marks

Bar Hill
Roman Fort

Sheep Hill Fort

VALLUM OF ANTONINUS PIUS

(unce

THE MOTTE
Duchal House

Renfrew Parish Church

glasgu
(dear green place)

Provan Hall

Houston Cross

CRAIG OF TODHOLES

Paisley Abbey
Crookston Castle

CRAIG OF TODHOLES

Aikenhead House

DECHMONT FORT

Rough Hill
Motte

MAINS CASTLE
and mound

Mearns Castle

BONNYTON MOUND
(The De'il's Plantin)

Eaglesham
House (farm)

DUMDRUFF HILL

of

al

land

ne

DUNDEE LAW
Mills Observatory
(site of vitrified fort)

Megginch Castle

Elcho Castle

Dunbarney House

Jackschairs Wood

St. Serfs Kirk, Dunning

Kincardine Castle

Millhill fort

The Ochil Hills

Loch Lobnuinn

Glassingal House

DUMYAT

Castle Law

ne Castle

Abbey Craig

STIRLING CASTLE

BRIDGENESS Roman Fort (site)

BODOTRIA AEST
The Firth of Forth

Plean Tower

Blackness Castle

Abercorn Castle (site)
Hopetoun House

on Bridge

site of Mumrills
Roman Fort

Linlithgow
Palace

St. Michael's
Church

Dolphington House

lark Stones
(Cumbernauld House)

Tomb
(uncertain origin)

Boudenhill Fort
Cockleroy Fort

Ochiltree Fort

Beechmount House
(Infirmary)

ST. GILES'
CATHEDRAL

CAIRNPAPPLE HILL
Neolithic Sanctuary

Huly Hill
(tumulus & standing stones)

Roseburn House
Edinburgh Castle

ARTHUR'S SEAT

Dun eadain
(Fort on a slope)

1. DUNDEE LAW to DOUNE CROSS	45¼ mls.		CASTLES and HOUSES
2. DOUNE CROSS to CAIRNPAPPLE HILL	25 "		open to the public
3. CAIRNPAPPLE HILL to BRIDGENESS	6¼ "		
4. BRIDGENESS to ARTHUR'S SEAT	17¼ "		BLACKNESS CASTLE
5. ARTHUR'S SEAT to DUNCOLM	50¼ "		CROOKSTON "
6. DUNCOLM to BEN LOMOND	17¼ "		DOUNE "
7. CAIRNPAPPLE HILL to ST. GILES' CATHEDRAL	17 "		EDINBURGH "
8. STIRLING CASTLE to DUMDRUFF HILL	33 "		ELCHO "
9. DUMDRUFF HILL to DUNCOLM	21 "		HOPETOUN HOUSE
10. DUMGOYNE to CRAIG OF TOPDHOLES	18½ "		LINLITHGOW PALACE
11. THE MOTTE to DECHMONT FORT	19¾ "		PROVAN HALL
12. MAINS CASTLE to BONNYTON MOUND	4¼ mls.		STIRLING CASTLE

A ley-line is no evidence of the existence of a right of way.

© Harry Bell 1977.

LEY-LINE PUBLICATIONS, EAST KILBRIDE

GLASGOW'S SECRET GEOMETRY

Harry Bell

Annotated and with additional commentary by

Grahame Gardner

An account of the discovery of the
Glasgow Network of Aligned Sites

Between 400 BC and 600 AD a network of straight tracks was formed on a barren plateau above the Nazca valley in the arid coastal area of Peru.

The tracks, or *pistas*, were made by a subtractive process reminiscent of that once used to make hill-figures in Britain. Dark soil and oxidised stones were lifted from the desert floor and sandy clay exposed beneath. Some of the tracks look like runways for jet aircraft, others radiate from mounds and piles of stones. Geometric figures, flowers and animal designs are laid out in the same way.

Also in Peru, in the former Inca city of Cuzco, *ceques* or invisible alignments radiate from the Temple of he Sun linking distant shrines and hilltops — somewhat similar to the alignments discovered at Camphill and the Necropolis. Because of all this, some of *Glasgow's Secret Geometry's* readers have asked — could ancient Britons have sailed the Atlantic? Did their descendants attempt to start a network of aligned sites in South America? It is an intriguing thought, but Harry Bell says there is no evidence for this whatsoever. The Glasgow alignments are, in fact, about 2,000 years older than those in South America.

Glasgow's Secret Geometry has acquired something of a cult status over the years, mostly by word of mouth, and now in this newly-revised format it is ready to meet a wider public. It's an heirloom of the future — take it home and check it out!

It would be a tragedy if this was discovered and lost in one generation — Glasgow Evening Times.

OBSERVATION

If you wish to see it before your eyes

have no fixed thoughts either for or against it.

— *Seng-t'san (d. AD 606)*

The Chinese say that a journey of a thousand miles starts with a single step. Just to be awkward, the journey I'm going to tell you about started on paper — with a neat row of four pencilled-in circles on a brand-new Ordnance Survey map of Glasgow and its surroundings.

Old Alfred's instructions, written over 50 years ago, were quite straightforward... First, pin your map onto a drawing board. Next, draw a circle around all the mounds, unworked stones, moats, holy wells, beacon points, crosses, crossroads, churches of ancient foundation and castles you can find. After that, stick a pin into an undoubted mark point (a mound or traditional stone), place a straight edge against the pin, and try to find four sites in a row.

Well, I wasn't too bad at the castles. I circled Mains, Crookston, Cathcart, Polnoon and Mearns before I ran out of ideas. For a church of ancient foundations I chose Glasgow Cathedral — but then, on second thoughts, I rubbed it out again. Nobody in their right mind would look for ancient trackways in the city nowadays. There had been so many changes during the eight years I'd been abroad, I could hardly find Anderston Cross, never mind holy wells and unworked stones.

What I needed to get me started was the undoubted mark point — a mound or traditional stone in the country somewhere. The only thing that I could think of in that category was a big, green mound I knew back in my cycling days. It was somewhere between Newton Mearns and Eaglesham; we used to pass it on the way back from the Malletsheugh Inn.

I chewed the end of my pencil for a while, and eventually the name came back to me — the De'il's Plantin. That was it — the Devil's Plantation. It was supposed to be haunted if I remembered correctly — not that I ever believed any of these old tales, but the place certainly had an atmosphere all its own. I always made sure I was in top gear when I cycled past in the dark anyway.

"It was supposed to be haunted, if I remembered correctly..."

The mound was marked on my map about a mile south of Mearns Castle, so I drew a neat circle round it and pressed in the pin. I put the edge of my plastic ruler to the pin, swivelled the ruler round, and then, to my surprise, a strange thing happened. The mound, Mearns Castle and Crookston Castle all fell into rough alignment. But Alfred had written "three points alone do not prove a ley, four being the minimum." So I thought for a bit, then extended the line past Crookston Castle. That way it passed through the grounds of Renfrew Parish Church, which was probably "of ancient foundation" as Alfred Watkins had specified. This meant I had the four sites in a row that I needed to start my fieldwork.

There was no way of knowing at the time, but by a stroke of sheer beginner's luck, I had picked one of the best possible places to start my travels.

The book that had inspired me in this line of research was *The Old Straight Track* written by the aforementioned Alfred Watkins in 1925. Watkins was a Hereford man, a gentleman amateur who observed that many of the mounds, moats, beacon hills and mark stones of his native county fell into alignment with each other. Between these points he found castles, churches, fords and wayside crosses which he thought might also occupy prehistoric sites. Watkins surmised that these landmarks were all that remained of a system of tracks used by prehistoric traders in salt, flint, and (later) metals, who had laid out their routes with staves and marked the way at intervals with stones. Many of these tracks passed through open woodland glades, and because of this Watkins called them leys, a name derived from an old Anglo-Saxon word meaning 'a forest clearing'. Though the original leys were now overgrown and invisible, Watkins maintained they could still be traced by careful map work and investigation in the field.

Archaeologists, of course, had several very valid objections to Watkins' theory. Firstly, there was the apparent uselessness of leys as trackways. What traveller would use a track that led him straight through forests, bogs and lakes? Then there was the question of dating. Could anyone be certain that alignments of medieval castles and churches followed prehistoric tracks? Finally, had Stone Age man been equal to the task of lining up sites across the landscape in an accurate manner? Without maps, surveying equipment, without even a pencil and paper? In the long run it was decided there was too much speculation in Watkins' work and not enough evidence. After Watkins died in 1935 his theory was ignored by the professionals and kept alive only by the efforts of dedicated amateurs and Sunday afternoon ramblers.

Half a century later, however, a new generation of enthusiasts were on the scene, all fully aware of the shortcomings of leys as trackways. Some postulated that they were underground water lines which could be detected by means of dowsing rods; some interpreted them as psychic power lines criss-crossing the countryside, radiating from storehouses of spiritual energy, and some claimed they were navigational aids for UFOs.

Accurate leys had been found all over England by this time. Was it possible that we had them in Scotland, too?

The mainstay of the ley theory is continued usage of the same site since prehistoric times, i.e. medieval castles built on top of prehistoric mounds, Christian churches now occupying pagan enclosures, wayside crosses replacing standing stones, etc. There are countless examples of this in Scotland, but none that I could think of were in straight lines. The whole idea seemed a bit far-fetched, but at the same time I could hardly say it didn't work. When I tried it out on the map it had worked first time. There was nothing to lose by investigating it in the field as well, and as the best place to start seemed to be the De'il's

Plantin, I made up my mind to cycle out there the following Sunday and carry on for a mile or two if the weather held.

The De'il's Plantin stands in the middle of a long, straight stretch of road in a quiet corner of the world some seven miles south of Glasgow. I arrived there around mid-day, left my bicycle in the lay-by on the north side, and climbed over the barbed-wire fence into the plantation. Through a ring of birch and beech trees I walked on to an inner mound where Spring sunshine printed dappled patterns of sunlight and shadow on the grass. There were two concave depressions on top of the mound, so I crouched down in one and spread my map out in front of me on bare earth swept clean by the wind.

The night before, I had noticed that my map line, if projected past Renfrew, led to a hill called Duncolm in the Kilpatrick Hills. The line looked fine on the map, but how did it look in the field? I added eight degrees to the grid bearing to compensate for magnetic variation, and with my prismatic compass I soon identified Duncolm as an unusual inverted-bowl shape sitting prominently on the long line of hills to the north. Mearns Castle, which I could see a mile away over the fields, was disappointingly out of alignment. I had to walk about 100m from the edge of the mound into the adjoining field before the castle and Duncolm lined up visually. It was hardly a promising start, but it was too early in the day to be discouraged, so I went back to my bike and started off along the back roads to the castle.

The auld keep of Mearns stands on a knoll that slopes towards a steep rock scarp overlooking a modern housing estate. Its history dates back to 1449 when King James II granted a licence to Lord Maxwell "to build a castle on ye Baronie of Mearnis in Refrushir" and to surround it

Mearns Castle.

with walls and ditches, iron gates and warlike appliances. After lying in ruins for years, the castle was restored under the auspices of the Renfrewshire Heritage Committee in 1971, and the newly-built Maxwell Mearns Castle Church was attached. This bizarre, symbiotic relationship with the kirk seems to have numbed the auld keep to a dull respectability. Robbed of its warlike appliances, besieged only by daffodils, it has lost the novelty it held for me in my boyhood. In those days, you could enter its draughty halls through a ground floor window, and climb a dilapidated corkscrew staircase up to the battlements. It was hazardous, but it was fun.

The adjoining church is built on an enclosure believed to be of an earlier date than the castle. Nobody knows when the enclosure was constructed, and now that the church is there it is impossible to guess.

Crookston Castle was the next site on my list; five miles further on as the crow flies. Tucked away in an odd corner of a Glasgow housing estate, this 15th century ruin stands within the ditch and bank of a medieval ringwork and occupies the site of an even

Renfrew Parish Church.

Photo: May Miles Thomas

earlier castle built in the 12th century by the Norman baron Robert de Croc, (hence Croc's-toun). Could de Croc have built his castle on a prehistoric site? Excavations have revealed only medieval relics, so there is no proof of this. But then who knows what the Normans found when they were building the castle?

The next two sites close to my line were churches; one in Renfrew and the other across the river in Clydebank.

Renfrew Parish Church is a well-kept building which retains an interesting 'olde-worlde' touch in the form of a 15th century tomb under an arch in the chancel. Here lie the sleeping effigies of Sir John Ross Hawkhead and his wife Marjory (not visible in the Brotchie sketch below). Legend has it that Sir John won the nearby lands of Inch by overcoming the champion of the English court in a wrestling match. During the bout, the Englishman rashly held out his hands to the Scot with the invitation, "Palm my arm". Ross seized his rival's wrists and with one jerk wrenched his shoulders from their sockets, thus winning the match and the lands. Ever after this, Ross was known as Palm-my-Arm.

Two earlier churches have occupied the same site as Renfrew Parish Church, and as far back as the reign of King David I (1084-1153) a parsonage stood there. The site, however, is flat, and has no known prehistoric connections. Nevertheless, because of its long history, I considered it a potential ley site.

The church at Clydebank was hardly "of ancient foundation". Common sense dictates that hundreds of churches must appear on alignments by coincidence, and somehow I felt that this was one.

Palm-my-Arm's tomb, Renfrew.

Next was the question of a fording place. It is difficult to assess the level of the Clyde in prehistoric times, but it is known than in the days before the river was made navigable for bigger ships, it was possible to walk across near Renfrew at low tide. Blaeu's map of 1654 shows an island called Sand Inch in the area where my map line crossed the river, so I considered that a plus factor.

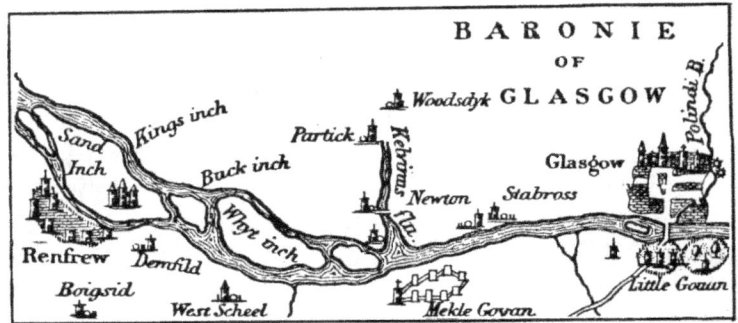

Section of a 1654 map, showing the islands in the Clyde.

What had I found, then? A string of five sites in a row — a mound, two medieval castles, a church and a possible ford. Basically a succession of unrelated features.

The least believable section of the line was the barren stretch between Mearns Castle and Crookston Castle. Five miles without a site seemed too long. The longer the line grows, the greater the likelihood there is of a site appearing on it by chance. I wasn't too happy about Mearns Castle either. It was not in true alignment with Duncolm. Yet the strange thing was that on days of exceptional visibility, when I looked at the castle from the De'il's Plantin, I could see the top of another peak in the distance, directly in line with the castle.[1] Was I reading too much into this, or were there other lines in the area that I had not detected? To check it all out in greater detail I bought 1:25,000 scale Ordnance Survey maps of the area.

[1] The "… peak in the distance, directly in line with the castle" is not identified. Possibly Ben Venue?

On Sheet NS55 of the 1:25,000 map, the De'il's Plantin is marked in Gothic letters as a tumulus (burial mound) at grid reference point NS 557535. To my surprise, I found that if I projected a line from this point through Mearns Castle it led straight to a site that was not marked on my 1:50,000 scale map. It was the site of Capelrig Cross, two and a half miles NNW of the tumulus. This 10th century cross is now in Glasgow Art Galleries, where it was taken to protect it from the elements.

On Sheet NS56, yet another point of interest showed up. Six miles further on from Capelrig, still in alignment with the castle and tumulus, is the site of long-demolished Inch Castle built by old Palm-my-Arm on the lands he won in the wrestling match.[2]

[2] Harry seems to have abandoned this alignment in favour of the one running through Renfrew Parish Church.

I soon found other lines in my travels. In a landscape dotted with ancient sites it is perhaps not surprising if a few sites fall into alignment here and there. What did surprise me, however, was the fact that the alignments themselves seemed to form a definite pattern. Sooner or later, they linked up with lines of sites leading to the hill called Duncolm.

Although it is only ten miles from Glasgow, I must confess I had never heard of the hill until I started tracing alignments. It is the highest of the Kilpatrick Hills and stands in the centre of the range some 401m above sea level on the north side of the Clyde, three miles from Erskine Bridge. Its name, in Gaelic, means 'fort of the dove' or 'fort of Columba', it could be either one.

Inch Castle.

At first glance it looks like a Scots cousin of Ayers Rock, the sacred site of the Aborigines in central Australia. Its distinctive outline could have made it a useful landmark for prehistoric travellers, but when I finally got to the summit and searched the area for tangible evidence of such a traveller, there was nothing to be found — no cairns, no earthworks, no visible remains.

So I looked for a place where my prehistoric traveller would have rested, and I sat there in a hollow sheltered from the wind, eating my sandwiches, and looking at the view. I could see the islands in Loch Lomond, and a prominent hill in the middle distance called Duncryne. Across the water behind Duncryne, a small peninsula known as Craigie Fort jutted out into the loch at Balmaha pier, and behind that again was the Ben itself. The scene before me changed constantly as clouds played hide and seek with the sun, casting huge moving shadows over the landscape. I was at peace with the world. Though I had found nothing of archaeological interest, I still felt that in some inexplicable way the presence of the early folk still lingered on Duncolm.

I sat gazing at the mountains vignetted into the mist on the far side of the loch, an infinite space where earth and sky dissolved; a place where greens and blues changed to grey in overlapping planes of perspective, like and old-time Oriental scroll painting — the Ben, the peninsula, and the hill of Duncryne — all in visual alignment...

Slowly it dawned on me that I could be looking at another sightline — two duns, a fort and an undoubted mark point!

But it was intentional or coincidental? There was no way of knowing, though the surrounding area had certainly been settled in prehistoric times. Dotted about the Kilpatrick hills are tombs dating back to early in the Neolithic era, a period that lasted roughly from 3500 BC to 1800 BC. Neolithic peoples were the founders of our civilisation. They introduced pottery to Britain, grew crops, raised cattle and changed the economy of the country from hunting and food gathering to agriculture. Nobody knows what form

"At first glance it looks like a Scots cousin of Ayers Rock, the sacred site of the Aborigines in central Australia."

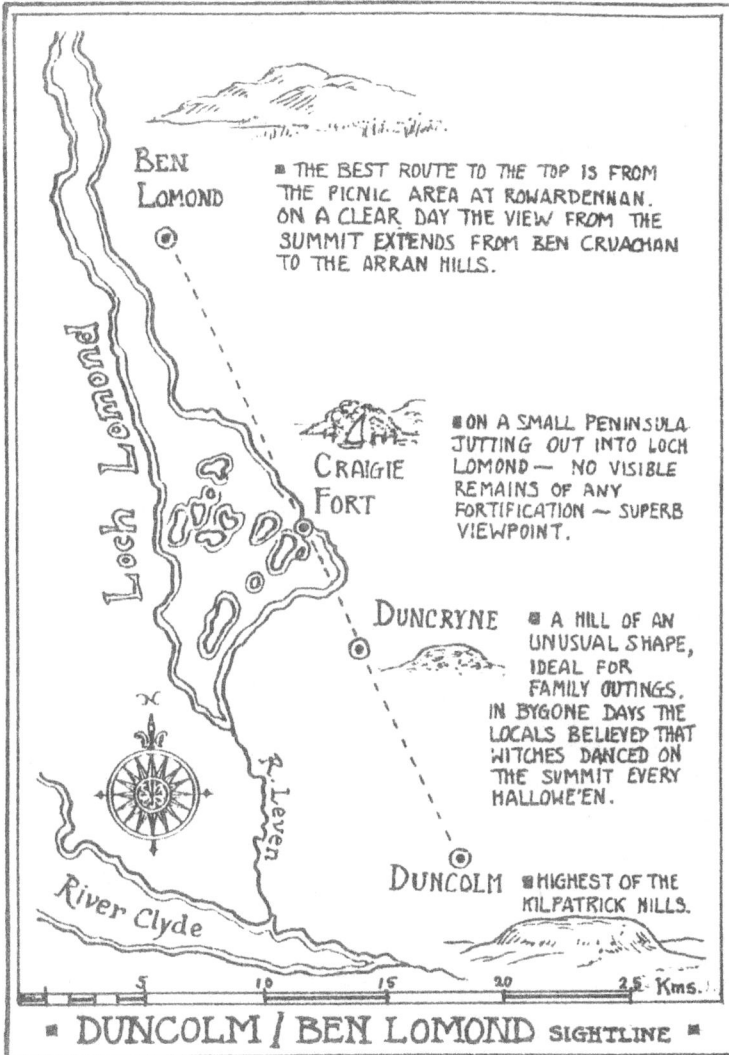

BEN LOMOND

■ THE BEST ROUTE TO THE TOP IS FROM THE PICNIC AREA AT ROWARDENNAN. ON A CLEAR DAY THE VIEW FROM THE SUMMIT EXTENDS FROM BEN CRUACHAN TO THE ARRAN HILLS.

Loch Lomond

CRAIGIE FORT

■ ON A SMALL PENINSULA JUTTING OUT INTO LOCH LOMOND — NO VISIBLE REMAINS OF ANY FORTIFICATION — SUPERB VIEWPOINT.

DUNCRYNE

■ A HILL OF AN UNUSUAL SHAPE, IDEAL FOR FAMILY OUTINGS. IN BYGONE DAYS THE LOCALS BELIEVED THAT WITCHES DANCED ON THE SUMMIT EVERY HALLOWE'EN.

R. Leven

DUNCOLM

■ HIGHEST OF THE KILPATRICK HILLS.

River Clyde

5   10   15   20   25 Kms.

■ DUNCOLM / BEN LOMOND SIGHTLINE ■

This map appeared in the first edition of Glasgow's Secret Geometry, but was omitted from subsequent versions, perhaps to save space? It is such a fine example of Harry's drafting skills that I wanted to reinstate it —*Ed*.

their trackways took, but it is believed they followed rivers and mountain ridges. Duncolm, Duncryne, Craigie Fort and Ben Lomond could have been very useful landmarks to a Neolithic community.

These thoughts were much in my mind when I tramped back down the braes of Cochno, heading in the general direction of Glasgow. This time my route marker was a distant hilltop showing blue-grey against the horizon almost 40 miles away. This landmark was Tinto Hill, a hill crowned by a huge cairn dating back to the Bronze-Age (c. 2000 BC to 600 BC). As I looked at the haze of the city with the blue bulk of Tinto lying behind it, I realised that the line from Duncolm to Tinto could also have been a suitable route for a prehistoric traveller. It leads through the fertile valley of the Clyde, the *Strath Cluith* of old — a prime piece of real estate in medieval times and still the same today.

It almost seemed as if by thinking on these things I had brought the old routes back to life. Imagination, of course, but for interest's sake I stopped to take a

Photo: Grahame Gardner

Duncryne Hill.

compass bearing which I traced out on my OS map after subtracting the magnetic variation. The results surprised me. The line from Duncolm to Tinto runs straight through the oldest part of Glasgow, and astride the line stands the church of ancient foundation that I had previously deleted from my list — Glasgow Cathedral.

It was then, for the first time, it occurred to me that the early settlements in the Glasgow area could have been laid out in accordance with some geometric plan completely unknown to modern man. It was a fascinating thought, one that was to recur again and again in the future, but it would take a lot more evidence than a few sightlines to support such a startling conclusion.

Between Duncolm and Glasgow there were two sites that interested me. The first I visited was at Castlehill, a wooded knoll near the fashionable suburb of Bearsden. Pottery sherds have been found here in the roots of fallen trees, but little remains above the ground to tell the story of the past. Crop marks, visible only from the air, tell the story to those who can decipher them; eighteen hundred years ago the 4th Cohort of Gauls guarded the Antonine Wall at this point. Deep in thought, I went on to the next site, Cairn Hill not far from Canniesburn Hospital.

I was unable to find information about any cairn that this hill could have been named after. At the time of my visit, Cairn Hill was a wasteland of thorny bushes that conspired to rip my casual attire. Through a labyrinth of sunken paths and nettles, I found my way to a wall that might possibly have been constructed with stones robbed from a cairn. It was all guesswork, but when I paused for a rest, and looked at the Kilpatrick Hills, the Campsies, and across the Clyde to the Renfrewshire Uplands, the all-round view, with Duncolm particularly prominent, made me think that this site could well have been settled in prehistoric times. It would have been high enough and dry enough; if early man liked a room with a view, he could have had one here.

Glasgow Cathedral stands on one of the oldest Christian sites in Scotland. As Dr Joseph Robertson put it in his *Scottish Abbeys and Cathedrals...* "Here the cross was planted and here was the ground blessed for Christian burial by a Christian bishop, while Iona was yet an unknown island among the western waves, while the promontory of St Andrews was the haunt of the wild boar and the sea mew, and only the smoke of a few heathen wigwams ascended from the Rock of Edinburgh". The bishop referred to was St Ninian, who around 400 AD consecrated as a Christian burying place a small space of ground on the hill between the fort of Cathures (also *Caer* or *Cathair*) and the Moldendinar Burn.

There has always been an aura of mystery about the selection of the exact site of the Cathedral. Back

Photo: Grahame Gardner

Glasgow Cathedral.

The Necropolis and John Knox statue.

in my schooldays, when civic pride was still popular, everyone knew the story of how the mystic St Mungo journeyed to the house of a holy man named Fergus, who died the night before he arrived.[3] Next morning, Mungo placed Fergus' body on a cart yoked to two wild bulls and commanded them to take it to "the place ordained by the Lord". At the place where the bulls finally halted, Mungo built a small wooden chapel. He was buried there in AD 612 and a shrine erected to his memory. Through time a stone church was built on the same site, and after many alterations down through the ages, this church became Glasgow Cathedral.

The interior of the Cathedral is much grander than its soot-grimed exterior suggests. The shrine of St Mungo (also known as St Kentigern) can be seen in the crypt, and in the Blacader Aisle a carved and painted boss overhead shows Fergus wrapped in his winding sheet lying on a cart. 'This is ye ile of Car Fergus' reads the inscription in Saxon letters. Beneath the flagstones at this point is the cemetery consecrated by St Ninian.

[3] According to *Life of Kentigern* and other accounts, Fergus was able to receive Mungo and instructed him on the disposal of his worldly goods, saying, "Dispose of my household and my life today, and tomorrow arrange for my tomb, according to your providence as you are inspired by God", before dying.

Cathedral roof boss showing Fergus on the cart.

Until 1789, the Bishop's Castle stood close by the cathedral. This structure seems to have been built within an existing oval ditch and bank sometime during the 13th century. A small granite monument and plaque in the Royal Infirmary forecourt car park marks its former location.

The site of the first cross of Glasgow is also in this vicinity, at the intersection of High St, Drygate and Rotten Row (a name alleged to be a phonetic version of *Rathad an Rath*, 'road of the ring fort'). Also of interest is the oldest house in Glasgow, Provand's Lordship, which was erected nearby in 1471.

Almost overlooking the Cathedral is the Glasgow Necropolis (Greek for 'city of the dead'). The Necropolis, which has been likened to a giant pincushion, is a hilltop cemetery bristling with obelisks, towers and memorials. Its use as a cemetery dates from 1833; before that it was known as Fir Park, and before that again it was part of the estate of Wester Craigs, bought in 1650 by the Merchants House.

At the top of the Necropolis, the stern, stone figure of John Knox in Geneva cap and gown gazes out

S. MUNGO'S SHRINE GLASGOW CATHEDRAL CRYPT

over the city. As I walked round reading the inscription on the base, I noticed that the statue stood on a slight mound. I wondered then, if before Knox's time, before even St Mungo came with teaching, men of an earlier religion had congregated on the hill. The feeling of the past was very strong there.

The Duncolm to Tinto alignment crosses the Clyde at Carmyle, so a few weeks later, just to be a thorough researcher, I went down to the place for a look. I look compass bearings and paced out the distance as a rough guide to the point where the line crosses the river. About 300m west of The Auld Boathouse pub there was a gap in the foliage at just about the right spot.[4] The banks of the Clyde are not normally accessible so near the city, but at that point I was able to walk in under the trees and down a gradual slope to the water's edge. It looked like an excellent place for fording the river.

A mile and a half after the line crosses the Clyde, it passes about 100m north of a scarcely visible mound that marks the site of Drumsargad Castle. When I was there, nothing could be seen for barley, but the castle is known to have been on the site of an earlier fort, and a Bronze-Age food vessel and cinerary urn found there were purchased by the National Museum of Antiquities in 1883.

The first site actually on the line is Cadzow Castle, an eerie old ruin in Chatelherault Country Park, two miles south of Hamilton. This area was settled centuries before the castle came into existence, because in St Mungo's day there was a King of Cadzow known as Rhydderch Hael.

Cadzow's mouldering ruins stand in ivy-clad loneliness high above a loop in the Avon Water, surrounded by tall oak trees. Branches push their way through cracks in the crumbling masonry and strange

[4] Harry later mentions a second ford called the 'King's Ford', which is marked on the 1888 OS map. This is located where the Kirk Burn enters the river, just downstream of the present Clydeford Road bridge.

scurrying noises are everywhere... the old castle talks in its sleep.

Gone are the halcyon days Walter Scott referred to in these lines:-

When princely Hamilton's abode

Ennobled Cadzow's Gothic towers

The song went round, the goblet flowed

And revel sped the laughing hours.

The castle itself has no known prehistoric connections, but, the remains of an Iron Age fort (c.600 BC to 400 AD) lie some 300m to the south still inside the Country Park.[5]

[5] This is thought to be the most likely site of Rhydderch Hael's castle.

While in the area, I visited a church in Larkhall that seemed to be on the same alignment. The site looked fairly modern so I didn't stay long; soon I was off on the way to Craignethan.

Craignethan Castle is about 100m off the line, which wasn't quite near enough for me, but as a Bronze-Age flanged axe was once found there, the site could be said to have prehistoric connections, so I decided to pay it a visit.

Craignethan is situated on a rocky promontory overlooking the steep wooded slopes that form the valley of the River Nethan half a mile from where it joins the Clyde. Tinto Hill is not visible from the ground but it can be seen from a mound near the entrance to the parking lot. Several antiquarians have suggested that this mound was once part of the original enclosed area.

It is a strange fact that apart from the main Tinto to Duncolm line, there appears to be another line half a degree off to the south. It leads from Tinto through the mound at Craignethan to a Bronze-Age monument

Craignethan Castle.

known as Fairholm Cairn (NS 754516), and from there to the Iron Age fort at Cadzow, after which it crosses the Clyde at King's Ford, 300m downstream from the ford I found at Carmyle. This baffled me at the time, but it made sense later on.

Tinto Hill was the last site on my line. The marker here is nothing if not conspicuous: one of Scotland's largest cairns 45m in diameter and 6m high crowns the summit. The name Tinto signifies 'hill of fire', and old records state that its summit was once "a place wheron the Druids lighted up their fires in heathen worship". A more authoritative documentary source, the RCAHMS *Inventory of the Prehistoric and Roman Monuments of Lanarkshire*, mentions that Neolithic stone axes of the Cumbrian type have been found here.

On this hill, the meeting place of four parish boundaries, I thoughtfully ended my Clyde Valley pilgrimage.

Tinto seen from Lanark Racecourse.

A Patriarch.

TCFB
Cadzow Forest

One of the mighty Cadzow Oaks, drawing by TCF Brotchie.

CLASSIFICATION

Working on the track and following up a ley

often leads to disappointments...

— (Watkins, 1925 p.189)

"This is really a magic place we live in. See all these hills and mountains in the distance? They've all got wee paths leading to them, with mounds and big stones marking the way... the paths are invisible now, but you can still find them. We're the only ones who know where they are."

Wee son thought this was great. It was better than Goldilocks any day.

"Now, I'm going to teach you the names of the hills", I said, "so if you ever have wee boys and girls of your own, you'll be able to tell them all about this."

I lifted him up onto the flat top of the boulder in front of us, held his arms out to steady him, and turned him gradually to face the south-east.

"See that hill away on its own in the distance? That one's called Tinto. You got that, son? Tinto Hill."

"Tin Toe Hill," he repeated knowledgeably, his round face unusually solemn beneath the fringe of his home-made haircut.

A row of new houses obscured the view to the south, so I turned him further round and pointed at the first recognisable landmark, a hill of unusual shape, its outline etched sharply against the sky.

"That's Dunwan Hill; you can see that one from your bedroom window."

I named as many as I knew and manoeuvred him round to face each one in turn.

"The blue hills in the distance are the Cowal Hills, the green ones are the Kilpatrick Hills; that one like a basin upside down is Duncolm... come on and I'll show you Ben Lomond."

I lifted him off the stone and straightened up his coat. Then we walked across the cropped, clipped New Town grass to a place where we could see the Ben. It was April, and there was still a little snow on the summit.

"That's it there, son, the big one away at the back. We could have seen it from the top of the stone if it wasn't for the new Health Centre."

Wee Son was listening intently, his head cocked to one side. For a boy of six his concentration was remarkable. This is how it all began in the Stone Age, I thought... a man teaching his boy on the hillside.

"Can you remember the name of any of the hills now?" I said. "Any one at all."

Proudly I watched, as eyes blackbird bright he scanned the horizon. How wise we looked, radiant with inner knowledge and secret smiles, a living repository of ancient wisdom.

At last he spoke.

"Daddy, is that an ice cream van?"

From somewhere on the outer limits of human hearing, a few faint bars of music floated up the hill, bringing me back to reality. I handed over the money for two cones and Wee Son was off and running to the tune of the William Tell overture. Civilisation was here at last. Last year this was a bare hilltop — this year we've got ice cream vans. As we ran downhill, past rows of neat new houses, I made a mental note to bring a camera on our next visit. There was still time to get a picture of the big stone and its surroundings before too many houses blocked the view. It was the only stone of that size for miles; for all I knew, it might even be an ancient route marker. It was aligned to the southern edge of the hillforts at Walls Hill and Duncarnock to the west, and to the mound at Craignethan Castle to the east.[6]

Whether by accident or design I could not say, but had the stone been a few inches smaller, or placed a few yards either way, a man of average height would have had difficulty seeing some of the landmarks. Given the circumstances, it was exactly the right size of stone in exactly the right place.

The following weekend I went out to Duncarnock and then on to Walls Hill. My hobby was fast becoming an obsession. In a sincere but crazy attempt to allocate numbers to ley-lines for reference purposes, I pursued my invisible alignments to the most surprising places. Then, when summer came, I tramped round archaeological sites all over the country, with guidebook, sleeping bag and wineskin, re-discovering an ancient world which to me was suddenly and vitally new.

Imagine my delight, then, when on one of my expeditions, far from anywhere, I found a lump of rock that looked to me like one of the stone tools I had seen in the glass cases at Kelvingrove Museum.

[6] I'm unsure of the location of this stone, but from the description is could possibly be Lickprivick Tumulus. That would tie in with the "new houses" remark. He later mentions it as being in Greenhills. There is a letter in the archives from Gordon Davies, Head of Planning for East Kilbride, informing Harry that the contractors were "...unable to find any trace of the stone".

The smooth, comfortable feel of the stone in my hand, its unusual colour and its battered cutting edge convinced me that at last I had something to show for my travels.

After miles of walking and several phone calls, I finally got in touch with an archaeologist who was prepared to take a look at it. I found her entombed in the study of a very old and very dusty building, walled-in by shelves of leather-bound books. Cautiously I entered her presence, carrying my heavy lump of rock wrapped up like the Koh-i-noor diamond.

"Hullo" I said, informal like.

"Hullo" she replied, with eyes all spectacles and suspicion.

"I think I've found a Stone Age hand axe." I said, unwrapping the precious implement and handing it over.

She peered at the rock suspiciously, turned it over in her hand and ran her forefinger lightly over the nibbled edge.

"And where did you pick this up?" she inquired.

"In the hills not far from here. At a place marked 'earthwork' on the map. It was on a sort of a ley-line; I've got the grid reference in my notebook."

She looked puzzled. "It was on a *what?*"

"It was on a ley-line. You know — the Alfred Watkins thing — the Old Straight Track and that."

Her brows puckered and she shook her head from side to side. I fished in the side-pockets of my rucksack and produced a crumpled notebook. I turned it to the appropriate page and held it out to her, but she ignored it.

"I hope you're not digging up archaeological sites on your own", she said. "You're supposed to inform us if you find anything."

"Oh I wasn't digging," I said. "The stone was sticking out the ground. The roots of a tree had sort of pushed it out."

"Hmmh."

She held the stone in the middle and bounced it disdainfully on a copy of *Discovery and Excavation in Scotland* that was lying on her desk. Then she handed it back to me.

"It's Quartz, with superficial iron oxide staining. The fissures on the surface are entirely natural and have been caused by the abrasive action of frost and weathering."

"It's entirely natural?" I said. "But it can't be — look, it fits my hand perfectly. It's chewed up in exactly the right place... it's as if somebody's been hitting something with it."

I tapped it on the cover of *D&E Scotland* to illustrate my point. The woman's eyes narrowed dangerously behind her spectacles and once more she lifted the stone.

"The working edge is in the wrong place. Stone Age man held tools this way..." She held the stone in the middle and rapped it on the book again.

It was my turn next.

"Do you mean to say that in the whole Stone Age, not one person ever held a stone the ordinary way —

like this?" I said, lifting the stone palm downwards and rapping the book again. Little dents were appearing all over the cover.

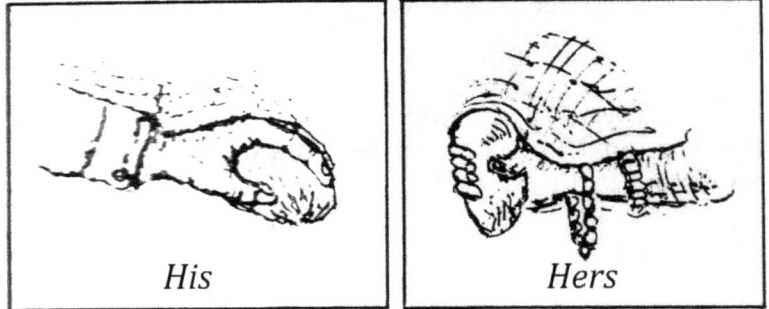

His

Hers

"How can you be sure? I mean — supposing he was left-handed or something, and held it a different way from everyone else?"

The woman, looking decidedly irritated, lifted the stone again; this time with her left hand.

"Left-handed people would have held the stone exactly same way — but in their *left hand*." She emphasised the last two words by thumping the book vigorously. She was wishing it was my head.

I could scarcely believe it — I had carried that big rock down from the hills for nothing.

"But — what if the man had a finger bitten off by a wild animal or something?" I said. "I mean, it happened a lot in those days. He could have had a bad hand." I lifted the stone in my left hand, and curled a finger into my palm, twisting the stone so that the chipped end became the striking surface again. For a moment I thought she was about to produce a whistle and call for the attendants. When I ventured a smile her nose twitched slightly and she drew me a look straight from the Pleistocene Ice Age. It was her turn with the stone but she didn't lift it.

It was time to go... my first archaeology lesson was over.

A few months later I took the worthless rock to Kelvingrove Museum and was given exactly the same opinion. The following week I enrolled in a course of evening classes at the Department of Archaeology.

When I last attended school the prevailing image of the ancient Briton was that of a man dressed in animal skins, carrying a club and dragging a woman by the hair. Recently, however, this concept had changed completely. The new image was of a man of skill and imagination, hampered by his environment, but capable of precise mathematical calculations and the prediction of lunar eclipses.

The study of lunar and solar alignments had become increasingly popular in the past decade, but what about terrestrial alignments — how had Watkins' theory progressed? As far as Scotland was concerned, not at all. Ley-hunting was purely an English pastime, I was told. Like cricket, it had never quite caught on in Scotland. Its eccentric devotees were firmly classified as the lunatic fringe of archaeology, just one step removed from the Flat Earth Society.

Clearly then, my idea of a Duncolm to Tinto sightline having any connection with early settlement in Glasgow was highly speculative; but for all that, it still interested me. I was working in Glasgow at the time, and often in the period between finishing work and starting classes, I would sit in the Mitchell Library in North St, browsing through all kinds of old books pertaining to the origins of my native city. Perhaps, like most researchers, I only took note of information that supported my own theories, but from what I read it seemed to me that at least the area around the Necropolis was considered important in the pre-Christian era.

Hugh Mackintosh, in his *Origin and History of Glasgow Streets* (1902) wrote "...in ancient times, anterior to our ecclesiastical history, a Druidical place of worship stood on the site of the present Necropolis..."

John Ure, in *History of Glasgow* printed in 1786 says "...before paganism was eradicated furth of the kingdom there were here a sort of priests called Druids, held in those days in great estimation, they had their residence here in cells near the Blackfryer church adjacent to the college, there were in those days many stately groves of oaks..."

Blackfriars Church stood about half-a-mile from the Necropolis, on a site now occupied by the High Street Goods Station.[7]

[7] The High Street Goods Station is long gone, now replaced by upmarket student accommodation.

Another reference showed up in a poem called *The Legend of St Mungo* written by Keelinvine (probably a pen name) in 1869.

> *Wi' that he stepped o'er the burn*
> *and gently clomb the hill;*
> *Nae sign of heathen rites appear'd*
> *the morn was lown and still.*
> *... Nae signal fires on Tintock blazed*
> *or Dechmont's sacred heights*
> *Nae smoke arose frae Cathkin braes*
> *to vex St Mungo's sight...*

In this poem, St Mungo enlists God's aid to suppress paganism and the alleged sacrificial rites of the Druids. He steps over the Molendinar Burn and goes on up the hill that later became the Necropolis. Then he looks for beacon fires on Tinto, Dechmont and Cathkin Braes. Where Keelinvine got his information from I do not know, but he seemed to have thought that these three places had Druidical connections. Curiously enough, I had visited each of those sites myself, in the course of tracing my alignments.

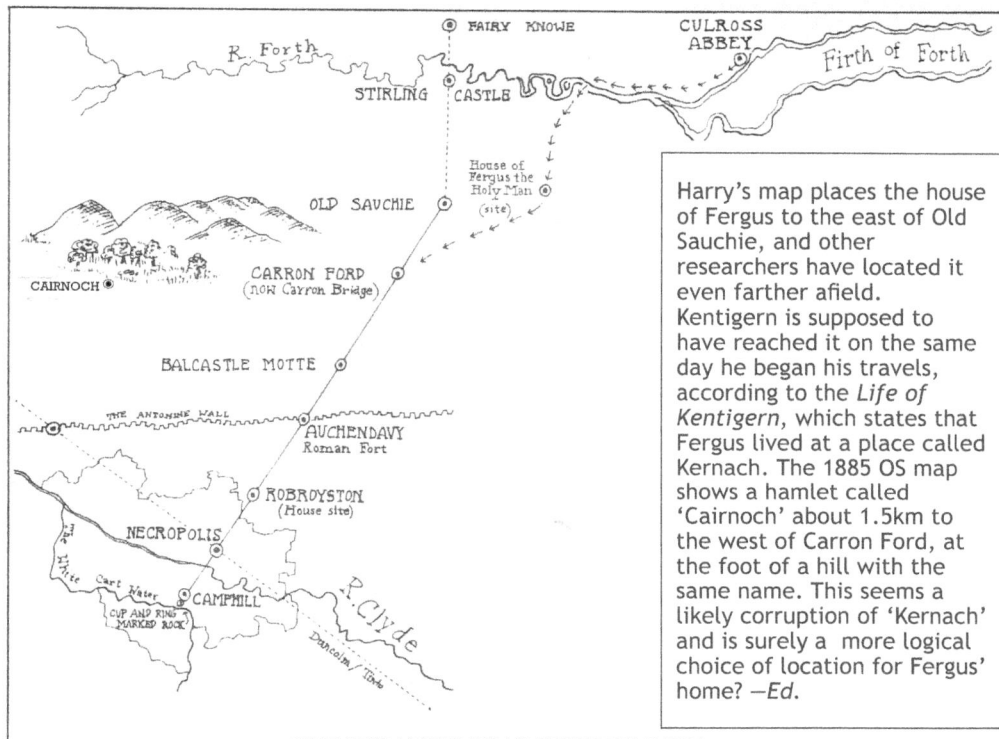

Harry's map places the house of Fergus to the east of Old Sauchie, and other researchers have located it even farther afield. Kentigern is supposed to have reached it on the same day he began his travels, according to the *Life of Kentigern*, which states that Fergus lived at a place called Kernach. The 1885 OS map shows a hamlet called 'Cairnoch' about 1.5km to the west of Carron Ford, at the foot of a hill with the same name. This seems a likely corruption of 'Kernach' and is surely a more logical choice of location for Fergus' home? —*Ed.*

THE STRAIGHT ROAD WITH NO PATH

St Mungo's journey started at Culross Abbey. From there he went on to the house of Fergus, the holy man. Perhaps, on his journey south he joined the 'Straight Road with No Path' along the way.

The 'Straight Road' descends towards Carron Ford from the Scots Pine trees on the skyline. Scots Pines are frequently found as ley markers and were often seeded by cattle drovers to mark their routes. The actual ford location is roughly at the bottom left of the picture, in front of the huts, where some stones are visible when the water level is low — *Ed.*

Photo: Grahame Gardner

My next step was to search for the earliest written account of St Mungo's journey to Glasgow. Perhaps in the record of this journey there would be a clue about the nature of early roads or tracks in the Glasgow area.

Many a tedious old volume I had to read through before I learned that when Bishop Jocelyn was rebuilding Glasgow Cathedral in the 12th century, he had commissioned a hagiographer from Furness Abbey to revise St Mungo's biography. Two copies of this book survive, one in the British Museum, the other in Dublin. To my delight, however, I unearthed a translated and edited version in the Glasgow Room of the Mitchell Library. In this book, *The Life of St Kentigern*, I finally found what I was looking for — the earliest known reference to a road or track in the Glasgow area. It appears in the following extract from chapter nine:

"And in truth, the bulls, in no way being restive, or in anything disobeying the voice of Kentigern, without any tripping or fall, came by a straight road. along where there was no path, as far as Cathures, which is now called Glasgu, along with Kentigern and many others accompanying; and then, with all gentleness, with the burden of the sacred earth laid on them, a beauteous sight, they halted near a certain cemetery, which had been long before consecrated by St Ninian."

Now, bear in mind that this extract is from the English translation of a book originally written in Latin 800 years ago. This Latin book, in turn, would have been hundreds of years old, so there was ample scope for errors in translation or changes in meaning to have occurred over the centuries. But, even allowing for that, one statement almost leaped out the page at me, *"the bulls ... came by a straight road, along where there was no path."*

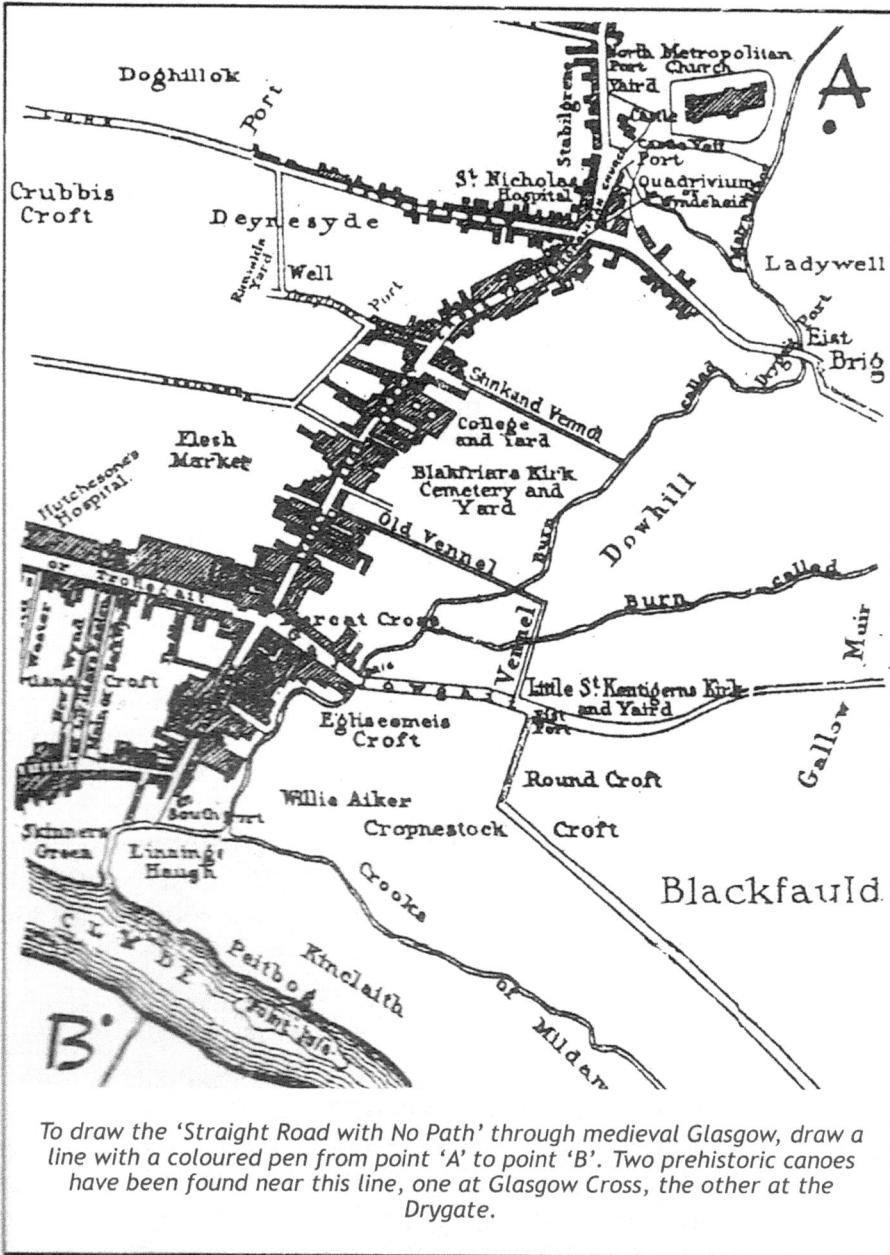

To draw the 'Straight Road with No Path' through medieval Glasgow, draw a line with a coloured pen from point 'A' to point 'B'. Two prehistoric canoes have been found near this line, one at Glasgow Cross, the other at the Drygate.

I was ecstatic... In a quiet corner of the reading room, I whispered the words over and over again to myself like a mantra, *"they came by a straight road along where there was no path"*.

But where was this straight road? It seemed to have led down through the Campsie Fells to the north of the city. The idea of a straight road through the Campsies was a bit unreal, but would the early chroniclers have added this detail to the story for no reason? I had already found a straight alignment through the Cathedral — was it possible there was another one in a different direction?

I pored over maps of all the old approach roads to Glasgow from the north and found nothing. With winter coming on, and the hills outside the city dusted with snow, the sensible thing to do was to leave the whole thing till springtime and research it then.

But it didn't quite work out like that...

A few weeks later, I was travelling northwards into Glasgow on a Corporation bus, sitting on the top deck, front corner seat. It was a wet, windy day, and rain pattered on the metal roof as rivulets of water ran down the windows, obscuring the world beyond. When the bus reached Queen's Park, I wiped some moisture from the fogged-up side windows so I could see better.

The park was one of my favourite places a child. Many a summers day we 'chipped in' pennies for lemonade and Paris buns, and made the long trek from the tenements of Cardwell Street across the road to Eglinton Toll and up Victoria Road to the park. We would enter by the big wrought-iron gates, climb the slope, and stroll on through the woods to the open space at the crown of the hill where the big stones were. They were smooth and polished-looking, sympathetic to the touch. You could play hide and seek when it was warm, or 'coorie in', share out the SDI lemonade, and shelter from the rain if it was wet. Rain or shine, the big stones were always there. It was almost a ritual to pay them a regular visit.

By the time the bus stopped to pick up passengers I was lost in reverie. Several stops later, I came to, and wiped the front window to see where I was. Now, the last thing I had seen through the side window before closing my eyes was the dark mass of trees leading up to the stones at Camphill earthwork; but when I opened my eyes again, the first thing I saw through the cleared space on the front window was the verdigris-coloured roof of Glasgow Cathedral two miles away. There is no direct road to the Cathedral from Queen's Park, but on a very short stretch of road the Cathedral happens to be visible from the top of the bus.

Somehow the images of Camphill earthwork and the Cathedral came together in my mind, and at that moment I realised I could be on the southern approaches of 'the straight road along where there was no path.' I had searched for this route from the northern side of the city so often, that my mind was completely closed to the possibility of finding it from the south.

When I got home later that night, I took out my map and protractor and found myself another alignment. It ran in a north-easterly direction from Camphill earthwork to the old ford a stone's throw from Carron Bridge, near Denny. It did not go through the Cathedral, but right through the highest point of the Necropolis where the John Knox statue stands.

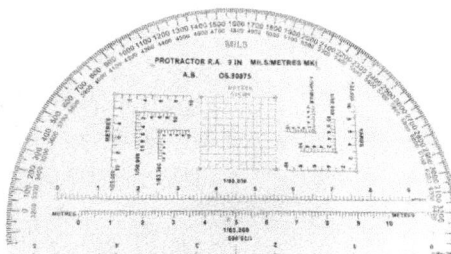

Military protractor as used by Harry.

This alignment crosses the Clyde in the vicinity of the tidal weir just upstream from the Albert Bridge. Before the Clyde was deepened, the average depth between low and high tide at this point was only 2 ft. 6 ins. so it would have been an excellent fording place. From here the line continues on through the west end of Glasgow Green and up into railway property built on the site of Blackfriars Kirk and Cemetery Yard (mentioned in Ure's book as the place where the Druids once lived). The line also runs very close to the course of the Molendinar Burn, where St Mungo baptised his first converts.

The Molendinar, which took its name from the Mill of the Bishop's Manor, is now an underground sewer. In earlier times, it ran sweet and clear round the foot of the Necropolis.

Some historians claim that a Roman road went down a glen and across the Clyde in this area. The alleged Roman road and the Straight Road with No Path could have been one and the same thing. It is interesting to note in this context, that my alignment to the old ford crosses the Antonine Wall within hailing distance of the Roman fort at Auchendavy.

Though this alignment provides a fascinating insight into Glasgow's past, it could scarcely be considered important in an archaeological sense unless the dates of the sites were contemporary. Aware of this, I decided to make a special study of site dates along the line, starting with Camphill earthwork. The results were bewildering — unlike anywhere else in this world, Camphill earthwork appears to be growing younger over the years.

On many old maps of Glasgow, Camphill is marked as a 'Celtic camp'. Yet, for some reason, generations of school children were taught that it was a Roman fort. After the excavations of 1951/52, however, the earthwork was re-interpreted as a Medieval defensive structure, which was later classified as a 'ringwork'. The last reference I found stated that the stones inside the ringwork, long thought to have historical significance, were left there by workmen building a road in Victorian times. (Barr, 1973, p71).

Dating evidence for the other sites on the line was also unconvincing. Archaeologically speaking, the Straight Road with No Path could be an assembly of coincidences and nothing else. But if that was the case, why did it tie in so well with the other alignments I had found? It would be a mistake to presume that because these alignments did not fit current archaeological theories they did not exist. It would also be a mistake to presume that since they apparently do exist, they must fit one of the wide range of theories evolved by researchers who had found similar lines in England.

From what I had read in *The Ley Hunter* magazine and elsewhere, it seemed that most English researchers now believed their ley-lines followed invisible 'lines of force' across the country. As the only lines I had found were simple overland alignments of hilltops and man-made features detected without recourse to dowsing or astronomy, I felt I could hardly call them ley-lines.

Some of my alignments were in line of sight between inter-visible points, others were connecting lines linking sites on different alignments — each line was joined, at an important point along its length, to another line. For this reason, I classified them, in the loosest possible sense, as prehistoric communication lines. But whether this was a definition or a supposition, I was by no means certain.

My first essential was to find out where these communication lines originated and where they terminated. To do this properly, it might be best to start at an undoubted mark point — but was there really such a thing? My mixed bag of castles, churches and cairns seemed to have been constructed for purely local purposes in no way connected with long-distance alignments. In fact, the only possible route marker I could think of was the big stone I had gone to with Wee Son at Greenhills, in East Kilbride. 1 wasn't too happy about that one, either. It was still something of an enigma — had it been levered into position by prehistoric surveyors, or was it a glacial erratic left high and dry after the Ice Age?

Maybe if I photographed the stone from every conceivable angle, measured it and took note of scratch marks, etc., there would still be time to get an independent opinion on it at the Department of Archaeology before my course of evening classes ended. If there was a possibility that the stone had been levered into position, I would carry on my research; but if it was merely a glacial erratic that had arrived in that position by chance there would be little point in continuing.

So it came to pass that one bright, cold December morn, Wee Son and I marched up to Greenhills to photograph the stone. The panorama of the surrounding hills seemed to rise to meet us as we reached the higher ground. We were superbly equipped for our venture; we had pencils, pens, graph paper, scale rulers, compass, maps, camera, two lenses and a relic from my National Service days —- one Protractor RA9 in mils/metres Mk 1, for the use of. We had left nothing to chance.

But when we rounded the corner of the newly-built shopping centre, I realised there was one thing missing — there was no stone.

Frantically, I knocked on the nearest door.

"Excuse me, but was there ever a big stone out here at any time?"

"Oh, I don't know... We're just new here."

I went to other houses and asked again. Some people had no recollection of it ever having been there. But finally I got an answer.

"A stone? Oh aye, the big one that was out there. It got taken away months ago. The ground got all muddy round it. The kids kept climbing up and falling off. It was a right nuisance."

We walked over to where the stone had been, a bare patch where already grass was beginning to grow. Soon there would be no sign of it ever having been there.

Wee Son stood on the bare patch, shaded his eyes and looked towards the distant horizon. Then slowly at first, but with gathering speed, he began to revolve like a lighthouse beacon. I waited till he lost his balance, then led him away. It had been a bad day for both of us. I had lost a route marker and Wee Son couldn't find an ice-cream van.

EAST KILBRIDE DEVELOPMENT CORPORATION

Atholl House
East Kilbride
Scotland
G74 1LU

Telephone East Kilbride 41111
Telex 779141

Our Ref: GD/FC

H Bell Esq
62 New Plymouth
Newlandsmuir
East Kilbride

2nd March, 1978

Dear Mr Bell

I refer to your letter regarding the location of a large stone which your studies have led you to believe was important in the prehistoric system of aligned sites.

I have attempted to locate the stone for you and have, through our Engineering Department, been in contact with the contractor who was recently working in that area of Greenhills. Unfortunately, we have been unable to find any trace of the stone. The contractors were, Daniel Campbell & Sons of Strathaven. Perhaps you might be able to pursue the matter privately with them.

I am sorry that we have not been able to locate the stone for you, and also that it has taken so long to pursue our enquiries.

Yours sincerely

Gordon Davies

Gordon Davies
Head of Planning

HYPOTHESIS

Begin to reason about it and you at once fall into error.

— Sermons of Huang-Po (d.850)

If, as John Ure suggested, the Druids inhabited the drumlins round Cathures before the coming of St Mungo, they must surely have found their way to the hilltop now occupied by Camphill ringwork in the Queen's Park.

The ringwork is a roughly oval-shaped enclosure, bounded by single rampart measuring 90m across at its larger axis. It slopes towards the western side of Camphill, so a wide range of landmarks — from Dunwan Hill in the south to Dumgoyne in the north — are visible from within its confines.

About 100m E of the ringwork, another vantage point presents itself in the form of the flagpole mound, a flat-topped artificial structure surmounted by a concrete and gravel platform. This platform affords views of Dechmont, Cathkin Braes and the hills above Eaglesham. Glasgow lies spread out to the north and west, with the Cathedral and Necropolis both visible despite the surrounding buildings.

Inside the ringwork, there are a dozen or so large stones gathered at the crown of the hill, and several other stones spread throughout the enclosure. Nobody knows how they got there. Neolithic farmers could have collected them when they cleared the land for the first time; Bronze-Age astronomers could

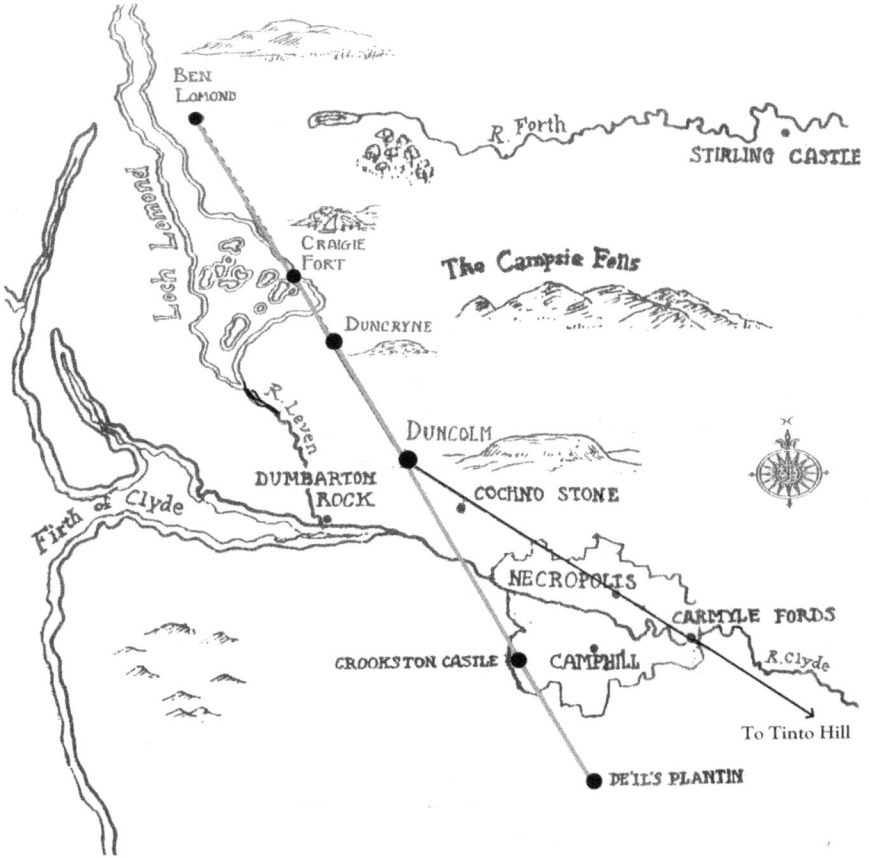

Another of Harry's first edition maps, this one shows the Dei'ls Plantin-Duncolm, Duncolm-Ben Lomond, and Duncolm-Tinto Hill PSAs (slightly modified for context and clarity —*Ed.*)

A snow-capped Ben Lomond.

have levered them into some now-forgotten alignment; Iron-Age Druids could have used them in a *nemeton*, or sacred grove — the possibilities are numerous. The stones might equally well have been shifted to their present domain when the fields of Pathhead Farm were landscaped to form a public park in 1857.

As I walked round the ramparts early one spring evening, I realised it was pointless weighing up the pros and cons. If there was any truth in my supposition that the straight road with no path led to Camphill, there should be other alignments leading out of the enclosure — where were they?

The stones in Camphill Ringwork.

In search of any possible clue, I walked **the area looking at each hilltop in the distance and touching every stone in my path. But where the early wayfarers are now they leave no footprints...** *one day, just like them, I will be five thousand years dead. But not today. Today it is my turn in the grove...*

Some 50m W of the main group of stones, I paused at an outlying boulder by the side of a lone birch tree.[8] And I stood there thinking on the last traveller to take the Straight Road. I thought on the questions

[8] This boulder lies due west of the main group of stones and could conceivably have been used as a marker for the equinox sunset.

I would ask him if I could, and I listened with my inner ear for the answers he might give me. Then I sat on the boulder on the edge of the glade, watching the sun search for spaces in the surrounding trees and wondering if in all the time to come, anyone would ever look for the Straight Road with No Path again. And for a while, it seemed that like the sun, the stones, the trees and the shadows, I too became part of the landscape.

When I rose again, I turned inwards towards the main group of stones — but I could not see them for the grass. So I stepped up on the boulder I had been sitting on, and the added height altered my viewpoint enough to allow me to see the tops of a few stones. I walked towards them then, and suddenly, with a rush of old memories recognised one particular stone as the 'den' we used years ago when I played hide and seek in the park. Whoever was 'het' had to kneel in front of this stone, with his head in his hands, chanting the litany "five, ten, double ten, five, ten, a hundred." When the requisite number was reached he would jump up on top of the den and scan the area hoping to espy his playmates.

As I was alone in the earthwork, I jumped up on the den for old time's sake and spun round quickly as

Gallowflat mound.

Photo: Grahame Gardner

if to catch childhood friends hiding in the grass... It was as that moment, in mid-spin it struck me — I could not see the outlying boulder. Yet from the boulder I had seen the den — how was this possible?

I ran down the slope to the boulder, then walked back to the den. It was the lie of the land and the height of the stones that had made the phenomenon possible. By this time, however, I had flattened the grass somewhat, and a temporary path now led through the damp grass from the boulder to the den. As I looked back along this path in a westerly direction, I noticed through the trees a wooded hill, far beyond the ringwork. I stood looking at this hill for a long time, then for interest's sake took a compass bearing in that direction. The compass bearing led straight to Crookston Castle.

A coincidence no doubt, but at the same time, the line felt somehow appropriate — as if a passage through the landscape had opened up and I was free to go. But in what direction? It seemed illogical to head from the den towards an outlier I could not see, so I chose to travel in the other direction — from the outlier to the den and beyond. At the flagpole, I took a back bearing on my line to Crookston, and for want of a better plan, I decided to follow this line till it reached the Clyde.

My methods until then had been rather haphazard, so as a guideline for future research I devised a working hypothesis, a supposition to be proved or disproved at a later date. My hypothesis was that Glasgow is built over a framework of prehistoric communications lines.

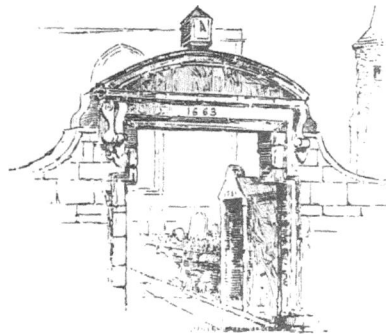

Rutherglen Port — the entrance to the Parish Church.

The line crosses the Clyde twice, first at Cambuslang and then at a point close to King's Ford, Carmyle. King's Ford was in daily use for centuries, but it is now covered by the bridge carrying the A763 over the Clyde at NS 644613.

On the same alignment, I also found Gallowflat mound in the east end of Rutherglen, a tumulus I did not know existed. According to Ure (1793, p124), during the alterations to this site... "a passage six feet broad and laid with unhewn stones was discovered, leading up to the top of the mound. Near to this passage was dug up two brass or copper vessels, shaped like a porringer ... They had broad handles, about nine inches in length, having cut upon them the name Congallus, or Convallus."

The vessels possibly date from the early Christian period when St Conval (or Convallus) is thought to have build a church in the Rutherglen area. The tumulus itself is surely earlier. If there were no houses intervening, Camphill could easily be seen from the top.

The line of sight from the tumulus to Camphill closely follows the street line of medieval Rutherglen. It runs parallel to Main St and King St (once known as Back Raw), the two oldest streets in the former burgh. Between those streets, right on the line, is the pre-Reformation tower of St Mary's Church, which has the gable of an even earlier Norman church attached to it on one side. This earlier church is believed to have replaced St Conval's wattled edifice, which survived till about the year 1100. (Shearer, 1922, p31).

The surface of the churchyard is about 1.5m above the level of the pavement outside. A large tumulus, said to have once stood here, is though to have augmented the height of the churchyard when it was levelled off. (Ure 1973, p84).

At the time of my visit, however, I knew nothing of any prehistoric connections, and to me it was just another churchyard. But the memories of yesteryear linger there like a heavy aroma, and within the bounds of this churchyard a strange notion took hold of me. I began to imagine I was retracing some ancient holy journey — a pilgrimage of sorts — on a network of unseen lines radiating outwards from the grove at Camphill.

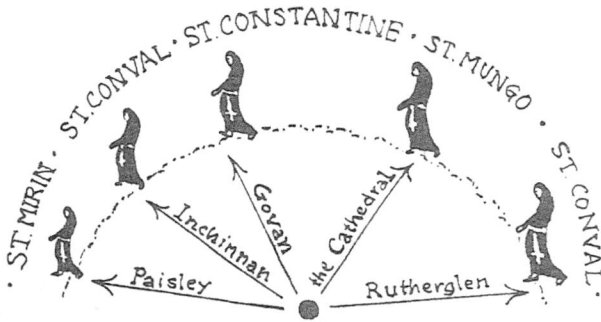

I walked round and round the churchyard in circles, lost in thought. Rutherglen Parish Church lies to the east of Camphill, Glasgow Cathedral lies to the north-east. I seemed to be moving a *widdershins* or anti-clockwise direction — where could I go next?

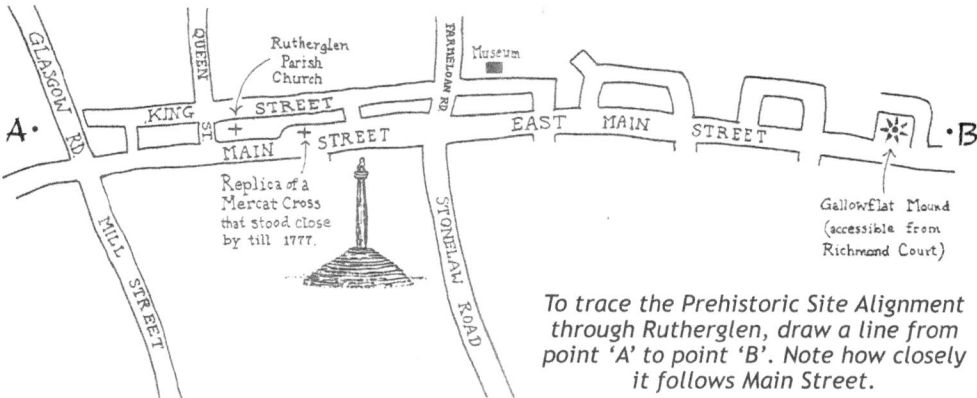

To trace the Prehistoric Site Alignment through Rutherglen, draw a line from point 'A' to point 'B'. Note how closely it follows Main Street.

Interlacing ornament in panels.

Sarcophagus of St Constantine, Govan Old Parish Church.

As I rested on the tombstone of a long-dead laird, a quotation from an old book came into my head, "there are few, if any, religious places in Scotland like unto the holy place of Govan."

In Fordoun's *Scotichronicon* it is written that Constantine, King of Cornwall, came to Scotland in AD 565, where he preached the Christian faith and founded a monastery at Govan. Other sources suggest that Govan was a pre-Christian place of worship, and this induced Constantine to evangelise the area.

Govan Old Parish Church is though to occupy the site of St Constantine's monastery. Close to the Clyde, it stands only a street or two from Water Row where a ford with stepping stones existed in Roman times. The churchyard is almost circular, a shape often associated with pre-Christian burial grounds. As at Rutherglen, the level of the graveyard stands higher than that of the surrounding ground. This is more noticeable from the back of the church that from the front. Five churches in succession have occupied the site, and it has been suggested that the

Photo: Grahame Gardner

The Sun Stone in Govan Old Church, thought to have Druidic connections.

churchyard was originally a fort which gradually flattened out in circular form throughout the centuries (Thomson, 1963, p6).

In a rare fit of piety, I attended Sunday evening service at Govan, and was afterwards shown round the remarkable collection of 26 stones which line the walls of the church. At one time, several of these stones were thought to have Druidic connections, but nowadays archaeologists believe they date from the 10th century onwards.

My next excursion took me across the river to the Cochno Stone (NS 504738), which is six miles from Govan churchyard but still in alignment with Camphill. This 13m by 8m outcrop rock is adorned with 90 sets of cup and ring marks, 110 cup marks, 2 four-toed footprints, a ringed cross and several other features.

In spite of its great size, I could not find the Cochno Stone anywhere. Unknown to me, the Department of Environment had covered it with a

Photo: Grahame Gardner

A section of the Cochno Stone, from the 2016 excavation.

[9] The Cochno Stone was fully excavated in 2016 by a team from Glasgow University led by Dr Kenny Brophy, to allow a full LIDAR and photogrammetry scan to be made, with a view to creating a replica if funding can be secured. After two weeks, the stone was reburied.

metre of soil to protect it from vandalism.[9] While I was hunting for the stone, I checked my position continually, and at one point took a compass bearing to far-off Tinto, to see if my compass was working properly. It was then I discovered that the Cochno Stone is in perfect alignment with King's Ford, the Iron Age fort at Cadzow, Craignethan Castle and Tinto Hill.

St Conval, who founded the church in Rutherglen, also founded the first church at Inchinnan, a village just across the river from the cup and ring marked rock. Inchinnan, therefore, was still in an anti-clockwise direction and seemed the logical place to continue my pilgrimage. St Conval is believed to have been buried there around AD612, and in the *Buik of the Croniclis* of Scotland a reference to his shrine appears in the following lines:-

> *Ane halie man of Scotland of great fame,*
> *That samin time, hecht Conwallus by name,*
> *Discipill als he wes of Saint Mungow,*
> *In Inchannane schort gait bewest Glesgo,*
> *His bodie lys quhair I myself hes bene,*
> *In pilgrimage and his reliques hes sene.*

The shrine of St Conval stood on a mound on the banks of the Black Cart Water. Other churches were subsequently built there, the last of the line being All Hallows Church which was demolished around 1969 during alterations to Glasgow Airport.[10]

[10] This is not marked on Harry's original map and is not mentioned in his Gazetteer, although it is on the alignment.

When the airport was built, 13 sculptured stones from All Hallows' churchyard were taken to the new Inchinnan Parish Church, a modernistic structure on the Old Greenock Road. Three of these stones, from the Early Christian period (7th-12th century) are in the covered area at the bell tower. The other ten, Templar stones and Ecclesiastical stones, are situated adjacent to the Session House.[11]

[11] Inchinnan New Parish Church is also on this same alignment.

Within a quarter of a mile of this site, on the east bank of the White Cart, close to its confluence with the Black Cart, stands a bluish-grey granite stone known as St Conval's Chariot. In bygone days it was believed that St Conval sailed over from Ireland on this stone.

'...many wonderful cures were achieved by the mystical stones near the old ford over the Cart.'

The story goes that Conval, son of an Irish king, was standing one day on the shores of Ulster, praying to be borne to the regions beyond the sea. Thereupon a miraculous thing happened. The stone on which he was standing stirred, and as if it had been a light boat, it conveyed the saint rapidly across the sea to the banks of the River Cart. Another story, a little less romantic, claims that the stone marks the place where St Conval first landed in Scotland.[12]

Beside St Conval's Chariot stands the Argyll stone, a sandstone pedestal through to have formed the base of a Celtic cross erected in honour of St Conval. This cross has long since disappeared. The pedestal become known as the Argyll Stone after an incident in 1685, when the Duke of Argyll, escaping from a company of militiamen, was captured as he rested there after crossing the ford.

Photo: Grahame Gardner

St Conval's Chariot and the Argyll Stone.

Both stones can still be seen today, imprisoned behind

[12] Both St Conval's Chariot and the Argyll Stone are thought to have been moved here from the riverside prior to 1836. There is some dispute as to which stone is which, with the so-called 'cross base' with the hollow in the top thought by many to be the true St Conval's Chariot. Rainwater gathered from the hollow was said to have great healing properties, and the visible wear of the moss on the top of this stone on the side nearest the railings suggests that the practice is still widespread.

rusting wrought-iron palings in the car park of the Normandy Hotel (NS 495678). Old books tell us that down to the eve of the Reformation the shrine of St Conval was the scene of great pilgrimages, and may wonderful cures were achieved by the mystical stones near the old ford over the Cart. Strangely enough, these same stones are in perfect alignment between Camphill ringwork and Dumbarton Rock.

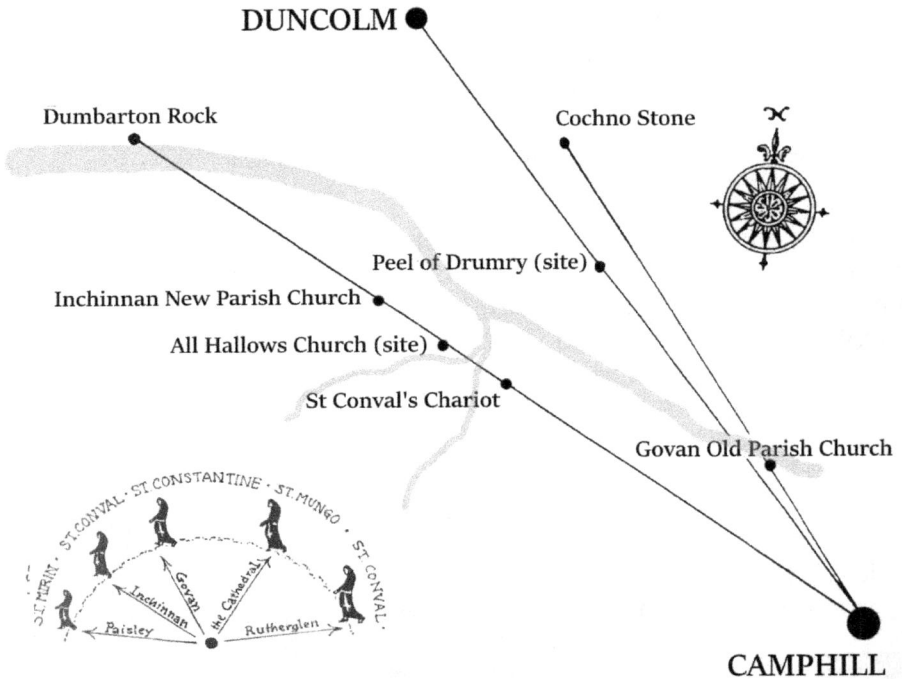

Three miles south of Inchinnan lies Paisley, a town whose patron saint is better known that most because a football team was named after him. St Mirin (or Meadhran) is Paisley's patron saint, a missionary from Ireland who evangelised the area in the 6th century and founded a church at a fording point of the White Cart Water. When St Mirin died, his church became a place of pilgrimage; centuries later, Paisley Abbey was built on the same site.

The Abbey stands on flat ground near a bend in the river. As with most town sites, the surrounding countryside is hidden by buildings, so to find any possible link with Camphill I had to resort to map-work. The only possibility that presented itself was an alignment I discovered on a 1935 Glasgow Corporation Transport map: it ran from Camphill through Ross Hall, Kilnside House and Auchentorlie House to a spot in the vicinity of Seedhill Craigs, a waterfall some 200m south of the Abbey.

I was disappointed the line didn't go to the Abbey, but when I looked into the history of Paisley, I found to my amazement that the river bank at Seedhill Craigs was the site of St Mirin's original settlement, destined to be abandoned for the Abbey site when the community grew too large for it. Tradition has it that the site was also occupied in pre-Roman times. (McCarthy, 1969, p 14).

Ross Hall stands near a bend in the White Cart, within half a mile of Crookston Castle. Its grounds are now a public park, but many years ago the vestiges of an ancient British Camp were found in the vicinity (Brotchie, 1923, p55).[13] According to Knox's plan of Paisley (1839 revised edition), Auchentorlie House was built on a knoll or mound. This structure, however, proved untraceable, as did Kilnside House.

Another possible alignment ran from the Iron Age hillfort at Walls Hill to Camphill, just missing Pollok House on the way. A near miss, I thought, when I plotted the line through the stable block. Later on, I found out that the stable block stands on a rock once occupied by Nether Pollok castle, built by Roland de Mearns in the 13th century.

It is quite common in Scotland for mansions to stand close to sites of former castles. This is because stones from the castles were often used for building the mansion. Bearing this in mind, I began to consider

[13] The "British Camp" mentioned is about 1.5km to the west of Ross Hall (hardly "in the vicinity"), and is not on the alignment. Auchentorlie House is on the alignment from Camphill; Kilnside House is about 70m N of it.

The Peel of Drumry.

historic mansions as possible sites on my alignment maps.

The Peel of Drumry, another historic old Glasgow house, was demolished in 1959. The site, near the junction of Dunkenny Road and Abbotshall Avenue in Drumchapel, was in use for at least 600 years and is in perfect alignment between Duncolm and Camphill. (The sketch of the Peel reproduced here was done by TCF Brotchie around 1909).

As my map shows, several other alignments converge on Camphill. One that still intrigues me is the line from Iron Age Dunwan Hill fort through the De'il's Plantin to the ringwork. It puts my early morning weather indicator, my staring-off point and my childhood playground all into perfect alignment.

Well, what did it all mean? Had St Mungo, St Conval, St Constantine and St Mirin built their churches in settlements that were once part of an ancient system of aligned sites? If so, who designed the network and what was it used for?

I drew maps of the network and showed them to several archaeologists at the evening classes I attended. If the alignments had been found in Peru or along the banks of he Nile they would have perhaps have shown more interest, but the idea of a network of prehistoric alignments running through Glasgow seemed completely unreal to them — why had nobody noticed it before?

In the first alignment maps I drew. I used the term PCLs — Prehistoric Communications Lines. This name proved unacceptable to archaeologists because it implied that A, my alignments existed, and B, I knew what they had been used for.

To get around this, I changed the name to PSAs – Prehistoric Site Alignments. No-one could argue with this name, because whether my lines were real or imaginary they were still prehistoric site alignments. By 'prehistoric' I meant that the site on the alignment dated to the time before recorded history *in that particular area*. This last part was quite important, as it gave me, in theory, a wider range of acceptable dates for the sites on my alignment maps.

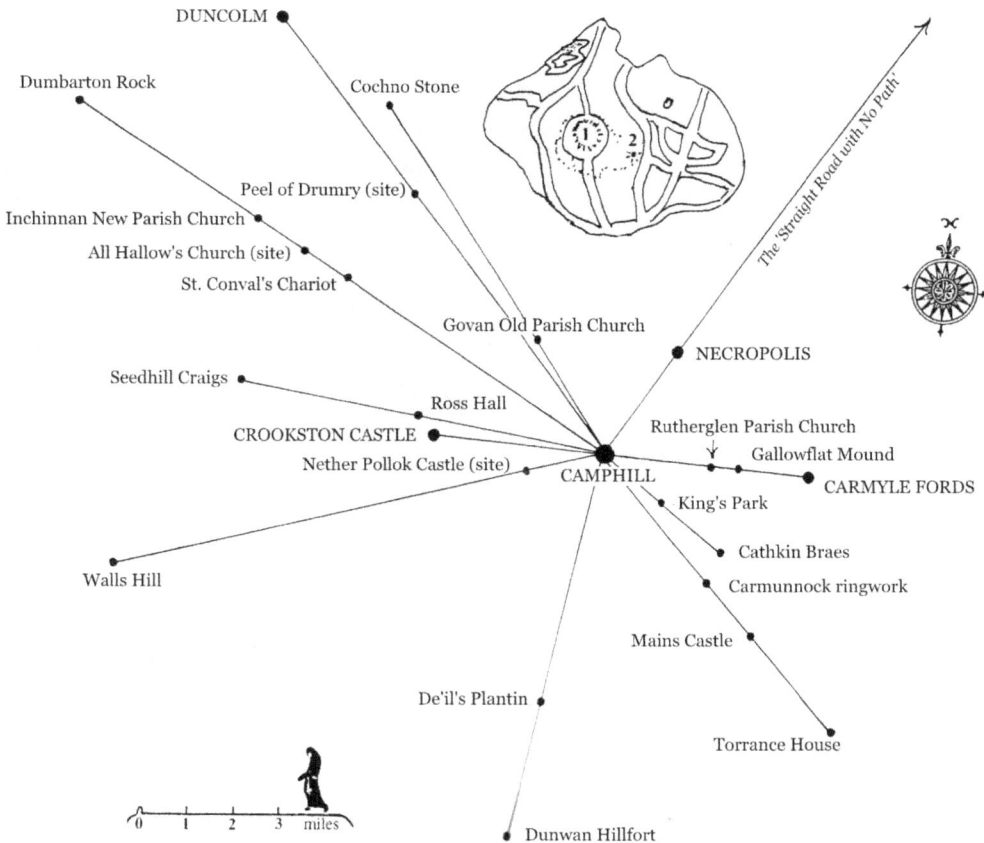

Visit Queen's Park and climb to the highest point of the hill. The ringwork is at the point marked '1' on the map; the flagpole is at the point marked '2'. The original sightline centre area was probably larger than the existing ringwork.

THE DE'IL'S PLANTIN: "... an inner mound where Spring sunshine printed dappled patterns of sunlight and shadow on the grass."

MEARNS PARISH KIRK: "... in the distance you will see the spire of Mearns Parish Kirk which is also built on a mound. A board on the outside wall states that the church was founded in 800AD."

EAGLESHAM MOOT HILL: "Possible site of the first wooden castle of the Montgomeries c. 12th century. Local tradition remembers it only as a venue for meetings and festivals."

ROADSIDE WALL AT CROSSLEES FARM: The large stone built into the wall is a Bronze Age cist grave cover slab, taken from a now-demolished cairn on the other side of the Humbie Road.

This alignment along the old Humbie Road, before it was re-routed to accommodate the Southern Relief Road, is a classic example of a Watkins ley. Harry did not include it in Glasgow's Secret Geometry, but discusses it at length on his 'Leyline Quest' website (see page 190). I felt it appropriate to include it here. (Note that the Eaglesham moot hill is not actually on this alignment and is included here for context only) —*Ed.*

PREDICTION

From one comes two, from two comes three

and from three the whole world.

— Lao-tzu (b.604 BC)

L ike all the other alignments I found, each one converging on Camphill is joined, at an important point along its length, to another line. Some of these lines lead to Crookston, so I went out there again for a second look at the hill on which the castle stands.

On arrival, I walked round the area taking compass bearings to the distant hills in the hope that I could find some new PSAs. When I checked my map, however, I found that the vast majority of my imagined alignments had no sites between the initial points to back them up. I would not even have picked out Camphill had it not been for the flagpole acting as a landmark.

Duncolm, of course, was clearly visible, but the only new alignment I found was one leading to the highest point of Cathkin Braes (192m) six miles away. It runs through the sites of three castles, all of which stood close to a river. Crookston, of course, overlooks the Levern Water; a mile and a half ESE, the line continues on through the site of 13th century Nether Pollok castle (mentioned previously) which once stood on a bend of the White Cart Water. Two and a half miles upstream from Nether Pollok, Cathcart Castle once guarded the gorge where the White Cart enters Linn Park. Since the name 'Cathcart' is allegedly derived from the Celtic *Caer Cart*, 'fort by the fertilising stream', there is a suspicion that an earlier fortification also occupied this site, though no traces of it have ever been found.

Mapwork subsequently showed that Crookston Castle is sandwiched in direct alignment between Walls Hill and the Necropolis. But the Necropolis cannot be seen from Crookston, so where was this PSA first surveyed from? To answer this question I first went out to Walls Hill and made a few calculations, then next I turned my attentions to the great hilltop cemetery of the Necropolis — I went in and out that place so often at weekends, the gateman must have thought I was a vampire.

It soon became apparent that there was more to Glasgow's secret geometry than I had ever imagined. Some PSAs appeared to converge on the Necropolis; others seemed to have been surveyed from the Necropolis to radiate outwards. The Duncolm/ Tinto and Seedhill Craigs/ Provan Hall lines passed through.

One PSA ran from Bronze-Age Harelaw Cairn through Lickprivick Tumulus in East Kilbride to the Necropolis via the site of Castlemilk House. The original tower of this building stood for nearly 600 years, until demolished in 1970. According to *Places and Characters of Old Glasgow* (1976, p.53) traces of a Roman road were found on the estate and prehistoric remains unearthed, including a keel made from black oak "with no marks of iron about it". The Necropolis can be seen from the sites when the light is right.

Some of my PSAs had only three sites on the line, but I included them in my maps if any of the three sites was an intersection on another alignment.[14]

[14] Although this seems a bit of a cop-out on Harry's part and goes against Watkins' (and his own) advice "…three points alone do not prove a ley, four being the minimum", he does later explain his reasons for this approach.

Crookston Castle

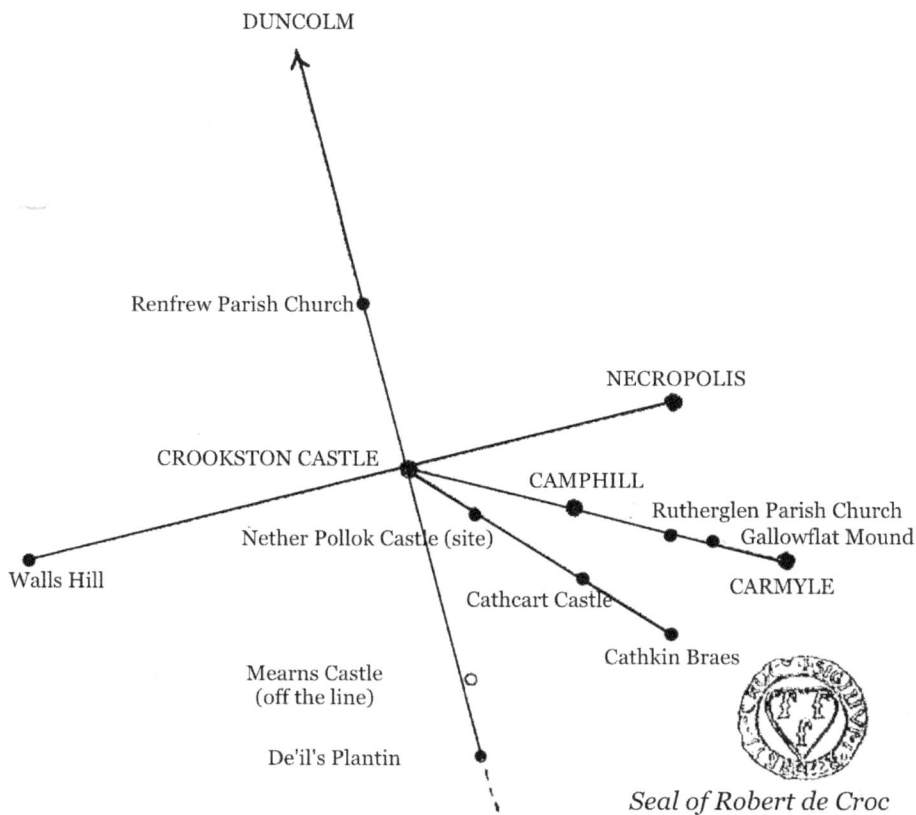

DUNCOLM

Renfrew Parish Church

NECROPOLIS

CROOKSTON CASTLE

CAMPHILL

Rutherglen Parish Church

Gallowflat Mound

Nether Pollok Castle (site)

Walls Hill

CARMYLE

Cathcart Castle

Cathkin Braes

Mearns Castle
(off the line)

De'il's Plantin

Seal of Robert de Croc

I had set out to find one sightline centre in Glasgow, but in fact I had found three. And the way my PSAs were heading, it looked as if there could be a fourth originating at Carmyle. This one was difficult to understand. Camphill, Crookston and the Necropolis are all on high ground — the fords at Carmyle are on low ground. The two fords are over 300m apart, so the sightline centre must have either have been on the banks of the Clyde between the fords, or some site now covered by the power station on the south side of the river near the weir.

A search through the record books in Edinburgh revealed nothing at that location, but I learned that a Bronze-Age burial ground was found in 1836 during construction of an iron works at NS 63856235, less than a mile from the fords, and precisely on my Duncolm/ Tinto line.

I was surprised to find that the site at Woodend Loch is connected to both the Necropolis network and the Carmyle Fords network. This puzzled me, because unlike any other site mentioned so far, Woodend Loch dates from the Mesolithic or Middle Stone Age era — the days of the hunters and food-gatherers (6000 BC to 3500 BC).

Since both the Necropolis and Carmyle East Ford are on the same line (Duncolm/ Tinto), it is reasonable to presume that the surveyors at Woodend Loch knew this line and attempted to link up with it. Does this mean that the Necropolis and Carmyle East Ford were also Mesolithic sites? Or does it mean the Woodend Loch site was inhabited long after the Mesolithic era had passed?[15] In an attempt to find an answer, I put on my 'wellies' and went out to the site, which is situated some 2 miles NW of Coatbridge, at NS708668. Nothing much could be seen on the reed-covered shores of the loch, but some 60m in from the water's edge there were two half-buried boulders that interested me. They were the only stones of any

[15] Although this alignment could have been surveyed starting from the Craw Stane, it is difficult to see how the Woodend Loch—Seedhill Craigs alignment was surveyed, as both termini are low points in the landscape.

size in the area. They stood about 13m apart, with the larger one at the SW end. I took a compass bearing from the smaller stone to the larger, converted it to a grid bearing and plotted the line on my map with a protractor. The line was within two degrees of alignment with the Woodend/ De'il's Plantin PSA.

In many ways, the Woodend/ De'il's Plantin line was one of the most puzzling I had yet encountered. The main problem was that the De'il's Plantin at c.160m above sea level seemed too low to be an initial sighting point. I wondered — was there another sighting point higher up? If there was, it might be marked with a stone or something.

There was no record of any such stone on my maps, but to satisfy my curiosity, I wheeled out my Iron-Age bicycle out of the garage one warm summer day and took to the road. At the first turning after the De'il's Plantin, I left the Humbie Road and pedalled painfully up the hill along the narrow, winding road that led to the higher ground of Bonnyton Moor.

I had marked a cross on my map where I expected the stone to be, and as I drew near the spot, I found myself standing up on the pedals, craning my neck to see into the next field. I was getting light-headed from all the exertion, and when I first saw the bump silhouetted against the skyline, it looked to me like a tree stump. But then — it began to look like a stone that looked like a tree stump.

It was about 50m nearer the roadside than I had expected, but in a much better viewpoint than the spot I had marked on the map.

Although I had predicted it would be there, I was still surprised to see it. I approached it warily, half-expecting an electric shock when I touched it. This time, however, I made no attempt to analyse the

Photo: Grahame Gardner

The Craw Stane, looking NW.

situation or relate the stone to its surroundings. I didn't even stand on it. I just walked round it slowly, took a photograph, and then went back to my bicycle.... *Like Tam o' Shanter on his auld grey mare (lest bogles catch me unaware) I sped downhill — puffin' and pantin' — turned to the right at the auld De'il's Plantin, ower the burns and past the farms, and away for a pint to the Eglinton Arms.*

I had just started on my second pint when an interesting thought came into my head — if the De'il's Plantin was not high enough to have been an initial point on the line to Woodend Loch, it would surely not have been considered high enough to have been an initial point on the line to Duncolm either — where, then, was the initial point on that alignment?[16]

16 Actually, as this picture shows, it is possible to see Duncolm (and Ben Lomond) from the De'il's Plantin on a clear day.

Photo: Grahame Gardner

If everything ran true to form, it should be somewhere in the hills above Eaglesham, perhaps at the junction of two PSAs. One of the PSAs would, of course, run from Duncolm through the De'il's Plantin and beyond. My map was opened out on the bar-room table, so I shuffled a few beer mats into service as a rough and ready straightedge. Supposing... just supposing the other line came from Carmyle East Ford. If it ran from Bar Hill and Provan Hall through the ford it would meet the other PSA at a place called Dumdruff Hill....[17]

A cold wind whistled through the weathered stones of Myres Cairn, and pewter-coloured clouds lumbered across a sky that threatened rain. My neighbour, Duncan Stoddart, stood 50 paces away, and his younger brother Stewart 100 paces away, their bright blue anoraks billowing out behind them with the wind. The three of us shuffled into alignment with a compass bearing to the point where my imaginary PSAs crossed half-a-mile away. Finally, we got it right.

"Scottish detachment, the lunatic fringe will advance... bring furrit' the tartan."

Our little procession started plodding up the deserted hillside, falling into holes, jumping over burns and sinking into the soft peat. But we stayed in alignment. Using a leap-frogging technique — where the 'back marker' ran to the front and lined up with the other two men before being replaced by a new back marker — we managed a fair approximation of a straight line. It was tedious, but it worked.

Myres Cairn.

Soon, however, I realised that there was no need to do our field test the hard way — amazingly enough, the route was already marked out for us. As long as we kept Myres Cairn in alignment with the centre of Dunwan Hill fort two miles away, we were travelling in the right direction.

[17] The name on the OS map is Drumduff Hill, yet he always calls it "Dumdruff" — possibly Harry is using a local sobriquet?

We kept looking back, lining up the cairn and hillfort behind it like a rifle sight, slowly drawing nearer the point where my PSAs converged.

At an estimated mark, Duncan and I began the countdown: three paces for every two metres... the wind was really strong... *"Ten, eight, six, four, two, zero."*

We stopped in an embarrassed silence some 50m from the summit of the hill. There was no stone, no ruined cairn, nothing to mark the meeting place of my PSAs.

We could hardly see for the wind blowing in our eyes.

"Hey — Duncan — Harry, come over here."

Young Stewart stood staring intently at the ground, 30m away. We ran forward and through our blurred vision saw first a line of reeds, then a moment later the almost imperceptible outline of a sub-rectangular turf-built enclosure — so low in the ground that in parts it had sunk out of sight.

Well, I'm told I did a lap of honour up there.

"You ran all round it waving your scarf and shouting. We couldn't hear you for the wind," Duncan and Stewart said later.

The truth is, I got carried away with the whole thing; I thought we had discovered some kind of prehistoric farming enclosure.

My two PSAs (from Duncolm and Bar Hill) joined our newly-discovered line that ran from Dunwan Hill fort through a Bronze-Age cairn to the spot I had marked on the map. To me, this seemed more than coincidental.

LICKPRIVICK TUMULUS: The highest point in East Kilbride and the highest point in Castlemilk are on the same alignment from Harelaw Cairn to the Necropolis.

SEEDHILL CRAIGS: These young anglers are fishing on the site of the earliest settlement in Paisley, just opposite the Watermill Hotel.

CARMUNNOCK: The golfer putting on the 13th green of Cathkin Braes Golf Course would be surprised to know that the green is inside an ancient ringwork, part of the Glasgow Network of Aligned Sites.

Photo: May Miles Thomas

POLLOK HOUSE: "A near miss", I thought when I plotted the alignment though the stable block. Later on I found that the stable block stands on a rock once occupied by Nether Pollok Castle, built by Richard de Mearns in the 13th century.

Harry on the Drover's Cairn, Dumbarton Muir, 1986.

Photo: Ian Marshall

Photo: May Miles Thomas

Dunwan hillfort.

But the more I walked round the enclosure the more baffled I became. Roughly 20m long in each direction, the rampart reached a height of about 0.4m at its highest point on the NE corner. Tinto Hill, Ailsa Craig, Dumgoyne and Loudon Hill were all visible from different parts of the enclosure.

Could it be a post-medieval structure built on a prehistoric site? Without excavation there was no real way of knowing.

As we walked back down the hill, Duncan had the last word on the subject. "I don't know what it is either, but I'll tell you this much, Harry — it's a lot better than that Stone-Age hand-axe you had for the left-handed man with one finger missing."

The following weekend I took a rest from archaeology and papered my bedroom wall — just one wall, 3.80m long by 2.15m high. Down came the pastel shade paper and up went 15 beautiful sheets of Ordnance Survey 1:50,000 scale maps, carefully pasted top to bottom, end to end, with faint blue vertical easting lines plumbline straight. From Dundee Law up in the top right-hand corner, to Lamlash down at the left, a whole playground of rivers, footpaths, ancient forts, mounds and Roman roads spread before me. To me, if no-one else, my wall looked beautiful.

Half-awake and propped up by three pillows on lazy Sunday mornings, I would gaze fondly across the room at my giant map, planning expeditions. Once I even imagined that an attempt had been made to link Ben Lomond, the Rock of Stirling and Dumdruff Hill in one giant triangle. The Duncolm/ Ben Lomond PSA is almost a continuation of the Dumdruff/ Duncolm PSA, and the Bar Hill/ Stirling PSA is almost a continuation of the Dumdruff/ Bar Hill PSA. This made my imagined configuration more of a pentagon than a triangle, but nevertheless the idea appealed to me.

So I went out to Stirling and followed the line (in parts) from there to Ben Lomond.

Before I went, I picked out two points along the line that I thought might possibly have been settled in prehistoric times. At the first, I drew a blank; at the second I had better luck. Visibility was poor by that time; I couldn't use Ben Lomond as a route marker so I had to rely on map-work to take me to the field in question. At the nearest farmhouse I spoke to John Turnbull who worked there, and asked him if there was a ford at the bottom of a certain field I pointed out to him. He said that there was, and that it was supposed to be part of an old drove road. When I asked him if anyone had ever found prehistoric remains in the vicinity, his answer stopped me in my tracks.

"Aye," he said, "Ah've fun' them ma'sel' in that very field when ah was oot ploo'in' eftur the rain. Stane arrows an' the heid o' an aix — like a tomahawk, ken."

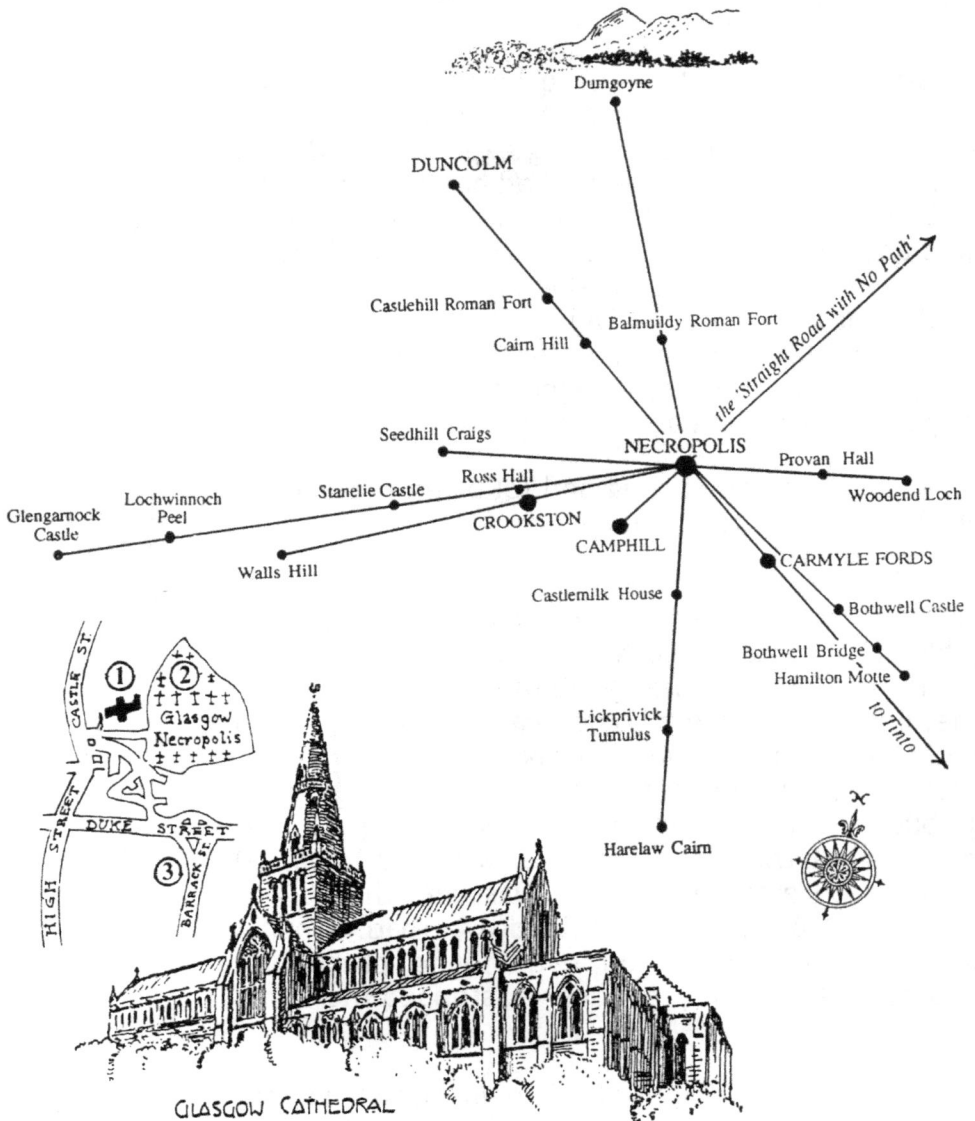

GLASGOW CATHEDRAL

The Necropolis is open daily from dawn till dusk. The entrance is not far from Glasgow Cathedral, which is marked '1' on the map. No. 2 is the John Knox statue; you can see Tinto Hill from there on a clear day. No. 3 is Barrack Street, about 400m away. A heavy deposit of oyster shells was found there in 1982, giving rise to speculation that the area was inhabited in Mesolithic times.

Rutherglen Port, the entrance to the Parish Church.

The Clyde at Carmyle East Ford.

Photo: May Miles Thomas

Bar Hill
Roman Fort

DUNCOLM

Cochno Stone

Castlehill Roman Fort
Cairn Hill

Woodend Loch

Provan Hall

NECROPOLIS

Viewpark (Bronze Age urn)

Bronze Age burial site
Kylepark (Bronze Age urns)

Gallowflat Mound
CARMYLE FORDS

Rutherglen Parish Church

Coatshill (Bronze Age cist)

CROOKSTON CASTLE
CAMPHILL

Cathkin Braes

Cadzow Castle

to Tinto

Meikle Dripps

De'il's Plantin

Craw Stane

miles 0 1 2 3

The west ford, known as King's Ford, is situated where the Kirk Burn joins the Clyde. The other possible ford is just off River Road. The sightline centre must have been somewhere between these fords, possibly on the south side of the river.

Queen Mary's Well, Cathkin Braes.

Did this prove the existence of my Ben Lomond/ Stirling/ Dumdruff configuration? At the time I imagined it did, but I have since grown away from that idea. Inevitably, PSAs can be selected that fit with other imaginary triangles. But it cannot honestly be presumed that settlers along the Forth had any knowledge of Dumdruff Hill.

For a while I wondered if the ridge near the trig point at Cathkin Braes was yet another sightline centre, but the PSAs I found there seemed to be aimed at sightline centres rather than at skyline markers. This made me think that the Braes PSAs were for some reason an addition to a network already in existence.

When I looked towards Camphill from the Braes, I noticed that the highest point of King's Park is also in alignment. I went down there for a look, and found a site which was eventually listed in *D&E Scotland*, 1977.[18]

After further research I traced this PSA right out to a Bronze-Age burial site on the banks of the River Leven (see PSAS 1943/4 pp 128-9).[19]

The most important site on this line is the Roman Fort at Old Kilpatrick. Once the terminal at the western end of the Antonine Wall, the site is now

[18] Recorded by a certain 'H. Bell'..!

[19] Bonhill Bronze Age burial site at NS 393793.

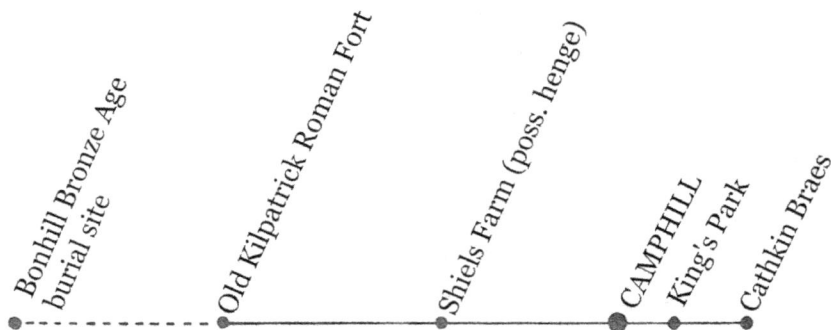

buried under the houses of Gavinburn Gardens, near the Forth and Clyde Canal. There is nothing to see there, but I liked the site, the view down the Clyde, and in fact, the whole area. Was it possible that a prehistoric site lay underneath?

"Nonsense", said a Romanist scholar I asked about this.

"The Romans chose sites to suit their defensive technique, they did not adapt their technique to suit available sites."

I was agreeably surprised to find out later on, that Bronze-Age cists (stone coffins) had been discovered at the site in 1923 and 1924. (See TGAS viii, 1933 pp55-61).

During my weekend jaunts, I found stretches of the rivers Clyde and Cart that had as many sites along their length as my PSAs. If I wanted the complete picture, not just 'the straight line picture', I could not discount the possibility that these stretches of river had also served as communication lines in prehistoric times. In fact, some of the most difficult sections to survey overland seemed to be linked in some way to the main rivers.

For instance, Bothwell Castle, Bothwell Bridge and Hamilton Motte are on the same PSA leading to the Necropolis, but they are also on the same stretch of river as the fords at Carmyle. A polished stone axe was once found in the bed of the Clyde beneath the walls of Bothwell Castle, and Bothwell Bridge spans an ancient ford, so both these sites could well have prehistoric connections.

MOAT HILL
HAMILTON·

The motte at Hamilton is thought to have been part of the ancient settlement of Netherton, but for all anyone knows, the motte could have been built over a prehistoric cairn. It is situated about 200m north of Hamilton Mausoleum.

One scorching Fair Monday holiday, I spent an interesting day cycling round the area, trying to figure things out as I went along.

The Netherton Cross.

[20] *The Borderlands of Glasgow*, p. 100.

When the drawing of 'the cross by the Clyde' was done, Netherton Cross stood 60m north of the motte. It isn't there any more; but an old man told me it had been moved to a churchyard, so off I went, cycling round the churchyards — one hand on the handlebars, the other holding an ice-cream.

Eventually I found the cross in the grounds of Hamilton Parish Church, off Cadzow Street. Over 2m high, of beautifully weathered golden sandstone, it is thought to be about 900 years old. As Theodore C F Brotchie stated in his *Borderlands of Glasgow* (1923)... "the tumuli and the cross witnessed the birth of medieval Hamilton; they saw its demise .... As objectives of an afternoon ramble, I can cordially recommend them to the attention of the wayfarer."[20]

Back in my schooldays I was an avid reader of Brotchie's books (which were old even then). Because of this, I knew my way round dozens of historical sites in the Glasgow area, and I was never short of ideas about where to go next. It is amazing how many of the sites that Brotchie sketched turned out to be on PSAs. It is almost uncanny — as if he sensed there was some connection between those places, but couldn't quite figure out what is was.

Before Brotchies's day, Hugh MacDonald had gone over much the same ground, but his books were not illustrated, and Brotchie's were. I read both as a schoolboy, but it was really the magic old Brotchie drawings that worked their spell and started me rambling.

My mental picture of the Clyde Valley landscape had changed considerably since I started archaeo-orienteering. The whole of the Glasgow area had become a giant game of snakes and ladders in which I was the only player. Rivers served as snakes, and PSAs served as ladders; it all made perfect sense. Once I got to know the hills and rivers I understood how people like the Australian aborigines could memorise routes through vast stretches of land associated with the Dreamtime wanderings of their ancestors... When the shape of hills and landscape features became familiar to me from different angles, I too, could go walkabout.

Bothwell Bridge.

In field tests at Camphill, Crookston, the Necropolis and Cathkin Braes, I could indicate the precise direction of dozens of sites that I could not actually see. Surprisingly, some of the skyline markers I used for this purpose — from Camphill for instance, could also be used to indicate different sites from Crookston and the Necropolis.

This marvellous network lay far beyond my own powers of invention. I began to wonder if it had been designed for settlers, rather than travellers. It seemed to have come into being at a time when improved farming methods led to an increase in population, so one of its functions could have been to space settlements out and avoid too many people living off the land in any one area.

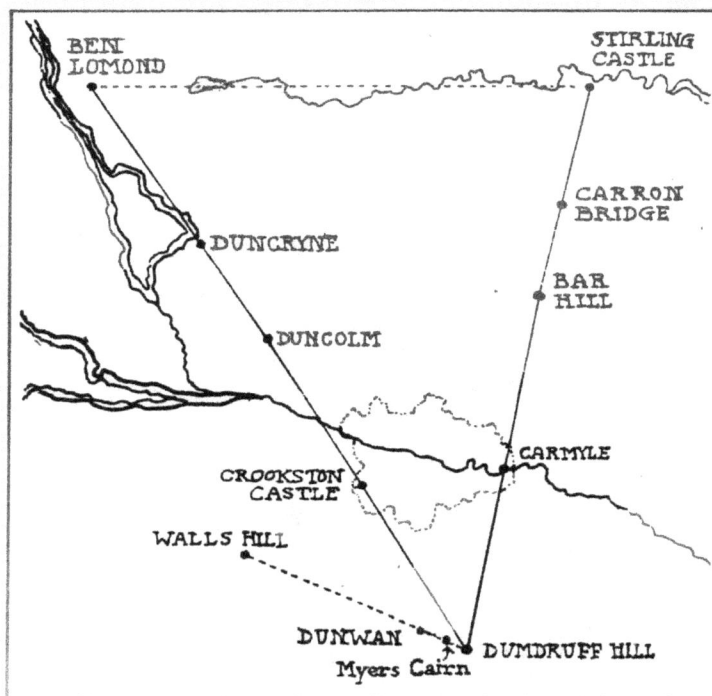

Map from the first edition of Glasgow's Secret Geometry, showing Harry's proposed Walls Hill to Drumduff Hill PSA. He later decided that there were too few sites to justify this alignment and did not include it in subsequent editions —Ed.

TEST

S ite by site, line by line, I pieced together a cat's cradle of alignments that could be interpreted as either total delusion on my part, or the abandoned plan of an ancient Trans-Clyde communications network.

The most amazing thing about this network is not so much the number of sites in any one line, it is the way the lines cross and recross the same points of the landscape. Radiating from only four main centres, they pass straight as a die through the oldest man-made structures in Glasgow, Paisley, East Kilbride, Hamilton, Renfrew, Kilsyth, Inchinnan, Govan, Rutherglen, Castlemilk and Easterhouse. The odds against this happening by chance are astronomical.

To me, this suggests that the present day idea of Glasgow as a medieval creation is only partly true: the real origins of the city lie back in prehistoric times, thousands of years earlier.

The four city networks interlock perfectly, forming a larger system which I call the Glasgow Network of Aligned Sites.

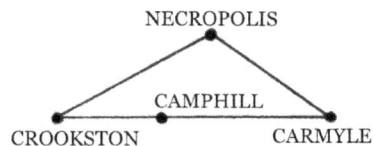

The Glasgow Triangle.

The source of this system seems to be a triangle with three of the four sightline centres on a single line at the base. I call this feature the Glasgow Triangle.

By walking the hills, looking at the sites from different views and angles, I found a possible sequence for the development of the triangle. First, a PSA surveyed from Duncolm to Tinto as a communication line up the Clyde Valley. On the way it would pass through the Necropolis (1) and Carmyle (2). Next, a shorter Camphill (3) Necropolis (1) line, possibly extended later because it was a suitable direction indicator to the tidal waters of the River Forth. (These two PSAs cross at the Necropolis, which ties in with the rather vague references in old books about travellers in earliest Glasgow walking along the west bank of the Molendinar Burn to join a road which ran along the ridge where the Cathedral now stands.)[21] Third, a PSA surveyed from Crookston (4) to Duncolm. This would not have been part of the triangle, but it would have established Crookston as a sightline centre. The line could later have been extended in the opposite direction to the De'il's Plantin and Dumdruff. (The next day or 500 years later, who knows?) For most of its length, this alignment runs within a mile or two of the River Cart. A Walls Hill/ Crookston/ Necropolis PSA and another from Crookston to Carmyle complete the triangle.

[21] This may refer to the old Roman Road that is thought to have run up the hill, roughly where John Knox Street is now. A Roman fort was thought to have stood at the top of the hill.

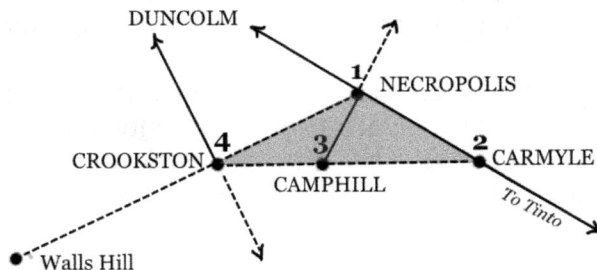

By the time I got round the 60 or more sites on my PSAs, I was in the final year of the Glasgow University

It's amazing how many of the sites that Theodore Brotchie sketched turned out to be on PSAs. It is almost uncanny — as if he sensed there was some connection between those places, but couldn't quite figure out what it was. Though drawn in Edwardian times, many of the sites still look the same today.

Harry at the Hill o' Many Stanes, Caithness.

Photo: Ian Marshall

Three Year Field Archaeology Certificate course, and was well aware that to most archaeologists, the idea of a network of prehistoric alignments in and around the city was somewhat unreal. So, seeking enlightenment, I gave out copies of my maps to ten archaeologists, professional and amateur alike, on the off-chance that someone could come up with a better explanation for my alignments than I had myself.

Immediately I was reminded by ten archaeologists that there is nothing remarkable about alignments. As well as alignments of ancient sites in Glasgow, there are also alignments of modern sites. Churches, schools, petrol stations, etc. can be found three and four in a row all over the city.

This is true, but when random alignments of this nature are compared as a group to the Glasgow Network of Aligned Sites, one significant difference emerges. Random alignments of modern structures cross similar random alignments at random points along the line — PSAs are far more selective. For example, some of the PSAs in my survey, around 15kms long, have five sites along their length. If these five sites — say a mound, a church, a castle, a cairn and a standing stone — were laid end to end they might add up to 300m of utilised space on the line. It could be said that approximately 2% of the PSA consists of space occupied by prehistoric sites, and 98% consists of unoccupied space.

By the laws of probability, any PSA crossing another should therefore have about one chance of passing through the occupied space, to 49 chances of passing through the unoccupied space.

Nevertheless, every PSA in the Glasgow Network has another PSA joining it or crossing it somewhere in this estimated 2% of occupied space. No amount of 'observer bias' on my part could bring about this result artificially — this is clear statistical evidence that a man-made network of alignments exists in Glasgow.

"Why then, have the sites on the network not presented a more consistent dating pattern?" my colleagues enquired.

The main reason, I believe, is that the bulk of my research was done in what is considered to be an archaeologically sterile area. Far from the astronomical alignments of Argyllshire and the Hebrides, further still from Watkins' Hereford, the city of Glasgow — with its original landscape almost obliterated by 800 years of housing and industrial development — is scarcely the best testing ground for an archaeological theory.

Another reason is that it is in the nature of communication lines of any type or period to have an inconsistent dating pattern. Years after railway lines have been laid, new stations are opened and old ones closed down. Bus routes change continually, airline terminals go in and out of fashion, telephone networks are extended — the multi-phase multi-period communication line is the norm.

One example of this is in the growth of Glasgow streets. As a boy, I often used to walk from Eglinton Toll to the shops in Renfield Street, a distance of one and a quarter miles. Though it looked like one long road to me it was actually five different streets: Eglinton St, Bridge St, Jamaica St, Union St and Renfield St. Each of these streets had been constructed at a different time: the sequence was Jamaica St, Bridge St, Union St, Eglinton St, then Renfield St. My sketch map shows these streets with numbers below them representing the order in which they were built. If PSAs and the sites that occupy them evolved in a similar way over a longer period, it is small wonder they present an inconsistent dating pattern.

The construction sequence of five Glasgow streets

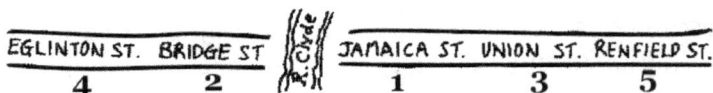

If PSAs evolved like this, they, too, could have undergone different phases of development — perhaps even into Early Historic times.

Archaeological remains would be at different levels underground — some discovered and excavated, others not... add to this the churches, mottes and castles that were build on vantage points and existing centres of administration in medieval times.

Surface traces are Medieval, and the lower layers are prehistoric. The result is an alignment with no apparent archaeological meaning — a typical PSA.

Eric Talbot, a likeable Welshman who taught and specialised in ringworks, mottes, and early medieval castles in Scotland, thought I had been too selective in the choice of sites for my maps. Why, for instance, were the ringworks at Camphill and Crookston represented, while other ringworks were conveniently left out?

I explained that the only other ringwork I knew was the one near the pond in Pollok Country Park, and as it was nearly 200m from the nearest PSA I naturally did not include it in my maps.

"But it's not fair if you include the ringworks that suit your purpose and leave out the ones that don't suit your purpose," Eric replied. "It gives a false picture."

He then went on to tell me about two other ringworks I was unaware of: one a semi-circular part-obliterated bank of earth, also in Pollok Country Park (see *D&E* 1973), the other, described in the Paisley Burgh Survey of 1980 as "a postulated Norman ringwork of earth and timber" was on private land. So in the interests of equal rights for ringworks, I looked up the map references and went out to visit both sites.

The one at NS 555624, 320m S of the ringwork near the pond in the Park, was in poor condition. The other had been landscaped into a rockery at a house in the Castlehead district of Paisley.

Sad to say, Eric was back teaching in Wales by the time I visited the sites. I would have liked to have told him personally that both ringworks are in perfect alignment with Camphill and Crookston, on the baseline of the Glasgow Triangle.

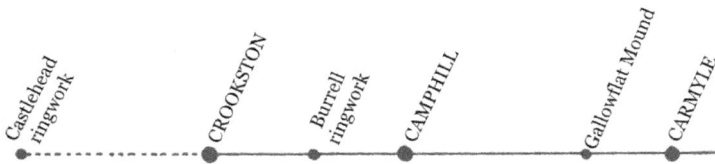

Elated as I was with this discovery, I realised that it brought new problems of interpretation with it. Did it mean that ringworks were being sited on Glasgow alignments up till the 12th century? Or did it mean that ringworks or the sites they were built on were much older than archaeologists suspected?

And what about the ringwork near the pond in Pollok Country Park — the one that wasn't on my line? A rare stroke of good fortune gave me some information on this one. In the course of collecting facts for an essay I signed out four books in the Mitchell Library. For some unaccountable reason the girl brought me five. The fifth one was called *Mary Queen of Scots at Langside*, written by one Ludovic MacLellan Mann in 1918.

On page 100 of this book, on the subject of early dwellings, Mr. Mann had this to say "...An underground galleried and alcoved house was brought to light at Crossmyloof. It was situated precisely on a line leading from the prehistoric, circular, defensive earthwork in Queen's Park to a similar, though smaller, earthwork in Pollok Wood."

The underground house was apparently discovered when the properties near the corner of Minard Road. and Waverley St were erected (see *Places and Characters of Old Glasgow*, p72). A line drawn from Camphill to the ringwork by the pond goes straight through that very corner. The strange thing about this alignment is that MacLellan Mann recorded it in 1918 — seven years before Watkins wrote *The Old Straight Track*...

Ludovic MacLellan Mann — I knew the name. There was a photograph of him at the Cochno stone in RWB Morris' book *The Prehistoric Rock Art of Southern Scotland*. I wondered if he too had been an alignment researcher.

Back to the libraries I went, and looked up anything Mann had ever written. In one book, *Earliest Glasgow, a Temple of the Moon*, I found an interesting section titled 'Ancient Land Surveys' on p10. It read as follows:

"The Neolithic philosopher and astronomer laid out the Glasgow area on a plan similar to a clock-face and like a gigantic spider's web, but rigorously geometrical. Its radii, usually set on a nineteenth divisional system (sub-divided at times into 38ths and 76ths) dictated the positions, and ran through loci of prehistoric importance.

"These lines were counted anti-clockwise beginning at the south-going radius which corresponds with the position of the clock-hand which indicates six o'clock on a modern timepiece.

"The 31st radius (on a dial of 38 radii) proceeds from the Cathedral to St Enoch's Square and passes in direct line through the centres of several sacred areas, usually made rectangular, and set cardinally and equidistantly. This radial line is one of many, but may here be specially noted as it recalls the story of St Enoch, a Glasgow notability...

"Her sanctuary with its curative well was situated in the present day St Enoch Square, which has always been communal property. Through it ran the little stream called the Glasgow Burn, and the spot was chosen because it lay at a vital locus within the spider's web.

Photo: Grahame Gardner

Built on an ancient site —
the former Travel Centre, St Enoch Square, now a coffee outlet.

"At this place, and drawn up into the little burn, was found a dug-out canoe overwhelmed with flood silt. The boat contained among other relics a Neolithic or Bronze Age polished green-stone axe-blade. It lies within the period 6000 BC to 1000 BC."

This was heady stuff. I knew about the canoe and stone axe: they had been found when the subway station at St Enoch Square was built, but the Cathedral/ St Enoch Square alignment was new to me. It interested me because at one time I had thought the Cathedral was a sightline centre. That was before I discovered that the lines going through it were actually bound for the hilltop cemetery of the Necropolis. It didn't seem likely that an alignment would stop at St Enoch Square, however. Was it possible MacLellan Mann's line was longer than he thought it was?

On Bartholemew's 1:20,000 scale City of Glasgow Streetplan, a map so accurate that the Ordnance Survey grid is incorporated, I held a piece of threat straight, so that it ran from Crookston Castle to the northern side of the Necropolis. The line went through St Enoch Square just north of the subway station and narrowly missed Glasgow Cathedral on the way to the Necropolis.

It was so close a miss that any sites on MacLellan Mann's line from the Cathedral to St Enoch Square would be incorporated my own line — the much longer Necropolis/ Crookston/ Walls Hill PSA — the NW side of the Glasgow Triangle.

Of the 38 radii and the "sacred areas, usually made rectangular, and set cardinally and equidistantly," I knew nothing, and MacLellan Mann, long dead, could not help me, so it remains a mystery. It's a strange, strange place this city of ours... Glasgow, a Temple of the Moon — Teotihuacan, eat your heart out!

"These lines were counted anti-clockwise" wrote MacLellan Mann. This, too, intrigued me. What had made him say that? I thought back to the day at the beginning of my research when I walked round Rutherglen churchyard in circles, always in the same *widdershins* or anti-clockwise direction. All the time I had a strange feeling that this was *the way*.

I began to wonder if some of the contemporaries of MacLellan Mann were still alive, and could help me somehow — men who were old now but who had known MacLellan Mann in their younger days.

The most likely candidate was surely the man whose book contained a picture of MacLellan Mann at the Cochno Stone — that grand old man of Scottish rock carvings, Ronald WB Morris. I managed to track him down at a cheese and wine party given in the Department of Adult and Continuing Education after the 'Art on the Rocks' conference held in honour of Mr Morris' 80th birthday (1983).

The only problem was how to get near enough to the guest of honour to speak to him about MacLellan Mann. Fortunately, in this I had an accomplice — an archaeology course classmate, Ian Marshall. Small, dapper Ian was one of the leading lights of the class of '84. A great talker, he was soon engaging the visiting dignitaries in conversation, creating a space beside Mr Morris who sat on the edge of the group. Wearing a tie for the first time that year, I moved sideways, back to the wall and quickly sat down beside the grey-suited, grey-haired octogenarian and introduced myself.

Mr Morris never knew Ludovic MacLellan Mann personally and he had never heard of Mann's 'Temple of the Moon' theory; but he was able to tell me a bit about the late Glasgow councillor's working methods.

"He infuriated everyone because he would never explain how he arrived at his conclusions, he'd just come out with a statement... like the time when he said he could decipher cup and ring marks. From studying the carvings he said there had been a solar eclipse at a certain hour, on a certain day, in a certain year..." (3 pm, March 27th, 2983 BC — see Cleugh Stone, p92 *Prehistoric Rock Art of Southern Scotland*, RWB Morris.) "Well, everyone knows you can't do that. There was one thing though — he was a great man for finding things — new sites, rock carvings, stone axes — he found more stuff than all the other archaeologists of that time put together. He seemed to know exactly where to go, he had an instinct for going to exactly the right place."

Well, here my file on MacLellan Mann was closed. But it was nice to know that with the whole of Scotland to pick on, the only two alignments he ever wrote about in detail radiated out from Camphill and the Cathedral ... a man after my own heart.

Although there are plenty of burial cairns in the Glasgow area, there are no known Bronze-age settlements or field systems, and curious about the nature of such things, I had to travel out to the Hebrides to see them. I didn't learn much from this exercise, but in a roundabout way it led to an opportunity to try something that had been on my mind for some time — a psychic 'reading' of one of the Glasgow sites.

It came about this way ... at a late hour in the bar of a Hebridean ferry bound for one of the islands, an assortment of holidaymakers, vagabonds, and one amateur archaeologist were telling travellers tales when the subject turned to ghost stories and the paranormal. Stories of shipwrecks, drookit' ghosts turning up at bereaved relatives' doors and grey dogs howling at the moment of their owner's death were legion. When it came to my turn, I told, not a ghost story, but a strange event that took place during my childhood.

It happened at the time when my first set of teeth were being pushed out by the second set, and my mother took me to the dentist to get several teeth extracted at one sitting. The deal was that if I went peacefully I'd get a little joiners' set and a saw with real teeth (to replace my own). If I didn't go peacefully I'd get a good 'skelp'.

I went peacefully, and saw the whole operation. I was up on the ceiling looking down at it. With my first whiff of anaesthetic I floated right up to the frieze and cornices of the old Georgian room, where to my amazement, I was able to turn over and watch the dentist and his assistant working on my inert form.

Looking down, I could see my feet sticking out from under the white sheet — wee bare legs with Sunday-best shoes on.

One moment I was up on the ceiling looking down, the next I was back in the dentist's chair. I kept changing position rapidly from one position to the other till eventually I stayed down in the chair.

My mother remembered me running into the waiting room, oblivious of blood, pain, and the carefully packaged joiner's set lying on the seat beside her.

"Mammy, mammy, there's two me's" I kept telling her over and over and over again. But she never really believed me.

Well, my mother didn't believe me, but Marsha made up for it. Marsha was one of the passengers on the Hebridean ferry — an American girl who had majored in psychology at UCLA and was a keen researcher of all things psychic. She was enchanted with my little tale, "a classic tale of astral-tripping" she called it.

Marsha had participated in dozens of psychic experiments and had a fair claim to having psychic powers of her own by virtue of the high scores she rated in controlled experiments with test cards.

We talked the night away, and it was agreed that when she came back to Glasgow, we would attempt a psychic 'reading' of the site at Camphill.

A week later, we met at Queen's Park gates. Marsha, suitably attired for a psychic reading, looked magnificent. A russet-coloured Arizona poncho, a loosely-knit scarf and a river of blond-tipped hair flowed in the wind as she walked towards me; around her neck dangled a pendant inscribed with runic characters.

We walked and talked our way up the ringwork through fields of knee-high rye-grass. Then, arms stretched out, palms facing downwards, she walked round the ramparts of the ringwork with a look of intense concentration on her face... she was doing her thing.

"There's a lot of energy here," she said. "Really, a lot of power. The vibes are absolutely rolling off this hill."

She stopped walking and closed her eyes for a while.

"There's really three circles here, not just one," she said, hopping off the rampart and walking towards the stones in the middle of the ringwork.

"I feel three circles overlapping — there's a bit in the centre that's common to all three."

I couldn't quite visualise this, so she took out a pen and drew me a diagram. She sat on the 'den' to do it. "Something like that," she said. "The people who used these circles lived a long time apart."

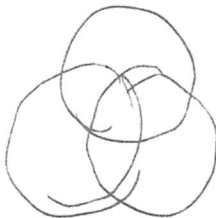

"How long?" I enquired.

"Oh, a long time."

"Hundreds or thousands of years?" I asked.

"I don't know," said Marsha, "but a long, long time."

We walked round to the flagpole area and looked out at the view.

Glasgow and its surrounding hills lay spread out before us. Did Marsha feel 'aware' of some of the hills and less aware of others? To ask her this would be a form of suggestion which could cast a shadow of bias over the test. Better, I thought, for her to tell me than for me to ask. But she never mentioned it, and with the soft breezes, blowing and the sun going down all thoughts of further testing went out of my head.

Still I couldn't say the reading was a failure. In a way, Marsha could yet be proved right. Since her visit, shards of Roman Samian ware have been recovered from the eroding bank at Camphill (*D&E* 1985, p45). This pottery originated in Gaul and was traded throughout much of central Scotland in the Iron Age, so it now looks as if the site was in use centuries before the Medieval ring-work was built there.

The ultimate test of the network took place one Sunday when a friend of mine, James Cairney, acquired the use of an Omni-Detector Kit: a neat little package consisting of two angle rods, a forked spring rod, and two pendulums. Nothing in my research had ever suggested to me that there was any connection between the art of dowsing and the Glasgow Network of Aligned Sites, but I wanted to stay open to other ideas and felt it was time to give dowsing a try.

Our venue for the test was the Moot Hill, Eaglesham, a site chosen less for archaeological reasons for its proximity to an old hostelry called the Swan Inn.

After reading the instruction booklet over a sizeable aperitif we emerged into the daylight and crossed the road to the Moot Hill — Jim with an angle rod in each hand, puffing away on an old calabash like an off-duty Sherlock Holmes in desert boots and denims. Trying hard not to look like Dr. Watson, I gripped the forked spring rod palms uppermost and vowed to follow wherever it led. It took me straight down to Mid Road, where, to my eternal discredit, I abandoned the whole enterprise at the first sign of a passer-by and pretended the dowsing rod was a dog leash.

Jim seemed to be having better luck at the Moot Hill — judging by the way his angle rods were swivelling, he had The Case of the Prehistoric Force Fields already solved. But when I drew nearer he shook his head. "It's only the wind", he said, "it's blowing the rods all over the place".[22]

TCFB °   ° EAGLESHAM·MOOT·HILL·   °AP·16·

The results of the Moot Hill test were, to say the least, inconclusive, but later that day I went out to Rough Hill Motte and the De'il's Plantin for other, more serious tests (with wristwatch off and eyes closed). I did my best, and several times experienced what I imagined was the 'dowsing response', but never at any time did I feel a pull towards any particular skyline feature or to any PSA.

When I got home in the evening, I wrote some more notes and took them upstairs to put in beside the rest of the bundle. Then I sat by the window in

[22] Although not exactly dismissive of dowsing, Harry did not think there was any connection between the lines dowsers found and his PSAs. On this occasion, both parties had zero dowsing experience and might have fared better after some dowsing training. On a subsequent outing with dowsers, he noticed that dowsers were picking up lines about 30m apart, but said that, *"whatever they were finding, it had absolutely no demonstrable connection with Prehistoric Site Alignments."* (see page 195).

Harry with dowsers on Eaglesham Moot Hill.

the bedroom of the giant map with a cup of coffee in my hand, looking out over the nearby spruce trees and away across the fields and meadows to Dunwan.

Sitka spruce grows quickly out our way, and soon I will not see Dunwan for the treetops. It will be sadly missed, because when I look at the old hillfort I can somehow see all the other sites of the network in my mind's eye — the mounds, the cairns, the kirkyards and the castles, each one linked to the one before and the one after — a whole Burrell Collection of antiquities caught in a timeless web.

How could I possibly explain it all?

My notes were a shambles, curling up at the corners in a cardboard shoebox bursting at the seams. Scraps of paper of all shapes and sizes were in there — potted essays on the back of library slips, unfinished drawings of cairns in the rain, flashes of insight scribbled on the margins of *The War Cry* on Friday nights... I heaped everything onto my desk and found a paperweight to hold it down — a wee, fat laughing Buddha I had picked up in Kowloon a long time ago.

I counted the beads round the Buddha's neck, then finished off my coffee and gazed out the window at Dunwan. But I found no peace there — I could feel the spruce trees growing.

My silent apprenticeship was over. I picked up a pen and started to write... *The Chinese say that a journey of a thousand miles starts with a single step.*

The Map

> The following pages contain a revised and updated version of the map for Glasgow's Secret Geometry. The original map was a larger sheet that came folded into a pocket in the front cover. Sadly, that method proved to be impractical in this compendium volume. To maximise size, the map is printed across two pages. By carefully folding the right-hand page across, you will be able to match things up correctly. All the sites are listed in the master gazetteer later in the book.
>
> To see a full interactive map of all the alignments in this volume, please point your internet browser to glasgowsecretgeometry.uk/map

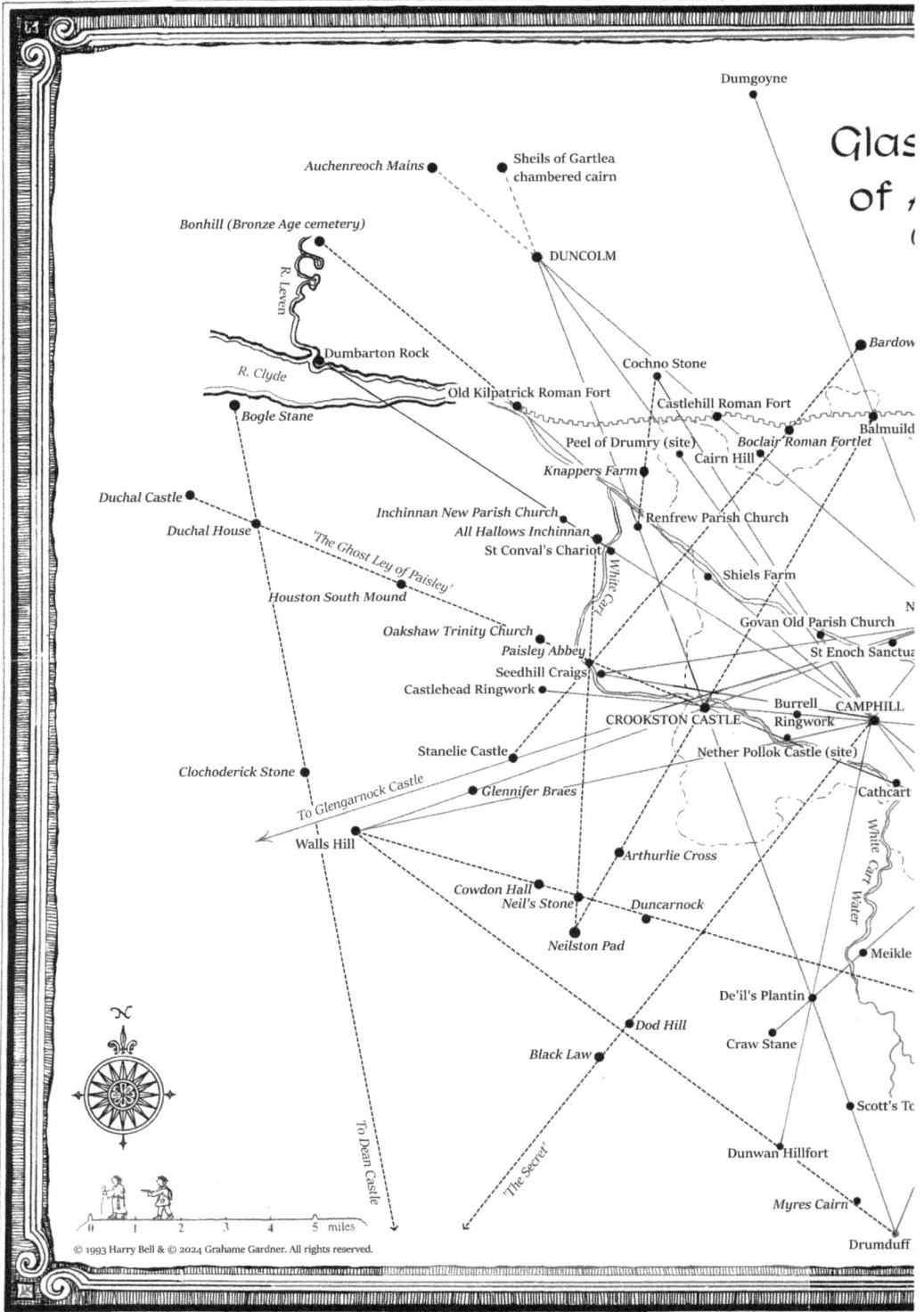

Dumgoyne

Glas
of
(

Auchenreoch Mains

Sheils of Gartlea
chambered cairn

Bonhill (Bronze Age cemetery)

DUNCOLM

Bardow

R. Leven

Cochno Stone

Dumbarton Rock

R. Clyde

Old Kilpatrick Roman Fort

Castlehill Roman Fort

Balmuild

Bogle Stane

Peel of Drumry (site)

Boclair Roman Fortlet

Cairn Hill

Knappers Farm

Duchal Castle

Inchinnan New Parish Church

Renfrew Parish Church

Duchal House

All Hallows Inchinnan

St Conval's Chariot

'The Ghost Ley of Paisley'

Shiels Farm

White Cart

Houston South Mound

Govan Old Parish Church

Oakshaw Trinity Church

St Enoch Sanctua

Paisley Abbey

Seedhill Craigs

Burrell

CAMPHILL

Castlehead Ringwork

CROOKSTON CASTLE

Ringwork

Stanelie Castle

Nether Pollok Castle (site)

Clochoderick Stone

Cathcart

To Glengarnock Castle

Glennifer Braes

Walls Hill

Arthurlie Cross

White Cart Water

Cowdon Hall

Neil's Stone

Duncarnock

Meikle

Neilston Pad

De'il's Plantin

Dod Hill

Craw Stane

Black Law

Scott's To

To Dean Castle

Dunwan Hillfort

'The Secret'

Myres Cairn

Drumduff

N

0 1 2 3 4 5 miles

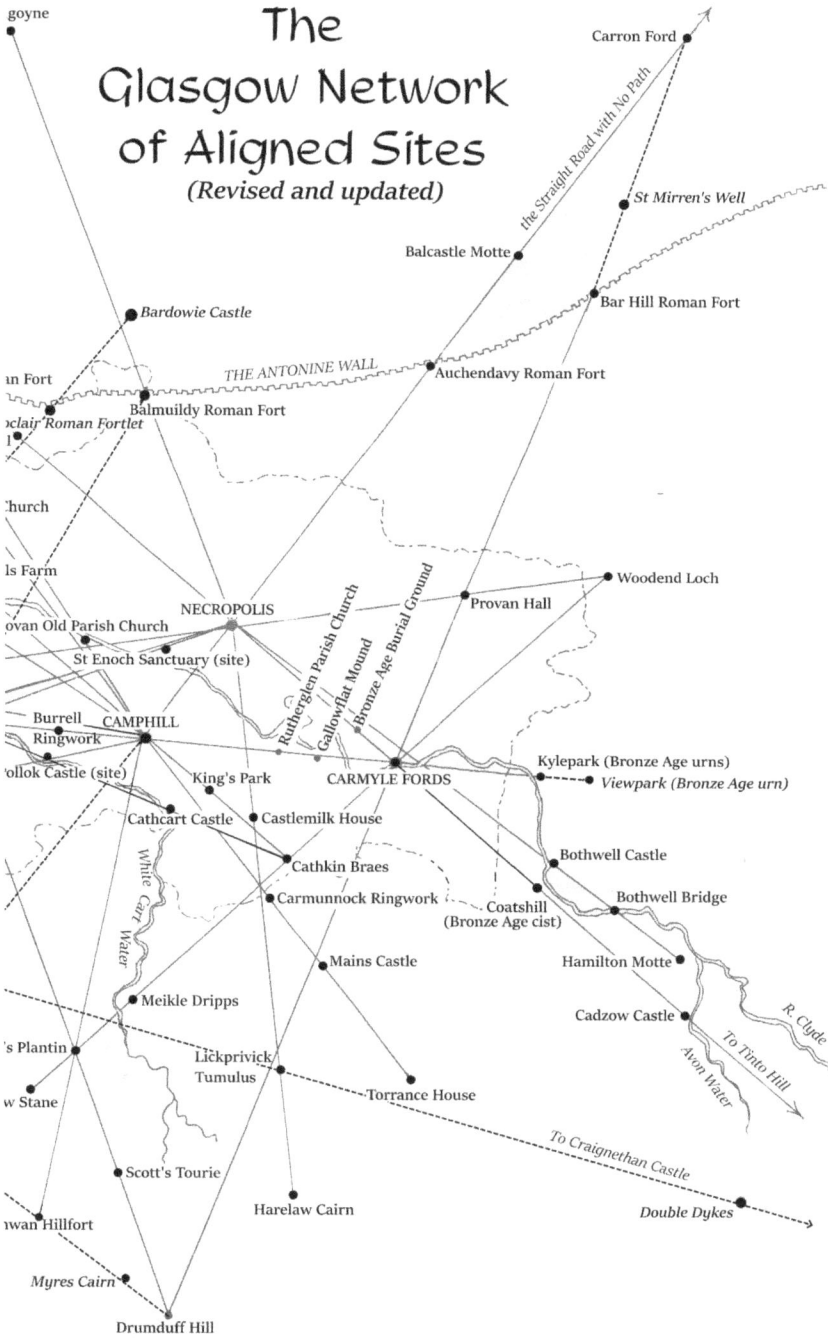

The Glasgow Network of Aligned Sites

(Revised and updated)

goyne

Carron Ford

the Straight Road with No Path

St Mirren's Well

Balcastle Motte

Bar Hill Roman Fort

Bardowie Castle

THE ANTONINE WALL

Auchendavy Roman Fort

an Fort

Balmuildy Roman Fort

clair Roman Fortlet

hurch

ls Farm

Woodend Loch

NECROPOLIS

Provan Hall

ovan Old Parish Church

St Enoch Sanctuary (site)

Rutherglen Parish Church

Gallowflat Mound

Bronze Age Burial Ground

Burrell

CAMPHILL

Ringwork

Kylepark (Bronze Age urns)

ollok Castle (site)

King's Park

CARMYLE FORDS

Viewpark (Bronze Age urn)

Cathcart Castle

Castlemilk House

Bothwell Castle

White Cart Water

Cathkin Braes

Carmunnock Ringwork

Coatshill
(Bronze Age cist)

Bothwell Bridge

Mains Castle

Hamilton Motte

Meikle Dripps

Cadzow Castle

R. Clyde

To Tinto Hill

's Plantin

Lickprivick
Tumulus

Avon Water

w Stane

Torrance House

To Craignethan Castle

Scott's Tourie

Harelaw Cairn

Double Dykes

Myres Cairn

Drumduff Hill

LEYLINE QUEST

Harry Bell

Edited & Annotated by

Grahame Gardner

Nowadays, most people who have heard of ley-lines associate them with dowsing and earth energies. They have also been associated with UFOs, geological fault lines, ritual funeral paths, Feng-Shui, planetary healing, crop circles, shamanic flight, the search for the Holy Grail and anything else that sells books. The subject has become so blurred by its many different interpretations that the general public is beginning to look on this wonderful part of our heritage as a joke ... Scots archaeologist Harry Bell invites you to join him in the search for a new approach.

Ed. Note: This section is essentially a printed version of Harry's former *Leyline Quest* website. Some content duplicated elsewhere in this volume has been removed. Some pictures were salvaged from the internet and consequently may not of the best quality.

The reconstructed web page can be visited at:
glasgowsecretgeometry.uk/leyline-quest/

Introduction

From the unreal, lead me to the real...

Lao-tzu (b.604 BC)

Alignment research has blown hot and cold on the fringe of archaeology since Sir Norman Lockyer published *Stonehenge and Other British Stone Monuments Astronomically Considered* in 1906. In it, Lockyer described some alignments in the vicinity of Stonehenge which had been drawn to his attention by the director general of the Ordnance Survey. Controversially, he included Salisbury Cathedral on one of his alignments because he thought it possible that the cathedral occupied an earlier site.

In 1912, Walter Johnson introduced this line of reasoning to a wider public in his popular *Byways of British Archaeology*, which demonstrated the continuity of religious tradition in Britain with instances of churches built on pagan sites, many of them within earthworks.

Alfred Watkins took this idea a step further in 1922 when he wrote *Early British Trackways*, and in 1925 when he wrote *The Old Straight Track* (ISBN 0 349 13704 8) and introduced the concept of leys.

Watkins was a Herefordshire man, a gentleman amateur who had observed in his travels that many of the mounds, moats, beacon hills and fords of his native county fell into alignment with each other.

Alfred Watkins.

Between these points he found castles, churches, mark stones and wayside crosses which he thought might also occupy prehistoric sites. Watkins surmised that these landmarks were all that remained of a system of tracks once used by prehistoric traders in salt, flint, and (later) metals, who had laid out their routes with staves and marked the way at intervals with stones. Many of these alignments passed through open woodland glades, and because of this Watkins called them leys, a name derived from an old Anglo-Saxon word meaning 'a forest clearing'. Though the original leys were now overgrown and invisible, Watkins maintained they could still be traced by careful mapwork and investigation in the field.

Archaeologists, of course, had several very valid objections to Watkins' theory. Firstly, there was the apparent uselessness of leys as trackways. What traveller would use a track that led him straight through forests, bogs and lakes? Then there was the question of dating. Could anyone be certain that alignments of medieval castles and churches followed prehistoric tracks? Finally, had Stone Age man been equal to the task of lining up sites across the landscape in an accurate manner? Without maps, surveying equipment, without even a pencil and paper? In the long run it was decided there was too much speculation in Watkin's work and not enough evidence. After Watkins died in 1935 his theory was ignored by the professionals and kept alive mainly by members of the Straight Track Postal Portfolio Club which lost momentum during the war and met for the last time in 1946.

The Watkins Country

Offa Street ley, Hereford. Mentioned in The Old Straight Track. The picture on the left is sighted on St Peter's Church, the picture on the right is sighted on Hereford Cathedral.

When on a bank overlooking the city these two churches are brought into alignment, there also lines up in the distance a wooded and mounded hill of circular enclosure, and in the foreground a small sighting-pond also aligns

— A Watkins, The Ley Hunter's Manual, 1927.

All Watkin's books and the records of the Straight Track Postal Portfolio Club are available for inspection at the Hereford Public Library in Broad Street, Hereford.[*] There is now a blue plaque on the wall of Watkins' old house at 5 Harley Court, near the Cathedral.

The National Grid Reference system was not in use in Watkins day, consequently the sites on many of his rural alignments are difficult to find if you are

---

[*] Also now available online at herefordshirehistory.org.uk/archive/alfred-watkins-collection/

unfamiliar with the area. His church alignments in Oxford are easy to find and will give you an interesting day out, but whether they date back to Neolithic times or not is a matter of opinion. Watkins believed the churches had been built on pagan sites to 'Christianise' them, and drew this sketch map "for all lovers of Oxford".

As you can see by Alfred's map, a five-church alignment crosses another of four at St Martins Carfax, the heart of the old Saxon town and the centre of early municipal life.

There has been a church at this busy crossroads since 1032, but the last one was demolished in 1896 and all that remains today is Carfax Tower. It is open to the public so you can climb the 99 steps to the top and gaze over Oxford's dreaming spires to the churches on Alfred's map.

St Mary the Virgin can also be visited as it now houses the Oxford Brass Rubbing Centre.

Confessions of a New Age Publisher

In 1976 I tried out Watkins' theory on my annual holiday. The end result was a map of alignments that zig-zagged across Central Scotland from the Kilpatrick Hills to Arthur's Seat. A redesigned version of the map accompanied by a brief plagiarised history of British alignment research went on sale in 1977 and half-a-century behind England, Scotland got its first book on ley-lines, *Forgotten Footsteps*. It could truthfully have been described as a crime against archaeology, but it sold well and financed further research.

The new generation of researchers had rejected the idea of leys as trackways, but were still finding them. Some postulated they were underground water lines which could be detected by means of dowsing rods, some interpreted them as psychic telegraph wires, and some claimed they were navigational aids for UFOs. I had no personal experience of any of this so my little booklet was a compendium of other people's ideas.

You can be an amateur archaeologist, an amateur artist, and an amateur photographer, but there is no such thing as an amateur publisher. Books are made to sell. Watkins might have visualised "a fairy chain of sites stretching from mountain peak to mountain peak", but I was a bit more commercially minded. With 2,000 newly printed books under the bed, I focused my thoughts on a fairy chain of bookshops stretching across Scotland through Glasgow, Edinburgh, Dundee and Stirling.

The main selling point was the map. It was more a record of my travels than anything else.

Don't take the results too seriously. Some of the alignments stand up to analysis, others don't. I followed Watkins' instructions as best as I could, but the Scottish landscape refused to conform.

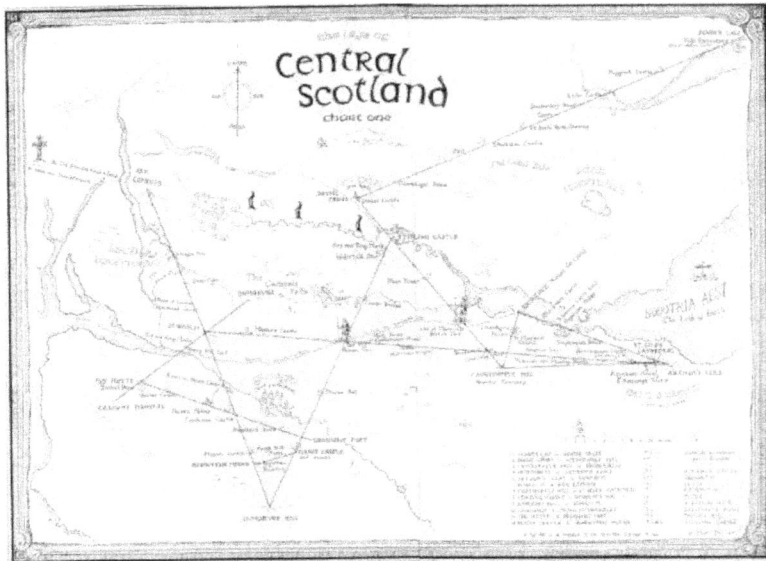

When I ran out of ley-line I covered the spaces in the map by placing some of the site names to the right and some to the left.

The Old Straight Track to Iona that filled a vacant space in the top left-hand corner is a piece of New Age nonsense inspired by the 'geomantic corridors' and long-distance ley-lines in vogue at the time. It was once said of it "only a crow or a holy man with a paraglider could travel that way".

'Plot the network on the do-it-yourself chart inside this book. Link the 62 sites with pencil and ruler and watch the sacred geometry of Scotland's past appear before your eyes — the results will amaze you!'

So said the blurb on the back cover...

One of the shops that sold my books was Bell, Book and Candle, next to the office of the East Kilbride News. Someone in the paper read the book and wrote an article about it. Thirty-four copies sold the next weekend and suddenly the book was on its way. In the weeks that followed, letters to the editor began to appear in the same newspaper and this, too, helped sales.

Nothing I have written since has been so poorly researched or so profitable.

Are they psychic telegraph wires?
Flying-saucer flight lanes?
Prehistoric trading routes?

FORGOTTEN FOOTSTEPS

Charted for the first time in 4,000 years

Trace them yourself in Glasgow, Edinburgh, Dundee, Stirling, etc.

Unique first-edition map inside

East Kilbride may be on UFO flight lane claims book

East Kilbride may be on the path of a flying saucer flight lane.

Another UFO?

MORE REPORTS ON STRANGE SIGHTINGS

During the summer of my alignment research, I was quite surprised by the amount of castles I found that were built on prehistoric sites. Even shortbread box picture castles like Eilean Donan and Edinburgh occupy Bronze Age sites.

In Argyllshire, many of the oldest castles occupy Iron Age duns (Dun is the Gaelic word for 'fort'). Some of these old sites seem to have the facility of storing and transmitting images from the past to those who are capable of receiving such images. Most of the castles on these sites are haunted by *glaistigs*, or fairy women, and some seem to be connected by ley lines.

This intrigued me, so my next literary project was to cram 50 ghost stories into a 48 page *Guide to the Haunted Castles of Scotland*. It was published in 1981 and reviewed in The Ley Hunter No. 97.[1]

The New Straight Track

Keep your eyes open when cycling or motoring on a bit of straight road for any hill point or mound, church or castle on a bank, which is not only straight in front, but keeps fixed in the same position as you travel; for such an observation almost certainly leads to the discovery of a ley through the point and on the road.

— *Alfred Watkins*, The Old Straight Track, 1925.

These words of Alfred Watkins come to mind on the Humbie Road between Eaglesham and Newton Mearns, in a quiet corner of the world some seven miles south of Glasgow.

The Humbie Road and the De'il's Plantin.

The first clue to a possible prehistoric origin for this stretch of road occurs when the road swerves to avoid Bonnyton Mound then continues on in exactly the same direction on the other side. Modern roads avoid obstacles, so this suggests that the road might be built over a track which went straight to the mound on purpose.[2]

This road has already been straightened. In 1825 it was re-routed through a burial mound it had previously run round at Crosslees Farm, and a cremation urn retrieved, apparently found inside a stone burial cist.

[1] The review, by Paul Devereux, says that Harry wrote it to pay for his 3-year Archaeology Field Certificate Course, and adds, *"Bell claims in passing that one of two of the haunted castles mentioned are connected by leys and speculates that there may be rudimentary evidence here of ghosts — whatever they are — somehow passing along the alignments. This is not a million miles from the contention of the old Chinese Feng Shui geomancers!"*

[2] Sadly, the Humbie Road no longer "continues on in exactly the same direction" due to its re-routing to accommodate the Southern Relief Road.

The cist cover slab is incorporated into a dry-stone dyke on the north side of the road.

The mound is known locally as the De'il's Plantin, or Devil's Plantation (NS 557 535). Carry on in the same direction and in the distance you will see the spire of Mearns Parish Kirk which is also built on a mound. A board on the outside wall states that the church was founded in 800 AD.

Cist cover slab in the wall at Crosslees Farm: Mearns Parish Kirk on the alignment.

The alignment passes through the site of the old Mearns Cross which stood on common ground till the village green was bisected by the Kilmarnock road in 1832.

A mile beyond this, in private land, stand the remains of an earthwork and part of the foundations of Pollock Castle on a high and conspicuous position on the point of a rocky ridge. This was the ancient seat of the Pollocks of Pollock who trace their ancestry to Fulbert de Pollock in the 12th century.

The terminal point of the alignment in the other direction is Ardoch Rig, a small, wooded hill eight miles SE of Pollock Castle.

In 1980, according to everyone I knew in Scottish archaeology, this alignment was purely coincidental. Nevertheless, I felt that it would be a mistake to presume my alignments did not exist because they did not fit current archaeological theories. It would also be a mistake to presume that since they apparently do exist, they must fit one of the wide range of theories evolved by researchers who had found similar lines in England.

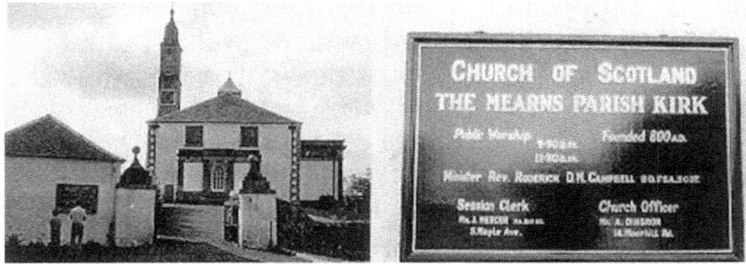

From what I had read in *The Ley Hunter* magazine and elsewhere, it seemed that most English researchers now believed their ley-lines followed invisible 'lines of force' across the country. As the only lines I had found were simple overland alignments of hilltops and ancient man-made features detected without recourse to dowsing or astronomy, I felt I could hardly call them ley-lines. They were not the same thing. Some of my alignments were in line of sight between inter-visible points, others were connecting lines linking sites on different alignments — each line was joined, at an important point along its length, to another line.

On the first alignment maps I drew, I used the term PCL's — Prehistoric Communication Lines. The name proved unacceptable in archaeological debate because it implied that A, my alignments existed, and B, I knew what they had been used for. To get round this, I changed the name to PSA's — Prehistoric Site Alignments. No-one could argue with this name, because whether my lines were real or imaginary they were still prehistoric site alignments. 'Pre-historic' meaning that the site was occupied before historical records were kept in that particular area. Even if the structure occupying a site is Medieval, the site itself can be very much older.

The third, and last, Leyline Publications offering to the public was *Glasgow's Secret Geometry* (ISBN 0950621919); first published in 1984. Without the UFOs and New Age sensationalism nobody noticed it except the dowsing societies. Many of their members had read books on energy lines and wondered if PSAs were the same thing, so a summer outing was arranged to introduce them to the subject. We met at the Eglinton Arms in Eaglesham, 'tuned up' at the Moot Hill on the village green, then set off along the Humbie Road alignment.

It was a great day out. As soon as we hit the Humbie Road every short pendulum, every long pendulum, every angle rod and every forked spring rod of the eighteen dowsers present pointed straight up that road! The instruments whirled like spinning tops in the ancient circular churchyard of Mearns Parish Kirk (one man was so overcome with 'the vibes' that he had to leave the party); energy lines whizzed off across the landscape in all directions from the nearby Craw Stane and both clockwise and

To Pollock Castle   MEARNS PARISH KIRK   De'il's Plantin   Crosslees Cairn (site)   EAGLESHAM   To Ardoch Rig

anticlockwise spirals were detected around the cup-marked rocks at Carlin Crags.

It was fun, but if I had redrawn each line the dowsers discovered on a 1:25;000 scale map with a pencil, the map would have been absolutely solid with graphite.

The Dowsing Response

West Kennet Avenue at Avebury.

Throughout the 1980s, a fascinating walking tour operated from one of the bookshops in Avebury. A guide appeared outside the shop at an appointed time and took the assembled party a walk round the stones. At one point to demonstrate the 'earth energy' in the area he issued forked spring rods and angle rods and asked everyone to walk in single file through a gap between two stones. The rods nearly jumped out of our hands. Everyone in the party experienced this; it was certainly not imaginary. Unknown to ourselves, we were walking over the site of a missing stone.

Dowsers all over the world have felt this type of response, but in Britain, by a leap of faith, some of them have managed to combine the ideas of 'earth energy' and ley-lines into one. Arthur Lawton of the Straight Track Portfolio Club suggested this as an alternative theory to archaic tracks in 1927 so the idea is not new.

Archaeology is perhaps more of a humanity than a science, but it must be tested using scientific principles and all science is based on repeatable experiments.

On field trips, outings, open days and lectures, I have witnessed the prowess of at least 40 dowsers in the field. No matter where the tests took place, no dowser ever walked more than 30 metres without picking up a line. They found lines everywhere; but spaced 30 metres apart, no two dowsers ever came up with the same lines.

Some were convinced they could trace the PSAs on my map by dowsing, but they had not allowed for map to field magnetic variation and were wrong in every instance.

They were honest, intelligent people, sensitive to the dowsing response. They were looking for alignments the same as I was, but whatever they were finding, it had absolutely no demonstrable connection with Prehistoric Site Alignments.

Shamanic Flight

A fair proportion of Americans visit my GNAS web site, and many of them, influenced by the Native American tradition, are interested in the concept of spirit travel or shamanic flight along leylines. I have never personally experienced shamanic flight, but I can at least claim to have reached first base with a vertical takeoff and three-minute hover job.

It was the time of life when the new teeth push out the old, and as I had quite a lot of extractions to be done, it was decided that I had to go to the Dental

Hospital. The deal was that if I went peacefully I'd get a little carpenter's set and a saw with real teeth, not rubber. If I didn't go peacefully I'd get a smack on the behind.

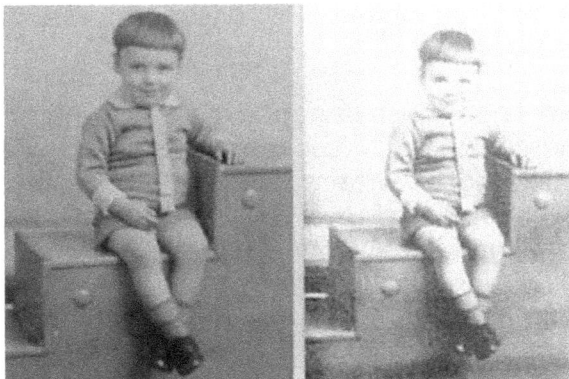

Been there, done that, got the carpenter's set...
the two me's.

I went peacefully and after the anaesthetic was administered I saw the whole operation. I was up on the ceiling looking down. From my vantage point somewhere between the entablatures and cornices of the old Georgian surgery I could see three people in white coats surrounding my inert form. I still remember my amazement at seeing myself down below. My arms were poking out of a white apron-type gown, and I could count the coloured bands on each cuff of my woollen jersey. One minute I was down below with dentists and nurses probing into my mouth, the next I was up on the ceiling. I changed from one state to the other continuously. When I was up on the ceiling I could move my legs and turn around, but nobody seemed to know I was up there.

When it was all over, my mother remembered me running into the waiting room, oblivious of blood, pain and the carefully packaged carpenter's set lying on the seat beside her.

"Mammy, mammy there's two me's" I kept telling her over and over again... but she never really believed me.

Shamanic illustrations from a panel of Bronze Age rock carvings at Kallsangen in Sweden.

The only account I have ever come across in Scotland that resembles shamanic flight or astral travel along ley lines is from Duchal Castle, an ancient fortress mentioned in the *Lanercost Chronicle* as the scene of a series of hauntings in 1296. The ghost first appeared at Paisley Abbey in a "hideous, gross and tangible" form, then for some reason it moved on to Duchal where it settled on the castle turrets. The garrison fired arrows and threw spears at it to no avail; anything that came within striking distance burned to ashes. One night, the Lord of Duchal's eldest son heroically engaged it in single combat. He was never seen alive again, but his torn and mutilated body was found in the castle hall next morning. After that, the ghost disappeared for all time.

During research for *The Guide to the Haunted Castles of Scotland* in 1981, the ghost's route was traced from Paisley Abbey to Duchal Castle and another ley was discovered in the process. For some reason, the ghost of Duchal seems to have used it in its travels. A straight line from Duchal Castle to Paisley Abbey runs through the grounds of Duchal House and prehistoric Houston South Mound on the way. Extended past the Abbey the alignment leads to

3 See 'The Ghost Ley of Paisley' in the Afterthoughts & Addenda section (page 218).

Crookston Castle, one of Glasgow's major sightline centres.[3]

A Psychic Test

We walked up to the ringwork through fields of knee-high rye grass. Then, arms stretched out, palms facing downwards, she walked round the ramparts with a look of intense concentration on her face... she was doing her thing.

"There's a lot of energy here," she said. "Really, a lot of power. The vibes are absolutely rolling off this hill."

She stopped walking and closed her eyes for a while.

"There's really three circles here, not just one," she said, hopping off the rampart and walking towards the stones in the middle of the ringwork.

"I feel three circles overlapping — there's a bit in the centre that's common to all three."

I couldn't quite visualise this, so she took out a pen and drew me a diagram. "Something like that," she said. "The people who used these circles lived a long time apart."

"How long?" I enquired.

"Oh, a long time."

"Hundreds or thousands of years?" I asked.

"I don't know," said Marsha. "But a long, long time."

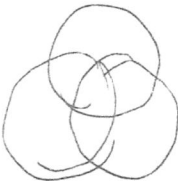

We walked round to the flagpole area and looked out at the view. Glasgow and its surrounding hills lay spread out before us. Did she feel 'aware' of some of the hills and less aware than others? To ask her this would be a form of suggestion which could induce a response and cast a shadow of bias over the test. Better, I thought, for her to tell me than for me to ask. But she never mentioned it, and neither did I.

At the time of the test Camphill Ringwork (NS 577 621) was firmly classified in archaeology as a medieval site. Several Prehistoric Site Alignments crossed there so I thought otherwise. It was a fair test as the American psychic who did it knew nothing about this.

The latest archaeological survey, by the Association of Certificated Field Archaeologists (Glasgow University) in 1996, now describes Camphill as "an earthwork of uncertain date and purpose, perhaps from the late prehistoric period, with some evidence of re-use in the medieval period..."

One professional archaeologist who visited the site suggested that the earliest construction date could be somewhere in the region of the 2nd millennium BC.

Terrain Echoes

I never knew what to call this phenomenon till John Billingsley used the term in an introduction to an article on Castlerigg Circle I wrote for Northern Earth, issue no. 79.[4] *Terrain Echoes* — an apt description for something that occurs all over the world – stones or mounds that seem to echo the shape of hills in the background, skyline, or horizon from a given point.

[4] This was the Autumn 1999 issue. Not included here, as the article is essentially a slightly edited version of this section, with the headline, '*DRAWING DOWN THE HILLS — Harry Bell, author of "Glasgow's Secret Geometry", ventures south to look at terrain echoes in the stones of Castlerigg.*'

One of the best places I know to look for them is Castlerigg in Cumbria.

Castlerigg Stone Circle (NY 291236) standing within a natural amphitheatre formed by the surrounding fells, is believed to be one of the earliest circles, possibly constructed as far back as 3,000BC. There are 38 stones in the circle, 33 of which are still standing. A further 10 stones are arranged to form a rectangular enclosure on the SE side. The average diameter of this slightly flattened circle is 30 metres.

According to Prof. Alexander Thom's *Megalithic Sites in Britain*, the stones of the ring show seven solar or lunar declensions, four of which cross in the centre of the circle.

As an occasional fell-walker, I have long been aware that the circle stands in direct alignment between Skiddaw and Hellvellyn. In fact, on my first visit there I found that two of the biggest stones in the circle, numbers 13 and 38, form a perfect alignment between the two fells. How, I wondered, did this tie in with the astronomical alignments?

Stone 38 in alignment with Skiddaw, stone 1 in alignment with Blencathra. Taken from the ringcairn.

Around 1980 I visited Castlerigg to see if any of Thoms' alignments married up with the landscape alignments I had marked on my map. They did not, but I spent a long time in the circle looking at the alignments of stones and distant hills till eventually I drifted into the north-east corner of the circle where this sort of this seemed to work better. Tired of carrying my rucksack around with me, I dumped it on the ground and walked round, lining up stones and hills, at no time needing to move more than a few yards from my rucksack to do this.

After a while two German girls appeared in the circle. Armed with archaeology books and leaflets they walked round the stones, till suddenly one of them pointed in my direction and both of them converged on my rucksack. I watched with interest but soon realised it was not my humble swag the girls were looking at, it was the faint circular feature surrounding it, an indentation about the circumference of a hammer-thrower's circle. I had never noticed this when I dumped my rucksack on the ground, but the girls had the feature marked on their National Trust leaflets.

Now the strange thing about this indentation is that, even yet, no one knows what it is. The most common archaeological guess is that it is a Bronze Age ringcairn, levelled by 19th century ploughing in the circle's interior. In 1885 Benjamin Williams reported

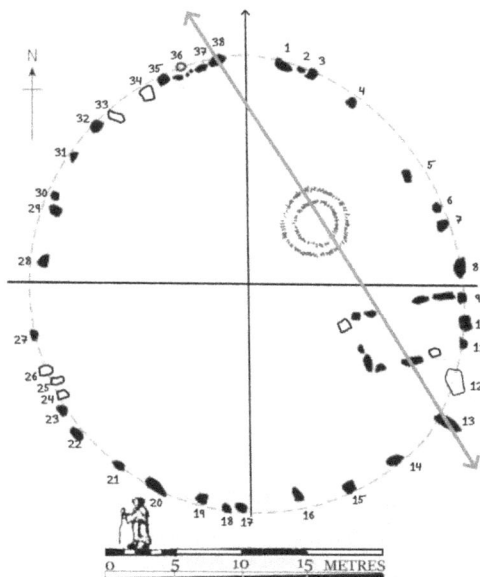

Plan of Castlerigg Circle, after CW Dymond (with different numbering system). The Skiddaw/ Hellvellyn alignment runs from stone 38 to stone 13 through the centre of the ringcairn. The tall upright, stone 13 pictured on the right, indicates Hellvellyn. The two stones in front of it echo the shape of the two hills in front of Hellvellyn.

traces of three cairns inside the circle but since then the other two seemed to have vanished.

When the fräuleins departed, I had a closer look at the indentation, and took compass bearings and photographs. It seemed to me that the full range of stone shape/hilltop shape alignments can only be seen from the ringcairn; it doesn't work as well anywhere else.

Left: Stone 4 from inside the ringcairn. Centre: Stone 4 from outside the ringcairn, but still inside the circle. Right: Stone 5 points to Great Mell Fell (with ditch-enclosed barrow on top).

Even the rectangular enclosure that has baffled archaeologists for years looks good from this angle because the double row of stones echo the shape of a low ridge of hills in the near distance and a higher line of hills beyond. This enclosure is a bit of a puzzle because its purpose is still unknown and nothing quite like it is found in any other stone circle.

An interesting point here is that the ringcairn is not in the centre of the circle. It is tucked away in the NE corner. There is a hint of conspiracy about this. It's as if the builders didn't want everyone to know exactly where the burial was inside the big circle, but at the same time they wanted to be able to find it for themselves. It might not even have been a burial. It could have been some sort of tribal relic or totem, who knows? There are also enough cross alignments with the surrounding hills to ensure that anyone 'in the know' could find their way to that very hillside again without difficulty. One way to do it would be to first place yourself in direct alignment between Hellvellyn and Skiddaw, then walk in the direction of

Skiddaw keeping your eye on the summit of Blencathra a little to the right. Stop just before the summit goes out of view behind Gategill Fells. (No dowsing rods or astronomical tables required.) This would lead you to exactly the right spot. It could have been done in prehistoric times, and it can still be done today.

My next visit to Castlerigg was years later with the Association of Certificated Field Archaeologists.[5] As an experiment, I positioned the members inside the circle, each facing a different stone and hilltop, and asked them to walk backwards keeping their designated stone and hilltop in alignment. Stopping when our shoulders touched we found ourselves right on the edge of the ploughed-out ringcairn. Slides of the stones and aligned hilltops photographed from the ringcairn, were shown at the 1994 AGM, and members were asked to vote whether they thought the stones had been placed in position to approximate the shape of surrounding hills or not. Twenty-two people voted; 17 thought the alignments were deliberate, 5 did not.

[5] See 'Cumbria Revisited' in The ACFA Papers section (page 245).

If these alignments were intentional, it suggests that whoever masterminded the layout of the stones did it from the ringcairn. If this is so, then the ringcairn must have been constructed before the circle and is thereby the earliest structure at Castlerigg. It's as simple as that. Castlerigg is a stone circle built round a burial. It is not a stone circle that had a ringcairn inserted later.

The method also works at Torhousekie Stone Circle in Wigtownshire (NW 382 565). Though the 19 smooth granite boulders there are graded in size towards the south-east and are unlike the shape of the hills, if you follow the stone/hilltop alignments round you'll find yourself walking the outline of the 'D' shaped ringcairn off centre inside the circle. Compared to the stones at Castlerigg, those at Torhousekie look like graded potatoes worn down in an automatic peeler. The skyline is lower and the total effect is rather like a Disneyland Castlerigg, but almost certainly based on the same principle.

At recently-discovered Wildshaw Burn Circle in Lanarkshire,[6] recumbent stones hidden in the grass can be pinpointed from an off-centre locus with no visible indentation. Yet at Long Meg and Her Daughters Circle (NS 571372), much nearer Castlerigg, the method proved useless.

Could the stones be aligned to the surrounding hills and to stars in the night sky at the same time? Personally, I don't see how this could be possible inside the confines of one stone circle. With a bit of stone shifting through the ages a landscape aligned circle could possibly have made 'astronomer friendly', but in my opinion the two ideas are mutually exclusive — take your pick! Next time you visit Castlerigg, check it out.

[6] This paragraph has been added from the Northern Earth article. Its origin is one of Harry's ACFA papers (see page 252).

Further Reading

Burl, A. *Stone Circles of the British Isles*, Yale University Press, 1976.

Farrah, RWE. *Mayburgh Henge*, Northern Earth. issue no. 85, 2001.

(This article explains how Blencathra comes in and out of view at significant points of Mayburgh Henge (NY 51922843) 15 miles east of Castlerigg. Farrah suggests that the contours of the entrance to the henge mirror the saddle shape of the mountain and Mayburgh was purposefully oriented towards Blencathra.)

Dymond, CW. *Transactions of the Cumberland and Westmoreland Antiquarian and Archaeological Society*, Vol. V 1881.

Thom, Prof. A. *Megalithic Sites in Britain'* Oxford Press, 1967

(There is no known astronomical alignment connecting stone 13 and stone 38, but according to Prof. Thom, stone 13 and stone 31 form an astronomical alignment between the Candlemas rising sun to the SE, and the most northerly setting moon to the NW.)

Research and Reminiscences

Between 1981 and 1984, I attended a three-year extra-mural course in Field Archaeology based at the Department of Adult and Continuing Education in Glasgow.

That's when I learned there was more to archaeology than churches, mounds and castles.

We visited chambered tombs, stone circles, round cairns, cairn-fields, burial cists, cup and ring marked rocks, ring-ditch houses, unenclosed platform settlements, enclosed platform settlements, vitrified forts, enclosed cremation cemeteries, early Christian cemeteries, shell middens, burnt mounds, ring groove houses, post hole houses, scooped settlements, Roman forts, signalling platforms, watch towers, mottes, duns and the astronomical alignments at Ballochroy and Kintraw.

Brochs, wheelhouses, crannogs, and Viking houses, were about the only sites we missed because of the distances involved, but to round out our education, most of us visited them in our own time.

It was a marvellous mind-expanding learning experience of lectures, field trips, surveys and discussions that gave me a far greater understanding of the prehistoric mind than I would ever have gained otherwise. Unlike my colleagues, however, I had come to archaeology for a specific reason — I wanted to find out how the alignments I had surveyed in my cross-country travels got there. Why did some of them keep crossing and re-crossing the same points on the landscape — who had designed all this? This subject was not on the curriculum, but during the course I learned a simple five-step process that for me changed an inexact science into something that could be analysed.

Observation, Classification, Hypothesis, Prediction, Test... five steps to clearer thinking. After the course I applied it to my own research, vowing that in future I would do everything 'by the book'.

Naturally I refrained from mentioning my publishing activities to my colleagues, but as readers of Billy Bunter's Schooldays might recall, the Cad of the School is always lurking out there waiting to play some thoughtless jape on the unsuspecting scholar ... in the final week of the course I found this cartoon tucked into my reference books.

The Straight Road with No Path

One of the strongest objections to my alignment maps in the early 80's was that there had never been any reference to alignments or anything of that nature in the early Scottish chronicles.

Everyone seemed quite certain of this, but had anyone ever looked?

All I had to go on was an account of the origins of Glasgow Cathedral.

St Mungo (aka Kentigern) is said to have led a burial procession down through the Campsie Fells to bury Fergus the holy man in a cemetery that now lies beneath the flagstones of the Cathedral crypt. I was curious about the route the bullock cart took to the cemetery so my next step was to search for the earliest written account of St Mungo's journey to Glasgow. Perhaps in the record of this journey there would be a clue about the nature of early roads or tracks in the Glasgow area.

Many a tedious old volume I had to read through before I learned that when Bishop Jocelyn was rebuilding Glasgow Cathedral in the 12th Century, he had commissioned a hagiographer from Furness Abbey to revise St Mungo's biography. Two copies of this book survive, one in the British Museum, the other in Dublin. To my delight, however, I unearthed a translated and edited version in the Glasgow Room of the Mitchell Library. In this book, *The Life of St Kentigern*, I finally found what I was looking for — the earliest known reference to a road or track in the Glasgow area. It appears in the following extract from chapter nine, in the very first sentence in any historical record ever to mention Glasgow:

And in truth, the bulls, in no way being restive, or in anything disobeying the voice of Kentigern, without any tripping or fall, came by a straight road, along where there was no path, as far as Cathures, which is now called Glasgu ...

I was ecstatic ... In a quiet corner of the reading room, I whispered the words over and over again to myself like a mantra, "they came by a straight road along where there was no path".

Archaeo-Orienteering

Bell's field work is admirable and he demonstrates that sightlines do indeed exist across his alignments and that after some time negotiating the surrounding landscape he was easily able to orientate himself in relationship to identifiable fixed landmarks and to know the direction of other, invisible, points on his alignments. He was able, like the Australian aborigine, to go walkabout without the aid of a map or compass. He named his lines Prehistoric Site Alignments (PSAs) to distinguish them from leys, which by 1984 were universally accepted as energy lines. Bell did not agree with this English consensus. His alignments are definitely sight lines. Bell makes no claims for universal networks or global grids. He doesn't invoke esoteric energy, lost knowledge or an extraterrestrial hypothesis. He relies on his own eyes and an open mind — he calls his approach archaeo-orienteering....

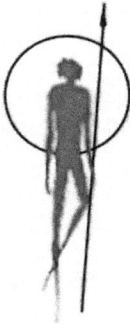

Review of Glasgow's Secret Geometry in The Ley Hunter *magazine, issue no. 130.*

The philosopher Ludwig Wittgenstein once said "the limits of our language set the boundaries of our world". This is very relevant to alignment research. Anyone who uses the term ley-lines in archaeological circles immediately loses all credibility.

Nowadays most people who have heard of ley-lines associate them with dowsing and energy lines. The meaning of the word has become so blurred by its many different interpretations that this wonderful part of our heritage has ceased to be taken seriously.

Alfred Watkins never used the term 'ley-line' in his life. He called his alignments leys until 1929, after which he referred to them as archaic tracks.

Unlike Watkins, I cannot find archaic tracks — my alignments cross the Firth of Clyde and the Sound of Bute so they are definitely not tracks. Unlike the dowsers, I am not interested in energy lines either — I am looking for something that can be observed, classified, measured, and mapped — what I find is Prehistoric Site Alignments.

PSAs are simple overland alignments of hilltops and ancient man-made features detected without recourse to dowsing or astronomy. Some are in line of sight between inter-visible points, others are connecting lines on different alignments.

Prehistoric Site Alignment-hunting is a clumsy term, so I call the process archaeo-orienteering.

I have found stretches of the Clyde, the White Cart Water and many other rivers that have more sites along their length than any of my PSAs. If I want the complete picture and not just 'the straight line picture' I cannot discount the possibility that these stretches of river also served as communication lines in prehistoric times. The overall effect is that of a giant game of snakes and ladders. Rivers serve as snakes, PSAs as ladders; once you know where they are it all makes perfect sense.

The photograph below shows Loch Quien crannog on the Isle of Bute (NS 062593), aligned to Holy Isle off Arran 20 miles to the south, and Loch Dhu crannog and Dunburgidale fort to the north.

Dunburgidale (NS 064661) fort is classified as a 'galleried dun' because of the chamber in the wall. If you stand on the moorland outside the fort you cannot see Holy Isle, but step up on the ramparts and away in the distance, the highest point of the isle comes into view.

Although they cannot be seen from Dunburgidale, the crannogs at Loch Dhu and Loch Quien are on the same alignment.[7] An important point about this alignment is that the two crannogs on it are believed to date from the Iron Age. The idea of building crannogs (artificial islands) came late in prehistory and earlier occupation of these sites is just not possible. This shows that the custom of using alignments was part of a continuing tradition which does not necessarily date from Neolithic times as most people seem to think.

Prehistoric Site Alignments do not form themselves into a network of tracks, they seem more like a collection of local landmarks with the same hills often used by different communities as a means of finding their bearings using skyline markers. There was no need to follow PSAs across the water or all the way up to the hilltops. Those who use stars for navigation don't have to fly to the heavens to get where they're going either, but they use the same principle.

[7] Harry seems incorrect here. There are two crannogs in Loch Quien. The photo shows the south one. Only the north crannog can be aligned with both Holy Island and the Loch Dhu crannog (although that is below the surface of the reservoir and cannot be seen). However, the alignment does not pass through Dunburgidale, it is some distance east of it, closer to the OS trig point at Acholter.

My research has shown that important sites in prehistoric times were very often placed in alignment between landmarks in the surrounding hills. The most likely reason for this would be to help you find your way back to them through the wilderness.

Obscurities and Objections

How can we tell the difference between a genuine alignment and an assembly of coincidences?

Alfred Watkins arranged 51 churches on the OS map of Andover into 29 three-point leys, eight four-point leys and one five-point ley. To see how many alignments were likely to turn up by chance, he marked out 51 crosses haphazardly on a sheet of paper the same size and found 33 three-point alignments, one of four points, and none with five. He concluded from this that three-point alignments are valueless as proof, while four points or more are exceedingly strong evidence.

The flaw in this apparently logical supposition is that for all we know we are narrowing down our research options because three-point alignments might have been perfectly acceptable in prehistoric times. Some of the churches in the Andover survey could have been like those on Watkins' Oxford map — strung out along main thoroughfares which were more the result of town planning than prehistoric surveying. This would have resulted in a strong bias in favour of the churches over the 51 random crossmarks.

Since Watkins' experiment, ley-line statisticians have concentrated on various complicated formulae to find the 'statistically significant alignment', with the more sites on the line the better. Again, the reasoning behind this is suspect. It almost suggests that the main aim of prehistoric peoples was to cram as many sites into a straight line as possible. The truth is that a single line in isolation doesn't prove very much. For all our calculations, there is still no real way of knowing the difference between a statistically significant alignment and a statistically significant coincidence.

The method that gives me the best results is to isolate an area for research and see where my PSAs originate and where they terminate. I consider three-point alignments quite acceptable if any of the three sites is an intersection on another alignment.

To cut coincidental alignments to a minimum, I chose the worst possible ground in Scotland for my biggest research project. Far from the astronomical alignments of Argyllshire and the Hebrides, further still from Watkins' rural Herefordshire, the City of Glasgow — with its original landscape almost obliterated by 800 years of housing and industrial development — could scarcely be considered a favourable testing ground for an archaeological theory.

Nevertheless, I tracked down every alignment I could find that passed through the city limits. Had my 31 alignments led to places like Hampden Park, Central Station, the Plaza Ballroom and the City Chambers, I would have folded my tent and crept off silently into the night.Instead, they led me into a fascinating interlocking Network dominated by four strategically placed sites, three of which are in perfect alignment.

Another Time, Another Place

It was my birthday and computers had discreetly registered the fact in undertaker's offices throughout Central Scotland. I had reached the point in life when 'pay for your funeral now' circulars outnumber the birthday cards.

Wee Son, now Big Man, back from an exchange year at Kansas University had invited me out for a meal. We sat pair-bonding in the roadhouse restaurant wearing matching grey sweatshirts with 'Kansas' printed on the front in blue slab serif lettering outlined in red ... I was reeking of duty-free aftershave.

He seemed very evasive about where we were going after the meal ... my curiosity was aroused when he turned off our usual route home and stopped at a newly-built office block not far from the same hilltop we had been to all those years ago.

We went into a ground-floor office, blinking under the fluorescent lights, and crossed the room to a computer console. He switched it on and it flickered into life. Silently I watched, as eyes blackbird bright he scanned the screen, radiant with inner knowledge, a living repository of hi-tech wisdom logging on to the Internet.

"Off we go, Dad", he said as the words Glasgow Network of Aligned Sites appeared on the screen.

"Click this button here".

A photograph of a hill shaped like a basin upside down gradually built itself up from a pattern of little squares on the screen ... Duncolm!

"Now on to the Hypothesis section", he said, deftly tapping the keyboard. "I've taken some of the photos from your book and scanned them in — you can add the text yourself later..."

And that was how my online education began... with a son teaching his father on the hillside.

AFTERTHOUGHTS AND ADDENDA

Grahame Gardner

Over the years that I've worked with Harry's network, several additional sites have come to light — some through more recent archaeological discoveries, others perhaps because Harry either chose to ignore them or was unaware of them at the time. Access to documentation has greatly increased with online mapping sites and historical databases like Canmore and it's now much easier to research this material.

We don't know for sure how many leys Harry surveyed, but there are a few more that he mentions in his *Guide to the Haunted Castles of Scotland* that I've listed in the Gazetteer and the Directory of Leys. Although most of these are three-point leys, therefore not conforming to strict Watkinsian standards, they are of some interest; in many cases I've managed to unearth additional sites on them. All of these additional PSAs can be viewed online at glasgowsecretgeometry.uk/map.

Dunstaffnage to Ben Cruachan

"Like many of Scotland's haunted castles, Dunstaffnage stands on a ley-line", says Harry, in *Haunted Castles*. He only mentions one intermediate site on this ley, namely Inverawe House, which has a ghostly connection with Inveraray

Castle involving a time-travelling spook. Like all good ghost stories, it began on a dark and stormy night in 1740, when Duncan Campbell, the Laird of Inverawe, gave shelter to a fugitive from the law. As Duncan lay in bed later that night, a ghostly apparition of his cousin appeared, bleeding from several wounds, warning him to "shield not my murderer". Duncan realised that the ghost must be referring to his fugitive guest, but under the rules of Highland hospitality, he could not challenge the stranger to a duel or otherwise do him harm inside his home. So, the next morning, he took the man to a cave on Ben Cruachan and left him to fend for himself. However, after the ghost returned on the second night, Duncan went back to the cave intent on challenging the stranger, only to find him gone. That night, the ghost appeared to Duncan for the last time. Pointing a bloody finger, it whispered "Farewell, Inverawe. Farewell, until we meet again at Ticonderoga." No-one in the family had heard of the name Ticonderoga at the time, but they kept a note of it in the family records. Some 18 years later, Duncan was serving in the Black Watch during the Seven Years War when he died of his wounds following an attack on the French-held Fort Carillon, a strategic outpost near the southern end of Lake Champlain on what is now the New York/ Vermont border. The Indians called the fort *Ticonderoga*.

At the time of this attack on Ticonderoga in 1758, a ghostly battle involving Highland warriors attacking a fort defended by French soldiers was seen in the skies above the Campbell stronghold of Inveraray Castle. It was witnessed by the physician Sir William Bart and two companions, and independently corroborated by two other ladies who had been walking the grounds. (Biltcliffe, 299)

The ghost of Duncan Campbell has also been seen at Barcaldine Castle, a few miles north of Dunstaffnage (but sadly not on this alignment).[*]

Glamis Castle to Finavon Castle

Harry mentions just one intermediate site on this ley — the four-poster stone circle in Carse Grey wood (although only three stones survive). However, in 2006, aerial photography revealed a linear crop mark near Berrymoss Wood (NO 397489) that indicated the presence of an underground souterrain, situated right on this alignment. Aerial photography of crop marks in the area around Carse Grey revealed more souterrains and evidence of a Late Prehistoric settlement.

Glamis Castle to Baldoukie

Another three-point ley. Harry only mentions the Pictish St Orland's stone as an intermediate site between the castle of Glamis and the prehistoric earthwork at Baldoukie; however, just south of Redford, at the side the A928, there is a small medieval chapel dedicated to St Ninian that lies on the alignment. It may have older provenance.

Crathes Castle to Muchalls Castle

The sole intermediate site on this three-point ley mentioned by Harry is the recumbent stone circle of Clune Wood, yet a 2004 excavation revealed a series of five aligned pits oriented north-east to south-west in the grounds of Crathes Castle and bang on Harry's alignment. The pits orient towards a prominent skyline notch marking the midwinter sunrise, and are believed to date from around 10,000 years ago. Analysis in 2013 confirmed a

---

[*] paranormaldatabase.com/highlands/Argydata.php

lunar connection with the alignment, making this the world's oldest known lunar calendar. There is also a later Early Neolithic timber structure associated with the site.

Interesting trivia – Crathes Castle holds an ornamental jewelled ivory horn in its collection, named the Horn of Leys!

Dunburgidale to Holy Island

Mentioned in his online *Leyline Quest*, Harry includes four sites on this ley – Dunburgidale, Loch Dhu crannog, Loch Quien south crannog, and Holy Island. However, getting things to line up is a little problematic. The alignment can only include the Loch Dhu crannog if the north crannog in Loch Quien is used, yet it is clear from his photograph that Harry is referring to the south crannog (see page 210). Even then, it doesn't align well with Dunburgidale. The trig point near Acholter is a better fit. Still, all is not lost, as the Iron Age promontory fort at Ardnahoe on the Bute coast sits nicely on this line.

Here are a few of my own discoveries.

The 'Ghost Ley' of Paisley

Finding myself in Paisley with an hour or two to spare while I waited on a local garage to finish some car maintenance, I took the opportunity to visit a few of Harry's sites, starting with Seedhill Craigs. This is where St Mirin's original chapel was located, according to Harry's research. As I mentioned earlier, it seems a poor location for a sighting centre due to its low position in the landscape, and this visit did nothing to disabuse me of that opinion. The section from here to the Necropolis would be devoid of other sites had I not added the Ramshorn Kirkyard (one of the oldest burial grounds in Glasgow) at the suggestion of Kenny Brophy.

Seedhill Craigs.

Ramshorn is a curious place name and its origin is obscure, but there is an interesting connection with St Kentigern/Mungo. A story tells of a thief who stole a ram from the bishop's flock, cutting its head off. The head instantly petrified and stuck to his hand so securely that he could not remove it. He reluctantly went to confess his crime to St Mungo, who absolved him of his sin and gifted the ram to him. The area where this happened became known as the lands of Ramshorn. (Foreman, 2008, 36)

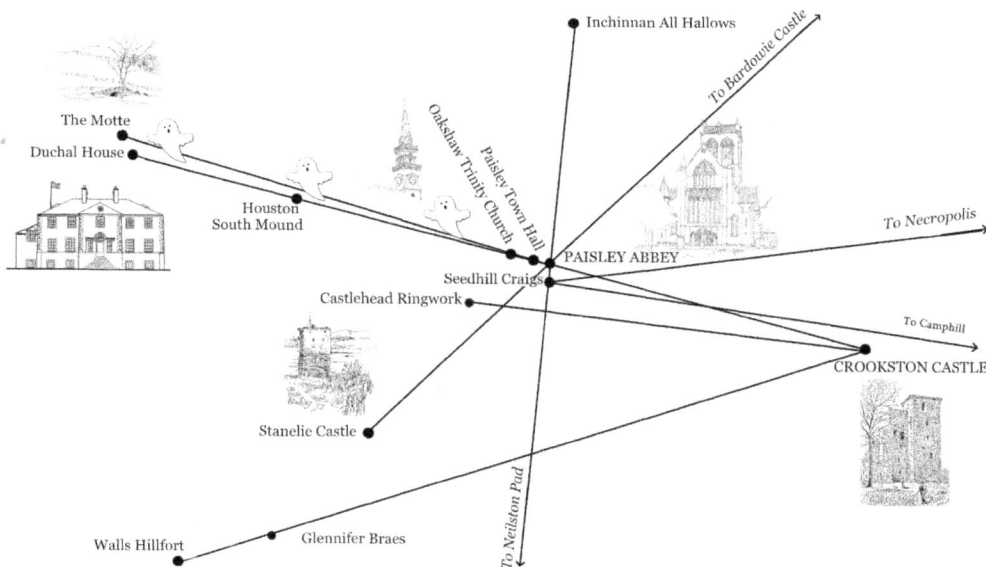

Moving the sighting centre to Paisley Abbey (as Harry had in *Forgotten Footsteps*) does not offer much hope regarding the PSA to the Necropolis,

Oakshaw Trinity Church

Photo: Grahame Gardner

although there is a good alignment running through there to Crookston Castle and Dechmont Hillfort in one direction, and to Duchal Castle in the other. I've identified two additional leys running through the Abbey — one runs NE from Stanelie Castle to Bardowie Castle, the other more or less north from Neilston Pad to the site of Inchinnan All Hallows Church.

Clearly the Abbey is a significant site, but again, it's not particularly elevated in the landscape so perhaps not the best sighting centre. The hilltop setting of the next site I wanted to look at, Oakshaw Trinity Church, offers a much better sighting centre and its spire is easily visible from Crookston Castle. Traces of a defensive Iron Age hillfort have been found here, and there is thought to have been a Roman Fort on the western slopes of the hill.

Moving the Seedhill Craigs PSAs to Oakshaw Trinity Church produces some interesting possibilities. The alignment running to Crookston Castle passes through no less than five former churches and chapels in Paisley, some dating back to the 16th century: the site of the old Mercat Cross in the town square, and the fishpond in Pollok Park (just missing the earthwork). Another alignment, extended as far as Provan Hall, misses the Necropolis but runs down the axis of Glasgow Cathedral. En route it passes through the old Stobcross Quay, where a Neolithic logboat was discovered, and, between the Cathedral and Provan Hall, a location where a funerary urn with cremated remains was unearthed at Milnbank, and also a medieval Glasgow boundary stone that once stood on the bank of the Molendinar.

But it is the alignment from Dechmont Hill to Duchal Castle (via Crookston Castle and Paisley

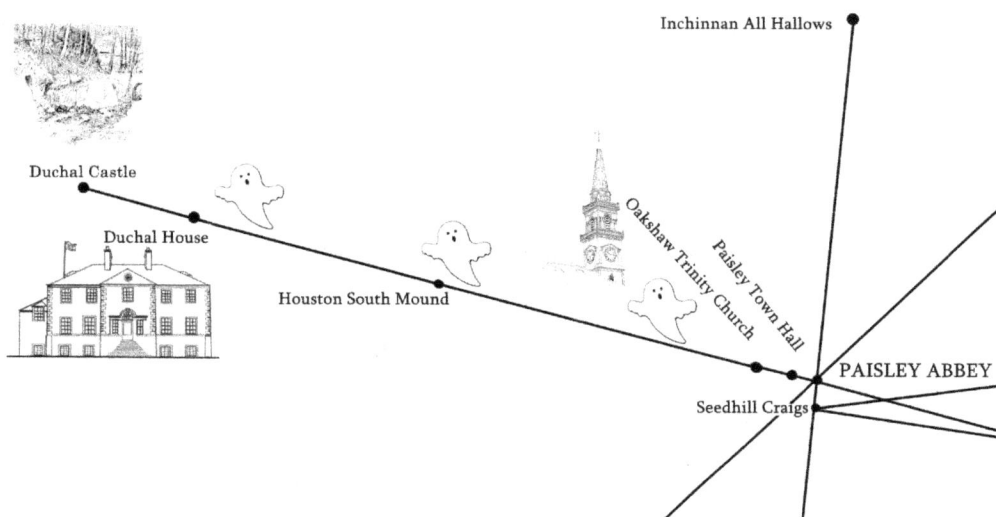

[1] See page 197.

Abbey), listed in *Forgotten Footsteps*, that I wanted to investigate further, as it has several documented hauntings in the section from Paisley Abbey to Duchal Castle. On his *Leyline Quest* website, Harry speaks of a ghost seen in a "hideous, gross and tangible form" at Paisley Abbey in 1296, documented in the *Lanercost Chronicle* written around the start of the 14th century.[1] The ghost moved to Duchal Castle, appearing as a black monk on the castle turrets. Any weapons that the garrison tried to use on it were burned instantly to ashes. One night, the Lord of Duchal's eldest son decided to tackle the spectre himself, but sadly, his mutilated body was found the next morning, apparently slain by the ghost.

This same alignment passes through Paisley Town Hall, which is not without its own ghostly resident. A local ghost hunting club reported unusual noises and being poked and pushed about by unseen beings when investigating the basement.

Oakshaw Trinity Church, the next point on the alignment, also has its own ghost in the shape of 'Wee Leitch', a stonemason who fell to his death while working on the steeple, and has been seen in the church. The pavement outside has a pair of glasses, a heart, and a handkerchief worked into the cobbles, said to mark the spot where he fell.

Between Duchal Castle and Oakshaw, but squarely on the alignment, is Houston South Mound, where a stone cist burial containing human bones, a flint knife, and a food vessel dated to the Bronze Age was unearthed in 1791. Some Neolithic pits have also been discovered in the vicinity. No hauntings are reported here, but it is tempting to imagine that the former occupant of the cist might be a wee bit grumpy at the disturbance.

Beyond Paisley, the alignment runs to Crookston Castle, where a shadowy figure has been seen in the ruins on a couple of occasions. Harry mentions this in his *Haunted Castles* book. A local ghost-hunting group found the ghost to be a female named Elspeth, and recorded that she "seemed rather tetchy".

Hauntings like these are fairly common on the 'energy leys' that dowsers find; it seems there is some energetic/ informational component that allows ghosts to travel along them. The Paisley Ghost Ley is a classic example of this behaviour.

Photo: Grahame Gardner

Wee Leitch's 'spectacles' in the pavement.

Some other alignments

These alignments are very much in the same vein as Harry's 3-site PSAs, included because they pass through sites that intersect with another PSA.

Stanelie Castle to Bardowie Castle

Another alignment through Paisley Abbey, this one has castles at each end, Paisley Abbey in the middle, with a Roman fortlet and a 20th-century crossroads for added flavour. There are no obvious prehistoric connections, apart from possibly Paisley Abbey, so technically it shouldn't be included, but it is a neat alignment.

Stanelie (or Stanley) Castle dates back to the 15th century and was originally situated on an island in a marsh. It was abandoned in the early 19th century and sold to the Paisley Water Company, who built the present reservoir that surrounds it. In the Gazetteer of *Glasgow's Secret Geometry*, Harry mentions that "a small medal of Roman date commemorating Titus' capture of Jerusalem was found there in 1829".

From Stanelie, the alignment runs in a northeast direction straight to Bardowie Castle. Along the way, it passes through Paisley Abbey and then it crosses the Clyde with no other sites until we get to Knightswood Cross, which, despite only existing since the 1920s, boasts four churches. Knightswood itself is mentioned on the William Roy map from the 1750s and was home to a small settlement of ironstone miners and brick makers but was otherwise unpopulated farmland and disused mine workings. The area wasn't developed into a housing estate until the Great Western Road was extended beyond Anniesland between 1924 and 1927.

Old Castle of Stanley

Bardowie Castle and Loch

Beyond Knightswood, the line passes through the postulated Roman fortlet at Boclair. Here, the Antonine Wall makes a sharp angle and an interval fortlet would be expected. However, a trial trench in 1961 revealed only the base of the Antonine Wall and no sign of the anticipated fortlet, which still awaits discovery. There is another Roman connection in Knightswood, where a Roman bronze coin was found in the garden of a house in Pikeman Road, a few tens of metres from Knightswood Cross, in 1950.

The A-listed Bardowie Castle on the shores of Bardowie Loch is in private ownership now, but there has been a castle on this site since the 16th century and the site was recorded as belonging to Clan Galbraith in 1244. Could it possibly be much older than that?

Neilston Pad to Balmuildy Roman Fort

Neilston Pad seems like it should be an obvious sighting centre for one of Harry's PSAs and its tree-covered profile is prominent on the skyline from the north of the city, yet strangely, it is not mentioned at all by Harry.

'The Pad', as it is known locally, has an earthwork on the top enclosing an area of about 26 acres that is mentioned in Canmore, although it doesn't go as far as calling it a hillfort. There are two alignments emanating from it that I have found. The first runs in a roughly northeasterly direction, passing through Crookston Castle on its way to Balmuildy Roman Fort. Before it reaches Crookston Castle, it passes through the site of the Arthurlie Cross, a 10th century sculptured cross-slab, which was rescued from acting as a bridge over a burn in the 19th century, only to be repurposed as a gate-post with an iron ring embedded in the face. It now stands within the protective embrace of railings at the corner of Springhill Road and Carnock Crescent, just a little way off the alignment.

Arthurlie Cross

Roger Griffith, Public domain, via Wikimedia Commons

The next site on this alignment is Crookston Castle, reinforcing its position as a major ley crossroads and an important nexus on Harry's Glasgow Network. From there, things get more tenuous as it passes through north Glasgow without encountering any further sites of interest until it reaches Balmuildy Roman Fort. Harry mentions this location as it sits on one of his PSAs running from the Necropolis to Dumgoyne. Balmuildy was a substantial fort with an internal area of around 4 acres. There isn't much to see of the fort nowadays other than traces of the ditch and outer mound, but Balmuildy was one of only two forts on the Antonine Wall that had stone ramparts rather than turf, and it guarded an important river crossing of the Kelvin. Harry suggests that the fort may have pre-dated the construction of the Wall to guard this frontier point; indeed, a geophysical survey in 2005 suggested that the site may date back to prehistoric times.[*]

Neilston Pad to Inchinnan All Hallows Church

In terms of the number of sites, this alignment looks very promising. Proceeding in an almost due north direction from The Pad, the first location it passes through is the site of Neil's Stone, which supposedly gave the parish its name. A tradition exists of a combat between two chiefs named Arthur and

_____

[*] www.antoninewall.org/system/files/documents/Balmuildy-%20Fort.pdf

Neil. Both died of their wounds, the former being buried at the site of the Arthurlie Cross while the latter was buried at Cross Stone Brae south of Neilston village, where a sepulchral cross is known to have been standing at the end of the 18ᵗʰ century.

There is another standing stone in Neilston, about 230m away in a field to the northeast, but little is known about it and it is not thought to be connected with this story.

Continuing northwards, our alignment next heads for Paisley Abbey, passing through the site of 'Our Lord's Cross' on Sauchel Hill, that was recorded in W M Metcalfe's *A History of Paisley*. (Metcalfe, 1909,23) (This site is also on Harry's Carmyle Fords-Castlehead Ringwork PSA).

After the Abbey, the ley heads straight to the site of the former Templar church of All Hallows at Inchinnan, which was home to several Early Medieval sculptured stones of the Govan School. now on display at Inchinnan New Church just along the road following the demolition of All Hallows in 1969 during the expansion of Glasgow Airport. Inchinnan All Hallows is thought to have been the burial place of St Conval, and is on Harry's alignment from Camphill to Dumbarton Rock.

Renfrew Parish Church to the Cochno Stone

Although it only comprises three sites, I mention this one as it has a connection to Ludovic Mann that Harry seemed unaware of, although he did include the Cochno Stone on his Network. Roughly halfway along this alignment, it passes over the site of Knappers Farm, a neolithic burial site, or the 'Druid Temple' as Mann called it during his excavation and over-inflated interpretation.

Mann was investigating the Knappers site as the same time as he was painting his own complex multi-coloured interpretative grid on the Cochno Stone just up the road, where he tried to prove his theory that it was a map of the heavens and that a particularly fine double cup-and-ring mark recorded a solar eclipse in the Glasgow area. Using his own drawing of the markings, he invented a mythological "eclipse monster" that devoured the Sun before the other planets came to its rescue, and claimed that the Knappers site was a commemorative temple to this event. His highly speculative excavation ultimately destroyed his reputation. Subsequent interpretations of the site suggest that it may possibly have been a henge or a Bronze Age barrow cemetery, but it has been so messed about with by Mann that it is impossible to say anything definitively. There are no visible remains.

Dean Castle to The Bogle Stone

Dean Castle in Kilmarnock was one of the retail outlets for Harry's *Guide to the Haunted Castles of Scotland* book, but after a group of schoolgirls claimed to have contacted a ghost they called 'The Grey Lady' with a Ouija board, the castle gardens were inundated by "unruly mobs" of schoolchildren at night, intent on laying the ghost to rest. Some of them were apparently carrying copies of the book, so it was promptly banned from sale in the gift shop!

The castle's ghostly reputation rests on an account from a maid in the year 1730, who experienced an apparition of a ghastly disembodied head that was later identified as William Boyd, the 4th Earl of Kilmarnock. Although he was still alive at this time, he was beheaded 16 years later for being on the Stuart side at the battle of Culloden.

The Palace at Dean Castle.

Photo: Fraser Sutherland, CC BY-SA 3.0

The alignment runs in a NNE direction, passing the ruined Cairn Duff, where three urns containing cremated human remains were found in 1810. The next site is the Clochoderick Stone, (sometimes called the Cloch-a-Druid stone), a glacial erratic to the north of Castle Semple Loch which used to be a 'logan' (rocking) stone. It was said to have been a Druidic meeting place where justice was dispensed, and it also supposedly marks the burial place of King Rhyderrich Hael of Strathclyde, whose castle was thought to be near Cadzow. In Harry's day, the Clochoderick Stone was better known as a convenient assembly point for cyclists heading off on a day out.

The Clochoderick Stone.

Next, the alignment traverses Duchal House, a location we have already encountered in the 'Ghost Ley of Paisley' alignment. However, it also features in a tale about the last location on this alignment, the Bogle Stane in Port Glasgow. This is actually a cluster of whinstone fragments beside the bus stop on Clune Brae, the remains of another glacial erratic. Folklore tells of a Bogle (mischievous spirit) that lived behind the stone and would jump out to scare people. If he caught you, he would eat you with his sharp teeth. The local minister, tired of this superstition, had the stone blown up and used the remains to make curling stones and dykes. The stone was said to have been nearly 4m high before this demolition.

An old folk tale tells of a farmer called Malcolm McPhee, who had inherited his farm but did not care for the hard work involved in running it. He dreamed of finding a way to support himself and his wife without having to work at all. One night, a stranger in the pub told him that the Bogle, if captured, would have to grant three wishes. The stranger had many other tales, including ones about a mermaid who'd told his fortune on the Port Glasgow shore, about a witch he'd danced with up near Lochwinnoch, and about a ghost he'd met up at Duchal. (These locations could all have been located on this alignment).

Thinking that catching the Bogle would offer the solution he was after, Malcolm stayed up all night at the stone, waiting for the Bogle to appear, but to no avail. He was too tired the next day to do any work on the farm, but resolved to stay up again the next night to catch the Bogle. He told his wife not to worry about the farm, "for when I catch the Bogle, I'll wish for a much bigger farm and enough labourers to work it for us". Well, this went on for some weeks, until one morning he came home to find his wife had packed up and left him and the crops in the fields were ruined. Despondent, he drowned his sorrows in the pub that night. However, on his way home past the Bogle Stone, this time the Bogle jumped out! Grabbing the Bogle by the arm, Malcolm said, "I've been looking for you for months! Now that I've caught you, you must grant me three wishes."

"Who told you that?" said the Bogle. "Was it a stranger in the pub? Who dances with witches and talks to mermaids?" For it was the Bogle who had played a trick on Malcolm.

"A Bogle can't grant three wishes, and you must work for what you want", continued the Bogle. "You have wished your life away, and now you are mine", he said, baring his sharp white teeth... *

The Bogle Stane, Port Glasgow.

Photo: Grahame Gardner

---

* talesoftheoak.blogspot.com/2010/10/malkie-and-bogle.html

Stirling Castle to Dumyat

On a recent visit to Stirling Castle, I noticed that the castle is in alignment with Abbey Craig and Dumyat hillfort at the end of the Ochil Hills (See the picture in *Forgotten Footsteps* page 52).

Abbey Craig is best known as the site of the Wallace Monument; but it is also a vitrified hillfort, yet is listed as 'Early Medieval' on Canmore. However, a worked stone flake recovered from a rabbit hole just inside the rampart at the back of the Wallace Monument suggests a more prehistoric use of the hill. It's a great location from which to view the carse below and William Wallace is said to have used it as a vantage point before the Battle of Stirling Bridge.

The alignment continues through the rather grandiloquently-named Blairlogie Castle, a relatively modest mid-16th century 2-storey plus attic tower house. Blairlogie is overlooked by the next site, Castle Law hillfort on the shoulder of Dumyat. Like Abbey Craig, this is a typical Early Iron Age vitrified fort, prominently situated at this southern end of the Ochil Hills, thought to be a northern outpost of the Maeatae group of tribes who inhabited an area between the Antonine Wall and the Ochils.

Dumyat summit boasts a memorial bench seat dedicated to Mr Michael Simpson, who was a long-serving member of the Open University. There is also a monument to the Argyll and Sutherland Highlanders, plus an OS trig point and a cairn supporting a beacon that was commissioned to mark the Queen's Jubilee in 1977, but is now full of 'wishing stones' left by visitors.

A fine polished green stone axe was found on the alignment just below the summit in 1927 and donated to the National Museum of Scotland.

A Victorian Church Ley

This is an example of an intentional 'geomantic corridor' created in Victorian times. Great Western Road in Glasgow was laid out in 1841 with the intention to be completely straight between St George's Cross and Anniesland Cross, a distance of around 4 kilometres. This involved the construction of a new high-level Great Western Road Bridge over the River Kelvin, replacing the old low-level carthorse bridge that crossed the river at an angle.

Great Western Road was a direct extension of New City Road, although you wouldn't know that nowadays as the latter was almost obliterated by the construction of the M8 motorway. The twin pipes carrying Glasgow's water supply from Mugdock reservoirs run under the full length of the road.

The Great Western Road ley is aligned to Beltane/Lughnasadh sunset (May 1/Aug 1).

Heading west from St George's Cross. The road points directly towards the sunset at Beltane (1 May) and Lughnasadh (1 August), providing Glasgow with it's own version of 'Manhattanhenge'.

To walk this alignment, one can start at the National Piping Centre, formerly Cowcaddens Free Church of Scotland a the top of Hope Street. Head west down the ramp onto the lower footpath and walk past Cowcaddens Subway station, turning left to go through the underpass leading to what's left of New City Road. Follow the road round to the right past 'Chinatown' and cross the road under the motorway. Continue westwards behind the new student flats, still on the route of the old New City Road until you pass St Georges Cross Subway station and reach the start of Great Western Road proper.

Along the route there are at least five church sites either on or within a few tens of metres of the road. Even today, the spires of St Mary's Cathedral, Webster's Theatre (formerly Lansdowne United Presbyterian Church), and Oran Mor (formerly Kelvinside Free Church) can be seen in alignment. It also includes three major crossroads, including St George's Cross where you can still see the splendid 1897 sculpture of St George with the dragon by J and G Mossman that was presented to the City by the St George's Cross Co-operative Society when their building was demolished in 1985.

Anniesland Cross was at one time considered the busiest road junction in Britain. Nowadays, perhaps its most memorable feature is the former public toilets on the south side of Great Western Road, now marooned on an island amidst a tangle of roads and traffic lights. During the pandemic of 2020 an enterprising local builder, anxious to keep his workers employed, started to convert the building into a tapas bar. (If completed, this is sure to present some interesting access challenges for pedestrians!)

Photo: Grahame Gardner

Oran Mor.

Anniesland Cross is the termination of the straight section of Great Western Road, but the alignment can be extended farther to Knightswood Cross, passing directly through St Margaret's church (there are another three churches in the vicinity), and even beyond to the site of Knappers Farm, the previously-mentioned site excavated by Ludovic McLellan Mann (see page 226).

The Royal Mile Ley

This is a well-known ley running from Edinburgh Castle down the Royal Mile to Holyrood Palace. Harry was certainly aware of it, as he mentions that St Giles' Cathedral "stands on a ley crossing" (his Bridgeness to Arthur's Seat ley).

The Royal Mile is a succession of different streets — Castlehill, the Lawnmarket, the High Street, Canongate and Abbey Strand. It is just slightly over one mile in length (1.8km). Starting from the Castle, the alignment passes through The Hub, formerly the Assembly of the Church of Scotland and a site once called the Witches' Knowe. It continues through St Giles Cathedral, the Tron Kirk, John Knox House, then St John's Cross (this marks the old boundary of Edinburgh and the Canongate estate, which in the Middle Ages was owned by the Knights of the Order of St John).

The alignment continues through the churchyard of Canongate Kirk and the new Scottish Parliament building before ending at the Palace of Holyrood, the monarch's royal residence when visiting Scotland.

Philip Coppens' The Lothian Line

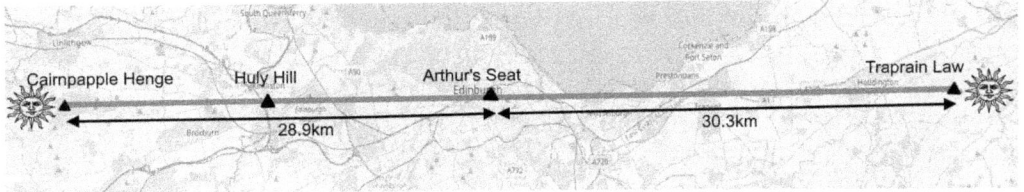

An east-west alignment between Traprain Law and Cairnpapple Hill passes through Arthur's Seat in the centre of Edinburgh. All three sites were of old under the domain of the Gododdin, called Votadini by the Romans. All three sites are inter-visible, and the late Philip Coppens noted that, as Traprain and Cairnpapple are almost equidistant from Arthur's Seat, an observer standing on its summit could watch the sun rise over Traprain Law and set over Cairnpapple at the spring and autumn equinoxes. (Coppens, 2007, 95)

May Miles Thomas' 'The Secret'

In May Miles Thomas' *The Devil's Plantation* iPhone app, a clock-face grid is revealed on completion of the quest. The grid has three sites and alignments marked — Tinto Hill, Ben Lomond, and 'The Secret', but the location of the latter site is not disclosed.

May confirms that I was the first person to figure out the Secret, which I did by overlaying her clock-face grid on my Google Earth file and adjusting the scale until Tinto Hill and Ben Lomond corresponded with their locations on the clock-face. This revealed that 'The Secret' was a small islet just off the coast of Troon called Lady Isle, which currently houses nothing more than a small automated lighthouse with some tumbledown outbuildings and a beacon pylon to guide boats into Troon harbour. Further investigation revealed that there is a fresh water spring in the centre of the isle, and that it once held a small chapel dedicated to the Virgin Mary. Timothy Pont's

1654 map shows a small structure on the island, presumably the chapel.[*]

The alignment is a continuation of Harry's 'Straight Road with No Path' as it extends from the Necropolis through Camphill, and my own research suggests that this corresponds with the direction of the major standstill moon-set, which occurs every 18.6 years.

There are three sites between Camphill and the Lady Isle that are worth mentioning. The first is Dod Hill (NS 493532), a name too good to exclude, as it reflects Alfred Watkins' assertion that the name 'Dod' refers to the 'Dodmen' with their sighting staves who marked out the ancient leys. There is a circular cairn about 19m in diameter on the summit of the hill, so it is a good sighting point.

The second site is Black Law (NS 464501), a hillfort site atop a volcanic plug that is prominent in the landscape. The slope of the ridge follows the alignment.

Cairn Duff (NS 420451), was once a large cairn covered with grass and trees on a prominent hill crest, although little remains nowadays as it has been almost completely robbed out. Three urns containing human bones were found in the cairn. Cairn Duff is also on the Dean Castle to Bogle Stone alignment.

References

Coppens, Philip, *Land of the Gods*, Adventures Unlimited Press/Frontier Publishing, 2007

Foreman, Carol *Hidden Glasgow* Birlinn, 2008

Metcalfe, William Musham, *A History of Paisley 1840-1916*, Alexander Gardner, Paisley, 1909

---

[*] wikipedia.org/wiki/Lady_Isle#Saint_Mary's_chapel

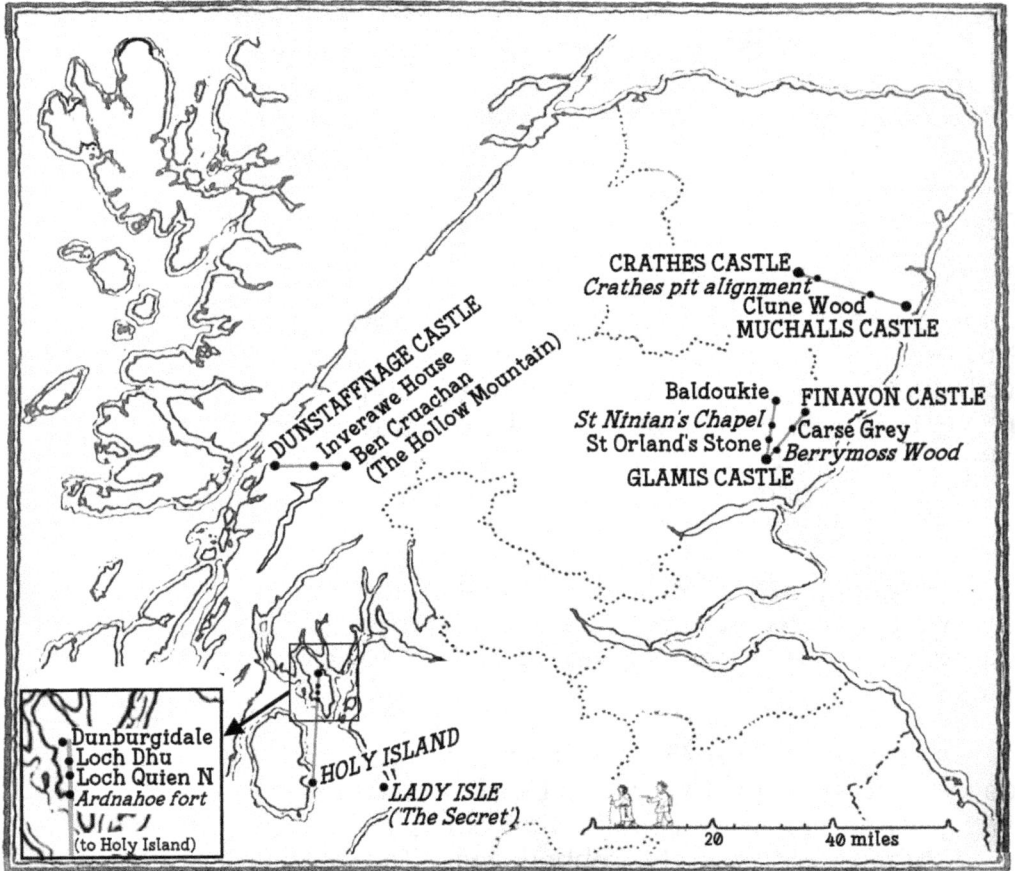

CRATHES CASTLE
Crathes pit alignment
Clune Wood
MUCHALLS CASTLE

DUNSTAFFNAGE CASTLE
Inverawe House
Ben Cruachan
(The Hollow Mountain)

Baldoukie
St Ninian's Chapel
St Orland's Stone
GLAMIS CASTLE

FINAVON CASTLE
Carse Grey
Berrymoss Wood

Dunburgidale
Loch Dhu
Loch Quien N
Ardnahoe fort

(to Holy Island)

HOLY ISLAND

LADY ISLE
('The Secret')

20   40 miles

Map showing the additional Harry leys from this chapter.
Sites added by Grahame are marked in italics.

THE ASSOCIATION OF CERTIFICATED FIELD ARCHAEOLOGISTS

THE ACFA
PAPERS

(& other ephemera)

Harry Bell

Edited and annotated by

Grahame Gardner

The very first ACFA AGM in 1987. Harry (sitting) bottom right.

Introduction

Grahame Gardner

In 1981, Harry attempted to bring some scholarly credentials to his work by joining evening classes at Glasgow University to train as a certificated Field Archaeologist. He thought this was a good way to expand his knowledge of the sites on his network and gain access to 'real' archaeologists.

The Association of Certificated Field Archaeologists (ACFA) arose from extracurricular work pioneered by Lionel Masters with the assistance of Eddie Peltenberg in 1976, who wanted to extend the training opportunities for their students and others through a series of evening classes. To gain certification, students were expected to complete 20 evening classes, two weeks of site visits and a residential field work week, submit four essays, and sit a three-hour examination. The final assessment was based on 25% written work, 25% examination, and 50% fieldwork portfolio. The first year class had 15 members, and the programme developed over the next decade, until ACFA was formally constituted in 1987.

Harry wrote a few 'occasional papers' during his years with ACFA, many based on reports of their field trips. He also contributed a couple of articles about Glasgow's Secret Geometry, in which he explained his military surveying methods. When he joined ACFA he was in his 40s, whereas most other members were in their early 30s. Harry felt a bit embarrassed by his lack of an academic background and initially lacked confidence in his studies. Yet he was pleased that he could have conversations with academics like Lionel Masters, an Oxford graduate, and his innate charm and sense of humour soon won him many friends and admirers amongst the ACFA membership.

It soon became clear that he was more interested in the kudos he gained from membership of ACFA than doing field surveys. He only ever completed one survey, at a former opencast coal mine called Chalmerston Down, near Dalmellington in South Ayrshire. It was during a driving snowstorm in December, and the students were tasked with measuring pit rows and slag heaps, something that held zero interest for Harry. His childhood friend and fellow ACFA member Ian Marshall recalls Harry exclaiming, "I didn't get into this to effing measure a slag heap!"

He was similarly unimpressed with site excavations. Once, after a particularly boring day excavating a Roman camp, Ian recalls him exclaiming, "Sod it, I'm not coming back to this!" Still, being immersed in the archaeological process did inspire his confidence. He was a big fan of Alexander Thom's surveying work on hundreds of sites around Scotland and Thom's concept of the Megalithic Yard, although his tutors and other students were somewhat less enthusiastic about these ideas. Harry admired Thom as he was an engineer, not an academic; perhaps he felt some kinship due to his own position on the fringes of academia.

Harry's knowledge of military operations sometimes provided insights about the archaeological sites they visited. On an ACFA visit to Inchtuthil Roman fort on the Gask Ridge, they learned about a buried hoard of nearly 900,000 nails weighing about twelve tonnes, discovered in 1951 and subsequently excavated by Sir Ian Richmond. The fort was planned to be the intended to be a large military hub housing 5,300 soldiers and covering some 53 acres, but was hastily demolished before completion when the Twentieth Legion was recalled south (Moffat, 2023, 38). Richmond's theory was that the nails had been buried to prevent them falling into the hands of the natives when the fort was abandoned, and that they may have been buried with some ceremony as a sacred offering. Harry, however, had a different idea. He joked that it was more likely that the quartermaster had accidentally ordered too many nails and was actively trading them with the locals! When told they were abandoning the fort, he had to act quickly to avoid discovery of this fiddle. Harry play-acted the part of the distraught quartermaster; "What, we're leaving? Quick, lads, dig a big hole here and let's chuck those nails in before we get found out!"[1]

Helen Maxwell recalls an ACFA trip to Cyprus, where Harry had been stationed during his National Service in the 1950s during the 'Cyprus Emergency'. Returning from a site visit, he asked her to divert off the main road to visit a remote hilltop village to look for the point where his squad had kept watch. Pulling up in the deserted square, he'd wistfully commented that "there might be a daughter or son of mine around here...". Ian Marshall adds, "He told me that he was frightened all the time (on that trip) that a wee boy would come running out, shouting, 'Daddy!'"

You will find many similar examples of Harry's wit in the articles and letters that follow. I hope you enjoy them. Unfortunately, most of these articles were transcribed from photocopies and regrettably, many pictures were not of sufficient quality to be used.

[1] Harry relates this tale in his 'Mysteries of the Roman North' article for Northern Earth (see page 313).

In the bathhouse at Chesters Roman fort on an ACFA field trip in 1994. Harry is second from left.

Cumbria Revisited

HARRY BELL GIVES US AN ACCOUNT OF THE VISIT TO CUMBRIA, 16TH TO 18TH SEPTEMBER 1994.

Our destination is never a place, but rather a new way of looking at things...

— Henry Miller

Seventeen ACFA members mustered outside the Angus Hotel, Carlisle, after breakfast on Saturday morning for the first item on our weekend agenda — a tour of the traces of Stanwix Roman Fort.

As our hotel had been thoughtfully built on the line of Hadrian's Wall, we didn't have far to go. Just round the corner to the car park of our neighbouring hotel, in fact.

After inspecting the remains, we drove to St Kentigern's Church in Aspatria (NY 1542) to see a replica of the famous ring-chain decorated cross which stands in the churchyard on the site of the original. Inside the church two hogback tombstones were also on view.

Allonby, on the coast (NY 0843), was our next destination. Here, Charles Dickens and a friend once stayed during a walking tour. Leslie Gray had somehow managed to find extracts from Dickens' diary about this episode, and produced a very creditable one-man show here, playing all the parts in true Peter Sellers style.

On to Crosscanonby (NY 0739) where we looked at the remains of an 18th century salt mining site and a neat little Hadrianic fortlet then down the road a bit to Maryport.

Senhouse Roman Museum, Maryport (NY 0336)

The museum lies adjacent to a fort which was the Headquarters Garrison of the Hadrian Coastal Defence system. From this fort, and the nearby Roman Civil Settlement (Alauna) most of the artefacts in the museum derive.

The fort was built sometime between 118AD and 123AD, and was garrisoned, virtually continuously, for around 280 years. The fields beneath which the Roman remains lie are in agricultural use and cannot be entered, so a look over a nearby wall must suffice.

This unsung little museum has the largest grouping of Roman Military Altar Stones and Inscriptions from any site in the country. It contains Romano-British artefacts in abundance, amongst them the celebrated 'Pin-up-Girl' — a column base depicting a gate of the fort with twin doorways and windowed gallery, beyond which stands a naked girl in provocative pose believed to be waiting to welcome soldiers on leave.

Paintings in the vestibule show various aspects of army life — recruitment, training, punishment for defaulters, etc. and an excellent bookshop backs up the exhibits with detailed information on both military and archaeological subjects. After our museum visit we indulged in a pub lunch at the Captain Nelson tavern in the same town.

Workington Hall (NX 9928)

The shell of this fortified manor house occupies a steep-sided knoll above the south bank of the River Derwent on the east side of Workington. It dates mainly from the 16th century, but incorporates a 14th century tower house.

Of Scottish interest is the (for once) fact that Mary, Queen of Scots slept here. After her defeat at the battle of Langside, Mary fled south and was given refuge at Workington Hall by Henry Curwen, Lord of the manor. A letter she wrote to her cousin, Queen Elizabeth I, from the Hall is now in the British Museum.

For most of its existence, Workington Hall was the home of the Curwen family whose history can be traced back to pre-Norman times. The family provided 28 High Sheriffs of Cumbria and represented the county in Parliament for at least 18 terms from 1371 onwards. It also provided the Hall with a ghost in the form of galloping Harry Curwen (1661-1725), a racehorse breeder and Jacobite rebel whose death throes can still be heard on a crumbling staircase leading to the courtyard (or so the guide said, anyway).

Cockermouth Castle (NY 1230)

This was next on our list but as it is never open and you can't see it for trees anyway, we opted instead for a walking tour of the old town.

Ignoring brightly-painted, half-timbered inns and the delights of the Friar Tuck fish and chip takeaway, we refreshed ourselves with a cottage tea at a twee tea shop in a recently converted pedestrian walkway. Serious business was at hand..........The Castlerigg experiment was about to begin!

Castlerigg Stone Circle (NY 291236)

There are 38 stones in this circle, 33 of which are still standing. A further 10 stones are arranged as a rectangular enclosure on the SE side, the average diameter of this slightly flattened circle is 30 metres. Castlerigg is believed to be one of the earliest circles, probably constructed around 3,000BC. According to Prof. Thom, the stones of the ring show seven solar or lunar declensions. Four of these cross in the centre of the circle.

Castlerigg is in perfect alignment between the summits of Skiddaw and Helvellyn. As Michael Caine would say, "A lot of people don't know that." There are also enough cross alignments with the surrounding hills to ensure that anyone "in the know" would be able to find their way to that very hillside again without difficulty. This could have been done in prehistoric times, and it can still be done today.

Around 1980, I visited Castlerigg to see if any of Thom's alignments married up with landscape alignments I had marked on my map. They did not, but I spent a long time in the circle looking at the alignments of stones and distant hills and eventually I drifted into the north-east corner of the circle where this sort of thing seemed to work better. Tired of carrying my rucksack around with me, I dumped it on the ground and walked round, lining up stones and hills, at no time needing to move more than about 5 yards from my rucksack to do this. The rectangular

Photo: Helen Maxwell

Harry explains his experiment to the ACFA team.

enclosure even looked good from this angle — the stones echoed the shape of a low ridge of hills in the near distance.

Suddenly two German girls appeared in the circle; armed with archaeology books and leaflets they converged on my rucksack. I watched them with interest but soon I realised it was not my humble swag they were looking at, it was the faint circular feature surrounding it, an indentation about the circumference of hammer-thrower's circle. I had never noticed this when I dumped my rucksack on the ground, but the girls had this feature marked on their National Trust leaflets, and for some reason wanted to look at it. Now, the strange thing about this indentation is that even yet, no-one knows what it is. In 1885 Benjamin Williams reported traces of three cairns inside the circle, but the other two seemed to have vanished. The most common archaeological guess is that it is a ploughed-out ring cairn.

During last year's Cumbria visit, each of the party stood in alignment of a stone and a distant hill. We all walked backwards together, stopped when our shoulders touched, and there we were — right on the edge of the indentation![2]

[2] Harry's argument is that the circle was originally surveyed from this position.
He discusses this in more detail in the 'Leyline Quest' section (see page 199).

Photo: Helen Maxwell

"...there we were — right on the edge of the indentation!"

This year the experiment was repeated to capture it all on slides to go on show at the AGM. Is it imagination, coincidence or what? Judge for yourselves when you see the slides. A similar experiment proved very successful at the recently discovered Wildshaw Burn circle, when using the same method, recumbent stones hidden in the grass were accurately pinpointed. Torhousekie stone circle in Wigtonshire is another place the method works. But there the 19 granite boulders bear no relation to the height of the surrounding hills. Nevertheless, follow the alignments and you'll find yourself walking the outline of the 'D' shaped ring cairn off-centre inside the circle.

We argued over the pros and cons of this all the way back to Carlisle.

[3] A pre-metric drinks measure. Harry is taking a jibe at the smaller English measures here. Scottish spirits were served in fifth of a gill quantities.

Back at the hotel, after a fine dinner and a few sixths of a gill[3], the 'mellowing out' process began. Soon, traveller's tales of the *Tokaido* (Eastern Way) in Japan blurred into stories of the Orient Express and then, when the 'megalithic hauf' was discovered — double sixths of a gill (ten of which will fit into any Bronze Age beaker with a capacity over 44cl) we got into ghost stories.

We started off by talking about Galloping Harry Curwen of Workington Hall and the 'haunted staircase' we had been to that day. Then, to our surprise this tale was relegated to second place by one of our own ladies who told us a great example of clairaudience (sounds beyond the natural range of the senses) which occurred at a lonely cottage when she heard the re-enactment of a murder committed years previously — a lady's voice singing quite happily... "...then — Bang! Bang! Two shots rang out and all was silent again........."

Nobody could top that story, and requests like "Anybody going to give us a song?" were quietly ignored. Pensively, we drained our glasses and trooped off to bed.

The Sunday programme started off with a drive to Penrith and a browse round the pre-Norman crosses and hogback grave markers of St Andrew's churchyard (NY 5130). As we drove, nine cars in all, at funereal pace around the churchyard looking for a place to park, one old man at the roadside doffed his cap with reverence. Either ACFA's fame had spread to Cumbria or he thought we were part of a funeral cortege.

From the churchyard, a short walk took us to Penrith Castle, an extensive red sandstone ruin of late 14th and early 15th century vintage. The sun was out and cameras clicked in every corner of the photogenic old fortress. At one point we risked all posing for a group photo under a very fragile looking vaulted roof.

Then there was **Long Meg and her daughters** (NY 571373), a large stone circle and cup and ring marked outlier in an area of much prehistoric activity. The circle is built on a slope and from some parts oi the circle the surrounding hills cannot be seen. The landscape alignment lobby, like the hills, kept a very low profile here.[4]

At nearby **Little Meg** circle, the light was just right for showing up the combined cup and ring and spiral carving on one of the stones. Another carved stone from the same site is on view in Penrith Museum.

We dined at Clifton House Hotel where we stayed on last year's trip, then drove to Clifton Hall, the remains of a 15th century manor house round which a detachment of Highland Horse on their retreat from Derby did battle with government dragoons on the 18th of December 1745.

[4] The outlier (Long Meg) is known to mark the winter solstice sunset, when her shadow is cast right across the circle. Spiral markings on Long Meg are probably related to this. The shadow theory may also apply to other dates.

Ian Marshall (or should it be Martial) ably described the skirmish that took place in the lanes around Clifton, a brief encounter that brought the Duke of Cumberland to a halt, and for a while delayed the inevitable.

With a black beret and two cap badges, Ian would make a very creditable stand in for Field Marshall Montgomery. Mel Gibson or anyone doing a biography of Monty please note........

Dacre (NY 4430) with its quaintly named 'Boot an Shoe' inn was the last village on our list. The castle there is not open to the public either, so after a short walk round the village green, we thanked Leslie for the effort he had put into the research and organisation of our trip, got back into our cars, and went "owre the border and awa'..."

Harry Bell

Cumbria Revisited — Part 2

In the last newsletter we read of the Castlerigg experiments where ACFA members were positioned inside the circle, each facing a different stone and hilltop, and asked to walk backwards. Stopping when our shoulders touched, we found ourselves right on the edge of a barely visible indentation believed to be a ploughed-out ringcairn.

Slides of the stones and aligned hilltops, photographed from the ringcairn, were shown at the 1994 AGM, and members were asked to vote whether they thought the stones had been placed in position to approximate the shape of surrounding hills or not. Twenty-two people voted, 17 thought the alignments were deliberate, 5 did not.

Well, what was it all about? Firstly, to see if anyone other than myself could see this phenomenon. If no-one else could see it, there would have been no point in writing this article. However, three-quarters voted positive, so let us proceed.

The full range of stone shape / hilltop shape alignments can only be seen from the ringcairn; it doesn't work anywhere else. Even the rectangular enclosure that has baffled archaeologists for years looks good from this angle because the double row of stones echo the shape of a low ridge of hills in the near distance and a higher-line of hills beyond.

This suggests that whoever masterminded the layout of the stones did it from the ringcairn. If this is so, then the ringcairn must have been constructed before the circle and is thereby the earliest structure at the Castlerigg. It's as simple as that. Castlerigg is a stone circle built round a burial. It is not a stone circle that had a ringcairn inserted later.

Now, an interesting point here is that the ringcairn is not in the centre of the circle. It is tucked away in the NE corner. There is a hint of conspiracy about this. It's as if the builders didn't want everyone to know exactly where the burial was inside the big circle, but at the same time they wanted to be able to find it for themselves. It might not even have been a burial. It could have been some sort of tribal relic or totem, who knows?

The method also works at Torhousekie in Wigtonshire. Though the 19 granite boulders there are unlike the shape of the hills, follow the stone / hilltop alignments round and you'll find yourself walking the outline of the 'D' shaped ringcairn off-centre inside the circle.

At recently-discovered Wildshaw Burn Circle, recumbent stones hidden in the grass were accurately pin-pointed from an off-centre locus with no visible indentation. Yet, at Long Meg and Her Daughters Circle, much nearer Castlerigg, the method was useless.

Castlerigg Circle is in perfect alignment between the summits of Skiddaw and Helvellyn. This and other cross alignments could have been useful navigational aids for finding the way to the circle or earlier ring cairn.

According to Professor Alexander Thom, the stones of Castlerigg show seven solar or lunar declensions, four of which cross in the centre of the circle.

Could the stones be aligned to the surrounding hills and to stars in the night sky at the same time? Personally, I don't see how this could be possible. With a bit of stone shifting through the ages a landscape aligned circle could certainly have made 'astronomer friendly', but in my opinion the two ideas are mutually exclusive.

If a theory is any good it should have some predictive capacity, so on the basis of the Castlerigg experiments let us make a prediction. If, in the future. Wildshaw Burn Circle is excavated, a ringcaim or similar structure of earlier date then the circle will be found at a locus slightly off centre from the circle. If it happens, remember, you saw it in the ACFA newsletter first!

Harry Bell.

Photo: Ian Marshall

Harry, impersonating Lionel Masters with pipe, pontificates at Dumgoyach (Duntreath) stone row.

Cyprus Trip

WHO WANTS TO BE A M1LLIONAIRE? AN ACCOUNT
OF THE ACFA TOUR OF KUZEY KIBRIS (NORTH
CYPRUS) 11TH - 18TH OCTOBER, 1997

Sixteen souls ventured forth — Lionel Masters, Campbell Provan, John Bray, Ann Bray, John Macdonald, Anne Macdonald, Ceci Alderton, Anna Pollock, Veronica Baker, Helen Maxwell, Valerie Bickers, Joan Nolan, Jim Anderson. Ron Rotchford, Bruce Henry and Harry Bell. Most of these are weel-kent ACFA members, the exception being Campbell Provan, a veteran of five seasons of excavations at Camster and longtime member of GAS.

We flew from Glasgow to London, then to Izmir in Turkey and finally to Ercan, North Cyprus where we picked up four white Renault 9 saloons and drove in state to the Club Tropicana, Ozenkoy, near Kyrenia. Accommodation was on a self-catering basis in two-storey semi-detached houses.

Overlooking the gardens and a medium-sized swimming pool which lay 10m west of a well-stocked bar.

The bar at the Club Tropicana is a light-roofed structure, 6.2m x 4.5m, with two windows. each 2.85m x 1.3m, open to the refectory on the south side. The sacred area, or gantry, is recessed and decorated with imitation pointed arches, lancets and foliated circles. The vessels on display on the gantry shelves contain wines of the Levant, Tekirdag Rakisi and Efes Bira. There is also a bottle of foreign origin containing Johnny Walker Red Label Scotch Whisky.

On our first evening in Kibris the 16 of us passed the evening at a rectangular table under a portico in the paved area, 3.8m south of the bar. That night four of the members discovered *Buzbag*.

SUNDAY

First a swim, then a Turkish breakfast at the poolside, then off to Kyrenia. Kyrenia (aka Girne) is one of the most attractive town in Kibris, particularly around the harbour area, dominated by the castle. The castle contains the Shipwreck Museum which houses the remains of a Greek trading vessel dated c.300BC. The cargo included over 400 wine amphorae from Rhodes, plates, oil jugs, and jars of almonds. Also within the castle grounds is the Lusignan Dungeon with a torture chamber, which proved particularly intriguing to those members of the party with S & M interests. The Full Monty — correction, the full horror — of the dungeon revealed itself only when your eyes became accustomed to the dim light within. (NB in this

Photo: Helen Maxwell

Relaxing in the bar. Harry 3rd from left.

context S & M has nothing to do with Shellfish gatherers/Mesolithic).

After lunch the next stop was the Abbey of Bellapais, founded around 1200AD by Aimery de Lusignan as a house of Augustinian canons, following the eviction of the order after the loss of Jerusalem in 1187AD. Spectacularly situated on an escarpment facing north, the abbey is entered from a gateway in the south-west corner. The view from the top of the cloisters takes in the coastline to the north and the Besparmak (Kyrenia) mountains to the south and is quite superb.

St Hilarion castle proved to be another spectacular viewpoint. This was the castle which Rose McAuly described as "a picture-book castle for elf kings". It occupies a magnificent position overlooking Girne (Kyrenia) from its perch 732m above sea level. The name comes from an anchorite, Hilarion, who lived in the 10th-11th century monastery which once stood here, and there is still considerable evidence of Byzantine masonry in the encircling walls, main entrance and gatehouse of the middle ward and the chapel. The castle's three wards are linked by crumbling passages and stairways, each of which merges into a rocky track at some point of another. It is quite a climb but the view wast to Cape Kormakiti was just reward for our efforts. There are not many tourists in North Cyprus which was why Jim Anderson and John and Ann Bray were surprised when they reached one of the highest turrets to find a small, heavily-set man there with an anxious expression on his face. "How did Dunfermline get oan on Setterday?" he enquired.

The Middle Bronze Age (1900-1650BC) cemetery of Karmani lies almost directly below St Hilarion. The site, restored and excavated by students of the Girne American University and the University of Melbourne, consists of several rock-cut tombs with either a shaft or a sloping 'dromos' for access to the burial chamber. One tomb, covered by a modern structure to preserve it, contains a human figure carved on the right-hand side of the dromos. During the long day we had sweated extensively, so, in the evening, we returned to the same tiled area 3.8m south of the bar. As the night wore on, four more members were introduced to *Buzbag*. The cult was growing...

MONDAY

This was the first day the banks were open, so a trip to Lefkosa (Nicosia) was arranged for the morning. Lefkosa is a divided city, the south part being the capital of Greek Cyprus. The 'Green Line' — the UN frontier — runs east-west under heavy military surveillance, and off-duty soldiers throng the streets everywhere. After a visit to the Museum of Turkish Cypriot Arts we changed our money at the astonishing rate of 280,000 Turkish Lira to the pound. Anyone with £4 to change became a millionaire! Although Lefkosa has interesting 16th century city walls, most of us headed for bazaars of the 'What Every Turk Wants' variety, returning after squandering untold millions on postcards, Turkish Delight, apple tea and raki. Anna Pollock, caught up in the general mood, bought two fertility symbols by mistake.

In the afternoon we drove 61km to Famagusta (Gazemagusa) at the east end of the island. The old part of the city is surrounded by walls and bastions made famous by the Siege of Famagusta, when a combined force of Greeks and Venetians tried to repel the Turks in 1570AD. The afternoon was spent in a leisurely stroll round the many places of worship and palaces, and here Bruce Henry and Campbell Provan proved their worth as tour guides, correctly identifying which mosque had been a Christian church, who had converted it, and when it had been converted. But the bars were open and the day wore on; at times we were sophisticated archaeologists, at times we were innocents abroad, and at times we were like extras in 'Carry On Up The Casbah'. When we emerged from the Mustaph Pasha Mosque we were behind schedule and had still not seen Othello's Tower. A group of us reached it 15 minutes before closing time at 4.30pm. The diminutive tower keeper pointed at his watch but let us in. We scurried up staircases, dived into dungeons and keeked into cannon ports, all the while in a time-crunch because the tower keeper kept coming round and pointing at his watch. Finally, we made it – only two minutes late!

Gallus and fearless now, because we could see the massive gate still open, we ambled up to the exit... and who did we see but the tower keeper, wreathed in toothless smiles, ushering two ladies IN. Our own dear Valerie Bickers and Joan Nolan had somehow sweet-talked him into it. Ignoring ACFA, eyelashes fluttering in the tower keeper's direction, tall blonde Valerie and raven-haired Joan swept past us on their way to a FREE guided tour.

By the time we got back to Club Tropicana we were starving. Nothing less than a banquet would suffice. Sixteen of us trooped up to The Old Mill restaurant, about half a mile away, and ordered up. Course followed course. Entrees of yoghurt, olives, sliced carrot, beetroot, mixed green salad and spiced onions were devoured in succession. Succulent kebabs followed, then delicately flavoured rice, omelettes for the vegetarians, sliced apples, iced grapes... wine corks popped all over the lamplit whitewashed room, shadows danced on the walls... Helen Maxwell and Anne Macdonald lit up cigars. The name of the red wine was easy to remember — *Buzbag*. The young Turkish waiter gave us the phonetic pronunciation — "Booze Bag".

Imported from the Turkish mainland, Buzbag is a robust little number, bursting with fruit, exploding on the palate like a hand grenade in a tea-cup, but quickly mellowing out, leaving a lingering aftertaste of scorched garters, lederhosen and plum jam. An acquired taste perhaps, but a positive steal at just under 250,000 TL a bottle.

We were on the wrong side of the Green Line for dancing and breaking plates, but it was a close-run thing!

TUESDAY

The first site visited today was Vrisi. Situated on a headland a few miles east of Catalkoy, in the rather incongruous surroundings of a large hotel complex, it is demarcated by a ditch on the landward side and a wall at the north end of the headland. The houses are curious in that they are built in great scoops in the bedrock, perhaps to provide some protection from the north winds.

Back in the cars again, a narrow, twisty road took us up the mountains to Kantara Castle at a height of 630m above sea level. Dating back to the 9th century, it was abandoned by the Venetians in 1525AD and left to the mercy of the elements. When we paused for breath, Veronica Baker read us extracts from her guidebook and from Lionel's notes. Calm and composed, in a crisply-ironed, ankle-length cotton frock and straw hat, looking for all the world like a prim Mem'sahib from the last days of the Raj, she told us stirring tales of bygone days and pointed out features like loopholes, ally ports, latrines and cisterns, as is she had known them all in a previous incarnation.

When we left the castle, we stopped for refreshments at an establishment called The Eagle's Nest Restaurant, situated on the left side of the road on a sweeping bend high above the sea. We had beer and orange juices and queued up to pay on the way out. The proprietor stood at the door selling jars of honey. Nobody was interested — the jars were too heavy and, for all we knew, the lids might open and spill the contents over everything in a sticky mess. "Good honey"', he intoned. "Good for all parts of the body – one spoon a day is enough." He had no takers. "For ALL parts of the body", he whispered to bearded brave-heart John Macdonald. Obviously a man with no need for dietary supplements for any part of his body for any reason, John gave him a withering look and walked on.

Behind John, a grey-haired man in faded blue shorts seemed to have difficulty in hearing. "EEZ AFRO-DEEZI-YAK", said the proprietor, carefully and clearly mouthing each syllable. Instantly, a hectic bargaining session began. A flurry of notes was seen and a hastily-wrapped package of merchandise changed hands. Though not a noted tea drinker, the grey-haired man murmured as he left the shop, "I've been looking for something to sweeten my tea for a long time."

Back in the cars again, we drove along the rocky coastline, conscious of the jagged, but graceful, silhouettes of pine-covered mountains vignetting into the distant skyline in front of us. Parched fields, sprinkled with tired grass, lined the road. Bamboo thickets and clumps of elephant grass came and went. Flock of sandy-coloured sheep strayed onto the road to slow us down. Goatherds in baseball caps stared at the passing four-car cavalcade from the shelter of gnarled olive trees twisted into shapes Van Gogh would have loved to paint. It was a nice drive.

After a long lunch break at Bogaz, we visited the Tombs of the Kings, burial place of the kings of Salamis in the 8th-7th centuries BC. The necropolis there contains rectangular, subterranean tombs and the skeletal remains of several horses. Cellarka was next. In the 1960s, over 100 rock-cut tombs had been excavated here within an area of just over 1,000 sq.m. Many of the tombs had been looted, but the 'dromoi' (some of them stepped) contained material which dated them to the 7th and 4th centuries BC.

The last stop of the day was at the Monastery of St Barnabas, 1km north-east of Enkomi. The monastery is now de-consecrated and serves as a museum for some of the finds from Salamis. Inside the church itself there is also a collection of richly-coloured icons.

WEDNESDAY

An idyllic scenic journey along the north coast took us to the Palace of Vouni, an Iron Age site close to the border with the Greek part of Cyprus. Beautifully situated overlooking a dreamy blue bay, the palace consists of a main building with a flight of steps leading down into a courtyard which contains a curiously carved stone. The stone is generally interpreted as being a wellhead, but John Bray put forward the suggestion that it might be a headless human figure which had been placed in its present position upside-down. After a bit of deliberation quite a few of us agreed with this. There is also a second courtyard and a temple to Athena to the south of the highest part of the hill. In spite of the occasional burst of self-loading rifle fire and belt-fed machine guns from a target range far below, the lasting impression of Vouni is that of otherworldly peace. The butterflies were there long before the Green Line and they are still there, fluttering with gently waving wings, silently stitching an invisible tapestry in and out of the rows of truncated pillars. Beneath them, alert sharp-eyed lizards darted, paused, and darted of again, flicking their tails across dusty mosaic floors decorated with beautiful spiral patterns.

The Guzelyurt Museum of Archaeology and Nature came as an anti-climax. There were finds from the Middle- to Late-Cypriot period and a church nearby with a large collection of icons. If you ask anyone who visited the place, however, all they will remember is the two-headed lamb in the Natural History hall!

Toumba to Skoura (The Mound of Darkness) is a Middle- to Late-Cypriot settlement which grew rich on the export of copper. You would never guess that if you saw it today. It has been bulldozed, vandalised and levelled... but still the presence of the early folk lingers. An excavation by Harvard University revealed the foundations of houses and underground chambered tombs. Rich finds included imported ostrich eggs, Minoan pottery and Syrian cylinder seals. These are all indicative of a high-status site, but, unfortunately, its exact status can now never be known.

In a cloud of dust, we drove off to the shrine of Myrtou Pighades. It lies on a plain at the foot of the Kyrenia mountains. Dated to the Late Cypriot period, the present remains comprise of two courts with rooms leading off and a tall, reconstructed altar,

Photo: Helen Maxwell

Harry with the 'Horns of Consecration' at the shrine of Myrtou Pighades.

surmounted by a Minoan-style 'Horns of Consecration'.

By the time we arrived at our next site, the ruins of Soli, some of our members were suffering from archaeo-fatigue, but, within the confined of the heavily-restored 2nd century AD theatre, a treat was in store. In the interests of archaeology, and to test the acoustics of the two-thousand year old theatre, Harry Bell and Anne Macdonald gave a rousing rendition of 'The Goodbye Song' from 'The White Horse Inn'. Standing centre stage, they belted it out with gusto, fortissimo, un poco braggadocio, secure in the knowledge that their captive audience were too exhausted to do anything but sit there and listen.

THURSDAY

There is as much chance of finding a quick-service restaurant in Kuzey Kibris as there is of finding a well-thumbed copy of the Chalmerston Report under a Spice Girl's pillow. All week, delicious lunches had been served to us by smiling restaurant staff, but it was all a bit too leisurely and whittled away some of our valuable archaeology time. By Thursday we were in a time-crunch and had Enkomi and Salamis to visit before driving out along the 'panhandle' of the Karpas peninsula to Andreas at the far end of the island.

First, there was Enkomi (Tuzla), one of the most extensively excavated Late Bronze Age towns. Enkomi was once a seaport but now it lies about a mile inland. The site measures about 400m north-south, but at least 300m east-west. The street plan is of the gridiron type so we all walked round the site with our green-covered 25-page printout open at page 17, plan of the town. Lionel had provided us with these printouts, containing information on each site we were to visit, at the start of the tour. It is from Lionel's printout that most of the archaeological information in this article is derived. Lionel is the perfect tour guide. Dressed for the climate in sandals, shorts, cool shades and NASA baseball cap, he was everywhere at once — pointing out the House of the Pillar, the Sanctuary of the Horned God, the House of the Bronzes and everything else anyone wanted to see. Those without sun hats followed him with eyes downcast, avoiding the blinding sun, not looking where they were going, but subconsciously following the pungent puffs of Condor ready-rubbed that Lionel wafted across the wilderness.

The second site visited that day was the city of Salamis — for many the most interesting site of the tour. It covers an area of approximately 1 square mile along the seashore to the north of the Pedios River. In mythology it was said to have been founded by Teucer, son of Telamon, king of the Greek island of Salamis. There is evidence of a city at this spot in the 11th century BC, when if replaced Enkomi, but there is little to see of this or later Archaic and Hellenistic cities. There are, however, extensive remains of the Roman and Byzantine cities, the most impressive of which are the Byzantine churches and a gymnasium and a theatre from the Roman period. Salamis was shaken by earthquakes in the 1st and 2nd centuries AD but, in spite of this, one of the memorable aspects of the site is the amount of tall pillars still standing.

The last site of the day for us was the early Neolithic settlement of Kastros at the end of Cape Andreas. The houses lie in the lee of a cliff a few metres above sea level, and probably represent a settlement of people who relied more on fishing than on agriculture. It was an idyllic site, scented by the tang of sea winds blowing in from Syria out in the blue beyond. Unfortunately for us, it seemed to be the home of a squadron of insects bent on attack. We were glad to get back into the cars and away back to the Club Tropicana before nightfall.

FRIDAY

This was our rest day, which was why Ron Rotchford only did a 10km run that morning. Pacing it out under a cloudless sky, inhaling the combined scents of jasmine, pine and acacia with every breath, Ron was in his element. The dogs were even getting to know him. First to break the silence was the one Ron nicknamed 'Barca', a big black mongrel who started it all off. Then the others began a canine cacophony of sound that echoed through the foothills till Ron turned off at the village of Ozenkoy. That's where the children were waiting for the school bus, waving and shouting encouragement at the wiry ex-Springburn Harrier as he passed. Even after the run, Ron was fit enough to take the optional excursion to Vounous.

The walk up to Vounous was a bit of a sporting event in itself. It involved the ascent of a steep path bounded by rubbish dumps on either side. After a mile of this, Lionel led us on a tour of some interesting Early- and Middle-Bronze Age rock-cut tombs on the lower slopes of the Besparmak mountains. The rest of the day was tailored to individual tastes. Helen and Veronica returned to their beloved Salamis, this time to investigate the underwater remains. Ceci Alderton vanished in a cloud of dust for a shopping tour, John and Anne Macdonald visited a military museum, others lazed by the pool.

In the evening, we had a 'finish off the duty-free' party at the Macdonald's and Bray's villa, followed by a farewell dinner at the refectory east of the portico, south of the well-stocked bar. After a great night of anecdotes, boisterous repartee and nonsense, the well-stocked bar was less well-stocked than it had been for a long time, and we all went home because we had an early start in the morning.

SATURDAY

All good things come to an end and it was time to go. At Ercan airport we bought our duty-free and trooped out to the aircraft, laughing and joking like soldiers on the way back to Blighty. The last man up the stairs turned on the platform and gazed back across the plain to Pentadyktalos, the Five-Fingered Mountain, for the last time. Then he walked into the plane looking up at the seat numbers on the luggage racks. He was carrying a plastic bag which all but concealed a very large jar. Something about the way he carried it alerted the hostess — for all the world he looked like a child carrying a jar of minnows home from the boating pond. The stewardess looked at him inquisitively. "It's all right", the man said. "It's just something to sweeten up my tea when I get back."

Harry Bell

(GSOH, own car, nights out or in)

MENORCA

Rough Guide to Menorca

Okay, she was a bit of a bimbo, but in a way you couldn't help feeling sorry for her; sitting there all pert and pretty in her First Choice uniform, working the Mahon Airport to Cala en Porter run giving her well-rehearsed sales talk to a clearly uninterested group of passengers.

"There's a Jolly Rodger castaway cruise with barbecue and free Sangria on Tuesdays and Thursdays, and a fun-packed cabaret night— not to be missed — every Wednesday at 8.30."

The whole busload of passengers rose as one, looked out the windows on the starboard side, then sat back in their seats again.

"For the ladies, there's a half day shopping trip to Ciutadella with wonderful bargains in perfume, lingerie and leather goods available."

"Perfume, lingerie and leather," growled Anne MacDonald, "she must think we're here to enjoy ourselves..."

The busload of passengers rose in unison, looked out the windows on the port side, then settled back down in their seats again.

Mandy the rep had never seen such a weird group of passengers since she'd worked the Transylvanian Castles run last summer... but she was observant, well-trained, and able to spot a trouble maker instantly.

"It's 'im,'"she decided. "The sun-tanned one wiv the beard — 'is 'ands give him away... 'e never interrupts me talk, but when 'e waves 'is 'and the whole bloody busload jumps up and looks out the window".[5]

Sometimes she thought she'd heard the words 'Taula' and 'Talaiyot' whispered, but she wasn't quite sure what they meant. Strange, strange people, Mandy thought ... and that was ACFA without the Edinburgh contingent.

Terminology

Talaiot (watch tower in Catalan): a circular, oval or square tower, up to 10m in height and between 10m and 20m in base diameter, built in dry-stone, in the form generally of a truncated cone. Some contain an internal chamber, approached from a ground level entrance passage; others have internal staircases, perhaps leading to an upper chamber. The talaiot is frequently surrounded by other buildings, including

Photo: Helen Maxwell

Es Tudons naveta (chambered tomb).

taulas, hypostyle halls and oval or circular houses. Over 200 have been recorded.

Taula: a vertical orthostat surmounted by a single capstone. This setting is normally within a stonewalled precinct. They are closely associated with talaiots, and are regarded as the religious focus for the talaiot settlement. 31 sites have been recorded in detail, but there are probably many others. Taula, (pronounced towel-ah) is the Catalan word for table.

Faulty Taulas

At Cala en Porter we were allocated spotless white-walled apartments furnished with dark varnished Spanish Colonial style sideboards and imitation maple shelving. Each room had a balcony overlooking the kidney-shaped swimming pool below. We were given keys at the reception desk and one passport per room taken for documentation purposes by a girl with the eyes of an El Greco saint.

Ten minutes later there was a knock at the door of *habitacion* D70. After struggling woman-fully up the stairs with a giant yellow holdall, Ceci Alderton had finally arrived.

"Wrong room, Ceci," said Bob Diamond at the door.

"But I'm supposed to be in D70 with Betty Rennie", Ceci replied. Bob showed her his room receipt and, ever the gentleman, brewed her a cup of soothing herbal tea while his room-mate went down to the reception desk to sort things out.

Spanish eyes had been replaced by Vinnie Jones in drag.

"Ceci Alderton and Betty Rennie are supposed to be sharing a room. Can you tell me room number, please?"

Vinnie looked at Bob's room-mate blankly. "No entiendo."

He tried again. "Senoras Alderton y Rennie are — eh-juntas, in the one habitacion." (He carefully pronounced the 'j' in 'junta' Spanish style, like an 'h'). "Que numero es la habitacion?"

"Junta" murmured the woman, leafing through the hotel register. "Habitacion A52". "Vale", said our hero, and away he went up to Habitacion A52 to see Betty.

Susan Hunter came to the door. "Betty Rennie's not here, I'm sharing with Dorothy Gormlie." "That's strange", said our hero. "The woman at the desk definitely said Habitacion A52." Then the *peseta* dropped, Susan Hunter / Susan *Junta*. (Betty and Ceci were finally re-united in Habitacion D22 and lived happily ever after.)

Le Transport

Three bright, happy little cars, red, white and blue, sat in the parking lot awaiting our arrival. The ACFA version of the famous Renault ad sprang to life when Nicole Maxwell and Papa Bell rushed out for a test drive. Nicole chose the blue Clio and was soon driving up and down the palm-lined streets, carefully stopping at each triangular *ceda el paso* sign. When she had practised enough, she stopped in a lay-by for the co-driver to take his turn.

Papa twirled his moustache thoughtfully and put on his reading glasses for a closer look at the gearshift sequence diagram. "This'll be reverse", he announced confidently, slipping the Clio into gear. It bounded forward and came to an abrupt halt in front of a hearing-aid beige coloured wheelie bin at the far end of the lay-by. Nicole smiled demurely and re-adjusted her seat-belt.

Meanwhile Bruce Henry had eased his 6-foot frame into the driving seat/ cockpit of the scarlet car and earned himself the sobriquet of The Red Baron for the rest of the week. Co-pilot Dorothy Gormlie and navigators Carol Primrose and Susan Hunter were recruited as aircrew.

John and Anne MacDonald and Scott and Ann Wood occupied the white car. When the Edinburgh contingent arrived, they piled into silver car No. IB-2290-DG, and led by Lionel's team in the yellow Seat 1400, our colourful cavalcade took to the road.

The Tour

ACFA's tour of Menorca concentrated on the sites and monuments of the prehistoric period. Apart from Talaiots and Taulas there are also about 60 *Navetas* on the island. Naveta (Spanish for boat) is a stone-built construction in the shape of an upturned boat. Some were used for burials, contemporary with the use of talaiots, and others were used as houses. The flat

Photo: Helen Maxwell

Negotiating a wall at Son Catlar poblat.

facade has a low entrance leading to an internal ground level chamber. In examples used for burials, just inside the entrance there is generally a gap in the roof, so that access may be gained to an upper chamber immediately above the ground level chamber.

Anyone interested in the island's archaeology should include in their itinerary a visit to The Museum of Menorca, situated in the Avinguda del Doctor Guardia in Mao (Mahon). Guidebooks and maps are available here. The Mapa Arquelogico de Menorca is recommended, but the coastal road coloured brown on the map is, in fact, a footpath. Beware!

Lionel provided everyone with a detailed 40pp printout which later became the prime source of archaeological information for this article, but since

Photo: Helen Maxwell

On top of the world at Torrellonet talaiot.

we were all in a holiday mood, and Lionel was available to answer questions, the printout was perhaps not studied as well as it deserved to be. Nevertheless, it was much appreciated and anyone considering a holiday on the island would be well advised to borrow it from any of the 20 ACFA members who did the trip.

La Llave

After a hot day traipsing round the Talaiots, it was bliss to relax on the balcony with a long, cool drink. On one such occasion, the occupants of Habitacion D70 came to the conclusion that instead of one key per room, they should really have one key for each occupant.

The Spanish dictionary gives the word for key as llave, pronounced "lyavvy", so armed with this knowledge, D70's self-appointed interpreter went down to the reception desk.

"Necesitamos una otra llave" he said.

Vinnie was her usual surly self.

"Una otra llave, por favor" repeated our hero, turning an imaginary key in the air.

Vinnie, clearly baffled by the heavily Glasgow-accented Spanish, thought for a moment, then repeated the word.

"*Llave?*"

"Si, una otra llave", nodded our hero, again turning his imaginary key. At that moment he felt a tap on his shoulder. "There's one in the bar," said the stranger. "First door on the right after the pool table -but watch yourself, the light switch is on the outside..."

Fashion Footnotes

In *fin-du-siecle* Menorca the ethnic look was in. On the first warm day of the tour, Lionel and John and Anne Bray appeared in tee-shirts adorned with geometric designs from the Nazca pampas of Peru. In an extravaganza of analogous harmony, hummingbirds hummed. condors did what condors do, and athletic monkeys disappeared up their own spiral tails.

Susan Hunter's tee-shirt represented the Nordic lands, with Bronze Age warriors and their domestic animals stepping out of the cold, sea-blue panels to warm themselves in the Spanish sunshine.

Twelfth-century descendants of these same warriors sailed to Orkney, searched for in Maes Howe chambered cairn, and left evidence of their exploits in the form of the largest collection of runic inscriptions to be found anywhere in the world. Lesley Gray had also sailed to Orkney, and proudly wore the largest collection of runic inscriptions to be squeezed into a tee-shirt anywhere in the world.

Isabel Black sported a tight-fitting maroon number decorated with Native American rock art motifs. When she laughed, five Sioux braves sashayed into a rain dance across her midriff!

Down under, in the dark demented dreamtime of Harry Bell's Aussie duffel bag, spirit beings stirred, wakened and went walkabout, casting spells over kangaroos bounding along the song lines to the deep drone of a bee-loud didgeridoo thrumming the hymn of Lamaluma the Thunderer.

R & R (Rest and Recuperation)

The most popular outings on our day off proved to be boat cruises round Mao harbour, liqueur sampling at the Xoriguer gin palace, and afternoon shopping in

Ciutadella. Most popular take-home gifts were perfume, gin and hand-crafted ceramic models of talaiots, taulas and navetas.

Our evenings were spent consuming paella, *calamares fritos* and whatever else took our fancy at La Palette and other Cala en Porter restaurants. The more adventurous drove off into the night to the old port of Es Castell where they strolled along in the smoked fish and hot olive oil atmosphere of the promenade, scanning each restaurant's *Menu del Dia*.

On Tuesday night both the red and the blue Clios converged on El Casino San Clemente for an evening of cool jazz. Richard Anderson, Veronica Baker *et al* sipped cold filtered San Mig to the soothing sounds of the saxophone augmented by a piano and the hypnotic rhythm of Brazilian bongo drums played with graceful flowing wrist movements by a one-time Errol Flynn lookalike.

The weather held up well, and it only rained at night, so a late autumn break in Menorca is certainly a holiday option worth considering. If you ever go there, and are serious about archaeology, remember to borrow the 40pp printout — hope you can still read it through the wine stains!

Glezga Acfaman, Cala en Porter, October 1999

Length of alignment 14.8km. MILITARY GRID BEARING 1716/4916 mils. OS map 64

The Alternative Archaeology Project 1

OCCASIONAL PAPER NO. 1

Since the Glasgow Network web site went online, more people have become aware of PSAs within the city. The Castlehead to Gallowflat alignment has attracted the most interest. The sites were known to archaeologists for many years but until *Glasgow's Secret Geometry* was published no one realised they were in alignment. With apologies to Hugh Grant *et al*, for the purpose of the article we will call this the FRF alignment (Four Ringworks and a Funeral).

FOUR RINGWORKS AND A FUNERAL
GAZETTEER OF SITES

1. Castlehead earthwork, Paisley (NN 4751 6333). Once thought to be of Roman origin, the site was excavated by EJ Talbot in 1973, when a trench 10m long and 2m wide was cut and fragments of medieval green-glazed pottery recovered.

"The place-name Castlehead is suggestive and the location of the 'camp' seems to indicate a Norman ringwork earth and timber castle, to which there are parallels nearby. The possibility that the remains here could be of Iron Age should, however, be borne in mind..." (Talbot, 1973)

2. Crookston Castle (NS 525 627). Two major periods are represented at this site, the earthworks of the late 12th century castle of Robert de Croc and the remains of an early 15th century tower.

A neolithic axe-head found in the vicinity was given to Paisley museum by Mr IP Perfect[1] in 1952. Excavations were carried out by EJ Talbot in 1973 but nothing was found that predated the stonework.

3. Pollok Park ringwork (NS 555 624). A 55m diameter semi-circular part-obliterated bank of earth, 320m S of Pollok ringwork recorded by Islay D Shanks and Eric Talbot in 1973. There are two ringworks in Pollok Estate; in *Glasgow's Secret Geometry* this one is called Burrell ringwork because of its proximity to the Burrell Collection.

4. Camphill Earthwork (NS 5776 6211). Measures overall 119m by 98m. The earthwork does not encircle the actual summit of the hill, but runs over the highest part and then curves down around the shoulder on the WNW side.

Partially excavated by Horace Fairhurst and Jack Scott 1950-51 who concluded that it was a "clay castle" of medieval date. Sherds of pottery "not later than 14th century" recovered. In 1980, Eric Talbot compared this site with others in the vicinity and suggested that it was a Norman ringwork earth and timber castle. The 1996 ACFA survey tactfully postulated earlier origins (as did Bell, 1984) and described Camphill as "an earthwork of uncertain date and purpose, perhaps from the late prehistoric period, with some evidence of re-use in the medieval period."

5. Gallowflat mound (NS 6230 6158). A round grassy mound measuring 31m in diameter and 1.6m high. This site was first recorded as a burial mound at the end of the 18th century (Ure 1793, pp124-5). Small finds recovered in the 18th century when the surrounding ditch was widened to make a fishpond comprised two Roman bronze paterae stamped with the maker's name *Congallus* or *Convallus*, three melon-shaped beads and the upper stone of a rotary quern. Tentatively identified as a medieval motte (Talbot 1974).

DISCUSSION

The anomaly of the FRF alignment is that the sites along its length seem to fit into two categories quite comfortably — prehistoric and medieval. There is no known alignment of four medieval ringworks in a perfectly straight 10km stretch anywhere in Britain, Ireland or France, but alignments of prehistoric sites have been noted in all three countries.

For this reason, let us temporarily disregard the handful of medieval sherds that so strongly influenced archaeological opinion in the past and reconsider the FRF alignment from a prehistoric perspective.

Castlehead earthwork: "The possibility that the remains here could be of Iron Age should, however, be borne in mind…"

Crookston Castle ringwork: Neolithic axe head found by IP Perfect in 1952.

Pollok Park ringwork: No finds from any period.

Camphill Earthwork: "…of uncertain date and purpose, perhaps from the late prehistoric period."

Gallowflat mound: Finds dating from the Roman Iron Age.

If the FRF alignment is to be reconsidered from a prehistoric perspective, one more site should perhaps be taken into account. John Ure, who first reported Gallowflat mound, also recorded a large tumulus that stood in Rutherglen Parish Churchyard and augmented the height of the parish burial ground when it was levelled off (1793 p84). Later antiquarians favour the opinion that the surface of the churchyard is 1.5m above the level of the pavement outside because of earth displaced by years of burials. It must be said, however, that the burial ground (NS 6133 6170) is situated precisely on the FRF alignment which closely follows the street line of medieval Rutherglen at this point by running parallel to Main St and King St, the two oldest streets in the former burgh.

For comparisons sake, let us now look at the two ringworks in the vicinity that Talbot mentions which are not situated on the FRF alignment. As the National Monuments Record of Scotland lists them as earthworks, this is the term we shall use. Again, both sites seem to have possible prehistoric connections as well as medieval.

Pollok Earthwork (NS 5566 6263). A roughly circular enclosure some 30m in diameter. Once thought to be prehistoric, it was regarded provisionally as a Dark Age homestead after excavations carried out by Glasgow Archaeological

Carmunnock ringwork on the 13th green.

Society in 1959-60. Talbot suggests a Norman ringwork.

Muir earthwork, Carmunnock (NS 6132 5777). A circular ditch with slighted rampart on the 13th green of Cathkin Braes Golf Course. Postulated as a prehistoric site in *Glasgow's Secret Geometry* (Bell, 1984). This prediction was dramatically confirmed in 1995 when Dennis Topen discovered that an aerial photograph in the NMRS collection which revealed a small enclosure 22.5m in diameter on the NE side containing a rectangular central feature 2m by 1m, thought to be a burial. "The discovery of this small satellite enclosure has swing the balance in favour of a prehistoric date." (Topen, 1996).[2]

[2] W Barr, in *Glaswegiana*, says that the 13th hole is named 'Camp' and was originally thought to be a Roman Camp, possibly connected with Watling Street, which was said to terminate in Castlemilk. (Barr, 73).

THE ALTERNATIVE ARCHAEOLOGY PROJECT

Occasional Paper No.2.

Some of you have inquired about the military grid bearing and the method employed in the computation of grid co-ordinates mentioned in the Castlehead to Gallowflats alignment article in the last newsletter.

Military compass bearings are always given in mils A mil is a unit of angular measurement used in gunnery equal to one six-thousand-four-hundredth of a circumference. I use them for the serious stuff because they are 17.7 times more accurate than degrees. Prehistoric man, of course never worked in mils, but by using them and visiting the sites at both ends of the alignment I can very often deduce which direction the alignment was surveyed from. This information is of prime importance when constructing an alignment sequence diagram.

On the left is a scaled-down print of an army protractor with a line leading from it through a ma with three sites circled.
In the bottom left hand corner you will find instructions on the computation of straight lines using grid co-ordinates (a far more accurate method than maps and rulers).

THE COMPUTATION OF STRAIGHT LINES USING GRID CO-ORDINATES

Method 1

1. Calculate the differences in Eastings and Northings thus: E = 1445, N = 3613

2. Take a suitable fraction of the length of line to give co-ordinates within the area you need them, e.g. 1/10

3. Take this fraction of the differences: i.e.
   144.5   361.3

4. Add their partial co-ords to the co-ords of A, to give 81686.5,   59383.3

These co-ordinates represent a point on the line AB. This point can be plotted and the point joined back to A.

Similarly 2 sets of co-ords midway between A & B could be found and there joined together not using A or B for drawing the line at all.

Co-ords of A: 81542 . 59022
Co-ords of B: 82787 . 62635
(Co-ords are always quoted Eastings first then Northings, as shown on any O.S. map.)

Harry's original front page for this article. NB there is a calculation error in his 'computation' example (a corrected version is given at the end of this article).

The Alternative Archaeology Project 2

OCCASIONAL PAPER NO. 2.

Some of you might have noticed an article in GAS Journal[1] 21, 1999, p67-69 by Dennis Topen entitled *A Circular Feature of Possible Prehistoric Date in the Growth of Langside College, Glasgow.*[2] One of the features was described as a "light oval, 4m by 3m". This brought to mind an entry I had placed in *D&E Scotland* away back in 1977:

> KING'S PARK: Enclosures, NS 595 605. At the highest point of the park, an oval outline roughly 12m by 7m with the suggestion of an outer wall on the N side. Also an oval crop-mark enclosure, 5m by 4m.

Two Roman coins, dated 193-211 AD and 253-268 AD had previously been found in the same grid square as my enclosures, so the area is now listed as one to be tested archaeologically if it is ever threatened by development.

As you can see by the map, Camphill ringwork, the new Langside College site, and the King's Park enclosures are all on the same alignment which eventually leads out to Cathkin Braes. This PSA was first mentioned in GSG in 1984, so the book has lost none of its predictive capacity.

[1] Glasgow Archaeological Society.

[2] Topen mistakenly identified this 'feature' as prehistoric. It is actually a WWII barrage balloon tether site. This does not in any way invalidate Harry's example alignment here.

The main objection to *Glasgow's Secret Geometry* has always been that orientations between two features known to be unrelated are considered unproven. This is quite logical, but it is also logical to suggest the custom of using alignments as landmark systems, territorial boundaries or anything else could have long outlasted the style and function of structures built along its length.

If a single site can have multi-phase, multi-period use, so can a PSA.

It is said that the dated excavation record is the archaeologist's bible. If that's the case then I'm an atheist.

The 1978 Lanarkshire Inventory states that 1800 Bronze Age sites have been recorded in the county believed to range in dates from 2,500 - 600 BC. If we classify those sites we find there are 1800 funerary sites and no habitation sites whatsoever. The funerary sites have only been 'discovered' because they are stone built. Farmers, builders and parish ministers have noticed them over the centuries and archaeology has inherited them. Even at that they average out at less than a burial a year between 2,500 BC and 600 BC so it is pertinent to ask — how many others went undetected?

Those who died in the Bronze Age probably lived within about 600m of their burial ground, yet with 1800 clues to their whereabouts, archaeologists have been unable to find a single house.

In any other profession this would have been looked on as a dismal failure; in archaeology nobody seems to have noticed.

No wooden or wattle and daub structure dating from the period between 2,500 BC and 600 BC has ever been recorded or excavated in the area of my survey. Hundreds of houses, farms, field systems and livestock enclosures have all disappeared without trace.

Nevertheless, the party line still seems to be: *The only sites worth including in your survey are those we have excavated.*

What this means is — we know it all already. Don't try to think things out for yourself, leave it all up to your betters. Buy our books, attend our classes, be a good consumer of our products and someday you might even work your way up to our standard (1,800 clues, zero results).

So how are new ideas received? Seemingly by following the advice in *Bluffer's Guide to Archaeology*, written by Paul Bahn.

"Deflect attention from a lack of ideas and solutions by attacking those trying to do some work and by trying to demolish their whole approach to the subject... Be sure to adopt the opposite view from your opponent."

Take a look at the questions and answers collected over the years during the fruitless quest for some intelligent feedback for my book:—

1984: THE PREHISTORIAN OBJECTION.

"Camphill is one of the most important sites in your book. Your alignment sequence diagram says it must be prehistoric but it was excavated by Scott and Fairhurst who proved it was medieval."

In 1996 the ACFA survey postulated prehistoric origins. One professional who visited the site suggested a date somewhere in the region of the 2nd millennium BC.

Coincidence.

1984: THE ROMANIST OBJECTION.

"You have Old Kilpatrick Roman Fort on a map of prehistoric sites — utter nonsense — the Romans chose their sites to suit their defensive technique, they didn't adapt their technique to suit available sites!"

In 1988 an account of two Bronze Age cist burials found inside the fort in 1923 and 1924 was discovered in TGAS viii,1933.

That sort of thing is the exception that proves the rule. (This means I'm still wrong even if I was right).

1984: THE EARLY HISTORIC OBJECTION.

"There is absolutely no record of alignments or anything of that nature in the early chronicles."

1985 — After a lengthy search an account of the route St Mungo took through the Campsies to bury the body of Fergus the Holy Man in Glasgow was found. In the very FIRST SENTENCE in any historical record to mention Glasgow, it states: "They came by a straight road along where there was no path. as far as Cathures, which is now called Glasgu ...."

Surely you don't take anything you read in those old books seriously?

1984: THE MEDIEVALIST OBJECTION.

"You have a photograph of Carmunnock ringwork in your book, supposedly on a Prehistoric Site Alignment. It's a Norman ringwork associated with Henry, son of Anselm who gifted the church of Carmunnock to the monks of Paisley around 1180."

1995, and an aerial photograph reveals an earlier site underneath believed to be a Bronze Age Burial.

Coincidence.

The trouble is that your average archaeologist knows nothing about the sites or the hills of the Glasgow Network and rather than admit this, many of them resort to some serious bluffing to make a point. Let us look at some of the alternative reasons given for the networks existence:

"It's all observer bias — the more you look into that kind of thing the more you see what you want to see."

(The gentleman making this assertion had not actually visited any of the sites and he couldn't point any of them out on the map. As he had observed nothing he had absolutely no bias.)

Next is the professional's favourite:

"Your survey is incomplete till you have listed all the sites that are not on your alignments."

(Funny, I don't remember anyone saying that to Euan Mackie — and sadly, Ronnie Morris, the grand old man of cup and ring markings went to his grave not knowing his surveys were incomplete because he hadn't bothered to make a list of all the rocks in Scotland without cup and ring marks on them.)

The most laughable of all was the suggestion made by one cartographically-challenged buffoon that he could probably find as good a network from four high rise fiats as I did from my four sightline centres.

A veteran of several two-day battlefield archaeology conferences, this armchair warrior seems to have taken on all the characteristics of a World War I general *i.e.*:

1. Maintain an unshakeable (and unfounded) belief in your own superiority.
2. Never visit the terrain in the field of operations.
3. Under no circumstances look at a map for more than two minutes.

Let me remind him that the Millennium Challenge is not just for one year — there is no time limit — and I hereby promise to pay one thousand United States dollars into his bank account on receipt of the grid references of the four tower blocks.

When I first started alignment research, my priority was to find out where PSAs originated and where they terminated. If they had led me to places like Hampden Park, Central Station, the Plaza Ballroom and the Barras I would have folded my tent and crept off silently into the night.

Instead they led rue into an interlocking Network dominated by four strategically placed sites.

Perhaps the average archaeologist, used to collecting all his information from books, is unable to see this; but with seven years Parachute Regiment training in overland navigation, reconnaissance, and communications analysis behind me, I recognised its importance immediately.

PSAs were not tracks or pathways. They were a means of finding your bearings using skyline markers. There was no need to follow them all the way up to the hilltops. Those who use stars for navigation don't have to fly to the heavens to get where they are going either, but they use the same principle. My research has shown that special sites in the area now occupied by Glasgow were placed in alignment with the hills.

in the wooded wilderness of prehistoric time this would help you find your way back to them.

Many of these sites were later built over, but the alignment can still be traced. Once you know the invisible pattern you'll never see Glasgow the same way again.

Harry Bell,

Tigli an Learscail Mhor, 5.12.2000

THE COMPUTATION OF STRAIGHT LINES USING GRID CO-ORDINATES

Co-ords of point A: 81542. 59022
Co-ords of point B: 82787. 62635

Co-ordinates are always quoted Eastings first then Northings, as shown on any OS map. Eastings run from left to right, Northings from bottom to top. The more digits in the reference, the more accurate the position.

Method 1

1. Calculate the differences in Eastings and Northings thus:
E (8287-81542)=1245,
N (62635-59022)=3613

2. Take a suitable fraction of the length of the line to give co-ordinates within the area you need them, e.g. 1/10

3. Take this fraction of the differences, i.e. 124.5, 361.3

4. Add their partial co-ords to the co-ords of A to give 81666.5. 59383.3

These co-ordinates represent a point on the line AB. This point can be plotted and the point joined back to A.

Similarly, 2 sets of co-ordinates midway between A & B could be found and there joined together not using A or B for drawing the line at all.

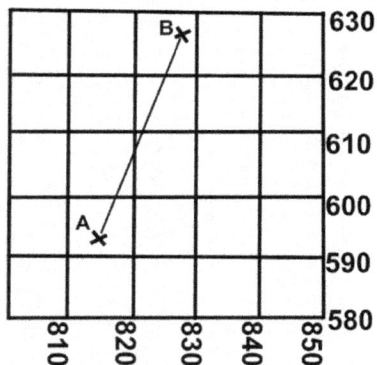

Tune in to the Network!

Do you ever feel archaeology is becoming a bit boring? As if the really interesting and exciting stuff was done years ago and there is nothing more to contribute? Well, don't give up hope, read on carefully and perhaps the enclosed map will change your mind.

The map is an updated copy of one originally drawn in 1984. It was not taken seriously at the time because alignments of sites from different periods in history seemed to be a map exercise with a pencil and ruler rather than the result of serious research... but that was 16 years ago, and since then questions have been answered by results.

The reason you've been given the map is to introduce you to the Glasgow Network of Aligned Sites. Some of you have never heard of it before and others are of the opinion that it's something I wrote about years ago and it's all in the past. For me it never went away. First thing every morning I look towards Dunwan for a weather check. If I'm driving into Glasgow, I know when I'm 'online' by the way Duncolm is framed in the centre of the Kilpatrick Hills. Coming up the M74 from England, I know I'm home when I see the outline of Dumgoyne in the distance.

At first glance Duncolm looks like a Scots cousin of Ayers rock, the sacred site of the Aborigines in Central Australia. Though only ten miles from Glasgow, it is surrounded by chambered tombs older than the pyramids. Some of the alignments passing through Glasgow originate here.

Standing stones at Duntreath, Stirlingshire, from the east. The site has been carbon dated to 3,250 BC. A solsticial foresight was discovered here by Euan Mackie, and also a natural foresight to the east, which could not be identified astronomically. The flat face of the centre stone indicates the unidentified foresight — it points straight to Duncolm.

One of the strongest objections to my alignment maps in the early 80s was that there was no known reference to alignments or anything of that nature in the early chronicles. After a lengthy search, I found the earliest reference to any road or track in the Glasgow area in a translation from Latin of The Life of St Kentigern in the Mitchell Library. The very first sentence in any historical record to mention Glasgow reads "...they came by a straight road, along where there was no path, as far as Cathures, which is now called Glasgu..."

Photo: Grahame Gardner

For many Glasgow archaeologists the only recognisable feature on the skyline is the University, pictured here on the left. To them, the hill at the west end of the Campsies is just part of the background, but the Romans knew it well, and 5,000 years ago the first Glaswegians used it as a landmark. Look on your map for Dumgoyne.

I live with it all the time. I'm a modern man in a beautifully scaled user-friendly prehistoric setting and I love it... welcome to my world.

In The Beginning...

Alignment research has blown hot and cold on the fringe of archaeology since Sir Norman Lockyer wrote *Stonehenge and Other British Monuments Astronomically Considered* in 1906. This was the book that paved the way for later researchers like Prof. Alexander Thom and Dr Euan MacKie.

Lockyer raised a few eyebrows when he included Salisbury Cathedral on one of his alignments because he thought it possible that the cathedral occupied an earlier site. Alfred Watkins took this idea a step further in 1925 when he wrote *The Old Straight Track* (ISBN 0349137072) and introduced the concept of leys, alignments of mottes, castles, beacon hills and churches which he was convinced occupied key sites on Neolithic trackways. Half a century later, a new generation of researchers had rejected the idea of leys as trackways, but were still finding them. Some postulated they were underground water lines which could be detected by means of dowsing rods, some interpreted them as psychic telegraph wires, and some claimed they were navigational aids for UFOs. They had been found all over England — were there any in Scotland?

In the early 70s, I tried out the theory on my annual holiday. The end result was a map of alignments that zig-zagged across Central

Scotland from the Kilpatrick Hills to Arthur's Seat. A redesigned version of the map accompanied by a brief history of British alignment research went on sale in 1977 and half-a-century behind England, Scotland got its first book on ley-lines. It could truthfully have been described as a crime against archaeology, but it sold well and financed a round-the-world trip and further research at Lockyer's alignments in Wiltshire and Watkin's' leys in Oxford and Herefordshire.

THE FIVE STEP PROCESS

The map in your possession is from the inside cover pocket of Glasgow's Secret Geometry. *By the time I did this I had been through the certificate course and we all know what a marvellous learning experience that was — a mind-expanding three years of lectures, essays, field trips and discussions. Unlike my colleagues, however, I had come into archaeology for a specific reason — I wanted to find out how the alignments I had surveyed in my cross-country travels got there. Why did some of them keep crossing and re-crossing the same points on the landscape — who had designed all this? No-one could help me on that subject, but during the course I learned a simple five step process that for me turned an inexact science into something that could be analysed. Observation, Classification, Hypothesis, Prediction, Test... five steps to clearer thinking. After the course I applied it to my own research, vowing that in future I would do everything "by the book".*

The alignments I had observed in Scotland were simple overland alignments of hilltops and ancient man-made features

Photo: Grahame Gardner

Camphill earthwork has been surveyed and partially excavated by Horace Fairhurst and Jack Scott (1950-51) who concluded that it was a "clay castle" of Medieval date. In 1980, Eric Talbot suggested it had been an earth and timber Norman 'ringwork' and the site became firmly classified as Medieval.

In 1984, alignment sequence research in Glasgow's Secret Geometry revealed that Camphill had prehistoric origins and the original sightline centre must have been larger than the ringwork — instant ridicule resulted.

In 1985. an American psychic visited Camphill for a 'reading' and drew a thought form diagram which suggested three separate phases of occupancy.

The 1996 ACFA survey describes Camphill as "an earthwork of uncertain date and purpose, perhaps from the late prehistoric period, with some evidence of re-use in the medieval period... "

One archaeologist who visited the site suggested a date somewhere in the region of the 2nd millennium BCE.

detected without recourse to dowsing or astronomy. Some were in line of sight between inter-visible points, others were connecting lines linking sites on different alignments. They differed in many ways from the ley-lines of English researchers so I classified them as Prehistoric Site Alignments (PSAs). 'Pre-historic' meaning that the site was occupied before historical records were kept in that particular area. Even if the structure occupying a site is Medieval, the site itself can be very much older.

It is said that the dated excavation record is the archaeologist's bible. This would be sensible if sites were untouched since the day they were built, but our prehistoric ancestors picked the most suitable sites and nobody put a 'listed building' order on them. In many cases they were used time and time again. "Only excavation can tell", archaeologists say. Is this true? Not if we tryout their own formula on their findings.

Observation: The 1978 Lanarkshire Inventory states that 1800 Bronze Age sites have been recorded in the county, believed to range in dates from c. 2,500 — 600 BCE.

Classification: Funerary sites — total 1800; Habitation sites — nil.

Conclusion: Stone built funerary sites survived; wooden dwellings disintegrated and left no trace.

Funerary sites discovered do not even amount to one burial a year between 2,500 BCE and 600 BCE, so it is pertinent to ask —

how many others went undetected? The people who had died had probably lived within 800m of their burial ground, yet with 1800 clues to their whereabouts archaeologists were unable to find a single house. In any other profession, this would be looked on as a dismal failure; in archaeology, nobody seems to have noticed. The dated excavation record is a very necessary part of archaeology, but it is biased towards stone-built sites and becomes outdated with every new discovery (for example, the platform sites discovered in Lanarkshire since 1978). Today we have x number of sites; fifty years from now we'll have $x + y$ and today's excavation record will be looked on as out-of-date and unreliable. If it will be unreliable in fifty years time, it is unreliable now. Why start research with an unreliable database? The true constants in the equation are the alignments themselves. Whether they were surveyed in prehistoric times or appear by accident, they are still constants. Fifty years from now the same alignments will still be there in the same place.

The only solution was to track down every PSA I could find within one specific area, and try to find out where they originated and where they terminated. To cut coincidental alignments to a minimum and avoid even a hint of bias I chose the worst possible ground in Scotland for testing an archaeological theory. Some of my alignments passed through Glasgow on the way to Duncolm, so as a guide-line for future research 1 devised a working hypothesis, a supposition to be proved or disproved at a later date. My hypothesis was that the city

One of the Camphill PSAs leads to the ringwork on the 13th green at Cathkin Braes Golf Course. Archaeologists of the 1980's were unimpressed — once again a Medieval ringwork was included on an alleged Prehistoric Site Alignment.

Thirteen years later, when ACFA did an archaeological survey of Cathkin Braes Country Park in 1997, an aerial photograph showed a smaller enclosure joining onto the NE side of the ringwork. "This is almost certainly a prehistoric burial..." p16, GAS Bulletin No. 36.

The Travel Information Centre in St Enoch's Square stands on the site of an old Medieval sanctuary and curative well. Going back even further, a dugout canoe and jade axe from the Neolithic era were found on the site when the subway was being built.

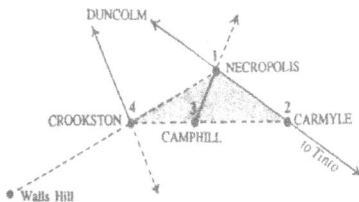

When the above alignment sequence diagram appeared on p62 GSG, one Medievalist asked why Camphill and Crookston ringworks were represented and others conveniently left out. He mentioned two lesser-known sites I had never heard of. Both ringworks, Castlehead and Burrell, were found to be in perfect alignment with Camphill and Crookston.

of Glasgow is built over a framework of Prehistoric Site Alignments.

THE MAP

Your map is the result of the testing of this hypothesis. Had I taken archaeologists advice I would not have included Roman or Medieval cites on my alignments. Camphill and Carmunnock ringworks would not have been on the map, and certainly not Old Kilpatrick Roman Fort at the western end of the Antonine Wall (none of us were aware that Bronze Age burial cists had been discovered inside the fort in 1923 and 1924). My research would have been slanted in the direction of what we in the 1980s, with our limited knowledge of excavation and dating techniques, thought appropriate. It would have represented what we allowed to be there, rather than the reality of what is there. There was no selection bias whatsoever, I plotted every possible alignment I could find within the city limits. Some of the alignments might be coincidental, some might be longer than I think they are, others may still lie undetected in the same area, so the map is not a route guide. Nevertheless, without any picking and choosing on my part, the PSAs run straight as a rifle shot through the oldest man-made structures in Paisley, East Kilbride, Carmunnock, Hamilton, Renfrew, Kilsyth, Inchinnan, Crookston, Govan, Rutherglen, Drumchapel, Castlemilk, Easterhouse and Old Kilpatrick. I mean this literally, no matter whether it is a cist, castle or church, the alignments pass through the oldest known site in each of these 14 communities. No amount of observer bias on my part could conjure up this result artificially. This is conclusive proof that Glasgow is indeed built over a framework of Prehistoric Site Alignments which are accurately sighted onto the surrounding hills. Check it out for yourself- it works perfectly on the map and it works in the field.

Anyone who thinks PSAs are imaginary can compare them against the random sample of sites to be found on a similar length of line anywhere on the 1600 kilometres of eastings and northings represented by the straight blue lines on your Glasgow Sheet 64 OS map. Observe how PSAs cross and recross the same points of the landscape. Count the sites on each line — there's no dubious two-point alignments twenty miles apart, no need to calculate sunrise or sunset over yonder hill in prehistoric times, no dowsing rods, knowledge of trigonometry or Greek math symbols required.

Every ACFA member has been given two maps to keep the knowledge alive in the next millennium. One is to enable you to transfer the PSAs onto an Ordnance Survey map and visit the sites. The second map is to be given away to anyone you know who might be interested. Armchair archaeologists can puzzle their skull with wonders measuring how straight the lines are on their Ordnance Survey map; the more adventurous can search for the Straight Road with No Path, admire the view from the Craw stane or go walkabout between the Deil's Plantin and the Fort of the Dove.

Cluster analysis indicates that the PSAs form four separate networks at the Glasgow

In July 1998, Daniel P Sullivan became the first archaeologist to test the accuracy of the Glasgow Network by transferring the alignments onto an Ordnance Survey map. His review of Glasgow's Secret Geometry appeared in Issue 130 of The Ley Hunter, *a magazine specialising in alignment research and folklore, which at that time included Aubrey Burl amongst its four editorial consultants.*

"...Bell's field work is admirable and he demonstrates that sightlines do indeed exist across his alignments and that after some time negotiating the surrounding landscape he was easily able to orientate himself in relationship to identifiable fixed landmarks and to know the direction of other, invisible, points on his alignments. He was able, like the Australian Aborigine, to go walkabout without the aid of a map or compass. He named his lines Prehistoric Site Alignments (PSAs), to distinguish them from leys, which by 1984 were universally accepted as energy lines. Bell did not agree with this English consensus. His alignments are definitely sight lines. Bell makes no claims for universal networks or global grids. He doesn't invoke esoteric energy, lost knowledge or an extraterrestrial hypothesis. He relies on his own eyes and an open mind — he calls his approach archaeo-orienteering..."

DP Sullivan, BA B. Arch, editor The Ley Hunter Magazine, *Cheltenham.*

Necropolis, Crookston Castle ringwork, Camphill and Carmyle. Alignments from these sites interlock perfectly to form the larger system I call the Glasgow Network of Aligned Sites. The odds against this happening by chance are astronomical. Mainstream archaeology has no record of this whatsoever — it's a new branch of the science and it's all out there awaiting your interpretation.

Further information can be found on the internet at glasgowsecretgeometry.uk.

A Linear Distribution of Earthworks in Glasgow and Paisley

HARRY BELL

SUMMARY

Though the sites discussed in this paper have been known for many years, it has gone unnoticed that they form an alignment almost as straight as the linear cemetery in the Kilmartin Valley though three times its length. There is no known alignment of five medieval earthworks of this type anywhere else in Britain.[3]

THE SITES AND THEIR EXCAVATION HISTORY

Castlehead earthwork, Paisley (NGR: NN 4751 6333). Once thought to be of Roman origin, only slight traces of the earthwork survive in the form of a much overgrown rampart with the possible indication of an external ditch. The mound is in private property and has been landscaped into a rockery (Fig 1).

"In January 1973, a trench 10m long and 2m wide was cut in the interior a little way behind the rampart. A sherd of late medieval green glazed pottery was recovered. An absence of stratification revealing occupation may be

[3] This article appears to be a variation of 'Four ringworks and a Funeral' in *ACFA Occasional Paper No. 1*, written for a more general readership, perhaps for submission to a journal or magazine. Whether it has been previously published is unknown. The original illustrations have been lost.

Photo: Grahame Gardner

Fig 1 The mound at Castlehead, landscaped into a rockery.

accounted for by 19th century landscaping here. The place name 'Castlehead' is suggestive and the location of the 'camp' seems to indicate a Norman ringwork earth and timber castle, to which there are parallels nearby (see NS56SW 4, NS56SE 32 and 33). The possibility that the remains here could be of Iron Age should, however be borne in mind." (Talbot 1973).

(NB The National Monuments Record of Scotland numbers Talbot referred to are those of Crookston Castle, Camphill earthwork and Pollok earthwork).

Crookston Castle ringwork, Glasgow (NGR: NS 5255 6272). Sir John Stirling Maxwell was a founder member of the National Trust for Scotland and donated Crookston Castle as their first property in 1931. It is still owned by the trust but administered by Historic Scotland.

Two major periods are represented at this site, the earthworks of the late 12th century castle of Robert de Croc and the remains of an early 15th century tower (Fig 2). Excavations within the stone castle, in the NW tower, the SW tower and the E end of the enclosure have revealed only sherds of 15th century pottery.

Photo: Grahame Gardner

Fig 2 Crookston Castle and surrounding ringwork.

"In 1975, an area was opened up N of the entrance within the defences. A stone building was uncovered at right angles to the entrance gap. It was set upon the slighted bank of the 12th century ringwork; this bank had been very carefully levelled (probably in the early 15th century when the tower house was constructed) to create a flat platform into which foundations had been cut. It was impossible to date or interpret the use to which this building had been put. Other indications of walling within the area investigated seemed to indicate a use for farm purposes."(Talbot, 1975).

Crookston is surrounded by the modern housing estate of Pollok, and at the time of its development in 1952, a Neolithic axe-head found on the hillside was given to Paisley museum by Mr I Perfect. As only a four-figure grid reference was recorded at the time, (NS 52 62), the precise location of this find has proved untraceable.

Pollok Park ringwork, Glasgow (NGR: NS 555 624) This 55m diameter semi-circular part-obliterated bank of earth, was recorded as a ringwork — an earth and timber castle which never contained a motte — in 1973 (Fig 3). It has never been excavated.

Fig 3 The ditch at Pollok Park ringwork.

Photo: May Miles Thomas

"At the NNE two apparent division walls across the ditch may outline a secondary small enclosure."(Shanks and Talbot, 1973).

Camphill earthwork, Glasgow (NGR NS 5776 6211). This structure was once part of Pathhead Farm which was sold to the City of Glasgow in 1857, formed into Queen's Park, and opened to the public in 1862.

The earthwork measures overall 119m by 98m; it does not encircle the actual summit of the hill, but runs over the highest part and then curves down around the shoulder on the WNW side (Fig 4).

It was partially excavated by Fairhurst & Scott (1950-51) who concluded that it was a "clay castle" of medieval date. Sherds of pottery "not later than 14th century" were recovered. (Fairhurst & Scott 1953).

Talbot (1973) compares Camphill with other sites in the vicinity and suggests it is a Norman ringwork.

Photo: Grahame Gardner

Fig 4 The ramparts of Camphill earthwork.

The 1996 Association of Certificated Field Archaeologists (Glasgow University) survey found no evidence of traces of occupation to support the 'clay castle' theory.

"It has to be said that the nature and location of the site do not immediately suggest a military or defensive purpose ... it is perhaps safest to conclude that this is an earthwork of uncertain date and purpose, perhaps from the late prehistoric period, with some evidence of re-use in the medieval period." (Topen 1996).

Gallowflat mound, Rutherglen (NGR: NS 6230 6158). In Richmond Court, on the N side of East Main Street, Rutherglen, stands a circular grassy mound measuring 31m in diameter and 1.6m high (Fig 5) which was first recorded at the end of the 18th century (Ure 1793, 124-5). At that time the mound measured 25m in diameter and 3.7m high.

In 1773, the ditch surrounding the mound was widened to make a fishpond for Gallowflat House, and "a passage six feet broad and laid with unhewn stones" was discovered leading to the top of the mound. (Ure, 1793). Small finds recovered comprised

Photo: Grahame Gardner

Fig 5 Gallowflat mound, Rutherglen.

two Roman bronze paterae stamped with the maker's name (Congallus or Convallus) three melon-shaped beads and the upper stone of a rotary quern.

Prior to redevelopment of the surrounding land in 1975, the fishpond was uncovered at the base of the mound. It appeared to have destroyed any evidence of an encircling ditch. Talbot (1974) suggests that the site is a motte, possibly the predecessor of the stone castle built on the N side of the medieval town.

DISCUSSION

It is important at this point to make a decision on whether we consider the alignment to be intentional or whether we regard it as an assembly of coincidences. The first essential is to find what is generally considered to be an intentional alignment.

The example that comes to mind is the linear cemetery, an alignment of chambered tombs and cairns in the Kilmartin Valley, Argyllshire. It is acceptable to most (but not all) archaeologists because of the following factors:

1. The straightness of the alignment.
2. The even distribution of the monuments on the line.
3. The similar function of the sites.
4. The high incidence of inter-visibility between them.

The monuments of Kilmartin valley and the earthworks of Glasgow and Paisley are clearly from different archaeological periods, but nevertheless, in the context of a discussion on alignments there is a reasonable basis for comparison.

1. The accuracy of the linear distribution of the five sites was determined by a computation of grid co-

ordinates taken to the nearest 10m square along an average grid bearing of 97/ 263 degrees calculated from both ends of the alignment (Fig 6). The Ordnance Survey maps consulted were 1:10,000 scale sheets NS 46 SE, NS 56 SW, NS 56 SE and NS 66 SW.

Fig 6 Location map of the linear distribution of earthworks. Left to right: Castlehead earthwork, Crookston Castle ringwork, Pollok Park ringwork, Camphill earthwork, (Rutherglen Parish Church),Gallowflat mound.

Castlehead earthwork: Starting point of the base line.

Crookston Castle: The alignment runs straight through the castle area, 13m N of the 10m grid square reference.

Pollok Park ringwork: This site is densely covered by trees and undergrowth that greatly hinders its interpretation so no 10m square grid reference has been recorded. The alignment runs 62m S of the estimated centre point of the 100m grid reference square (possibly 30m S of the small secondary enclosure postulated by Shanks & Talbot in 1973).

Camphill earthwork: The alignment passes through the earthwork 12m N of the 10m grid square.

Gallowflat mound: End of base line.

(Castlehead earthwork and Gallowflat mound appear in perfect alignment because the grid co-ordinates were calculated from end to end through these sites.)

It is difficult to judge the intentions of the medieval surveyor by modern methods. No matter how straight an alignment is desired, the landscape cannot be altered to suit. To modem man, calculating from the centre point of an imaginary grid square, Pollok Park ringwork appears 62m off the line. Rather than devote thousands of man-hours to a land-shifting project, medieval surveyors could have considered this to be quite acceptable.

If Pollok Park ringwork is regarded as a coincidence and left out of our calculations, the other four sites form an alignment straighter than the linear cemetery at Kilmartin.

2. The average distance between the five sites on the alignment is 3.7 km. The shortest distance between sites is the 2.4 km between Pollok Park ringwork and Camphill, the longest is 5.1 km between Castlehead and Crookston.

3. Four of these sites have been described as Norman ringworks, and one as a Norman motte, so it seems likely that at one time they served a similar purpose.

4. In spite of the built-up nature of the surroundings, the level of inter-visibility between sites on the alignment is excellent. Crookston and Camphill in particular are spectacular viewpoints.

It must be said, however, that the earthwork at Camphill only faces the direction of Pollok Park, Crookston Castle and Castlehead. Any sighting point in the other direction must have been from the region of the flagpole mound, 100m to the east.

If there were no intervening buildings Camphill would be visible from Gallowflat mound, especially if the mound was at its old height of 3.7m.

Critics of the Kilmartin Valley linear cemetery alignment point to the amount of similar sites in the vicinity and the possibility of observer bias arising because of this. By no stretch of imagination can this be said about the Castlehead to Gallowflat alignment. If, for comparisons sake, we look at the earthworks of the same type mentioned by Talbot in the vicinity which are not positioned on the alignment, we find there are only two.

Pollok Earthwork, Glasgow (NGR: NS 5566 6263) This earthwork forms a roughly circular enclosure, some 30m in diameter, 320m N of Pollok Park ringwork. Once thought to be prehistoric, it was regarded provisionally as a Dark Age homestead after excavations carried out by Glasgow Archaeological Society in 1959-60.

The puzzle here is why two earthworks were built so near each other. It seems unlikely that both were owned at the same time by the same family. Talbot (1974) suggests that both sites are Norman ringworks and the reason for placing them in such close proximity is that one could have been constructed to protect a besieging force attacking the other.

(If this was the case, Pollok Park ringwork on the higher ground of the alignment is likely to have been the oldest of the two sites because it holds the strategically superior position which would surely have been chosen first. The second site could have been built much later).

Muir Earthwork, Carmunnock (NGR: NS 6132 5777). The earthwork stands on the 13th green of Cathkin Braes Golf Course on high moorland country previously forming part of Muir Farm, 5.7km SE of Camphill. It is surrounded by a well-defined circular ditch 54m in diameter, 5.5m wide and up to 1m deep. The interior has been artificially raised in height and stands about 1m above the surrounding ground.

Opinions vary as to the period and purpose of this monument. Feachem (1965) implies that it is an Iron

Age homestead, while Talbot (1974) suggests a ringwork castle built by Henry, son of Anselm, who gave Carmunnock church to Paisley Abbey about 1180.

A reassessment of the site was made in 1995 when a soil and shadow feature attached to the rim of the enclosure was identified from an aerial photograph in the National Monuments Record of Scotland collection (photo AP F22 0045 24.11.54.) The new site is a circular ditched feature 22m in diameter overall; the ditch is 2.5m broad and contains a central rectangular feature 2m by 1m, thought to have contained a burial cist. (Topen 1996).

CONCLUSIONS

It is beyond the scope of this paper to speculate on the reason for the construction of the alignment. Multi-period use of some of the sites hints at earlier origins than medieval. As is often the case in archaeology, there are too many variables and not enough evidence at the present time to pursue this idea further, Suffice to say that in the opinion of the author the alignment is not coincidental and is worth recording for future generations with more sophisticated equipment than we have at our disposal today.

ACKNOWLEDGEMENTS

The author would like to thank the staff of the National Monuments Record of Scotland for their assistance during the preparation of this paper. A belated thanks is also due to all those researchers, particularly Eric J Talbot, whose efforts in the past provided a starting point for my own research.

BIBLIOGRAPHY

Fairhurst, H and Scott, JG. *The Earthwork at Camphill* in Glasgow, Proc. Soc. Antiq. Scot., 85 (1953), 146-56.

Feachem, RW. 1965 *The North Britons: the prehistory of a border people*. London. Shanks, ID, and Talbot, EJ. 1973. *Pollok Estate, Medieval Ringwork*, Discovery and Excavation in Scotland, 1973, 27.

Shearer, WR. 1922 *Rutherglen Lore*. Glasgow.

Talbot, EJ. 1973 *Excavations at 'The Mound', 12 High Road, Castlehead, Paisley*. Glasgow Archaeo. Soc. Bulletin, 2,1, 1973, 3-4. (NB The address is actually 12 Main Road, Castlehead).

Talbot, EJ. 1974 *Early Scottish Castles of Earth and Timber— Recent Field-Work and Excavation*, Scottish Archaeological Forum, 6,4974) 48-53.

Talbot, EJ. 1975 *Crookston Castle*, Discovery and Excavation in Scotland, 1975, 31.

Topen, D. 1996 *An archaeological survey of Queen's Park, City of Glasgow*, Association of Certificated Field Archaeologists (Glasgow University), Occasional Paper no 16.

Topen, D. *1996* Recent discoveries on the Cathkin Braes, Glasgow, Glasgow Archaeo. Soc. Bulletin, 36, 1996, 14-20.

Ure, D. 1793 *The History of Rutherglen and East Kilbride*. Glasgow.

Mysteries of the Roman North

HARRY BELL DONS IMPERIAL GARB AND GOES OFF IN SEARCH OF A WANDERING LEGION AND A BRITISH SACRED GROVE[4]

[4] Originally published in *Northern Earth* issue 83, Autumn 2000. Reprinted with permission.

Britain was the last place on earth the Roman soldier wanted to see on his marching orders. It was *Ultima Thule* — the end of the world as far as the old sweats of the Roman Army were concerned.

It had a reputation as a land of ghosts and strange spirits; further discouragement came from the historian Tacitus in the form of the first recorded comment on British weather, "unpleasant; though not cold, it rains much".

Worst of all was the rumour that turned hardened veterans pale be neath their suntan — it was said that Britain was a land where grapes never grew … and if there were no grapes, there would be no wine!

When the Romans were not fighting off the natives, they were building roads through the wilderness. Road-building was an integral part of the army's duties. The biggest rocks a man could lift were bedded into damp sand to form a foundation; hammers pounded gravel through the cracks and the crunching wheels of chariot traffic did the rest. It was rough and ready but it worked; 1,900 years later there are still 6,000 miles of Roman roads left in Britain. Much has been resurfaced, but parts of the old Military Way still exist; neglected, forgotten, deeply rutted by the wheels of army supply chariots.

The ruts are 4' 8½" apart — amazingly enough, this measurement survived the centuries to re-appear when the first railways were constructed. The standard gauge of British railway lines today is the exact width of the Roman Army supply chariots.[5]

The most impressive feat of Roman military engineering in Britain is undoubtedly the stone wall built in the reign of Emperor Hadrian to keep out the 'wild and unprofitable peoples' of the north.

It took eight years to build and stretches for over 73 miles in an unbroken line across the neck of England from Wallsend on Tyne to Bowness on the Solway. Here the garrison army of 5,500 cavalry and 13,000 infantry kept vigil against attacks from the north and in more peaceful times regulated trade after the fashion of a present-day Customs post.

The Lost Legion

Communication between Rome and North Britain was patchy in those days, and modern historians are conscious of gaps in the record. One such gap concerns the fate of the of Ninth Legion, *Legio IX Hispana*, which was attested in Spain then posted to North Africa and later to Britain. They possibly took part in the building of Hadrian's Wall and were at one time stationed in Luguvalium (Carlisle). The latest date of their presence in Britain is from a building inscription in York dated to AD 108.

They seemed to have vanished without trace after that and speculation has filled the void. For many years it was thought that they had been massacred by the "wild and unprofitable" people between the two walls and their name erased from military records to save the army embarrassment.

[5] This piece of urban folklore is categorised as 'partly true' by fact-checking website snopes.com, which adds that it is "probably just coincidence" and may have more to do with the width of a horse's behind.

This version of events is at odds with evidence from Nijmegen in Holland, where tiled stamps dating to AD 130 were found bearing the legion's name. Whether this was a reformed unit or the same old Ninth has long been a matter of conjecture. Nowadays most historians prefer the latter view.[6]

The legend of the lost legion was revived by the BBC twenty years ago in a six part serial called *The Eagle of the Ninth*, which portrayed the adventures of one Marcus Helvius Germinus, a young Roman who came to Britain to discover the fate of his father who had served in the vanished Ninth. The eagle in the title was the emblem on the legion's battle standard.

Opting for a bit of military realism, the BBC recruited volunteers from the 15th Scottish Parachute Regiment (TAVR) to serve as legionaries and be filmed in Roman attire marching through the Kilpatrick Hills N of the Clyde with eerie dawn mist swirling round their kneecaps.

[6] *(Note from John Billingsley, NE editor):* On a remote piece of moorland on the boundary between West Yorkshire and Lancashire, the Heptonstall-Thursden road crosses Birkin Clough. Here beside the road an old cross is incised on a boulder. However, if you set off upstream, after about 150 yds, you should come across, in a most lonely spot indeed (SD 917 337), a stone overhanging the stream; it has a flat vertical face on which some wag, who knows when, has carved the inscription 'SPCK IX' (9th Legion). Those guys really were lost... JB

The writer, gathering material for this article.

To the delight of the Territorials, the eerie dawn mist failed to materialise and they were paid for a weekend's sunbathing at Equity scale wages. On the afternoon of the second day, in the cruel heat of the Scottish summer with not a cloud in sight, 15 Para assault pioneers arrived from Glasgow with smoke grenade canisters and saved the day. The photograph shows your author 'between takes'...

The Inchtuthil Hoard

By far the largest Roman structure in Scotland is the 20 hectare fortress at Inchtuthil, on the N side of the River Tay between Perth and Dunkeld. Situated within the private grounds of Delvine House, there is little of the fort visible today, though it once housed a legion of 5,500 men. Due to the regular and thereby predictable layout of Roman military installations, barrack-blocks, granaries, HQ buildings, hospital, workshops and storehouses have all been identified by excavation.

Inchtuthil's unsolved mystery concerns the find of a large hoard of assorted nails up to 200mm in length buried within its confines. Excavation revealed that when the fort was abandoned, the buildings were demolished, the ramparts slighted and pottery systematically smashed. Had the wild and unprofitable people struck again? Did the Romans vandalise the fort to prevent it being used against them later? Why did they leave the unused nails — did they intend to come back and dig them up in more peaceful times?

I pondered these alternatives during my Field Certificate Archaeology Course in Glasgow. One of the requirements in the second year of the course was an essay entitled 'The Characteristic Features That Define A Roman Military Site In The Field'. With a title that length I felt compelled to pad out the essay a little, and for some reason I embarked on a treatise on a possible solution to the Inchtuthil mystery. It lay in the human frailty of the invading army. In the most academic terms, I postulated that the hoard could have resulted from a large-scale quartermaster's fiddle that involved the sale or barter of nails to the natives. When ordered to return south the miscreants must have buried the nails to avoid detection.

The Romanist who marked the essay was not impressed and rewarded me with the lowest mark of any essay I ever handed in. Apparently Inchtuthil had been abandoned because of the withdrawal of a legion from Britain in AD 86 which led to a reappraisal of commitments in North Britain and the subsequent abandonment of several forts in Strathmore.

The hoard, he informed me, consisted of 12 tonnes of hardware, amounting to almost a million nails, so my explanation was quite ridiculous.

The reason so many nails were left behind is still a mystery, but at least we solved the problem of what to do with them after the Romans had gone. Nowadays, finding a museum in Scotland without a display of Inchtuthil nails is as difficult as finding a castle Bonnie Prince Charlie never slept in.

The Forgotten Sanctuary

Ten years after Hadrian's Wall was completed, the Antonine Wall was built to form a barrier across the narrowest part of Britain, where (in the words of the first-century historian Tacitus), "the firths of Clota and Bodotria, being carried far inland by tides from opposite seas, are separated by but a narrow strip of land". (Clota, the divine cleanser, is the River Clyde, Bodotria the River Forth).

The wall warranted only the most fleeting mention in the biography of Antonius Pius, the Emperor who ordered its construction. "He subdued the Britons through Lollius Urbicus, the governor, and after driving back the barbarians, erected another wall, this time of turf."

The defences consisted of a 4m deep ditch backed by a turf rampart built on top of a stone foundation 4.5m broad. The garrison occupied forts which, with the exception of Bar Hill, were attached to the rear of the rampart and linked by a military road.

One of the best place-name sources for Roman Britain is a list compiled by an anonymous cleric in a book called *The Ravenna Cosmography*. No early manuscripts survive, but there are three from the Middle Ages.

On or near the Antonine Wall the Ravenna Cosmographer gives a list of ten places which he said were joined by a road in a straight line — *recta trainite una alteri connexae* — implying some sort of line on his source map (ley-hunters please note). The source map dating from Flavian times, was used by Marinus and through him, by Ptolemy.

Photo: Grahame Gardner

2. Bar Hill bath-house.

It is difficult to identify these sites with the Antonine forts because the original map was modified during the campaigns of Severus and names set down carelessly, some to the E of the forts, some to the W, according to spaces left on the paper.

One site is called Medionemeton, a name derived from two Gallo-Brittonic words: *medio* meaning 'middle' and *nemeton* a 'sanctuary' (an open sanctuary in the Celtic religious tradition, not a Roman-style roofed structure).

The only known sanctuary in the Forth-Clyde Isthmus is at Cairnpapple Hill, a multi-period ritual and burial site dating from 3,000 BC onwards into the Early Iron Age. When Professor Stuart Piggott excavated the site 1947-48 he suggested in his report in *The Proceedings of the Society of Antiquaries of Scotland* that Cairnpapple Hill was the Medionemeton of the Ravenna Cosmographer.

As Cairnpapple is only six miles from the Firth of Forth and over 30 miles from the Clyde Estuary, it is difficult to see how the Romans would have described it as a 'middle sanctuary'.

Before starting to theorise, let us first examine the factors common to other Celtic sanctuaries in existence at that time. According to Caesar, Druids in France met annually "in the centre of all Gaul, in the land of the Carnutes". Over in Ireland, Druidic assemblies were held at the Hill of Uisneach in County Westmeath. This hill is so centrally situated that it is often called the Navel of Ireland. Might not Medionemeton occupy a similar location in Scotland?

Revie and Smith in *Placenames of Roman Britain* (1979) suggest that Medionemeton could also be interpreted as 'middle grove' meaning perhaps a site halfway along the Antonine Wall or between two natural features.

The Antonine Wall today probably features more industrial than Roman remains, but there are still sections that are well worth a visit. The ditch at Watling Lodge retains almost its original profile; the fort at Rough Castle is noted for its ten rows of defensive pits (called *lilia*, or lilies) which; if planted with staves and covered with twigs and leaves, were guaranteed to stop any intruders, and Bar Hill has interesting ditch and rampart sections and a small bathhouse (Fig.2).

Bar Hill is the highest of the Antonine forts, but the highest point along the Wall is 200m to the NE, where the ditch is incomplete for 25 metres due to impenetrable dolerite. The wall is no longer visible here, but just beyond this point the ditch runs towards Croy in a deep gully that somehow still gives a lingering impression of the frontier of a mighty empire marking out its territory across the countryside.

Overlooking this section lies Castle Hill (Fig.3), a small Iron Age hillfort whose multiple ramparts and ditches are cut by the Roman frontier line. An information board at the entrance gives an artist's impression of what the palisaded fort looked like in Pre-Roman times.

Castle Hill predates the wall and is, in fact, closer to it than Bar Hill fort, which, unlike any of the others, is detached from the Wall, some 30m to the S.

At some unknown date, the Romans destroyed the ramparts of Castle Hill and reduced them to terraces, but no one is sure why they did so. Standing 155m above sea level, Castle Hill is higher than any of the Antonine forts and from the triangulation point on its summit both the Forth and the Clyde can be seen on a clear day. It is 14 miles from the Firth of Forth and 15 or less to the point where the Clyde met the sea in ancient times.

3. Castle Hill.

If there was ever a middle sanctuary in Scotland, there could have been no better place for it than Castle Hill (NS 709761).

Castle Hill is ten miles E of Glasgow and easily reached by road or rail (Croy station).

Motorists should drive to Kirkintilloch then take the B8023 for three miles to Twechar. Leave your car at the Twechar Enterprise Park, cross to the Quarry Inn, and 30m beyond you'll find a sign pointing up to Bar Hill.

Inside the fort is a well where votive objects have been recovered and the foundations of a small bath-house where the sequence of rooms from hot to cold can still be traced. Follow the path through the fort to the highest point of the Wall and there you will find Castle Hill.

Further Reading:

Breeze, DJ. *Roman Scotland A Guide to the Visible Remains*, 1979

Johnstone, F. *The Wild Frontier*, 1986

Piggot, S. *The Druids*, 1968

Revie, A. and Smith, C. *Place Names of Roman Britain*, 1979

Robertson, AS. *The Antonine Wall*, 1990.

Relics of the Antonine Wall and nails from Inchtuthill can be seen at the Hunterian Museum in Glasgow University and the Royal Museum of Scotland in Chambers Street, Edinburgh.

Cumbria's Sacred Landscapes

Harry Bell, East Kilbride

I read with interest Robert WE Farrah's article on Mayburgh Henge in NE85. Particularly intriguing were the references to how Blencathra comes in and out of view at significant points in the surrounding area, as if the henge was built to accommodate this.[7]

I have noticed a similar phenomenon at Castlerigg stone circle (NY 291 236), 15mls to the W. Readers can find a reference to this in the *Terrain Echoes* chapter of my 'Leyline Quest' website.[8] On the subject of overland prehistoric navigation it states:

There are also enough cross alignments with the surrounding hills to ensure that anyone "in the know" could find their way to that very hillside again without difficulty. One way to do it would be to first place yourself in direct alignment between Helvellyn and Skiddaw, then walk in the direction of Skiddaw keeping your eye on the summit of Blencathra a little to the right. Stop just before the summit goes out of view behind Gategill Fells. (No dowsing rods or astronomical tables required.) This would lead you to exactly the right spot. It could have been done in prehistoric times, and it can still be done today.

The 'exact spot' referred to is the entrance to the henge.

[7] This is a letter from Harry Bell published in *Northern Earth* #87, Autumn 2001. Reproduced with permission.

[8] See page 199.

⁹ Megalithic Sites in Britain.

Robert Farrah replies: With reference to Harry Bell's article, the 13-38 stone alignment, in direct line between Helvellyn and Skiddaw is one of the most significant lines of Castlerigg. The two stones are where the arcs of the flattened circle commence ant Thom also gives Stone 13 as marking the midwinter rising sun from the centre (Thom, MSB⁹, p.150). I must check this out because it will rise somewhere in the region of Helvellyn; there are echoes of Mayburgh.

Letters

A selection of correspondence, both to and from Harry, included here as they provide insight into some references elsewhere in this volume.

Typewritten letter from TC Welsh

c/o Department of Geography,
The University,
Sheffield S10 2TN

20th February, 1977

Mr H. W. Bell
62, New Plymouth,
Westwood,
East Kilbride.

Dear Mr Bell,

I note your entry on p56 of D&E 1976 regarding Nethercraig, Eaglesham. I felt I ought to draw to your attention that there is an alternative explanation available for these features, although I would emphasise, I am not claiming to be in a [position to say your interpretation is mistaken.

I published a note on these remains in D&E 1969, where I had understood from the farmer at Nethercraig that these were the foundations of the original farmhouse, rebuilt in the last century on the present site. However that was eight years ago, when

I was less careful and less observant than I would be now. I haven't looked closely at the site since, but I recall at the time being very intrigued by the rock-cut foundations. I would be inclined to suspect earlier remains, but would suggest you establish how much of it is recent, i.e. part of the old farmhouse. Several old farmhouses in the area are built on older structures. You could get the information from the Eglinton Muniments Farm Plans by John Ainslie 1789m in West Register House, Edinburgh, which should be for farm number 37. These plans are well worth looking through anyway; I had time to try one group before I moved to Sheffield, see D&E 1975 p 45/6, and found them very rewarding. I also know that there was a bridge across the White Cart at Nethercraig, the remains of the footings are still visible.

As regards the two D&E entries, I hope you won't feel awkward: it happens often. I've just done the same to one of Mr Newall's sites after only two years (D&E 1976 p30 cup marks, D&E 1974). If you plan to take an active interest in fieldwork in this area I wish you every success.

Yours sincerely,

Thomas C. Welsh.

Typewritten reply from Harry

62, New Plymouth
East Kilbride
5. 3. 77

Dear Mr. Welsh,

Many thanks for your letter informing me about your 1969 D&E entry. I went to the Mitchell Library last Saturday to look it up, but owing to Strathclyde

Region spending cuts the library is now closed at week-ends.

I still don't know the grid reference of your 'find', but there is a possibility that both of us have investigated different parts of the same field. At the time of my own 'find' I asked the farmer if anyone from and archaeological society had ever questioned him about the 'dun' before. He said that no-one had, but years ago a man had asked him about the way the rock had been cut down hear the roadside; "He was awful interested in it — I think he was a student or something."

Could this have been you?

I am going to Edinburgh next Wednesday and I'll have time to look up the Eglinton Muniments Farm Plans as you suggested. Not just for Nethercraig, but for other farms in the vicinity.

The site at Nethercraig looks to me like one of the outer earthworks of what a real archaeologist might call a "nucleated fort." There are four large earthworks and a few minor ones in a half-circle covering what the army would call "the dead ground" approach to North Highcraig. On the southern approach to North Highcraig there are no earthworks because the ground slopes gradually and the central position is sufficient for all-round observation.

The site at High Northcraig[10] seems to have been built on in the last few centuries, so I sent particulars of the lesser site at Nethercraig to D&E because it was in better condition.

[10] I'm unclear whether this is a different site to North Highcraig, or just a spoonerism on Harry's part?

Although it probably looks less convincing, the High Northcraig site must have been the most important of the two.

When I was up there, I noticed that the fort at Dunwan Hill can be seen peeping over the sky-line; a beacon lit there could be seen from High Northcraig quite easily. There were too many coincidences so I figured the site was genuine enough. Unfortunately, I didn't know enough about archaeology to explain it all. I remember thinking at the time, "the only one who might know anything about this is that bloke whose name was in D&E with all the Renfrewshire discoveries last year."

There were nine Thomas Welsh entries in the phone book, but no Thomas C Welsh, so I abandoned the idea of phoning you. As far as I know the site at North Highcraig has still not been reported. If I find out more about it in Edinburgh, I might put it in D&E 1977.

Your reference to the bridge across the Cart at Nethercraig intrigues me. I'd go down and have a look but my car is stuck in the garage with a broken sub-frame.

I think there's been a few settlements in this area that have been overlooked. In my naivete I presumed that D&E entries were subject to scrutiny by some panel of experts before their inclusion in the book. I hope I haven't given any false information about Nethercraig that would mislead researchers in the area, but to paraphrase Shakespeare, "what's dun is dun."

Many thanks for your letter and the information it contained,

Yours sincerely,

(Signed) Harry W. Bell.

Response from TC Welsh

c/o Department of Geography,
The University,
Sheffield S10 2TN

10th March, 1977

Dear Mr Bell,

Your letter prompts me to write again — though it would be against my principles to interfere with someone else's fieldwork — this time to offer advice.

You do not give me any idea about yourself which would enable me to aim such advice at the right level, but I judge from your letter than you fall into the same age category as I did when I wrote not dissimilar descriptions of sites. If I am wrong, please excuse my presumption. The advice I offer is not intended to be patronising, and I hope it will not be ill-received.

1). Professionals don't like amateurs, and this is particularly true of archaeologists, and most especially true of archaeologists in Scotland! It is also applicable to seasoned amateurs who regard themselves as virtually 'professionals'. So be warned. I am trying to speak fairly when I say that your description of features at Nethercraig and North Highcraig would get a very stony reception from the 'professionals'. I am all too familiar with responses such as, "take a course in archaeology at evening classes", "join the archaeological fieldwork group and learn from the bottom", "you should start off with a seasoned archaeologist until you have enough experience", "Renfrewshire is a very hard area to survey and you easily get confused", "we've already been over the area, and we can assure you, you should take the advice of older and more experienced field-workers". I still get this advice by the way.

What I am trying to say is <u>get your facts right and present them precisely and clearly, and above all make sure there are no obvious holes in your argument</u>. If you are likely to be patronised or given a brush off, at least don't give then an easy excuse. The commonest professional reply in my experience is "Yes, we'll look at it sometime", which is archaeo-slang for "Don't call us, we'll call you". If you present your case well, and if it's accurate, you have a better chance.

2). <u>A little knowledge is dangerous</u>. Advice which came to me through geography, and would have been invaluable if I had realised it when I started amateur archaeology. <u>It is necessary to approach with extreme caution all features with which you are not personally familiar or experienced</u>. Book descriptions, and excavation papers are all very well, but rather remote and ideal compared with what you are likely to encounter on the ground. Set your sights at the level of your experience and work upwards. I learned that the hard way. I doubt if you'll appreciate this. If you do, my letter will have been pitched at the wrong level, and all I've said won't be new to you. I could put it another way and say that the more experienced I get, the more aware I am of my limitations and the need to be cautious.

3). <u>At all costs avoid lining up or linking sites</u>, unless you are absolutely certain. <u>Treat linear features with extreme caution, whether wall, earthworks or tracks.</u> It would help to familiarise yourself thoroughly with (a) basic geology and geomorphology (i.e. natural landforms) (b) soils and drift, and the erosion processes associated (c) agricultural and industrial archaeology, right down to the fine details — wall building, road making, field systems, farming methods, mills, kilns and so on.

More often apparent links are merely a succession of features of different periods.

4). <u>Familiarise yourself with the styles of other amateurs</u>. Mr Frank Newall and associates have been publishing in D&E since it first appeared, but you probably won't get back volumes before 1965, unless you consult the complete set in the National Museum of Antiquities Library in Edinburgh. Although I started in 1968 (that is, in D&E) my style would be rather misleading as I was then 18, and I haven't really sorted out my ideas even now. If you can get hold of a copy of Archaeological News bulletin for CBA Group 3 No 14 April 1976 (from Mrs D. B Charlton, 28, Jesmond Park West, Newcastle upon Tyne 7), it will probably cost your 20 or 30 pence, you can get some idea of my methods pages 14-18. Otherwise follow through D&E 1969-1973 for <u>Sutherland</u>.

5). Purchase and use some practical texts. I found invaluable — H. W. Feachem "The North Britons" and "A Guide to Prehistoric Scotland"; Ordnance Survey "Field Archaeology in Great Britain" which is extremely valuable; Collins' Field Guides on 'Archaeology', which is a very useful early reference to which I owe a great deal, though I seldom use it now, and on 'The British Landscape' by JRW Cheatle, which is very recent, and which I wish I had had in the sixties — it covers landforms, soils, vegetation, architecture and basic archaeology. I have also found invaluable Christopher Taylor's 'Fieldwork in Mediaeval Archaeology', and I would advise you consult a book on industrial archaeology.

6). Get hold of your area material. Royal Commission on Ancient Monuments Inventory is in print, but they have up-to-date reports on prehistoric and Roman remains in Lanarkshire. Ordnance Survey Archaeology Division Record Cards can be consulted by appointment at 43, Rose Street, Edinburgh EH3 3NL. Set up your own card index and build from there.

My own index for Eastwood District, to date July 1975, is in the care of Strathclyde Regional Council, Department of Physical Planning, above SMT bus station. It is based on OSA record cards. Alternatively there is an account, to date August 1975, in the care of Eastwood District Library, Capelrig House, Newton Mearns, for public reference (this, I should emphasise, is in part personal opinions, and therefore not necessarily accurate).

I hope you find some of this of use. It is meant sincerely in the hope that you may be able to avoid the mistakes I made.

Yours sincerely,

Thomas C. Welsh.

1299   **rate**

rasp (räsp), *v.t.* **1.** to scrape or abrade with a rough instrument. **2.** to scrape or rub roughly. **3.** to grate upon or irritate (the nerves, feelings, etc.). **4.** to utter with a grating sound. —*v.i.* **5.** to scrape or grate. **6.** to make a grating sound. —*n.* **7.** the act of rasping. **8.** a rasping sound. **9.** a coarse form of file, having separate pointlike teeth. **10.** any similar surface. [ME *raspe(n)*, t. OF: m. *rasper* scrape, grate, t. Gmc; cf. obs. G *raspen* grate]

raspberry (räz′bə ri, -bri), *n.*, *pl.* **-ries. 1.** the fruit of several shrubs of the rosaceous genus *Rubus*, consisting of small juicy drupelets, red, black, or pale yellow, forming a detachable cap about a convex receptacle, being thus distinguished from the blackberry. **2.** one of these plants, as the **red raspberry**, *R. idaeus*, of Europe. **3.** dark reddish purple. **4.** *Slang.* a sound expressing derision or contempt made with the tongue and lips. [f. *rasp(is)* raspberry (orig. uncert.) + BERRY]

rasper (räs′pə), *n.* one who or that which rasps, as a machine for rasping sugar cane.

rasping (räs′ping), *adj.* harsh: *a rasping voice.*

The entry for 'Raspberry' from the Encyclopedic World Dictionary, with its (orig. uncert.) attribution, irritated Harry enough that he was prompted to put pen to paper and send in a correction.

A handwritten letter from Harry

62 New Plymouth
East Kilbride
G75 8QB

The Editor,
Encyclopaedic World Dictionary

Dear Sir,

It has come to my notice that on p. 1299 of your Dictionary (1971 Edition) you appear uncertain of the origin of Raspberry "(4. *Slang*. a sound expressing derision or contempt made with the tongue and lips [f. rasp(is) raspberry (orig. uncert.) + BERRY])"

As a craftsman in the printing trade, familiar with written and spoken English in all its forms, I can perhaps be of some assistance to you in this matter.

The word 'raspberry' in its '4. Slang' context, is similar to 'China' (p.296) in that is derivation lies in Cockney rhyming slang.

Raspberry is actually abbreviated rhyming slang for 'raspberry tart', i.e. fart (see p.580) Taboo – n. 1. an emission of wind from the anus, esp. an audible one [ME ferten, OE feortan c. GMG Ferzan]

In the interests of the origins and correct usage of English, I hope you can correct this small fault in later editions of what is otherwise an excellent publication.

Yours sincerely,

Henry Walker Bell.

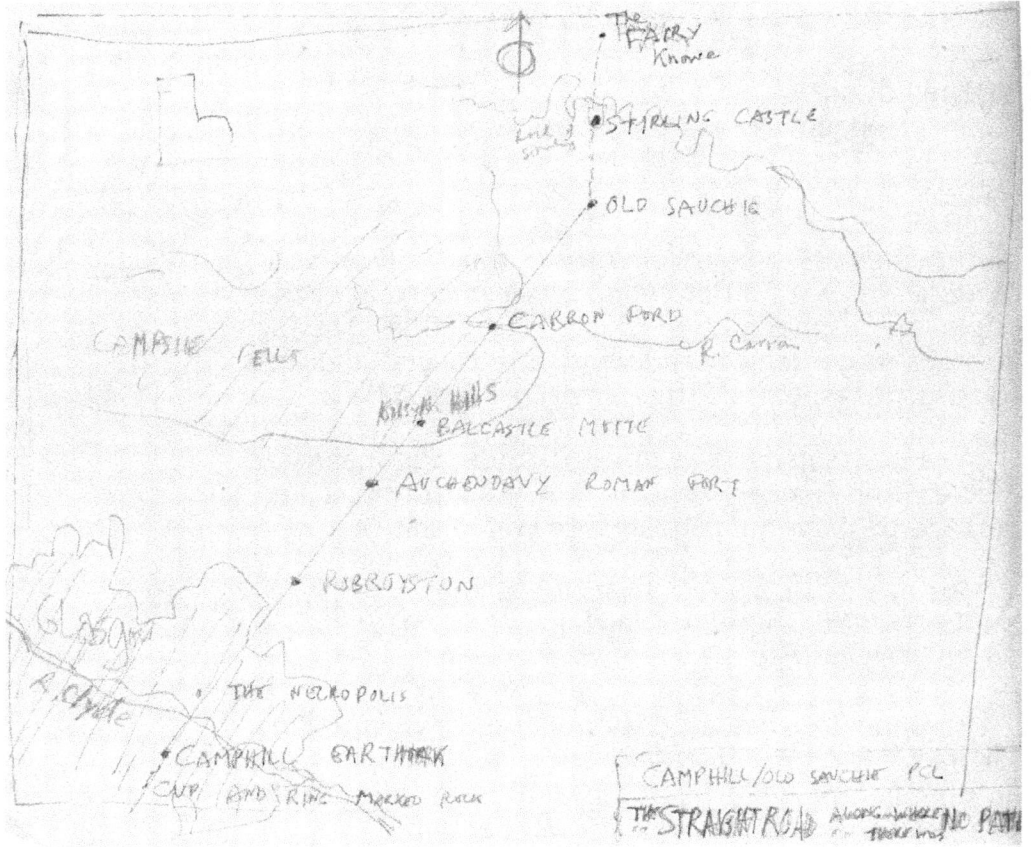

An early sketch by Harry of 'The Straight Road with No Path'

APPENDICES

DUMGOYNE

DUNCOLM

DUMBARTON ROCK

COCHNO STONE

BAR HILL Roman Fort

River Clyde

NECROPOLIS

WOODEND LOCH

SEEDHILL CRAIGS

CROOKSTON CASTLE

CAMPHILL

CARMYLE FORDS

To Glengarnock Castle

WALLS HILL

CATHKIN Braes

HAMILTON Mains

□ MAPWORK □

MOST OF THE SITES LISTED IN THE GAZETEER APPEAR ON THE ORDNANCE SURVEY SHEET 64 MAP OF GLASGOW (1:50,000 SCALE). SITES LISTED WITH A FOUR FIGURE REFERENCE AFTER THE NAME —i.e. AUCHENDAVY ROMAN FORT 6774 — CAN BE FOUND BY USING THE NUMBERS LIKE CLUES IN A CROSSWORD. CONSIDER 6774 AS 67 ACROSS, 74 UP. THE 'ACROSS' NUMBERS (KNOWN AS 'EASTINGS') ARE PRINTED IN BLUE INK AT THE TOP AND BOTTOM OF EACH MAP; 'UP' NUMBERS (KNOWN AS 'NORTHINGS') ARE PRINTED AT THE SIDES. FOLLOW THE BLUE LINES TO THE APPROPRIATE GRID SQUARE, AND THERE YOU WILL FIND THE SITE.

SOME SITES ARE LISTED IN THE GAZETEER WITH A FULL GRID REFERENCE OF TWO LETTERS AND SIX NUMBERS AFTER THE NAME. THESE SITES ARE WITHIN THE GEOGRAPHICAL AREA COVERED BY SHEET 64, BUT ARE NOT MARKED ON 1:50,000 SCALE MAPS (SOME — i.e. CARMUNNOCK RINGWORK NS613577 — APPEAR ON 1:25,000 SCALE MAPS). NUMBER 613577 SHOULD BE INTERPRETED AS 61 AND ½ ACROSS, 57 AND ½ UP. THE THIRD AND SIXTH NUMBERS ARE USED TO DIVIDE THE MAP INTO 100m SQUARES.

ONE SITE IN THE GAZETEER — CUP AND RING MARKED ROCK NS57216132 — HAS AN EIGHT FIGURE GRID REFERENCE. THIS NUMBER CAN BE USED TO SUBDIVIDE A LARGE-SCALE MAP INTO 10m SQUARES. FURTHER INFORMATION ABOUT GRID REFERENCE CAN BE FOUND IN THE RIGHT-HAND MARGIN OF SHEET 64, UNDER THE HEADING 'INCIDENCE OF ADJOINING SHEETS AND NATIONAL GRID REFERENCE SYSTEM'.

SITES WITH NO NUMBERS AFTER THEIR NAME —i.e. BEN LOMOND, DUNGOYNE, etc.— ARE OUTWITH THE GEOGRAPHICAL AREA COVERED BY SHEET 64.

A MORE DETAILED WORKSHEET CAN BE MADE BY TRANSFERRING ALL THE PCLs FROM THE ABOVE MAP ONTO SHEET 64 (GLASGOW) OF THE ORDNANCE SURVEY 1:50,000 SCALE, SECOND SERIES.

DEIL'S PLANTIN Mark Stone

TORRANCE HOUSE

DUNWAN HILLFORT

HARELAW CAIRN

DUMDRUFF HILL

IT IS DIFFICULT TO ASSESS THE WIDTH OF A PCL. IT CAN BE AS NARROW AS A PATH BETWEEN TWO STONES, OR AS BROAD AS A DISTANT HILLFORT — IT ALL DEPENDS ON THE LINE OF SIGHT OF THE OBSERVER.

SOME PCLs, LIKE THE DUNCOLM/TINTO LINE, APPEAR TO HAVE BEEN SURVEYED FROM POINT TO POINT. OTHERS MAY HAVE BEEN EXTENDED OVER A LONG PERIOD. FOR EXAMPLE, THE DUNCOLM/DUMDRUFF LINE MAY ORIGINALLY HAVE BEEN A DUNCOLM/CROOKSTON LINE WHICH WAS LENGTHENED CENTURIES AFTER ITS ORIGINAL CONSTRUCTION.

A' the best,
Harry.

Map from the first edition of Glasgow's Secret Geometry.

FROM FOOTSTEPS TO GEOMETRY

AN ARCHAEOLOGICAL ASSESSMENT OF THE VERACITY OF HARRY BELL'S GLASGOW NETWORK OF ALIGNED SITES

Kenneth Brophy

Preamble

Harry Bell occupies an important place in the historiography of the study of prehistoric Glasgow, with his book *Glasgow's Secret Geometry* (1984) a love letter to Neolithic ingenuity and surveying skills in the Clyde Valley and beyond. However, you are unlikely to see his research referenced or discussed in any archaeological textbook or in a paper in the pages of an academic journal. This is because Bell's work, despite his archaeological leaning and fieldwork, was at the time — and still largely is — regarded as existing on the fringes of the discipline, dismissed in much the same way as any study that even hints at ley lines continues to be. In this chapter, I want to look back on Bell's work and evaluate the archaeological value of his arguments and fieldwork, something that has never been attempted before in a serious way. To do this, one must contextualise the work of Bell within the deep-rooted historical suspicions that have existed between archaeologists and the ley hunting communities for over a century now, both camps that Bell belonged to. It is also worth considering Bell's (Figure 1) book from another perspective, as a fine piece of writing that presents an innovative study of urban deep time and a creative approach to landscape archaeology.

Figure 1: Harry Bell at Stonehenge.

A brief history of the relationship between archaeologists and ley hunters

lfred Watkins, who amongst other things was a more than proficient photographer, came to his ley-revelation late in life. Active in the local archaeology scene in Herefordshire, Watkins first developed the concept of ley lines during and immediately after a walk in Blackwardine in June 1921 (Pennick & Devereux 1989, 17; MacFarlane 2014, xii). Mapwork on his return led to a revelation that a straight line between two locations — Croft Ambury and Stretton Grandison — passed through many other points of interest (Stout 2008, 176-7). The concept was quickly expanded and explored through maps and fieldwork, and he would subsequently publish several books about his theory, including the seminal *The Old Straight Track* (Watkins 1925) and *The Ley Hunters Manual* (1927). Watkins believed that invisible straight lines through the landscape passing notable anthropomorphic landmarks (and some natural features) were in fact ancient routeways, including sightlines, to be followed by traders in prehistory. These lines, according to Watkins, were marked in various ways and can still be read into the landscape today through many different types of physical markers, from megalithic monuments to medieval churches that may have been built in previously pagan places. Watkins argued leys were set out in the Neolithic period (Williamson & Bellamy 1983, 32) and could in some instances even be recalled in local folklore and place names (Watkins 1925; 1927).

Watkins was very clear that to find leys, and then prove them on the ground, one had to carry out mapwork, followed by fieldwork (Screeton 1977, 38). Harry Bell himself (1984, 2) characterised the first part of the process thus: "Old Alfred's instructions ... were quite straightforward... First, pin your map onto a drawing board. Next, draw a circle around all the mounds, unworked stones, moats, holy wells, beacon points, crosses, crossroads, churches of ancient foundation and castles you can find. After that, stick a pin into an undoubted mark point (a mound or traditional stone), place a straight edge against the pin, and try to find four sites in a row". Ordnance Survey maps were thus the weapon of choice for anyone wanting leads in the hunt for these abstract lines in the land.

Fieldwork was also an important component part of this activity. Indeed, Watkins argued that this was the "chief objective" (1927, 69). Guides to ley-hunting include lengthy lists of types of sites and features to look out for while in the field, and how to identify them on the ground (e.g. Watkins 1927; Devereux & Thomson 1979; Pennick & Devereux 1989). These lists, including barrows, megaliths, camps (or forts), castles, ponds, roads, and crossroads, are often accompanied by morphological descriptions to help recognition in the field, and as such are reminiscent of lists found in archaeological fieldwork guides such as Wood (1963). More recent accounts draw on archaeological evidence such as cropmarks (Pennick & Devereux 1989, 48ff.) which are not visible from the ground, thus suggesting research in sites and monuments records is now also a requirement. Pre-reformation churches (despite the evidence for many of these being built in pagan locations being very slim (e.g. Williamson and Bellamy 1983, 77-9; Grinsell 1986; Hutton 2013, 331-3)) are also commonly used points on leys. Paradoxically, the presence of a site on an alignment elevates their significance and makes them more likely to be prehistoric, a dubious and self-fulfilling chain of logic.

Stout outlines the dramatic impact that these ideas had on the public, promoting fieldwork and visits to the countryside, and the formation of clubs (2008, 190). Although most of these folk did initially adhere to the principles and ideas that had been set out by Watkins and his imitators, even during his lifetime attempts to read more esoteric meanings into leys were emerging (Stout 2008, 203-4). Through time, Watkinsonian ley-hunting lost momentum, but was revived and began to move in different directions from the 1960s onwards, initially because of a connection made with UFO flight paths (Hutton 2009, 321). This revitalisation and reconceptualisation of leys was secured with books such as John Michell's 1969 *The View Over Atlantis*, allowing a shift in the meaning of leys from being ancient tracks to mystical earth energy lines that could be identified by dowsing, using a pendulum (e.g. Lethbridge 1972), or taking magnetic readings (entirely new areas of methodology in ley-hunting which were considerably removed from archaeological practice compared to Watkins' approach). The post-Watkinsonian 'earth mysteries' turn for leys led to a wide range of theories and arguments made as to their nature, form, and origins (e.g. Devereux & Thomson 1979, 53ff.; Hutton 2009, 321-4), and it is these ideas in particular that have contributed to the negative view most archaeologists have towards ley theory.

Although Watkins' books sold very well, he did not get the approval of the archaeological establishment and *Antiquity* editor OGS Crawford that he so craved (Stout 2008, 182-4). As well as refusing to carry advertisements for Watkins' books in *Antiquity* or mention him by name in print (an oft repeated slur: see Devereux & Thomson 1979; Daniels 2006; Stout 2008; Charlesworth 2010, 139), Crawford later wrote that *The Old Straight Track* was, "one of the craziest books ever written about British archaeology" (1953, 269). Crawford's reaction was typical of the general approach of archaeologists to leys since the 1920s, ranging from apathy to ridicule (Stout 2008, 188), part of a general move to establish archaeology as a serious discipline of which Crawford was very much a leading figure (Hauser 2008; Barber 2016). Crawford's successor as editor of *Antiquity* Glyn Daniel for instance called ley lines, in an editorial in that journal, 'extravagant nonsense' and 'dottinnesses' (Daniel 1970, 174). Indeed, serious academic consideration of leys has often been replaced by patronising commentary (Figure 2). In an open letter sent to one ley-hunting correspondent to *Antiquity*, Crawford dismissively wrote, "it would be possible to align factory-chimneys or haystacks" (quoted in Hauser 2008, 112), while a similar mocking claim was made by Atkinson regarding the alignments of red telephone boxes (Ruggles 2005).[1]

[1] In the editorial of the December 1969 issue of *The Ley Hunter* magazine, editor Paul Screeton quotes a letter from avowed earth mystery sceptic John Cleary-Baker PhD, then Chair of BUFORA — The British UFO Research Association — who writes, "*...to my way of thinking, one could construct equally convincing ley lines by the use of public houses, telephone booths or branches of F W Woolworth's.*"

These attitudes persisted and persist. Much later Colin Renfrew stated leys were a "remarkable tissue of beliefs" studied by those "blinded by some personal obsession" (1989, 37-8), while Francis Pryor (2001, 167) in one brief footnote dismissed the whole concept as a twentieth century invention. As with the fate of other eccentric characters without professional status who were carrying out archaeological work across the twentieth century, such as John Pull (Russell 2001), Ludovic McLellan Mann (Ritchie 2002) and Alexander Thom (Thom 1995; MacKie 2021), Watkins was shut out of academic publication and attacked in the pages of august books and journals with no obvious right or route to reply, and this continued long after his death.

'*This book shows how the roundabouts on the M4 are built on a system of ancient burial mounds, and on clear nights you can see a headless motorist . . .* '

Figure 2: Barry Fantoni cartoon, printed in the editorial for Antiquity *in March 1970.*

Those with an interest in leys have in turn been critical of mainstream archaeology, often in the form of outdated stereotypes and misconceptions about archaeological practice. Accusations of an elitist, closed-minded, vested interest nature have been commonplace (e.g. Screeton 1977, 22-4; Devereux & Thomson 1979, 43-4) fuelled by the treatment of Watkins, and this perception has been maintained to an extent even today (e.g. Charlesworth 2010, 139-40). Michell (1969, 64) claimed that archaeologists indulged in "treasure hunting and grave robbery", while the dynamic nature of archaeological theory has been used as evidence archaeologists cannot be trusted to get the past right because they keep changing their minds (Screeton 1977, 63-4).

More damaging, and relevant to when Watkins was working back in the 1920s and 1930s, was the charge archaeologists viewed prehistoric people as primitive, and thus unable to logistically organise or intellectually conceive of something so complex as the ley system. Bell himself argued that, "Until the 1960s, the common image of the ancient Briton was a man dressed in animal skins, carrying a club and dragging a woman by the hair" (1977a, 3). Even in the 1960s, this would have been a wholly outdated perception of what prehistorians thought, although such attitudes amongst some archaeologists persisted towards the middle of the century. In a gentle critique of Watkins, archaeologist Wood conceded, "*primitive man* would have used prominent marks to guide him through the wilds" (1963, 133, my emphasis), the use of the word primitive here being an unhelpful rebuttal. Hutton (2009, 322) also detected a certain nostalgia for antiquarianism in the ley community, illogical given the largely dismissive views William Stukeley and others had of the capabilities of pre-Roman occupants of Britain.

Serious archaeological engagement has been thin on the ground where ley lines are concerned, another bone of contention for ley-hunters. Devereux and Thomson (1979, 43) noted that, "we are hard pushed to find any meaningful discussion of leys ... on the part of archaeologists" although that was soon to be rectified. Williamson and Bellamy's 1983 book *Ley Lines in Question* remains the only in-depth serious, methodological, and statistical analysis of the Watkinsonian ley phenomenon from an archaeological perspective. This study highlights and, I would argue, convincingly demonstrates a range of problems in the data sets used to identify leys, including poor chronological resolution, selective use of evidence, unsubstantiated claims of prehistoric origins for historic and natural features, and a general lack of awareness of the formation and nature of the archaeological record. Their analysis focused on 350 named and mapped leys from eight key books on the topic including Watkins (1925, 1927), Michell (1969), Screeton (1977) and Devereux and Thomson (1979). They concluded none stood up to archaeological and statistical scrutiny (Williamson & Bellamy 1983, 54-5). There have, since, been useful amelioratory statements on leys from archaeologists such as Ruggles (2005) and Johnson (2006, 50), albeit it the latter merely supportive of 'sympathetic' rather than brusque critique.

Such serious – and measured – scrutiny of leys and ley-hunting by archaeologists is rare however, and where leys are discussed, it is usually in the context of 'alternative archaeology' or pseudo-archaeology, what used to be known unkindly as the lunatic fringe (cf. Fagan 2006; Derricourt 2012; Feder 2017). There has been a gradual change in attitude towards so-called fringe ideas in archaeology since the 1990s, part of a broader post-processual turn in archaeology, with motivations ranging from facilitating alternative voices to be heard and engaged with; looking for synergies, shared interests and useful insights; and a realisation that archaeologists needed to counter dehumanising and racist narratives (such as the alien archaeologies of von Daniken) rather than simply ignore or mock them (Schadla-Hall 2004; Holtorf 2005). Notable examples of this new approach include the broad acceptance of some of the principals of archaeoastronomy in archaeology (Ruggles 2015; Mackie 2021), and dialogue with the Mother Goddess community at Çatalhöyük, Turkey (e.g Meskell 1995).

Such new ways of engaging with 'non-archaeologist' interest-groups did not go uncontested. Renfrew argued that such thinking undermined the empirical and rational underpinning of archaeology, opened the door to 'rampant relativism', and gave equivalency and legitimacy to all manner of extreme views and opinions on the past. This was based on his assertion that aforementioned theoretical developments in archaeology in the 1980s and 90s left, "no criteria with which it could reject the astrological predictions, the ley lines, the chariots of the gods of Other Archaeology" (1989, 34). However, a set of principles outlined by the Lampeter Archaeology Workshop (LAW 1997) countered such arguments based on empirical relativism (the concept that evidence is needed to prove a theory!), and the necessity to weigh-up alternative opinions based on the discipline's internal ethical value system. A simple truth was also contained within the argument of this collective: "supposing the group concerned [such as ley-hunters] simply reject all these arguments and continue to maintain their beliefs...?" (LAW 1997, 171). This happens because different interest groups are often, 'talking past each other' (Rountree 2007). As I have already suggested, this is the case with leys, which are still searched for and studied today despite the empirical and logical dismantlement of the concept by Williamson and Bellamy (1983). Indeed, this book appears to have made little impact, not mentioned at all for instance in later 'ley textbooks' such as Pennick and Devereux's *Lines on the Landscape* (1989). When reviewing *Ley Lines in Question,* Burl (1984, 69) suggested, "ley hunters will not like it, and most will ignore it...", while more recently Williamson himself has acknowledged that, "archaeologists weren't particularly interested, and ley-line people were hostile".* There remains, even today, an impasse in relations.

It is within this tense context that Harry Bell was working in the 1970s through to the 1990s. Biographical information about Bell contained in this book shows that during this time he increasingly engaged with the archaeological community, but at heart it seems he was an alignment hunter much to the well-meaning amusement of his friends (Figure 3). The remainder of this chapter will assess through his writings and research how successful Bell was in straddling these two very different intellectual and fieldwork traditions, both applied to the study of prehistory.

Figure 3: Cartoon gently mocking Harry's relationship with his fellow amateur archaeologists in the 1980s.
(reproduced courtesy of Ian Marshall)

First footsteps

Harry Bell's 1977 book *Forgotten Footsteps* was his first in-depth published study of alignments, with this slim self-published work including the "first chart of Scottish ley-lines ever published" showcasing — as *Glasgow's Secret*

* www.theguardian.com/theguardian/2000/may/13/weekend7.
weekend1

Geometry would also do — his impressive artistic skills. This book is in many ways a straight-down-the-line ley study, presenting Bell's own research into a network of 12 alignments across central Scotland that connect "churches, castles and standing stones" (1977, map). This book was notable for its geographic focus given that – Bell argued – up until then leys had been regarded as "purely an English pastime" (1984, 19). These dozen alignments were regarded as having their origins over 4000 years ago (the Neolithic and early Bronze Age) although the meaning ascribed to these lines in the landscape was a mixture of Watkins-style and earth mysteries interpretations.

In many ways this is an esoteric publication, far removed from mainstream archaeology despite the undoubted archaeological content. Topics of discussion, sometimes framed as musings rather than opinion, includes energy stored in standing stones, psychic abilities of prehistoric people, ESP, and UFOs (Figure 4), while places as diverse as Glastonbury, Tibet and the Nazca lines are mentioned. The book takes as its starting point the Watkins method, but then moves on to consider the potential energy within leys, and how prehistoric and later peoples interacted with this energy. One section discusses the dark-skinned, golden-eyed nature of Neolithic monument builders, although this quickly defers to archaeological evidence on the matter of physicality; however, his vision of Neolithic and Bronze Age folk as peaceful seekers of spiritual enlightenment now seems hopelessly naïve and out-dated.

The book also contains a decent summary account of what we know about Scotland's ancient and more recent past, again with evidence of consultation with recent scholarly work on these matters. This narrative is very much of its time, and there is an emphasis on mystical elements of these cultures. This contextualised the leys that run across central Scotland from Iona to Dundee Law, connecting a host of archaeological sites, historic buildings, and notable natural places. As would also be the case with *Glasgow's Secret Geometry*, these nodes were chronologically all over the place, ranging from genuine prehistoric sites such as Cairnpapple Hill henge, West Lothian; Huly Hill cairn and standing stones on the edge of Edinburgh; and several cup-and-ring marked stones, to castles, churches, and forts both Iron Age and Roman. Some of the landmarks and sites were to become incorporated into the Glasgow Network of Aligned Sites (GNAS) presented in *Glasgow's Secret Geometry*.

This book therefore is very much a mixed bag, with content that contains serious and daft assertions, and a narrative that jumps all over the place. There is no doubt that this is a ley line book, and it seems to me that Bell was formulating his own thoughts on the matter as he wrote. *Forgotten Footsteps* is, however, also an endearing little volume where Bell began to explore his own unique style.

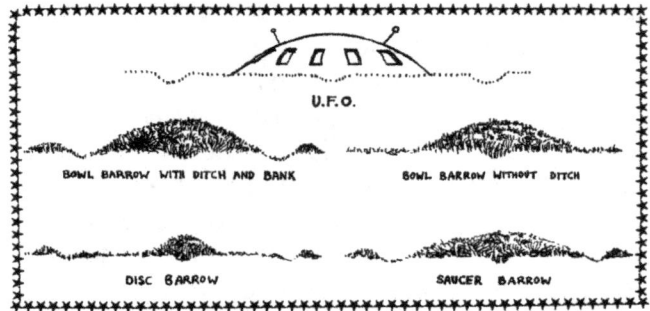

Figure 4: UFOs and barrow similarity: illustration from Forgotten Footsteps (Harry Bell).

Elsewhere in this book it has been argued that Bell's involvement from the early 1980s with the Association of Certificated Field Archaeologists (ACFA) including attending a night class in archaeology at the University of Glasgow, and taking part in formal fieldwork projects, changed or modified his views after *Forgotten Footsteps* had been published. This seems to me very clear when we consider the differences between *Forgotten Footsteps* and his next book on the topic, the ambitious and influential *Glasgow's Secret Geometry*.

An archaeological assessment of Glasgow's Secret Geometry

Glasgow's Secret Geometry (henceforth GSG) is a remarkable book, now a highly sought after collectable. It is a very well written and engaging exploration of Glasgow's recent past and deep time, reflecting a deep love of history and landscape, backed up by extensive research and fieldwork, and it is beautifully illustrated by Bell himself. Here, I want to present the first archaeological assessment of Bell's book, reflecting on the aims, methodologies and results presented therein. Ultimately, GSG is a book that tells us little about the socio-cultural lives of the people who lived in the place we call Glasgow in prehistory, but it is a creative and engaging piece of work.

From the start, Bell's study is situated in the tradition of Watkinsonian ley line fieldwork and research: the aforementioned "old Alfred's instructions" (1984, 2). However, unlike *Forgotten Footsteps*, GSG presents a critical view of ley lines as a concept and avoids, where possible, using the term. Bell felt that leys had become too associated with earth mysteries theories — 'lines of power' — and this did not describe what he was finding in his studies (1984, 4). He came to regard such ideas as "New Age nonsense inspired".[2] He also listed the arguments made by archaeologists against Watkins' leys — their uselessness as trackways, difficulty in surveying in prehistory, and chronological issues. "In the long run it was decided there was too much speculation in

[2] See page 188.

Watkins' work and not enough evidence" (1984, 4). However, he did not rule out alignments as a valid line of research even if the idea did seem "far-fetched" (ibid) and so Bell experimented early on with maps and a ruler using sites he was familiar with. Throughout he was cautious about the potential of coincidence (random unrelated things in lines) although he acknowledged that seeking alignments became an 'obsession' (1984, 16) that saw him go so far as to wallpaper his bedroom with giant maps (Figure 5).

Figure 5: Harry's map-covered bedroom wall.
(Photo courtesy of the family)

The identification of what Bell called PSAs (Prehistoric Site Alignments, not to be confused with Polished Stone Axes, which coincidentally form two points on his alignments) was undertaken via a combination of mapwork, research and fieldwork. Books on Glasgow history and archaeology were poured over to find hints and tips of ancient origins for more recent sites and buildings. Maps were consulted, with features highlighted and lines connected between using ruler and protractor, with four points, fairly closely spaced, the minimum needed to make a PSA.

An interesting element of Bell's approach was his improvised fieldwork. He visited sites, often by bicycle, to both see them for himself but also ground-truth the lines he was identifying on his maps. "The line looked fine on the map, but how did it look in the field?" (1984, 5). Equipment used was basic: 1:25,000 scale maps, prismatic compass, protractor,[3] camera, and in some cases, this involved camping overnight. Bearings were taken to prominent hilltops and viewpoints to confirm map readings or find new leads. Sometimes others went along to help, standing apart in a line to help confirm distant alignments. Some lines were walked to identify new points or test them; here we might recall his words in *Forgotten Footsteps* (Bell 1977a, 20)[4] that "a genuine ley-line followed on foot will soon reveal an amazing amount of unmarked sites". Dowsing was attempted at a later stage of the process but with little success.

[3] Military protractor, calibrated in mils.

[4] See page 78.

Bell's alignments were, he suggested, routeways across the landscape used from the Neolithic period into the Bronze Age, and he also argued, "the early settlements in the Glasgow area could have been laid out in accordance with some geometric plan completely unknown to modern man" (1984, 10). He also called PSAs "prehistoric communication lines" (1984, 25) and suggested they did not exist in isolation but as part of a network – the Glasgow Network of Aligned Sites (henceforth GNAS). Bell pondered if this network was, "designed for settlers, rather than travellers … one of its functions could have been to space settlements out and avoid too many people living off the land in any one area" (1984, 58). This rather mixed bag of interpretations essentially demonstrates that Bell did not really know exactly what his network of alignments was created for, but he was convinced that he had found the handiwork of prehistoric peoples, and this did not relate to energy lines or UFOs.

The eclectic nature of the sites on the alignments is deeply problematic as Bell himself was aware of; he was often told this by archaeologists and friends as he did his fieldwork. He described the points on his alignments as a "mixed bag of castles, churches and cairns" (1984, 25) but the coherence of the PSAs depended on all points on each line being occupied during the Neolithic or early Bronze Age periods (4000-2000 BC). Churches were included using the same logic that Watkins had adopted, that these were likely places of long-term sacred significance and were probably preceded by ancient pagan temples or prehistoric occupation, although as noted above evidence for this assertion is thin on the ground. Natural places were included as they might have facilitated movement in the landscape – hilltops such as Dumgoyne and Duncolm for orientation, and river crossing points and fords.

In preparation for this analysis, I looked at all the sites featured on the GNAS map. The analysis was based on the third and final edition of GSG, published in 1993. In total, 59 places were included on the map on one or more alignment; I have used the names given to each site by Bell (with more commonly used names given in Table 1). For the purposes of this study, I have not included sites named in the text of GSG that were not included on the map e.g. Polnoon Castle, Capelrig Cross, Craignethan Castle, or a 'church in Larkhall'. Nor did I consider other alignments mentioned (Duncolm to Ben Lomond; Tinto to King's Ford via Cadzow fort) which again were not included on the map. Table 1 summarises my understanding of each site based on Bell's own notes and current archaeological thinking, drawing on the National Record of the Historic Environment (NRHE) online portal Canmore*. (The Canmore ID is the number in italics below the site name).There is a fairly even distribution of sites across Bell's study

---

* canmore.org.uk/

Site name	Council	NRHE Class	Notes	Category
Auchendavy Roman Fort 45201	E Dunbartonsh.	Roman Fort	A Roman Fort	Roman
Balcastle Motte 45883	Stirling	Motte (12th-13th C)	Likely a medieval earthwork. Bell notes the discovery of a polished stone axe 400m away.	Medieval
Balmuidy Roman Fort 44476	Glasgow	Roman Fort	A Roman Fort	Roman
Bar Hill Roman Fort 45920	E Dunbartonsh.	Roman Fort	A Roman Fort	Roman
Bothwell Bridge N/A	S Lanarkshire	NA	Bell notes historic tradition of there being a ford here.	Natural feature
Bothwell Castle 44879	S Lanarkshire	Polished axe-head (stone)	Nothing more is known about the date or context of discovery.	Neolithic
Bronze Age burial ground 45068	Glasgow	Burial ground (Period unassigned, Cairn (possible), Urns etc.	Known as Clyde Iron Works in NRHE. Wilson (1863) suggested Bronze Age objects were found in a tumulus.	Bronze Age
Burrell Ringwork 44322	Glasgow	Ringwork	Also called Pollok Park ringwork. Excavations in 2008 suggested this is at the earliest a Medieval enclosure, with some agricultural function. (Driscoll & Mitchell 2008)	Medieval
Cadzow Castle 45740	S Lanarkshire	Castle	A castle, with no evidence on site of earlier activity, although a possible Iron Age fort is located a few hundred metres away.	Medieval
Cairn 43465	W Dunbartonsh.	Burial cairn (Bronze Age)	Known as Auchenreoch Mains. This is a damaged cist, probably Bronze Age.	Bronze Age
Cairn Hill 281293	E Dunbartonsh.	Enclosure (Possible)	Prominent little hill, possible earthwork on top (Welsh 2006) but of unknown date and origin.	Place name

Site name	Council	NRHE Class	Notes	Category
CAMPHILL 44292	Glasgow	Earthwork (Period unassigned)	Enclosure of unknown date, despite several excavations (Fairhurst & Scott 1973). It is possible it is later prehistoric.	Iron Age
Carmunnock Ringwork 44949	S Lanarkshire	Earthwork (Period unassigned)	Also known as Muir. A much-denuded earthwork enclosure on a golf course, could be Iron Age or Medieval.	Iron Age
CARMYLE FORDS N/A	Glasgow	NA	Natural fording point on the Clyde.	Natural feature
Carron Ford N/A	N Lanarkshire	NA	Natural fording point on the Carron.	Natural feature
Castlehead Ringwork 43154	Renfrewshire	Earthwork (Period unassigned)	Nothing left here, at best this was some kind of Early Medieval or Medieval earthwork.	Early Medieval
Castlehill Roman Fort 44510	E Dunbartonsh.	Roman Fort and Possible Roman Fortlet	A Roman Fort	Roman
Castlemilk House 44894	Glasgow	Tower House (Medieval), House	Bell notes that there is historic tradition of prehistoric items being found in vicinity as documented in Old Glasgow Club 1976, 53.	Medieval
Cathcart Castle 44305	Glasgow	Ringwork (Possible), Tower House (Medieval)	A 15th century castle, no evidence of anything earlier here.	Medieval
Cathkin Braes 44909	Glasgow	Cairn (Period unassigned)	Not clear what this site refers to, there are several cairns and possible cairns in the park. Best known is Queen Mary's cairn which was probably Bronze Age.	Bronze Age
Coatshill Bronze Age cist 44860	S Lanarkshire	Cist (Period unassigned)	A single cist with a Food Vessel (Davidson 1940).	Bronze Age

Site name	Council	NRHE Class	Notes	Category
Cochno Stone 44535	W Dunbartonsh.	Prehistoric cup and ring marked stone	Large rock art panel, probably late Neolithic. (Brophy 2018)	Neolithic
Craw Stane N/A	E Renfrewshire	NA	Probably a glacial erratic.	Natural feature
CROOKSTON CASTLE 44400	Glasgow	Chapel (Medieval), Ringwork, Tower House	A castle which has an earthwork component of unknown date and origin.	Medieval
De'il's Plantin 43921	E Renfrewshire	Possible cairn (Period unassigned)	Might be a motte, a natural mound or — unlikely — a prehistoric tumulus.	Early Medieval
Drumduff Hill 43759	E Renfrewshire	Enclosure (Period unassigned)	Watching brief found no evidence of a date for the earthworks here. (Hastie 2009)	Post-medieval
Dumbarton Rock 43376	W Dunbartonsh.	Castle; Possible early medieval fort	Castle, with early Medieval origins in the form of Alt Clut. (Alcock & Alcock 1990)	Early Medieval
Dumgoyne N/A	Stirling	NA	Hill	Natural feature
DUNCOLM N/A	W Dunbartonsh.	NA	Supposed enclosure on top of this hill looks to be nothing.	Natural feature
Dunwan Hillfort 43771	E Renfrewshire	Fort (Prehistoric)	Multivallate hilltop enclosure probably later Prehistoric.	Iron Age
Gallowflat mound 45075	S Lanarkshire	Mound (Roman), Beads (Roman), Patera (Roman)	No evidence this is any earlier than the Iron Age and not clear what type of site it could have been. (see Talbot 1975, 51-2)	Iron Age
Glengarnock Castle 42179	N Ayrshire	Building (Medieval)	14th / 15th C building with associated earthworks.	Medieval
Govan Old Parish church 44077	Glasgow	Burial ground (Medieval) etc	Early Medieval power centre, possible barrow at Doomster Hill nearby.	Early Medieval
Hamilton Motte 45683	S Lanarkshire	Motte & Bailey (Medieval)	Small flat-topped mound, probably some kind of Motte.	Medieval

Site name	Council	NRHE Class	Notes	Category
Harelaw Cairn 44823	S Lanarkshire	Cairn (Prehistoric)	A robbed out prehistoric Cairn.	Bronze Age
King's Park 44364	Glasgow	Enclosure (Period unassigned)	Cropmark enclosure, 12m x 7m, identified by Bell himself. (1977b)	Unknown
Kylepark (Bronze Age urns) 45043	S Lanarkshire	Cinerary Urns, Food Vessel, Human remains	Bronze Age burials disturbed by urban expansion in late 19th Century. (Duncan 1885)	Bronze Age
Lickprivick Tumulus 44979	S Lanarkshire	Mound (Period unassigned)	Flat-topped mound, much interfered by urbanisation, 24m across, more likely a motte than barrow / cairns. Also known as the Greenhills Mound.	Medieval
Mains Castle 44915	S Lanarkshire	Moated site & Motte (Medieval)	Also known as Laigh Mains, this is beside a castle, which presumably replaced it.	Medieval
Meikle Drips 43848	S Lanarkshire	Moot Hill / Mound (Period unassigned)	Mound with stone associated, probably Medieval in origins.	Medieval
NECROPOLIS 45014	Glasgow	Cemetery (19th C)	19th century cemetery. Bell suggests a tradition of ancient use, and Mann called this a 'Temple of the Moon' (1938). No evidence to support this.	Modern
Nether Pollok Castle 44308	Glasgow	Castle (Medieval), House etc	13th C castle on site of Pollok House in bend of a river.	Medieval
Old Kilpatrick Roman Fort 43276	W Dunbartonsh.	Cist (Prehistoric), Cremation (Prehistoric), Food Vessel etc.	Roman fort, but with Bronze Age burials in the same location. (Callander 1930)	Bronze Age
Peel of Drumry 44570	Glasgow	Tower House	Tower House, no evidence of anything earlier.	Medieval
Provan Hall 44985	Glasgow	Laird's House (16th C)	Fancy house, with no evidence of anything early.	Medieval

Site name	Council	NRHE Class	Notes	Category
Renfrew Parish Church *44181*	Renfrewshire	Church (19th century)	An earlier church sat on this site but there is no evidence at all of anything pre-dating this.	Medieval
Ross Hall *N/A*	Renfrewshire		Bell notes, "...many years ago, the vestiges of an ancient British camp were found in the vicinity" (Brotchie 1923, 55) but this is not in the place Bell said it was.	Error
Rutherglen Parish Church *268490*	S Lanarkshire	Church (12th Century), Tower (Medieval)	There may have been an even earlier church, but no evidence of anything before that.	Medieval
Scott's Tourie *43943*	E Renfrewshire	Cairn (Period unassigned)	A robbed-out cairn, probably of Bronze Age date, also known as East Revoch.	Bronze Age
Seedhill Cralgs *N/A*	Renfrewshire	NA	Natural ford. Bell cites tradition that this was used in pre-Roman times but no evidence for this.	Natural feature
Shiels Farm *44173*	Glasgow	Settlement (Period unassigned)	Excavated in 1973-74 (Scott 1974). Earthwork enclosure 42m x 36m, with possible structure inside. Might be an Iron Age settlement site. Unlikely to be a henge.	Iron Age
Shiels of Gartlea *43454*	W Dunbartonsh.	Chambered cairn	Very likely to be a Neolithic chambered cairn, in quite a bad state these days.	Neolithic
St Conval's Chariot *43064*	Renfrewshire	Cross (Period unassigned)	Perhaps the base of a carved cross, but may not be in the original location. Lots of mythology about this site but few facts.	Early Medieval
St Enoch Sanctuary *44301*	Glasgow	Polished Stone axe, Logboat	Stray finds of a polished stone axe and logboat during development, and possible Holy Well tradition. (Mann 1938)	Neolithic

Site name	Council	NRHE Class	Notes	Category
Stanelie Castle *43150*	Renfrewshire	Castle (Medieval)	Fortified house of 15th C date now in the middle of a reservoir.	Medieval
Tinto Hill *47525*	S Lanarkshire	Cairn (Neolithic / BA)	Largest prehistoric cairn in Scotland sits atop this prominent hill.	Bronze Age
Torrance House *44980*	S Lanarkshire	Motte (Medieval)	Mound or promontory enclosure, origins unknown, probably Medieval.	Medieval
Walls Hill *43011*	Renfrewshire	Fort (Iron Age)	Very large multi-vallate hillfort. One flint flake found at some point.	Iron Age
Woodend Loch *45770*	N Lanarkshire	Lithic implements (Stone)	A Mesolithic lithic scatter found on the edge of the loch (Davidson et al 1951). No evidence of later activity here.	Mesolithic

Table 1 — Summary of the sites named on Bell's map showing the Glasgow Network of Aligned Sites. Place names capitalised on the map are also capitalised here. Category refers to my best reasonable guess as to the earliest origins of each place, or the reason why the site was included on the map.

Council area	No. of sites
E Dunbartonshire	4
East Renfrewshire	5
Glasgow	17
North Ayrshire	1
North Lanarkshire	2
Renfrewshire	7
South Lanarkshire	15
Stirling	2
West Dunbartonshire	6

Table 2 — Sites on the Glasgow Network of Aligned Sites, by Council area.

Site category	No. of sites
Mesolithic	1
Neolithic	4
Bronze Age	9
Iron Age	6
Roman	4
Early Medieval	5
Medieval	18
Post-medieval/ Modern	2
Unknown	1
Natural feature	7
Place name alone	1
Included in error	1

Table 3 — Sites on the Glasgow Network of Aligned Sites, by probable age.

area of Greater Glasgow and the Clyde Valley. However, the majority of the 59 sites — 54% — are located in Glasgow and South Lanarkshire Councils (Table 2), while a preponderance of sites is to be found south of the River Clyde (60%) with two further sites being in the river itself (fords at Carmyle and Bothwell). Council boundaries, it should be noted, have no bearing on Bell's work and indeed the current boundaries post-date the first edition of the map and book.

The range of sites chosen to be included on the map as points on the PSAs that form the GNAS has an extremely wide chronological currency spanning some 8,000 years, from the Mesolithic lithic scatter at Woodend Loch, to the 19th century Necropolis cemetery. Of the 59 sites, seven are natural features, and 51 are artificial in some way. (One last site, which Bell named Ross Hall, appears to have been an error on his part, the site referred to being located several hundred metres to the west.) As noted above, he included genuine prehistoric sites but also more recent sites, places, and buildings that he hoped or suspected had deep time origins. Some sites made it into the Network because of the placename alone (Cairn Hill) or due to some historical tradition associated with a relatively modern place (such as Castlemilk House (Old Glasgow Club 1976, 53) and the Necropolis (Mann 1938)). For each of the sites in the GNAS, I have allocated these to a period in the past based on taking back each site as far as it is reasonable to do so, and in some cases I have given Bell the benefit of the doubt. Some of the Iron Age sites may well be later for instance. The results are listed under 'Category' in Table 1, and summarised in Table 3, using a fairly traditional sub-division of time periods. Bell would likely have called the Early Medieval centuries the Dark Ages.

What is remarkable about this assessment is that only four of the 59 sites (7%) are actually Neolithic, the period that the alignments are supposed to date back to. Of these four, two are the findspots for polished stone axes which were both found in the Clyde; it is extremely unlikely that these 19th century findspots represent the place where these axes were deposited in the river. Therefore, only two reliably located Neolithic sites — the Cochno Stone rock art panel, and Shiels of Gartlea chambered cairn – sit on the Network, but even here the former has never been dated (Brophy 2018). Bell himself was puzzled by the inclusion of a Mesolithic lithic scatter on his own alignment, with his fieldwork at this site identifying boulders at the edge of Woodend Loch a weak attempt to find later activity. This is resolutely a Mesolithic assemblage hinting at a nearby hunter-gatherer-fisher camp (Davidson et al. 1951; Finlay 2015). The nine Bronze Age sites (all burials) might reasonably be argued to belong to Bell's alignment tradition and a few of these are cairns that were either excavated or destroyed pre-20th century so might have Neolithic origins that we don't know about. The only 'standing stone' included, the so-called Craw Stane (Figure 6), is likely a glacial erratic and is not included in the NRHE. Taken together, this

Figure 6: The Craw Stane with Ian Marshall and a copy of Harry's GNAS map

seems a weak basis upon which to assign these alignments as far back in time as pre-2000 BC.

In GSG, Bell tries to connect later sites with Neolithic activity, either through noting sites and objects of that period nearby, or falling back on historical tradition drawn from his extensive research. For instance, he records that Neolithic stone axes had been found near Balcastle Motte and Crookston Castle, but as noted above such stray finds are unreliable indicators of the exact location of Neolithic sites or settlements. Some sites are suggested as being possible prehistoric burial mounds or cairns, notably any motte or mound site (there being several in the list), but there is no evidence that the De'il's Plantin (Devil's Plantation) (Figure 7), Lickprivick Tumulus, or Gallowflat Mound, were Neolithic or Bronze Age, although the latter has revealed an assemblage of Roman Iron Age artefacts (Talbot 1975). Historical texts suggesting that there was a prehistoric site at the Necropolis (e.g. Mann 1938) and have no corroboration or evidence. The classic Watkinsonian inclusion of churches on leys is rarely repeated here, with Bell only including two churches, his focus being more on the latent

Photo: May Miles Thomas

Figure 7: The Devil's Plantation — natural knoll, prehistoric barrow, or Medieval motte?

prehistoric potential of mounds, ringworks, and fortified enclosures.

In some cases, Bell appears vindicated in his argument, most notably when discussing Old Kilpatrick Roman Fort, where he speculated "was it possible that a prehistoric site lay underneath?" (Bell 1984, 56). This indeed was the case as he goes on to note, with the discovery of two Bronze Age burials at the fort during excavations in 1923-24 (Callander 1930). But this has not been repeated at any of the other Roman sites included in the Network (four other forts in all). In some cases, fieldwork has taken place after Bell passed away, but very little of this has strengthened his argument. Welsh (2006) recorded some kind of enclosure atop Cairn Hill but it is not a convincing account and this site —if site it is — has no obvious date. Excavations at the Pollok Park (Burrell) ringwork have confirmed this is likely Medieval at earliest and probably associated with agricultural activity (Driscoll & Mitchell 2008) while investigations on Drumduff Hill included excavation of an earthwork which found no dating evidence (Hastie 2009) and we could hazard a guess this is post-medieval. Work at the Cochno Stone in 2015-2016 did not date the site but confirmed its location (Brophy 2018). On the other hand, excavations at Netherton in 2015 in advance of M74 improvements discovered an Iron Age dagger deposited beneath the floor of a post-Medieval building close to Hamilton Motte, with the excavators suggesting this rusty thing was found and deemed to be an ancient object with "special or talismanic qualities" (Arabaolaza et al. 2021, 42); remnants of the prehistoric past continue to be found, transforming our understanding of more recent places.

To summarise, there is no doubt that some of the sites on the GNAS were Neolithic and Bronze Age in origin, and that other sites have the latent but untested potential to be older than they first appear.

However, taken together they are an eclectic and self-selected group of sites that do not coherently suggest they were placed in relation to one another between 4000 BC and 2000 BC. As Bell himself acknowledged, genuine prehistoric sites in the Greater Glasgow area, such as Bronze Age cemeteries found in Victoria Park in 1886 (Gunning 1995) and Greenoakhill quarry, Mount Vernon, in 1928 (Mann 1928) were not included on any alignment, when far less convincing prehistoric examples were. Curiously, the Druid Temple site at Knappers, made famous by Ludovic Mann in the 1930s (Mann 1939), was also not included, despite Bell's admiration for Mann, calling him "a man after my own heart" in GSG (see Brophy 2019 for more on the Mann / Bell relationship). It is also worth noting that were Bell to be working now, he would have a completely different dataset to work with, with hundreds of previously unknown sites found in the region by development-led archaeology, some of them prehistoric sites. So, in Bell's favour, GSG is based on a very incomplete dataset, so we can perhaps forgive his partial representation of Neolithic life.

Creative practice but not prehistory

The archaeological legacy of Bell's work is difficult to assess. There is no doubt that he was poorly treated by professional archaeologists when he, in good faith, sought their advice or opinion. It is amusing to speculate on the identity of the various archaeologists and museum curators that Bell recounts awkward conversations within the pages of GSG. On the other hand, the progression in thinking, and an increasingly critical evaluation of the concept of leys, evident between *Forgotten Footsteps* and GSG, is testament to Bell's deepening involvement with field archaeology through ACFA and the friendship and advice of fellow amateur archaeologists.

Ultimately, in my view, the concept of PSAs, and the GNAS, do not hold up to scrutiny. The Neolithic origin of this network is, at best, unproven, and its reality underpinned by a combination of misguided and wishful thinking, and confirmation bias in research and fieldwork. The use of earthworks instead of churches shows a development from the work of Watkins (these being more likely to have prehistoric pre-cursors than churches) but far too few of the sites are demonstrably prehistoric; a lot of luck would be required for even ten of the sites on the map to be dated back to the Neolithic period in my view.

There is no archaeological evidence that such a network as envisaged by Bell ever existed or would have been needed. The concept of routeways in the landscape has been given some considerable thought in Neolithic studies since Bell's time, with movement linked to pilgrimage, sacred routeways, journeys to and from resources, and transhumance (e.g. see contributions to Leary 2014; Leary & Kador 2016), and mobility across wide geographic areas attested to by stable isotope studies, but none of these require, nor is there evidence for the use of, straight lines. Similarly, we have some sense of Neolithic settlement patterns in lowland Scotland (Brophy 2016), but these are not arranged in geometrical patterns. In the Neolithic, movement between spaces would have had to be navigated in a largely woodland world, with extended views to hills and other landmarks obscured by vegetation (Edmonds 1999), rendering straight lines impractical and near impossible to survey.

However, this is not to dismiss the value of Bell's work and that of other ley-hunters. It is timely that archaeologists reconsider and engage with practices associated with the search for prehistoric trackways and sightline leys. The mapping and fieldwork practices involved have for some time been undergoing a re-evaluation within other disciplines which, like archaeology, have a concern with embodied approaches to interpreting landscape. For instance, Thurgill (2015) has argued that the Watkinsonian school of ley-hunting is a process of 'deep mapping' revealing sensory and spiritual insights into the land, with implications for the practice of cartographers and experimental geographers. He notes, "walking a ley line allows for an intense sense of mobility; a way of revitalising one's connection with the environment" (Thurgill 2015, 649). Following this line of argument, Bell's GNAS might be described as a "deep map...allowing us to explore the contours of narrative and place" (Thurgill 2015, 649) and, I would argue, explore Glasgow's deep time as well (Brophy 2019).

Embodied mapping of this kind requires being on foot, and so ley-hunting accords well with the recent 'walking turn' in the arts and humanities, from subversive urban and industrial exploration (e.g. Edensor 2008; Garrett 2013), to walking as a means of bodily engagement (e.g. Ingold and Vergunst 2008; Solnit 2008). Watkins (1925, 1927) saw walking as vital in his methodology and theories — these were and are lines to be walked, guiding the body and the eye, in the past and the present, and Stout (2008) associated ley-hunting with other countryside hobbies such as hiking. One way of looking at leys is that they in effect allow us to enact walking tours through a lost prehistoric landscape that transcend time and offer radically different ways of experiencing familiar landscapes. Walking is a central, yet strikingly under-played and under-theorised, methodology in undertaking archaeological phenomenological fieldwork (Tilley 1994), and so engaging with leys by walking along them may offer some insight into practices that move between prehistoric sites and monuments in the contemporary landscape. Leys are a means, as Hutton (2009, 323) notes, to enable, "a

sensuous personal relationship with prehistoric sites",
and in this respect, it is prudent to recall Tilley's
(2008, 275) argument that, "to be a good
phenomenologist is to try to develop an intimacy of
contact with the landscape akin to that between
lovers".

Thurgill (2015, 645ff.) walked along a self-
identified ley alignment in Norfolk, an exercise in
deep mapping through bodily movement and sensory
engagement. This process enabled unexpected
encounters, and insights and connections to be made
that would not have been possible from (detached)
mapwork. The walk started as an academic exercise
and became an affective experience, impacting on
the walker, who as he became attuned to his task
began to sense that the path 'unfolded' before him
(ibid., 646). This walk became, as far as I can tell
from the account, an exercise in self-reinforcement,
with discoveries increasingly fitting the narrative of
this being a ley. I have had similar experiences when
walking along a Glasgow city centre alignment
described by both Bell and Mann between St Enoch's
Square and the Necropolis (Brophy 2019). This kind of
experiment accords with psychogeographical
practices which attempt to replicate old (invisible or
obscured) routeways and subvert twentieth century
urban rigidity through mapwork and walking
(Coverley 2010; Richardson 2012). Landscape
engagements such as this can inspire creativity and
different ways of thinking about the past, with no
need to accept any kind of reality of leys in
prehistory; these are ways to think with our feet.

Such alternative strategies for re-imagining,
reconstructing, and trying to make sense of past
activities in our contemporary landscape (the only
setting within which we can study prehistory) are of
a piece with the ideas of Watkins, who despite
himself, appears to be in the process of becoming re-
evaluated as something of a figure ahead of his time

regardless of the acknowledged flaws in his logic. The aesthetic quality and simple elegance of his approach to lines in the landscape have been celebrated by artists such as Richard Long and Hamish Fulton (Daniels 2006). Others have argued that Watkins' background in photography informed the visual component and aesthetic of his view of landscapes and allowed him to manipulate images to give the impression of the rural past in the industrial present (Daniels 2006; Charlesworth 2010). It is perhaps no coincidence that Harry Bell was also gifted in the visual arts. In this respect, then, practices and imagery associated with leys can and should be considered as relevant to any discipline that has an interest in landscape history and mapping as a means to make sense of our engagements with the past in the present including archaeology.

Conclusion

In a letter sent to Bell in 1977 by TC Welsh, himself an 'amateur archaeologist' who has had challenging relationships with professionals, the advice was, "at all costs avoid lining up or linking sites unless you are absolutely certain".[5] Bell's books leave the reader in no doubt — he was certain that he was right. Yet the power of coincidence can lead one to ascribe more conviction to something than it deserves; in preparation for writing this chapter I realised that one of Bell's alignments passed right by the house I grew up in in Larkhall, and Bell even visited a local church that I went to from time to time, as it was bang on this line. Excavations at one of only two Neolithic sites on the Network — the Cochno Stone — were directed by me. I have written elsewhere (Brophy 2019) about the convincing experience of playing with maps and rulers. This is not proof however of anything other than that any of us can be seduced by information bias and pareidolia.

[5] See page 330.

Yet the history of relationships between ley hunters and archaeologists shows us that despite disciplinary differences, there is much in common between those searching for Watkinsonian leys and prehistoric archaeologists. Both groups (and some as with Harry Bell would characterise themselves as belonging to both categories) share an interest in the ancient past, and have a deep respect for the intellect, capabilities, and agency of prehistoric people. Moreover, those who search for ancient routeways and tracks, and archaeologists, share common fieldwork practices, from using maps, note-taking and photography, to ground-truthing fieldwork and the use of surveying equipment. Excavation was even proposed by Watkins as a means by which to find leys: in *The Ley hunters Manual* (1927, 71-2) some brief notes and guidance were offered on how to find tracks and confirm mark-stones by digging, and he carried out his own basic excavation at the Queen Stone, Herefordshire (Burl 1993, 161). Bell carried out his own walkover survey work, prospection, and research, which in some cases discovered possible new sites, such as an enclosure in King's Park (Bell 1977b), and he was involved in many traditional archaeological surveys in his ACFA days. The discovery of previously unknown sites, often deep in the undergrowth, is noted by Michell (1982 [2007], 118) as a side benefit of following leys wherever they might take you.

In the course of my research for this chapter, I plotted a line that had been so significant to Bell, a personal journey for him that connected up many dots in ways that made perfect sense for him. One does not need to align oneself to his outcomes to admire what he did to get there. My own disciplinary expertise and experience has led me to reach a very different conclusion to Bell about the veracity of his Network. But by doing as Bell did — accepting areas of convergence and mutual understanding between the core and periphery of archaeology — appears to me to be a means by which we can move the debate on from repeated impasse. The example of Harry Bell, who stuck to his convictions but abandoned UFOs, and was pragmatic enough to adopt alternative methodologies and critical thinking, should be an example of the creative power of keeping an open mind.

Acknowledgements

I would like to thank Grahame Gardner for allowing me to contribute to this book and for the conversations we have had about leys over the years. Many thanks also to Ian Marshall for allowing me access to Harry Bell's archival materials and taking me to see some of the Eaglesham sites. Gordon Barclay commented on earlier versions of part of this text, but the final version is all down to me, warts and all. Finally, thanks for some last-minute help from Francis Young.

Kenneth Brophy is a senior archaeology lecturer at Glasgow University. In 2015-2016, he directed the full-scale excavation of the Cochno Stone. He maintains an active presence on social media as The Urban Prehistorian.

Bibliography

Alcock, L & Alcock, EA 1990 Reconnaissance excavations on Early Historic fortifications and other royal sites in Scotland, 1974-84, *Proceedings of the Society of Antiquaries of Scotland* 120, 215-87.

Arabaolaza, I, Baillie, W, Cross, M, Ferguson, N & Mooney, K 2021 *The road to rediscovery: Netherton Cross during the M8, M73, M74 Motorway Improvements 2014-15.* Archaeological Reports Online 41: GUARD Archaeology Ltd.

Barber, M 2016 Capturing the Material Invisible: OGS Crawford, Ghosts, and the Stonehenge Avenue. *Bulletin of the History of Archaeology* 26(1): 6, 1-23.

Bell, H 1977a *Forgotten Footsteps.* East Kilbride: Ley-line Publications.

Bell, H 1977b Glasgow, King's Park, enclosures. *Discovery and Excavation in Scotland* 1977, 17.

Bell, H 1984 / 1998 *Glasgow's Secret Geometry*. 1st edition / 3rd edition. East Kilbride: Leyline Publications.

Brophy, K 2016 On ancient farms: Neolithic settlement in mainland Scotland, in Brophy, K, Ralston, IBM and Macgregor, G (eds) 2016 *The Neolithic of mainland Scotland*, Edinburgh University Press, pages 200-235.

Brophy, K 2018 'The finest set of cup and ring marks in existence': the story of the Cochno Stone, West Dunbartonshire, *Scottish Archaeological Journal* 40, 1-23.

Brophy, K 2019 Glasgow's occult ancient geometry: the obsessions of Ludovic McLellan Mann and Harry Bell. In Hing, R, Malkin, G, Silver, S & Paciorek, A (eds) *Folk Horror revival: Urban Wyrd volume 2 Spirits of Place*. Wyrd Harvest Press. Pages 57-80.

Brotchie, TCF 1923 *The Borderlands of Glasgow Tramway Guide to The Countryside around the City*. Aird & Coghill Ltd. Glasgow, 55

Callander, G 1930 Prehistoric graves in the Roman Fort at Old Kilpatrick, Dumbartonshire. *Transactions of the Glasgow Archaeological Society* 8.2, 55-61.

Charlesworth, M 2010 Photography, the Index, and the Nonexistent: Alfred Watkins' Discovery (or Invention) of the Notorious Ley-lines of British Archaeology, *Visual Resources* 26:2, 131-145.

Crawford, OGS 1953 *Archaeology in the field*. London: Phoenix House.

Coverley, M 2010 *Psychogeography*. Harpenden: Pocket Essentials.

Daniel, G 1970 Editorial. *Antiquity* 44 (175), 169-74.

Daniels, S 2006 *Lines of sight: Alfred Watkins, photography and topography in early twentieth century Britain*, *Tate Papers* No. 6, (www.tate.org.uk/research/tate-papers/06/lines-of-sight-alfred-watkins-photography-and-topography-in-early-twentieth-century-britain)

Davidson, JM 1940 Bronze Age burials at Blantyre and Milngavie, *Transactions of the Glasgow Archaeological Society 9.4*, 305-8.

Davidson, JM, Phemister, J & Lacaille, AD 1951 A Stone Age site at Woodend Loch, near Coatbridge, *Proceedings of the Society of Antiquaries of Scotland* 83, 77-98.

Derricourt, R 2012 Pseudoarchaeology: the concept and its limitations, *Antiquity* 86 (332), 524-531.

Devereux, P and Thomson, I 1979 *The ley hunters companion. Aligned ancient sites, a new study with field guide and maps*. London: Thames and Hudson.

Driscoll, ST & Mitchell M 2008 Pollok North Woods, Glasgow (Eastwood parish), excavation. *Discovery and Excavation in Scotland* New Series 9, 89-90.

Duncan, JD 1885 Note regarding cinerary urns recently discovered at Uddingston. *Proceedings of the Society of Antiquaries of Scotland* 19, 337-40.

Edensor, T 2000 *Walking in the British countryside: Reflexivity, embodied practices and ways to escape, Body and Society* 6.3-4, 81-106.

Edmonds, M 1999 *Ancestral geographies of the Neolithic*. London: Routledge.

Fairhurst, H & Scott, J 1963 The earthwork at Camphill in Glasgow. *Proceedings of the Society of Antiquaries of Scotland* 85, 146-56.

Fagan, GG 2006 *Archaeological fantasies. How Pseudoarchaeology Misrepresents the Past and Misleads the Public*, London: Routledge.

Feder, KI 2017 *Frauds, Myths, and Mysteries: Science and Pseudoscience in Archaeology*, Oxford University Press.

Finlay, N. 2015 The Mesolithic in Keo, T. (ed) *Essays on the Local History and Archaeology of West Central Scotland*. Glasgow: Culture and Sport Glasgow (Glasgow Museums). Pages 31-48

Garrett, B 2013 *Explore Everything: place-hacking the city*. London: Verso.

Grinsell, L 1986 The Christianization of Prehistoric and Other Pagan Sites, *Landscape History* 8, 27-37.

Gunning, A 1995 *The Fossil Grove*. Glasgow.

Hastie, M 2009 Whitelee Wind Farm, Eaglesham, excavation and watching brief, *Discovery and Excavation in Scotland* New Series 10. Pages 63-64.

Hauser, K 2008 *Bloody Old Britain: OGS Crawford and the Archaeology of Modern Life*, London: Granta.

Holtorf, C 2005 Beyond Crusades: how (not) to engage with alternative archaeologies. *World Archaeology* 37.4, pages 544-51.

Hutton, R 2009 Modern druidry and earth mysteries. *Time and Mind* 2.3, 313-332.

Hutton, R 2014 *Pagan Britain*. Yale University Press.

Ingold, T and Vergunst, JL (eds) 2008 *Ways of Walking: ethnography and practice on foot*, Ashgate.

Johnson, M 2006 *Ideas of Landscape*. London: Wiley-Blackwell.

Lampeter Archaeology Workshop 1997 Relativism, objectivity and the politics of the past, *Archaeological Dialogues* 4.2, 164-198.

Leary, Jim (ed.) 2014 *Past Mobilities : Archaeological Approaches to Movement and Mobility*, Taylor & Francis.

Leary, J & Kador, T (eds) 2016 *Moving on in Neolithic Studies: Understanding Mobile Lives*, Oxbow Books.

Lethbridge, TC 1972 *The legend of the Sons of God*. Arkana.

MacFarlane, R 2014 Introduction (to reprint of A Watkins [1925] *The Old Straight Track*). Head of Zeus.

Mackie, E 2021 *Professor Challenger and his lost Neolithic world: the compelling story of Alexander Thom and British archaeoastronomy*. Archaeopress.

Mann, LM 1928 Bronze age colony: its manner of life. *The Glasgow Herald*.

Mann, LM 1938 *Earliest Glasgow: a Temple of the Moon*. Glasgow.

Mann, LM 1939 *The Druid Temple Explained* (4th edition). London and Glasgow.

Meskell, L 1995 Goddesses, Gimbutas and 'New Age' Archaeology. *Antiquity*, 69 (262), 74-86.

Michell, J 1969 *The View over Atlantis*. London: Abacus.

Michell, J 1982 [2007] *Megalithomania. Artists and antiquarians at the old stone monuments*. The Squeeze Press.

Old Glasgow Club 1976 *Places and Characters of Old Glasgow*. Glasgow.

Pennick, N and Devereux, P 1989 *Lines on the Landscape. Ley lines and other linear enigmas*. London: Hale.

Pryor, F 2001 *Seahenge. New Discoveries in Prehistoric Britain*. London: Harper Collins.

Renfrew, C 1989 Comments on archaeology in the 1990s, *Norwegian Archaeological Review* 22, 33-41.

Richardson, T (ed.) 2012 *Walking inside out: contemporary British psychogeography*. Rowan and Littlefield.

Ritchie, G 2002 Ludovic McLellan Mann (1869-1955): 'the eminent archaeologist', *Proceedings of the Society of Antiquaries of Scotland* 132, 43-64.

Rountree, K 2007 Talking Past Each Other: Practising Multivocality at Çatalhöyük, *The Journal of Archaeomythology* 3 (www.archaeomythology.org/publications/the-journal-of-archaeomythology/2007-volume-3/2007-volume-3-article-6/).

Ruggles, C 2005 Ley Lines. *Ancient Astronomy: An Encyclopedia of Cosmologies and Myth*, Bloomsbury.

Ruggles, C (ed.) 2015 *Handbook of archaeoastronomy and ethnoastronomy*. Springer.

Russell, M 2001 *Rough quarries, rocks and hills. John Pull and the Neolithic flint mines of Sussex*. Oxford: Oxbow Books.

Schadla-Hall, T 2004 The comforts of unreason: the importance and relevance of alternative archaeology, in Merriman, N (ed.) *Public Archaeology*, 255-71, London: Routledge.

Scott, JG 1974 Govan, Shiels, ditched enclosure, *Discovery and Excavation in Scotland* 1974, 82-3.

Screeton, P 1977 [1974] *Quicksilver Heritage. The mystic leys: their legacy of ancient wisdom*. London: Abacus.

Solnit, R 2000 *Wanderlust: a history of walking*, New York: Viking.

Stout, A 2008 *Creating Prehistory: druids, ley hunters and archaeologists in pre-war Britain*. Oxford: Blackwell.

Talbot, EJ 1975 Early Scottish castles of earth and timber – recent fieldwork and excavation. *Scottish Archaeological Forum* 6, 51-2.

Thom, AS 1995 *Walking in all of the squares: biography of Alexander Thom, engineer and archaeoastronomer*. Argyll Publishing.

Thurgill, T 2015 A strange cartography: leylines, landscape and 'deep mapping' in the works of Alfred Watkins, *Humanities* 4.4., 637-52.

Tilley, C 1994 *A phenomenology of landscape*. Oxford: Berg.

Tilley, C 2008 Phenomenological approaches to landscape archaeology, in David, B & Thomas, J (eds) *Handbook of Landscape Archaeology*, pages. Leftcoast Press. Pages 271-6

Watkins, A 1925 *The Old Straight Track*. London: Methuen.

Watkins, A 1927 *The Ley hunter's Manual. A guide to early tracks*. London and Hereford.

Wood, ES 1963 *Collins Field Guide to Archaeology in Britain*. London: Collins.

Williamson, T and Bellamy, L 1983 *Ley Lines in Question*. Tadworth: The World's Work Ltd.

Wilson, D 1863 *Prehistoric Annals of Scotland* volume 2. London.

MANN, MYTH, AND MUNGO

LUDOVIC MANN, HARRY BELL, AND GLASGOW'S SECRET GEOMETRY* — A PSYCHOGEOGRAPHIC EXPLORATION OF 'THE STRAIGHT ROAD WITH NO PATH'

Grahame Gardner

The enigma that is Ludovic McLellan Mann casts a lengthy temporal shadow down through the decades. One of the "most original and significant figures of early Scottish archaeology" (Ritchie 2002), his ideas regarding prehistoric astronomy and metrology were never adequately explained in his writings, leaving subsequent researchers struggling to make sense of his extraordinary claims. He held some highly individual views on the history and layout of Glasgow, as detailed in his treatise *Earliest Glasgow — a Temple of the Moon*, where he imagined Glasgow laid out on a clock-face style grid centred on the Necropolis by some prehistoric geographer (Mann 1938, 10-11; Brophy 2019).

The image of Mann posing on his inventively painted Cochno Stone cup-and-ring marked stone, West Dunbartonshire, is well-known (see Brophy 2018, Figure 4) and has captured the imagination of

* Originally published in the Scottish Archaeological Journal 42 Supplement, October 2020

many researchers ever since. Where does this grid come from? What does it mean? Unfortunately Mann found few adherents to his belief that the Cochno Stone was a star map of the Glasgow area, as hinted at in *The Druid Temple Explained* (Mann 1939), or that there was a total solar eclipse in Glasgow in 2983 BC, six days after the spring equinox at 3pm in the afternoon (Glasgow Herald on 17 September 1930), so his theories remain largely unexplored today. Yet there is no denying the publicity value of a painted Cochno Stone in boosting his reputation and attracting visitors to the site (Brophy 2018, 7).

Someone who later connected tangentially with Mann's work was Harry Bell, an amateur researcher into alignments in Scotland (e.g. Bell 1977, 1984). He was an enthusiast of Alfred Watkins' work on leys (e.g. Watkins 1925, 1927), and saw some echo of Watkins' alignments in Mann's idea of a Glasgow grid. In his 1984 work *Glasgow's Secret Geometry*, Bell documents his search for alignments in the area, culminating in his discovery of what he believed to be the earliest mention of a road or track in the Glasgow region, a passage in Jocelyn's *Life of Kentigern* describing the route taken by the young saint on his

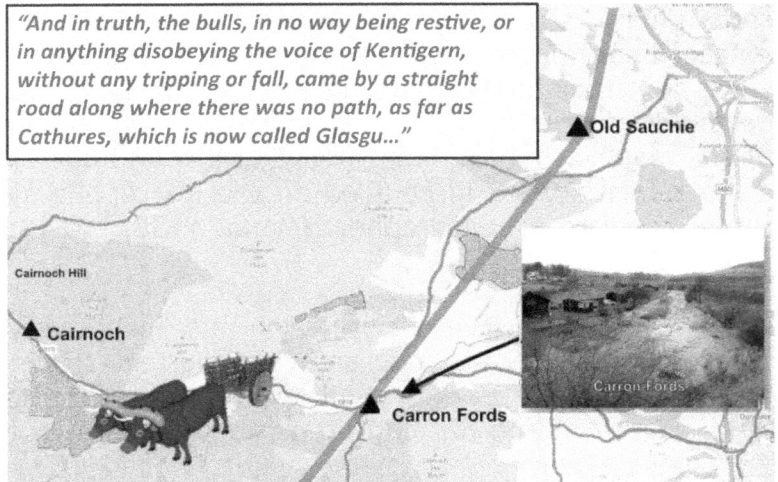

"And in truth, the bulls, in no way being restive, or in anything disobeying the voice of Kentigern, without any tripping or fall, came by a straight road along where there was no path, as far as Cathures, which is now called Glasgu…"

Figure 1: The 'straight road with No Path'.

journey to Glasgow with a pair of oxen pulling a wain carrying the body of the holy man Fergus (Figure 1): "And in truth, the bulls, in no way being restive, or in anything disobeying the voice of Kentigern, without any tripping or fall, came by a straight road, along where there was no path, as far as Cathures, which is now called Glasgu ..." (quoted in Bell 1984, 20).

Bell was convinced that this meant a ley, and this became a primary alignment in his schema of the Glasgow Network of Aligned Sites. During fieldwork, he tried to locate the Cochno Stone on another alignment from Duncolm to Tinto Hill, unaware that the stone had been buried in 1965 to protect it from damage (Brophy 2018). Bell did eventually plot such an alignment from Cochno to Tinto, but unlike the Duncolm line it missed running through the Necropolis, the central node point in Bell's network.

Ludovic Mann was also interested in Kentigern's story. In *Earliest Glasgow*, he claimed that Kentigern was the initiated head of a Druidic lunar cult centred on the hillfort of Dun Chattan, better known nowadays as the Glasgow Necropolis. His justification for this theory seems based on some questionable Gaelic etymology. He breaks down 'Kentigern' into Caen-Tigh-Ern, which he translates as 'Head (of the) House (of the) Moon' (Mann 1938, 12). Kentigern's mother was St Tenew, Tenau or Thenew, from which we get St Enoch (St Enoch is a corruption of her name). In medieval times, Glasgow had a holy well and chapel dedicated to her in the vicinity of St Enoch's Square, her supposed burial site, and two later churches graced the site until 1926. Trongate and Argyle Street were known as St Thenew's Gait until around 1540, when it was a simple country road leading to her chapel and well (Macintosh 1902, 47).

To fully understand Mann's interest in Kentigern, we need to look at the 'mythtory' of his origins. His mother Tenew was the daughter of King Lot or

Lleuddn, who gave his name to the Lothians. Lot was head of the Gododdin people, whose main base of operations was the hillfort of Traprain Law in East Lothian. Mann equates Lot with the god Lugh, who he claims was a lunar deity (Mann 1938, 5), despite most other historians placing him as a sun god. Philip Coppens, for instance, claims that Traprain Law was once a centre of sun worship, based on his discovery of the 'Lothian Line', an alignment running through Arthur's Seat in Edinburgh to Cairnpapple Henge in the Bathgate Hills, West Lothian. Both Traprain and Cairnpapple are almost exactly 30 km equidistant from Arthur's Seat and the alignment is east-west, so a person standing on Arthur's Seat at the spring or autumn equinoxes could witness the sun rising over Traprain Law and setting over Cairnpapple (Coppens, P 2007) (Figure 2).

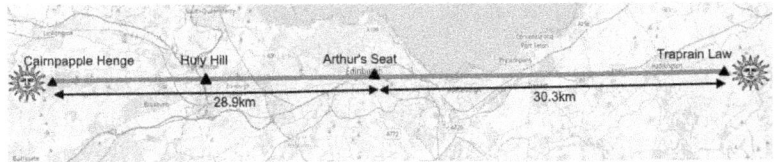

Figure 2: The Lothian Line.

The story goes that Urien, the king of Rheged, was visiting King Lot accompanied by his son Owain, with the intention of brokering a marriage contract with Tenew. However, she was not in favour of the idea, and so her affronted father banished her from the hillfort to live with the common folk below, where she worked in the fields as a shepherdess. Owain, besotted with her beauty, tracked her down and raped her, causing her to become pregnant. As she was unmarried, her furious father condemned her to death and had her thrown from the cliffs of the Law.

Miraculously surviving the fall, she was taken to Aberlady, East Lothian, on the Firth of Forth, where she was cast adrift in a coracle and left to her fate. Yet rather than drift out to sea, thanks to the intervention of the sea-god Manannan, whose magical crescent-shaped boat 'Wavesweeper' was given to him by Lugh, she instead made her way upriver, eventually making landfall at Culross, Fife, where there was a monastic community under the leadership of St Serf. There she gave birth to Kentigern, who was brought up within the community and given the pet name Mungo, meaning 'dear one', by St Serf.

By the age of 25, Kentigern had acquired a respectable tally of miracles, (many of these are told pictorially on the Glasgow coat of arms), such as bringing a robin that was beloved of his master back to life. He decided to leave the monastery to seek his fortune or, as more cynical commentators have claimed, he was bullied into leaving by his resentful fellow students who were jealous of his favoured status. But how did he get to Glasgow? Without resorting to a risky boat crossing of the Forth, the most logical place to get across the river is just upstream of Stirling Castle, near the confluence with the River Teith. From there, he could proceed in a south-westerly direction through the Campsie Hills.

For Harry Bell, his 'straight road along where there was no path' began at Old Sauchie, an ancient settlement south of Stirling, before proceeding directly towards Carron Ford and over the hills in the direction of Glasgow. On the skyline above the Ford there is a clump of Scots Pines, which are often found marking ley alignments, and thought to have been deliberately seeded by cattle drovers to mark their routes (Figure 3). This was once the main route between Stirling and Kilsyth and is part of a network of ancient drove routes in the area.

On the way, Kentigern is said to have visited a holy man named Fergus who, on his deathbed, had expressed a wish to meet and pray with the young boy-priest. Fergus lived in a place called Kernach or Carnock, which various commentators have placed in

[1] See page 115.

diverse locations over southern Scotland. Bell placed it somewhere east of the settlement of Old Sauchie (1983, 23 map)[1], yet there is a hill and a settlement named 'Cairnoch' that appears on old OS maps about 1.2km west of Carron Bridge, which seems a far more likely candidate to me (see Figure 1). 'Cairnoch' (Caer Cnoc) basically means 'Castle Hill' in Gaelic, so it is a common enough place name.

Marker trees?

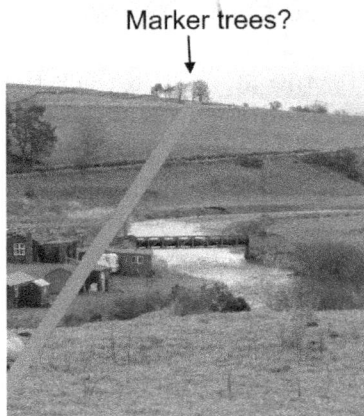

Figure 3: The 'straight road' from Carron Ford — Note the Scots Pines on the skyline.

Having placed the body of Fergus on a wain yoked to a pair of oxen, Kentigern proceeds along the 'straight road with no path' towards Glasgow. Today, the route roughly follows the Tak Ma Doon Road to Kilsyth, but Bell's next stop is Balcastle Motte, North Lanarkshire. This is said to have been constructed by the Earls of Lennox in the 12th Century (Bell 1983, Glossary), yet Bell reports that a Bronze Age polished stone axe was found nearby, right on the line of the alignment, implying a much older use of the site (1983, Glossary). From here, with good visibility it is possible to see Glasgow's Necropolis and Duncarnock hillfort, East Renfrewshire, on the skyline beyond (another 'Carnock' place name).

After this, the antiquity of Bell's sites on this line becomes more questionable. His alignment passes through Auchendavy Roman fort, East Dunbartonshire, on the Antonine Wall. Little remains of this fort, but five Roman altars were found here, one of which was dedicated 'to the Spirit of the British countryside', a reference to the genius locus. The final site on Bell's 'straight road' before reaching the Necropolis is the Wallace Monument in Robroyston, Glasgow, which marks the location of the house where Wallace often stayed and was ultimately betrayed to the English. Although there seems no direct connection with Kentigern, the monument is positioned right on the alignment. Nearby is Wallace's Well, where the great hero would presumably have refreshed himself.

The end point of this line is the Necropolis and cathedral area. The Necropolis is believed by some to be the site of an ancient Druid temple, Dun Chattan. Hugh Macintosh, in his *Origin and History of Glasgow Streets* (1902, 20) writes: "In ancient times, anterior to our ecclesiastical history, a Druidical place of worship stood on the site of the present Necropolis...".

The central node point of Bell's network is situated, not at the highest point where the John Knox statue is, but farther south on the shoulder of the hill, near to the Monteath mausoleum and above the now-capped Lady Well, which pre-dates the city itself and was the last public well to be closed following the opening of the Loch Katrine aqueduct in the 1860s. Other significant wells in the area include St Mungo's well, which is now enclosed in a corner of the cathedral crypt, and the Priests' well, which used to be located on the banks of the Molendinar Burn adjacent to the Bridge of Sighs but is now hidden beneath a drain cover. Another important city well previously mentioned is St Tenew's well, dedicated to Kentigern's mother and located near what is now St Enoch's Square.

Ludovic Mann placed great importance upon this latter location, calling it a 'sanctuary' and writing that, "the spot was chosen because it lay at a vital locus within the spider's web" (Mann 1938, 11) referring to his clock-face geometry. In a feat of impressive etymological juggling, he manages to equate Thenew, by way of Tennay/ Tenau to Danu, the hypothetical Celtic Mother-Goddess of the Tuatha De Danann. Not much is known about her, but she does have some associations with water and rivers (the Danube is thought to be named after her), and was also associated with the moon according to Mann:

> *She was descended from the Mother Moon, Danu, whose tribe was the Tuatha de Danann, and, it would seem probable, far-off cousins of Diana. An immaculate mother and water-goddess, she gave birth to Kentigern in a crescent boat (Mann 1911, 5).*

You will recall that the 'crescent boat' was Wavesweeper, given to Manannan by Lugh himself.

On this somewhat shaky edifice, Mann builds his theory of the moon cult centred on Traprain Law under the aegis of King Lot/ Lugh, connecting it with Kentigern's final destination in Glasgow:

> *The Calendric datings of Lug show that he was of the family of the Moon and was not a Sun-god as usually stated ... To the Celt he was monarch of the outstretched 'silver-hand' and was 'Lug of the Long Arm.' His bow, like a curved golden thread, was spread against the dark heavens like the gliding and shining wings of a bird ... He made the rivers to bend into his own shape and the shores of the seas and lochs to twist into bays, and so to encircle his sanctuaries. And this he did at Glasgow... (Mann 1938, 5).*

Mann's insistence on this lunar connection contrasted with Coppens' solar equinoctial Lothian Line prompted me to wonder if there were similar astronomical links relating to Bell's alignments at the Glasgow end of Kentigern's tale. Extending Bell's 'straight road' from the Necropolis takes it through Camphill Earthwork in Queen's Park, another significant node in Bell's network. The azimuth of this line is 212°, which I discovered is the azimuth of the major southern standstill moonset at this latitude. Observers on the Necropolis would see the standstill moon setting over Camphill and Duncarnock hillfort. Does the existence of this lunar connection therefore support Mann's claim that Kentigern was the head of a lunar cult? Referring to the Necropolis/Dun Chattan, Mann says:

> At Glasgow the lunar temple was placed on the rising ground nearest to the apex on the river's bend and above the flood plain. (1938, 2).

Also consider the tale of Kentigern's journey to Glasgow, following the two oxen along the 'straight path'. The crescent-shaped horns of the oxen naturally link the animal to moon symbolism. Mann again:

> Among emblems of moon-worship were a rounded bay, a river-loop, a staff with a hooked handle, and the crescentic horns or tusks of an animal, and at times the animal itself. (1938, 9).

Then there is the lunar symbolism of Manannan's crescent-shaped boat and Tenew's shepherds' crook in the tale, both suggestive of a lunar connection; we might also consider Tenew's fall from the cliffs of Traprain Law as an allegorical indication of a significant solar or lunar alignment.

So, it seems plausible that there may be some kernels of astronomical truth embedded as allegory in Kentigern's story. There are certainly other significant astronomical orientations from the Necropolis that are marked by Bell's network — his alignment to Bar Hill Roman Fort, East Dunbartonshire, which he claimed was the Druid sanctuary of Medionemeton (Bell 1977, Robb 2013, 50-53) marks the summer solstice sunrise, with the sunset occurring behind

Duncolm in the Kilpatrick Hills, a site that Bell felt was worthy of further archaeological investigation. Tinto Hill, South Lanarkshire, another 'Druid' site with its Bronze Age cairn, marks the winter solstice sunrise, and the cross-quarter day sunrise at Imbolc/Samhain occurs in the direction of Bothwell Castle and Hamilton Motte (Figure 4).

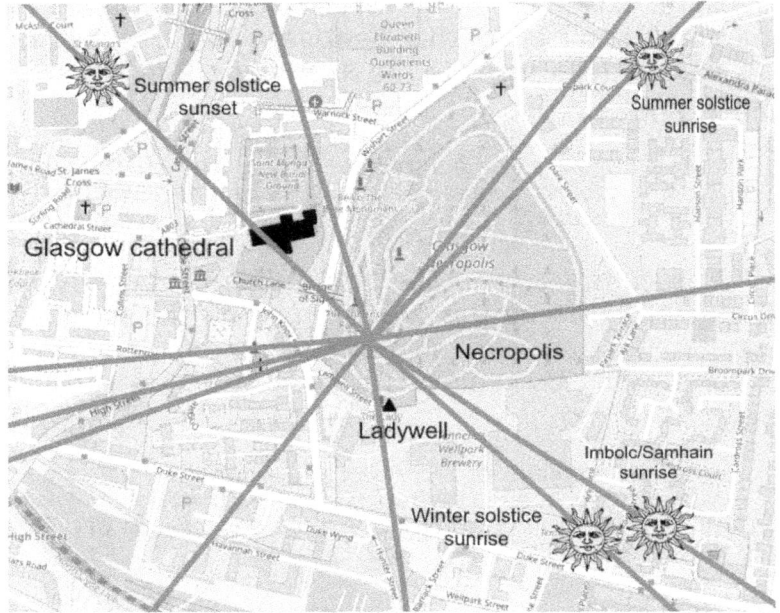

Figure 4: Necropolis alignments.

I also decided to test Mann's theory of the clock-face grid against Bell's alignments. If there was any truth to Mann's idea, then we should expect some correspondence:

> *The Neolithic philosopher and astronomer laid out the Glasgow area on a plan similar to that of a clock-face and like a gigantic spider's web, but rigorously geometrical. Its radii, usually set on a nineteenth divisional system (sub-divided at times into 38ths and 76ths), dictated the positions, and ran through loci, of prehistoric importance. (Mann 1938, 11).*

Overlaying a radial grid of 19 divisions immediately shows a general correspondence with at least four or five of Bell's alignments (Figure 5); if we increase the radials to 38 than another three or four would align. It is not perfect by any means but, given the vagaries of my own mapping of Bell's network, I think it is close enough to suggest that Mann was indeed on to something with his idea of the radial geometry.

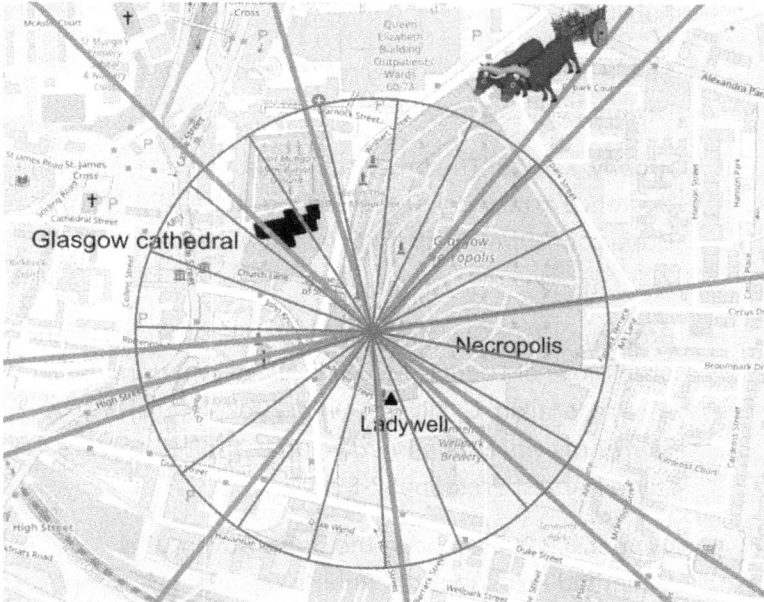

Figure 5: Mann's 19-radial grid overlaid on Bell's network.

Yet other questions remain. Was Kentigern really the head of a lunar cult, as Mann claimed? Is Kentigern's life story actually a veiled astronomical parable? Are there other Celtic saints with similar astronomical connections? I feel there may be a whole new area of research opening up here!

Geomancy is about defining our relationship with landscape and place. The weave and overlay of historical data, folklore, psychogeography, geometry, astronomy and so on, creates a multi-layered, multidimensional picture that enables us to work with and within the landscape, enhancing our connection with the Spirit of Place and revealing novel means of interaction with our consensual reality. I hope that this essay has left you with a fresh appreciation of the numinous landscape that is all around us.[*]

Bibliography

Bell, H 1977 *Forgotten Footsteps*. East Kilbride: Leyline Publications.

Bell, H 1983 *Glasgow's Secret Geometry*. East Kilbride: Leyline Publications.

Brophy, K 2018 'The finest set of cup and ring marks in existence': the story of the Cochno stone, West Dunbartonshire. *Scottish Archaeological Journal* 40, 1–23.

Brophy, K 2019 Glasgow's occult ancient geometry: the obsessions of Ludovic McLellan Mann and Harry Bell. In Hing, R, Malkin, G, Silver, S & Paciorek, A (eds) *Folk Horror revival: Urban Wyrd* volume 2 *Spirits of Place*. Wyrd Harvest Press, pp57-80.

Coppens, P 2007 *Land of the Gods*. Adventures Unlimited Press/Frontier Publishing, p95.

Mann, LM 1938 *Earliest Glasgow. A Temple of the Moon*. Glasgow and London.

Mann, LM 1939 *The Druid Temple Explained*. Glasgow.

Macintosh, H 1902 *Origin and History of Glasgow Streets*, Citizen Press. p20

Ritchie, JNG 2002 Ludovic McLellan Mann (1869-1955): 'the eminent archaeologist'. *Proceedings of the Society of Antiquaries of Scotland* 132, 43–64.

---

[*] You can watch a video presentation of this article at youtu.be/e5eaGiCiSGo

Robb, G 2013 *The Ancient Paths,* London: Picador 2013, pp50-53

Watkins, A 1925 *The Old Straight Track*. London: Methuen.

Watkins, A 1927 *The Ley Hunter's Manual. A guide to early tracks.* London and Hereford.

Searching for alignments in Carnac.

GAZETTEER OF SITES

This section contains details of all the sites listed by Harry in *Forgotten Footsteps* (FF), *Haunted Castles* (HC), *Glasgow's Secret Geometry* (GSG), and *Leyline Quest* (LQ). It also includes additional sites and alignments added from my own research (*shown in italics*). You can see all the sites and alignments on the map page at glasgowsecretgeometry.uk/map/

The numbers in italics below the National Grid References refer to the site reference number on canmore.org.uk

Abbotsford Parish Church (now called Waterfront Church) NS 498701 *196664*	Harry says this is "probably a coincidental alignment". He also cites a possible low-tide ford over the River Clyde near here as an alignment point. In days before the river was dredged to allow shipping, monks from **Paisley Abbey** were thought to ford at this point. The late John McMillan, who was a painter in John Brown's Yard, put forward the name *Abbotsford* in recognition of this.
Abbey Craig NS 810957 *74628*	Hillfort that is now the site of the Wallace Monument. Canmore records it as 'Early Medieval', yet a worked stone flake found just inside the rampart at the back of the Wallace Monument in 1984 suggests a more prehistoric occupation of the hill.
Abercorn Castle (site) NT 080792 *49136*	"Remains of a low motte are visible in the trees. The site is near stage nine on the Nature Trail from **Hopetoun House**. **Bridgeness** and **Blackness Castle** can be seen in alignment from the nearby promenade." (FF) The castle was a stronghold of the Black Douglas, which was captured and partially destroyed during a four-week bombardment by James II in 1455.

It has been suggested that the castle occupied the site of an earlier Roman fort, one of a supposed chain of forts between Cramond and the Antonine Wall. However, no Roman finds have been found to support this claim.

Aikenhead House
NS 59602
162873

Once a museum in King's Park, Glasgow. Now closed. Harry may be referring to another site near here, not the house itself. See also **King's Park**.

Ardnahoe Fort
NS 066574
40242

The remains of a small promontory fort are situated at the edge of the escarpment forming the old shoreline SW of Ardnahoe. Not mentioned by Harry but fits neatly on his Bute ley between **Dunburgidale** and **Holy Island**.

Ardoch Rig
NS 627467

A site mentioned in Harry's *Leyline Quest* website as the termination of an alignment extending along the Humbie Road to **Pollock Castle House**.

Argyll Stane/ St Conval's Chariot
NS 495678
43064

"Beside St Conval's Chariot stands the Argyll Stone, a sandstone pedestal thought to have formed the base of a Celtic cross erected in honour of St Conval. The pedestal became known as the Argyll Stone after an incident in 1685, when the Duke of Argyll was captured as he rested there after crossing the ford." (GSG)

Tradition has it that the 6th century St Conval was resting on the stone, considering founding a new church, when the stone floated out to sea, carrying him across the Irish Sea and up the Firth of Clyde before depositing him at Renfrew. St Conval then went on to found his church at the confluence of the Black Cart and White Cart waters at Inchinnan *(cf. Inchinnan All Hallows church)*. Pilgrims and sick people were said to drink the rainwater that gathered in a hollow on the top of the stone, believing it to have healing properties. Judging by the wear on the moss covering most of the stone, this tradition continues today. The hollow on the stone seems too shallow to have supported a cross-shaft, so it is likely that this stone is the real St Conval's Chariot.

Both stones were moved to their present location some time before 1836 when the land now occupied by the Normandy Hotel formed part of Blythswood Estate.

Arns Tomb
NS 805755
302174

Shown on the map as 'Tomb (uncertain origin)', but not mentioned in the text or the gazetteer of *Forgotten Footsteps*.

Canmore describes it as a 19th century burial enclosure. Arns was part of a larger estate, based just 650m to the south at Garbet, owned by the Melville family and it is assumed that it is their family burial ground.

Arrochymore Dun
NS 412919
43482

The remains of a dun about 17m in diameter occupy a rocky knoll 350m NW of Arrochymore Farmhouse. Not mentioned by Harry but clearly on the **Duncolm** to **Ben Lomond** alignment.

Arthurlie Cross
NS 499585
43006

The cross is thought to have stood in Cross-stane Field on the Arthurlee estate, but by 1785 it was being used as a bridge over a burn in the field. Around 1870 it was erected in the grounds of Arthurlee House on a contemporary base, and sometime prior to 1942 it was moved to its current position. The original site is believed to have been at NS 497581.

Not mentioned by Harry, but on an alignment between **Neilston Pad** and **Crookston Castle**.

Arthur's Seat
NT 276728
52561

"A hill in the King's Park, Edinburgh, crowned by the scarcely visible remains of a prehistoric fort with an estimated area of 20 acres. Hundreds of visiting exiles responded to its ley-line magic and climbed the summit to see the sunrise during the 1977 International Gathering of the Clans." (FF)

Hill fort defences are visible round the main massif of Arthur's Seat at **Dunsapie Hill** and above Samson's Ribs, in the latter cases certainly of prehistoric date. These forts are likely to have been centres of power of the Votadini, who were the subject of the poem *Y Gododdin*, which is thought to have been written about 600 AD. Two stony banks on the east side of the hill represent the remains of an Iron Age hillfort and a series of cultivation terraces are obvious above the road just beyond and best viewed from Duddingston.

Auchendavy Roman Fort
NS 677749
45201

"Syrian bowmen were once stationed here but there is not much visible now, as the fort was partly destroyed in the building of the Forth & Clyde Canal and the Kirkintilloch-Kilsyth road. During the construction of the canal (1771), five Roman altars were found. One was dedicated *Genio Terrae Brittanicae*, 'To the Spirit of the British Countryside'."(GSG)

Auchendavy is the only known Antonine Wall fort to have never been excavated. The fort is now mostly covered by buildings and a car park and there are no visible remains of the fort on the ground.

Auchenreoch Mains
NS 432803
43465

A cairn on Dumbarton Muir that was certainly visited by Harry, extending a putative alignment through **Duncolm** on the map of *Glasgow's Secret Geometry*. This is a Bronze Age burial cairn on the slopes of the 'Hill of Standing

Stones'. The cover stone has been removed, and a fencepost inserted within the cist. One of the sides and the foot of the cist is broken up and used as packing for the post.

Auchentorlie House
NS 494635

"According to Knox's plan of Paisley (1839 revised edition), Auchentorlie House was built on a knoll or mound. This structure, however, proved untraceable." (GSG)
Noted by Harry in the text as it falls on the alignment between **Seedhill Craigs** and **Camphill**, but he could find no other historical information about the site.

Balcastle Motte
NS 701781
45883

"Fashioned out of a natural knoll at the junction of the two streams on the lower slopes of the Kilsyth Hills, this motte is believed to have been erected by the Earls of Lennox in the 12th century. The structure was originally called *Kevisith* (Kilsyth), a name later transferred to the 15th century castle. A polished stone axe was found at Braehead Farm 400m away, right on the line of the 'Straight Road with No Path'"(GSG)

Baldoukie
NO 467588
33697

The remains of a tumulus and souterrain, now much reduced by cultivation.

Balmuildy Roman Fort
NS 581717
44476

"Scarcely visible remains of a fort that guarded a crossing of the River Kelvin. This fort pre-dated the Antonine Wall, and it has been suggested that native traffic crossed the frontier at this point." (GSG)
Nothing of the fort is visible on the ground today, but traces of the ditch and outer mound are visible in the field east of the farm buildings on the north side of Balmuildy road. Balmuildy was one of only two forts on the Antonine Wall which had stone ramparts, rather than turf. Excavations have revealed several buildings, including the headquarters, two granaries, the commanding officer's house, barracks and workshops. The fort was constructed and probably garrisoned by soldiers of the Second Legion. A building inscription was found here, featuring the name of Lollius Urbicus, the general and governor of Britain who was responsible for the construction of the Antonine Wall.

Bardowie Castle
NS 578737
44505

Not part of Harry's alignments, but an interesting alignment through **Paisley Abbey** to **Stanlie Castle**. Bardowie Castle consists of a tower, evidently completed by 1566, and additions made from the late 17th or early 18th century onwards; the latter are still inhabited as a modern mansion.

Bar Hill Roman Fort
NS 707759
45920

The highest fort on the Antonine Wall. The fort is unique along the Antonine Wall as it is not directly connected to the line of the wall, but is set back about 30m to the south, with the military way running between the fort and the rampart of the wall. A well and the foundations of the bathhouse are well preserved.

Bar Hill (Castle Hill)
NS 709761
45919

Harry speculated that this is the site of the "lost Druid sanctuary" of Medionemeton, which was situated midway between the Forth and Clyde, a theory supported by Graham Robb in *The Ancient Paths* (2013), who notes that **Bar Hill** is exactly in the middle of the Antonine Wall.

In 1895, An altar to Silvanus, with a separate stone plinth, was ploughed up on **Castle Hill**. The altar, now in the Hunterian Museum, Glasgow, is 1m in height, and a translation of its inscription reads: 'Erected to the God Silvanus by Caristanius Iustianus, Praefect of the first cohort of Hamii, in willing payment of a vow.' It may have formed part of a small shrine, either on the Castle Hill itself, or beside the military way.

Barrack Street
NS 603651
45020

A heavy deposit of oyster shells was found there during housing development in 1982, giving rise to speculation that the area was inhabited in Mesolithic times.

The street is named after an 18th century military barracks that used to occupy the site. Evidence of earlier 17th/18th century pottery works and other early industries were found during excavation in 2011.

Beechmount House
NT 212731
130571

Beechmount House, a loosely classical mansion built in 1900 to designs by John Watson, was bequeathed to the Royal Infirmary of Edinburgh in 1926 and opened as an auxiliary hospital c. 1928. The hospital was transferred to the National Health Service in 1948 and latterly was used as a convalescent home mostly for elderly patients. It closed in 1989-90 and returned to private ownership.

Harry notes that the ley site is just outside the hospital wall to the NE on the south shoulder of Corstorphine Hill.

Ben Cruachan
NN 069304

Mentioned in Harry's *Haunted Castles* as one end of a ley from **Dunstaffnage Castle**.

Ben Lomond
NN 367028

"One of Scotland's best-known mountains. The cairn at the top doesn't look prehistoric, but who can say when the mountain was first climbed and for what reason?" (FF)

Ben Lomond is the most southerly Munro (mountains over 3,000ft/914m), at 3,193ft/974m. Being close to Glasgow, it's one of the most popular hill-walks in Scotland.

Berrymoss Wood NO 397489 *285814*	A linear cropmark that is suggestive of a possible souterrain (underground passage), N of Ballindarg Burn, has been recorded on oblique aerial photography.
Black Law NS 464501 *43017*	Iron Age hillfort and volcanic plug. The ridge aligns to May Miles Thomas' 'The Secret' alignment.
Blackness Castle NT 055802 *49519*	"A 15th century castle built in the shape of a ship. In the Middle Ages, Blackness was the third most important port in Scotland." (FF) Built in the 15th century by one of Scotland's most powerful families, the Crichtons, Blackness was never destined as a peaceful lordly residence; its enduring roles were those of garrison fortress and state prison. Two burials, thought to be Bronze Age, containing cremated remains were found when digging a ditch on the crest of the ridge which has the castle at its far end. One grave contained an adult and child, the other two adults accompanied by a food vessel.
Blairlogie Castle NS 827969 *47163*	On the alignment between **Stirling Castle** and **Dumyat**. Originally consisted of a small tower, erected by Alexander Spittal in 1543, and a wing added in 1582. Both tower and wing are two storeys and an attic in height.
Boclair Roman Fortlet NS 568725 *44485*	A Roman interval-fortlet would be expected at the southwest angle of the Antonine Wall on Crow Hill; however, trenching in 1961 revealed only the stone base of the Wall.
Boghall roundhouse NS 678992 *45346*	A Late Prehistoric ring-ditch house was identified from crop markings. There is a larger ring-ditch enclosure a few metres to the north. A putative alignment from **Doune Cross** to **Duncryne**, although there are few sites across the marshy terrain to mark this alignment.
Bogle Stane NS 336736	A glacial erratic made of whinstone, at the top of the Clune Brae. It measures about 3m x 3m with a maximum height of 1m. Bogles in Scots myth were mischievous spirits, and the Bogle Stane was once the supposed abode of a bogle who used to hide behind it and scare folk. The local minister, tired of this superstition arranged to have the stone blown up, with the remains used for curling stones and dykes. Before the minister destroyed the stone it was said to have been nearly 4m tall.

Bonhill Bronze Age cemetery
NS 393793
42372

"A Bronze Age burial site on the banks of the River Leven (see PSAS 1943/4 pp128-9)" Harry mentions this in the text but doesn't elaborate on its name or location. (GSG)
Bonhill is mentioned in a charter of 1225 giving the monks from **Paisley Abbey** fishing rights on the east bank of the River Leven at the Linbrane pool. The village of Bonhill itself featured an early church and a ford across the River Leven on the drovers' road to Glasgow. Several cists of Early Bronze Age type containing human remains without urns have been found in Strathleven Sand and Gravel quarry.

Bonnyton Mound (De'il's Plantin)
NS 557535
43921

On the Humbie Road between Newton Mearns and Eaglesham; the peace now shattered by the Southern Relief Road. The site Harry chose to begin his research.
This cairn appears to be largely undisturbed suggesting that archaeological information is likely to survive beneath its surface. Two depressions in the top of the mound are said to have been dug by two labourers c. 1900 at the behest of the local laird.

Bothwell Bridge
NS 710577
45690

"Scene of Monmouth's defeat of the Covenanters in 1679, but the bridge spans an ancient ford." (GSG)
On the 22nd June 1679, a Royalist army on the north of the river, commanded by the Duke of Monmouth. bombarded the bridge and the Covenanter army, who were encamped at Hamilton. While the Covenanters were still preparing for battle, Monmouth's forces crossed the bridge and advanced, throwing the Covenant forces into disorder. Around 1,200 men surrendered immediately, and the rest fled.

Bothwell Castle
NS 687593
85621

"A ruined 13th century castle on a steep bank above a bend in the River Clyde, where a stone axe was once found." (GSG)
Bothwell Castle guards a strategic crossing point of the Clyde and played a key role in Scotland's Wars of Independence, changing hands several times.

Bowdenhill Fort
NS 977745
31283

A contour fort, 3/4 mile from **Cockleroy**.
This prehistoric fort is situated on Bowden Hill, where in 1791 the minister reported in the Statistical Account that there were "some remains of a circumvallation and rampart....nearly 200 yards in diameter".

Braehead Enclosure
NS 525664
44189

The Braehead enclosure was fully excavated in 2001 and was found to be a prehistoric ditched and palisaded enclosure. measuring approximately 76m x 60m. The enclosure included at least four roundhouses and several pottery and stone artifacts were found.

Until at least the 18th century, the site was an island in the River Clyde, called King's Inch (a name that is preserved in the name of the road that bisects the site).

Bridgeness Roman Fort
NT 014816
49567

"At the eastern end of the Antonine Wall. No visible remains. A fortlet is believed to have stood on the site now occupied by Bo'ness Tower." (FF)

The location of the eastern terminus of the Antonine Wall has been an unresolved matter ever since the Venerable Bede described the Wall around AD 730. Although various locations have been suggested, including **Abercorn**, Carriden, and Kinneil, the 1868 discovery of the Bridgeness Distance Slab confirmed that the Wall must have reached at least as far as the eastern end of Bo'ness. The original Distance Slab is now located in the National Museum of Scotland in Edinburgh. (antoninewall.org)

Bronze Age Burial Ground, Clyde Iron Works
NS 638623
45068

"I learned that a Bronze-Age burial ground was found in 1836 during construction of an iron works at NS 63856235, less than a mile from the fords, and precisely on my **Duncolm/ Tinto** line." (GSG)

What appears to have been a Bronze Age burial ground was uncovered during the construction of the Clyde Iron Works. An 1836 excavation found "two cinerary urns filled with ashes, two bronze bridle bits, and various other relics, supposed to have formed portions of horse furniture", but it is not certain that the bronzes were associated with the urns. (Canmore)

Bronze axehead found
NS 530616
44372

A flat bronze axehead was found in material apparently dredged from the River of Cart in the angle between Brockburn and Barrhead Roads, Pollokshaws. It was acquired for Glasgow Art Gallery and Museum.

Bronze axehead (Kilmacolm)
NS 350689
42252

An Early Bronze Age flat axe measuring 106mm by 63mm, now in the British Museum. A cast of it was exhibited in Glasgow in 1911, on loan from Ludovic McLellan Mann.

Buchlyvie Fairy Knowe (Broch-rems)
NS 585942
44651

Close to postulated **Doune Cross** to **Duncryne** line. Some human bones encased in a cist were found in 1796. Excavation in 1976 discovered remains of a broch constructed over an earlier wooden roundhouse, possibly 1st century AD.

Occupation of the broch was associated with Roman artefacts including bronze coins, pottery and glass.

Burrell Ringwork
NS 555624
44322

"There are two ringworks in Pollok Country Park, and this one, a semi-circular part-obliterated bank of earth, lies in the woods about 300m N of the Burrell Collection (See D&E 1973)". (GSG)
Not to be confused with the **Pollok Earthwork** to the north.
The site is part obliterated. It comprises a semi-circular earthen bank 180' (55m) in diameter, open towards the S, and varying in width from 12' - 30' (3.6-9m), with an inner ditch 20' - 30' (6-9m) wide. (Canmore)

Cadzow Castle
NS 734537
45740

"This area was settled centuries before the castle came into existence, because in St Mungo's day there was a King of Cadzow known as Rhydderch Hael. The castle itself has no known prehistoric connections, but the remains of an Iron Age hillfort lie some 300m to the south." (GSG)
The castle itself possibly dates from the 12th century, but most (if not all) of the present ruin is of a tower house of 1540, with outbuildings and a courtyard, also dating from the 16th century. It is an early example of a castle built to withstand artillery, probably built by James Hamilton of Finnart as with his castle at **Craignethan**.

Cadzow Earthwork (Chatelherault hillfort)
NS 734534
45727

"Possible Iron Age promontory fort listed in the Lanarkshire Inventory (1978)." (GSG)
During 1989 excavations a silver denarius of the Emperor Marcus Aurelius was found.

Cairn Duff
NS 420451
42922

The remains of this turf-covered cairn are situated on a prominent hill crest. Cairn Duff was almost entirely removed about 1810. It was a large mound of stones covered with grass and trees. Three urns containing cremated human bones were found in it.

Cairn Hill
NS 543709
281293

"I was unable to find information about any cairn that this hill could have been named after. At the time of my visit, Cairn Hill was a wasteland of thorny bushes that conspired to rip my casual attire...Roman coins were found in nearby Stirling Avenue in 1950." (GSG)
A possible earthwork enclosure was recorded at the top of Cairn Hill during field work by TC Welsh. The site is located on a strip of overgrown land between 2 housing estates. Two banks were noted, around 3-4 metres in width and with a possible ditch alongside. The area enclosed is around 80m x 50m and the banks are rounded at the corners. A stony area, possibly the remains of a cairn, was noted in the NW area of the enclosure.

Cairnpapple Hill
NS 987718
47919

"Archaeologists will see a cairn, stone circle and enclosing ditch dating back to 2,500 BC. Ufologists will see a perfect replica of a flying saucer made with the only materials readily available to primitive man, earth and stones. Don't miss this one!" (FF)

Henge & tumulus, regarded as the most important mainland archaeological site in Scotland. The 'cairn' is actually a concrete dome erected after the 1947 excavations to protect the cist burials inside. The main cist contained the body of a woman wearing a carved wooden mask and offerings including a grooved beaker, now in the National Museum in Edinburgh. Cairnpapple was a centre of worship and burial for over 3000 years. First the burial ground, then a henge of 24 large stones, and then an enormous cairn; in all five phases of ritual burial and cremations, with concentric rings of pits, ditching and banking. One theory suggests a continuity of use over 5,000 years that started with the henge and later burials before moving to the original chapel and then the subsequent Preceptory in Torphichen. There is certainly evidence that suggests a link between the cup-marked sanctuary stone in the kirkyard at Torphichen and a stone unearthed at Cairnpapple.

Philip Coppens records an equinox alignment between Cairnpapple and **Arthur's Seat**.

Camphill Ringwork
NS 577621
44292

"On many old maps of Glasgow, Camphill is marked as a 'Celtic Camp'. Yet for some reason, generations of school children were taught that it was a Roman fort. Later re-classified as medieval, yet shards of Roman Samian ware pottery have been recovered from the eroding bank... it looks as if the site was in use centuries before the ringwork was built." (GSG)

In his later website *Leyline Quest*, Harry records that "the latest archaeological survey, by the Association of Certificated Field Archaeologists (Glasgow University) in 1996, now describes Camphill as 'an earthwork of uncertain date and purpose, perhaps from the late prehistoric period, with some evidence of re-use in the medieval period...'"

Canongate Kirk
Edinburgh
NT 265738
52356

The Canongate Church, or Kirk, is a post-reformation building of great ecclesiastical and historical significance to the City of Edinburgh. Opened in 1691, its plan by James Smith is unique among 17th century Scottish churches. A set of antlers of a deer sit atop the gable; these are real antlers, renewed from time to time.

The kirk is the parish church for the **Palace of Holyroodhouse**, the official home of the British Monarch in Scotland, which explains the Royal pew at the front of the church and the military colours hanging over the nave. The churchyard contains the remains of many famous Scots, including economist Adam Smith, poet Robert Fergusson, and Mrs Agnes McLehose (Burns's Clarinda).

Capelrig Cross (site)
NS 545575
43906

"This 10th century cross is now in Glasgow Art Galleries, where it was taken to protect it from the elements." (GSG)
All four faces of the cross-shaft bear traces of relief carving, in each case consisting of two panels of interlace ornament within plain flat-band frames.
The boulder base is plain apart from a small incised cross.

Carlin Craigs
NS 546520
43967

On top of a small rocky crag, some 15 small cups were located on one or two natural rocks. There are many water-worn fissures in association, but no trace of rings or other artificial markings. The features may be authentic, or merely weather-worn cavities.(Canmore)

Carmunnock Ringwork
NS 613577
44949

"Circular ditch with slighted rampart on the 13th green of Cathkin Braes Golf Course." (GSG)
in 1997, when the Association of Certificated Field Archaeologists were doing an archaeological survey of **Cathkin Braes** Country Park, an aerial photograph of the ringwork showed an additional smaller enclosure joining onto the north-east side of the ringwork. (*"This is almost certainly a prehistoric burial..."* p16 Glasgow Archaeological Bulletin, No. 36)

Carmyle Fords
NS 646614
351047

"Two fords, 300m apart. The West Ford, where the Kirk Burn joins the Clyde (under a bridge) has been known as King's Ford and Thief's Ford. The East Ford has no known history. It looked like an excellent place for fording the river." (GSG)
The 1st edition of the OS 25-inch map (Lanark 1864, Sheet XI.1) depicts a ferry crossing on the River Clyde at Carmyle. Canmore records it at the east ford location.

Carron Ford
NS 743837
45983

"This ancient ford lies a stone's throw to the east of Carron Bridge (first built on the old Kilsyth-Stirling road 1695, and rebuilt many times)." (GSG)
"Named 'Carronfoorde' on Timothy Pont's 17th century map.
The ley crosses the river where the stones protrude from the water to the east of the present bridge." (FF)
The alignment from **Bar Hill** continues to **Stirling Castle**.

Carse Grey
NO 462538
33744

Three stones situated in the wood near to Carse Gray mansion house. They are said to be Druidical remains. According to Harry, these are situated on a ley between **Glamis** and **Finavon** Castles. The remains appear to represent a later prehistoric settlement comprising surface houses and souterrains or semi-subterranean storage buildings.

Castlehead
Ringwork
NS 474633
43154

"Described in the Paisley Burgh Survey of 1980 as 'a postulated Norman ringwork of earth and timber.' On private land." (GSG)
There is a possibility that the remains could be of Iron Age provenance, according to Canmore.

Castlehill Roman
Fort
NS 524727
44510

"On the Antonine Wall. No visible remains, but a circle of beech trees roughly marks its position. There may be both a fort and an earlier fortlet on the site (GAJ 7 pp80-84). Pottery sherds have been found here in the roots of fallen trees, but little remains above ground to tell the story of the past. Eighteen hundred years ago the 4th Cohort of Gauls guarded the Antonine Wall at this point." (GSG)
The existence of a Roman fort on Castlehill was indicated by the discovery of an altar in 1826 and a column capital in 1847.

Castle Law
(Dumyat)
NS 832973
47117

Castle Law on the shoulder of **Dumyat** is essentially similar to a number of neighbouring Early Iron Age forts whose walls contain vitrified material (e.g. **Abbey Craig**) This is one of two forts that stand on hills bearing a placename derived from the ancient tribal grouping of the Maeatae (Watson 1926, 59, 100). (Canmore)

Castlemilk House
(site)
NS 607597
44894

"Demolished 1970, but low walls can still be seen. Prehistoric remains have been unearthed in the vicinity, including a black oak boat keel (Places and Characters of Old Glasgow, 1976 p53)." (GSG)
Castlemilk estate was the largest property in the parish of Carmunnock. The house was the ancestral home of the Stirling-Stuart family and was built around the 15th century Cassiltoun Tower during the 18th and 19th centuries. The house and Castlemilk Estate were purchased by Glasgow Corporation in 1938, with the house serving as a children's home until it was closed in 1969 and demolished the following year.

Cathcart Castle
(rems.)
NS 587600
44305

"15th century castle demolished in 1980 following a partial collapse." (GSG)
The castle is around 100m north of the alignment.

Cathkin Braes
NS 614584
44919

"An excellent viewpoint. four Bronze Age burial cairns have been found in the vicinity, but their stones were removed for dyke-building during the 19ᵗʰ century." (GSG)
Site of a cairn listed on Canmore, close to the trig point.

Cist, Duntocher
NS 488726
43263

A 'stone coffin' containing human remains was found about 1817 in the second field to the east of the Ocean Field. The skull was for a long time in the office of the Milton Mill, but its present location is not known (Canmore).

Cleddans Roman Fortlet
NS 508722
44555

Not mentioned by Harry, but on his **Torrance House** to **Duncolm** PSA. A Roman fortlet that predates the Antonine Wall which abuts it at the north-east corner at a sharp angle. The north-west corner had been much disturbed by ploughing but the Wall would have joined it some way south of this angle.

Clochoderick Stone
NS 373612
42329

A glacial erratic 'logan' (rocking) stone, reputedly once used for Druidic justiciary purposes; supposedly the burial place of King Rhyderrich Hael of Strathclyde.
The name is supposedly a corruption of *'Cloch o' Druid'* - i.e. the Druid's Stone.

Clune Wood
NO 794949
36696

Occupying a low rise in a grass-grown clearing within the southern margin of Clune Wood, this recumbent stone circle stands side by side with a ring-cairn in a position that before the trees grew up commanded extensive views out across lower Deeside.

Coatshill Cist (site)
NS 683584
44860

"A Bronze Age cist containing a food vessel was found on this site in 1939. The site is right on the **Duncolm/Tinto** PSA." (GSG)
The food vessel, now in Glasgow Art Gallery and Museum, was standing upright near the centre of the cist.

Cochno Stone
NS 504738
44535

"This 13m by 8m outcrop of rock is adorned with 90 sets of cup and ring marks, 110 cup marks, 2 four-toed footprints, a ringed cross and several other features. In spite of its great size, I could not find the Cochno Stone anywhere. Unknown to me, the Department of Environment had covered it with a metre of soil to protect it from vandalism." (GSG)
One of the most significant rock art panels in Scotland, the Cochno Stone was fully excavated in 2016 by Glasgow University archaeology students under the direction of Kenneth Brophy. The surface was fully scanned with photogrammetry and LIDAR. The stone was then reburied. It is hoped that a replica can be created at some point.

Cockleroy fort
NS 989745
48000

"Surrounded by a ruined wall 130m by 65m. Accessible from a minor road 1.5 miles south of Linlithgow." (FF)
The gap between the two summits of Cockleroy is known as Wallace's Cradle or Wallace's Bed where there were ancient remains of a late Bronze Age / Iron Age fort. This is said to be where William Wallace took rest. It is claimed that Wallace watched Edward I's forces from here as they made camp on their way to meet Wallace's army at Falkirk. A stone arrowhead was discovered nearby.

*Cowdon Hall
(rems.)*
NS 466571
43009

Not mentioned by Harry, but on the **Walls Hill Fort** to **Craignethan Castle** PSA.
Stands on a prominent hillock overlooking the Levern Water.
Probably a 17th century laird's house and farmstead with 18th century additions, although a building may have stood on or near to the site prior to the seventeenth century as indicated by the name 'Kouden' that is recorded on Timothy Pont's Renfrewshire map that dates from between 1583 and 1596.

Craigie Fort
NS 416909

"On the West Highland Way, above the Pass of Balmaha. No visible remains of any fortification. From the subsidiary summit, **Duncryne** and **Duncolm** can be seen lining up in the distance. Now part of the West Highland Way." (FF)
The highlight of the trail is the wonderful view from Craigie Fort. This fort once formed a large enclosure around the summit of the hill. However, little remains today of the ancient site. This is still an incredible place to visit, as you can look out over Loch Lomond and its islands and can even admire the view of **Ben Lomond** in the distance.

Craigmarloch Wood
NS 341723
75473

Canmore records this as 'enclosure (period unknown)'. A roughly rectangular turf and stone walled foundation, the W wall with a gap at its S end. The wall spreads c. 2m to 3m to enclose an area c. 6m square, but the inner NW corner is rounded due to inward expansion.

Craignethan Castle
NS 815463
46563

"A Bronze-Age flanged axe was found here. Open to the public. 5m SW of Lanark." (GSG)
Craignethan is built on an imposing site above a bend in the River Nethan. The castle comprises a low central keep, within a rectangular walled courtyard. To the west is a deep ditch and beyond, a larger outer courtyard.

Craig of Todholes
NS 312647
42333

"Ley Line Publications have asked for a site in this area to be investigated." (FF)

Harry gives no indication of any significance to this site. There is a rectangular structure several metres to the south that may be what he intended as the location.
Canmore records two oval enclosures, 30m apart, on the SW hilltop at NS 312648.

Crathes Castle
NO 734968
36693

The castle bears the dates 1553, 1554 and 1596. It was built for the Burnetts of Leys who received the charter for the land from Robert the Bruce in 1323. Within the castle is held a jewelled ivory horn, the Horn of Leys, which is said to have been presented to Alexander Burnett by the Bruce when he received the charter.
This castle is haunted by a ghost referred to as 'The Green Lady'. A publication in 1900 described it as an "apparition of a lady dressed in green, with a child in her arms". It is said that 'The Green Lady' was once a servant girl who worked in the castle who fell pregnant out of wedlock – by who we don't know, but perhaps is the reason why she fled the castle. 100 years later in the 1800s, workmen were repairing the castle and uncovered the skeletal remains of a woman and a child beneath the hearthstone of the fireplace.

Crathes Pit
Alignment
NO 737966
36671

Canmore records a series of five aligned pits, excavated in 2004 and thought to be Mesolithic, running from NE to SW and the remains of a rectangular Early Neolithic timber structure.
The find was analysed in 2013 and is considered to be the world's oldest known lunar calendar dating from 8000 BC to about 4000 BC. This dating would make the structure up to five thousand years older than previously recorded time-measuring monuments in Mesopotamia.

Craw Stane
NS 545523

"...this stone could occupy the site of a robbed-out Bronze-Age burial cairn." (GSG)
It's probably a glacial erratic, but its high position caused Harry to choose it as a sighting point on the **Devil's Plantation** to **Woodend Loch** alignment.

Crookston Castle
NS 525627
44400

"Remains of a 15th century castle on the site of a castle built by Robert de Croc in the 12th century (hence Croc's Toun)." (FF)
"A stone axe found in the vicinity was presented to Paisley Museum in 1952." (GSG)
Harry speculates that the site might be prehistoric, although no archaeological evidence has been found to support this hypothesis.

The castle is the second oldest remaining building in Glasgow, after **Glasgow Cathedral**. Sir John Stirling-Maxwell presented the Castle to the National Trust for Scotland in 1931 as its first property. The two western towers were destroyed in the 15th century when the castle was besieged by James IV, who brought the cannon Mons Meg through from Edinburgh.

Crosslees Cairn (site) NS 564529 *43910*	"Urns containing calcined human bones were found beside a stone cist under a cairn in 1831." (GSG) The slab which covered the cist is now built into the wall on north side of the road. A benchmark has been inscribed on it.
Cumbernauld House NS 770756	"A group of six mark stones on the hilltop near Castle Way, about 200m south of Cumbernauld House. Uncertain origin." (FF) These stones are about 60m south of the alignment.
Dean Castle NS 436394 *42815*	Mentioned in Harry's *Haunted Castles* webpage. "It seems that some local schoolgirls who had seen the film (Ghostbusters) got hold of a Ouija board and took it to the castle to see if they could raise a ghost. They came back saying they'd been in touch with a ghost called '*The Grey Lady*'."
Dechmont Fort NS 656582 *44867*	"Situated between East Kilbride and Cambuslang. Beltane fires were lit here until the beginning of the 19th century." (FF) Little is now visible of the fort that occupies the central portion of **Dechmont Hill**, which is a ridge lying roughly ENE and WSW.
Devil's Head or Fairy Stone NN 725018 *24761*	In the past, children would hold hands in a ring around it and sing this song: "Olie, olie, peep, peep, peep; Here's the man wi' the cloven feet. Here's his head but where's his feet? Olie, olie, peep, peep, peep." Could this be a reference to this being the 'head' of the ley from Cairnpapple? A possible extension of the **Cairnpapple** to **Doune Cross** alignment.
De'il's Plant'in (Devil's Plantation) NS 557535 *43921*	"It was supposed to be haunted, if I remembered correctly." (GSG) On the Humbie Road between Newton Mearns and Eaglesham. Though some archaeologists claim it's a motte, urns containing calcined human bones are said to have been found. It is likely that the urns in question were actually found in a cairn that once stood near **Crosslees** Farm, also on the Humbie Road.

It appears to be a tumulus rather than a motte although the possibility of its being such cannot be ruled out. The deviation of the road is caused by the natural hillock on which the mound is situated, not by the mound itself (Canmore).

Dod Hill
NS 493532
88320

Too good a name not to include! On May Miles Thomas' 'The Secret' alignment to **Lady Isle**.
A circular cairn measuring 19m in diameter is situated on the summit of Dod Hill, at an angle in the stone march-dyke. It has been heavily robbed to provide material for the dyke and for the small semi-circular enclosure that encloses its W side. (Canmore)

Dolphington House
NT 158769
184733

No details are given in the text of *Forgotten Footsteps*. The ruined workers' cottages at Dolphington may be a better fit on the alignment.

Doomster Hill (site)
NS 555658
44078

Site of a large 5m high, 45m diameter stepped moot hill.
Not mentioned at all by Harry, which is a curious omission. Maybe he was unaware of it? A ceremonial pathway once connected it to the site of **Govan Old Parish Church**.
In 1845, a few planks of black oak, some small fragments of bones, and a bed of what seemed to be decayed bulrushes was found.

Double Dykes
NS 764479
45585

Also called Sodom Hill. Not mentioned by Harry, but right on his postulated **Craignethan Castle** to **Walls hill fort** alignment.
This fort occupies a large promontory formed at the N end of Sodom Hill by the gorges of the Cander Water on the E and the Avon Water on the W. (Canmore)

Doune Castle
NN 728010
24738

"Built on a mound and dating back to the 15th century. The official guidebook mentions the possibility that the castle ditch is of prehistoric origin." (FF)
Now most famous as a location in *Monty Python and the Holy Grail* and 'Castle Leoch' in the TV series *Outlander*.
Doune's history goes back at least as far as the Romans, who probably had a fort here in the area later occupied by Doune Castle. The discovery of medical instruments suggests the Romans also had a hospital here, on the site of what is now Doune Primary School.

Doune Cross
NN 727015
24744

"One of the best known Mercat Crosses in Scotland, dating from around 1696. In 1745, Prince Charlie's Highlanders rested from their march and supped brose on its steps." (FF)
King Charles I ordered that public executions should take place at the Cross instead of at the castle. Legend says:

'When Ye Cross of Doun,
Turns its Heid Roun
Ye End of Ye World is Neare Cum'
Harry lists Doune Cross as the termination of the PSA from **Cairnpapple Hill** that runs through **Doune Castle**, but the castle seems well off the alignment.

Dovehill
NS 599648

On the **Necropolis** to **Camphill** PSA, although not known to Harry. The name 'Little Dovehill' comes from the mound miraculously raised by St Mungo so the crowd he was preaching to could better see him. This is where the phrase "Let Glasgow flourish by the preaching of the word" comes from. (Past Glasgow).

Drumduff Hill
NS 583462
43759

"A turf-built enclosure (D&E Scotland 1977). Roughly 20m long in each direction, the rampart reached a height of about 0.4m at its highest point on the NE corner. **Tinto Hill**, Ailsa Craig, **Dumgoyne** and Loudon Hill were all visible from different parts of the enclosure." (GSG)
Harry always calls this 'Dumdruff Hill', probably a typo?
The enclosure is about 50m southeast of the summit of Drumduff Hill.

Drumsargad Castle
NS 666597
44858

"...the castle is known to have been on the site of an earlier fort, and a Bronze-Age food vessel and cinerary urn found there were purchased by the National Museum of Antiquities in 1883." (GSG)
Some remains were extant about 1775, but there is now no trace of the castle to be seen.

Drymen Parish Church
NS 474880
43419

The present church was built in 1771, but a number of earlier gravestones in the burial ground, one of which is dated 1618, suggest that this is a much older site. It sits well on a speculative alignment from **Duncryne Hill** to **Doune Cross**.

Duchal Castle (site)
NS 334684
42298

"A straight line from Duchal Castle to **Paisley Abbey** runs through the grounds of Duchal House and prehistoric **Houston South Mound** on the way. Extended past the Abbey the alignment leads to **Crookston Castle**, one of Glasgow's major sightline centres. During research for *The Guide to the Haunted Castles of Scotland* in 1981, the ghost's route was traced from **Paisley Abbey** to Duchal Castle and another ley was discovered in the process. For some reason, the ghost of Duchal seems to have used it in its travels.
"The ghost first appeared at **Paisley Abbey** in a 'hideous, gross and tangible' form, then for some reason it moved on to Duchal where it settled on the castle turrets. The

garrison fired arrows and threw spears at it to no avail; anything that came within striking distance burned to ashes. One night, the Lord of Duchal's eldest son heroically engaged it in single combat. He was never seen alive again, but his torn and mutilated body was found in the castle hall next morning. After that, the ghost disappeared for all time." (LQ)

There are now only fragmentary remains of Duchal Castle, on a high rocky crag, naturally defended on three sides by steep slopes.

Duchal House
NS 352679
42247

"Private residence built near the old castle of Duchal mentioned in the *Lanercost Chronicle* as the scene of a series of hauntings in 1296. The ghost, a former laird of Duchal, was also seen at **Paisley Abbey**." (FF)

See 'The Ghost Ley of Paisley' (page 218).

Dumbarton Rock
NS 399745
43376

"The name is said to be derived from *'Dun Breatainn'*, Fort of the Britons. Traces of a timber and rubble rampart found here have been given a radiocarbon date of around AD 600." (GSG)

Excavations were carried out in 1974-5 at Dumbarton Castle, anciently known as Alt Clut or Clyde Rock. They revealed a timber and rubble defence of Early Historic date overlooking the isthmus which links the rock to the mainland. Finds include the northernmost examples of imported Mediterranean amphorae of the 6th century AD, and fragments from at least six glass vessels of Germanic manufacture. (Canmore)

Dumgoyach
standing stones
(aka Duntreath)
NS 532807
44605

"The site has been carbon dated to 3,250 BC. A solstitial foresight was discovered here by Euan MacKie, and also a natural foresight to the east, which could not be identified astronomically. The flat face of the centre stone indicates the unidentified foresight — it points straight to **Duncolm**." (Harry Bell, ACFA occasional paper)

This setting of standing stones originally comprised four stones aligned from NE to SW; two field-gathered boulders have been added in recent times.

Dumgoyne
NS 541827

"This prominent hill, some 427m high, can be seen from **Camphill**, **Cathkin Braes** and many other vantage points in the Glasgow area. Archaeologists have suggested that the remains of a cairn on the summit might have been part of a Roman signalling station." (GSG)

"A structure on this hill has been reported and is awaiting investigation." (FF)

Dumyat NS 835976 *47117*	A finely-polished greenstone axe was found near the summit of Dumyat in 1927. The hilltop has a memorial to the Argyll and Sutherland Highlanders, a bench, a trig point, and a cairn with a beacon on top that was commissioned to mark the Queen's Jubilee in 1977.
Dunbarney House NO 110187 *113121*	A 17th C. country house with remains of a vaulted tower mill and dovecot dated 1697 in the grounds. Not mentioned in the text but appears on Harry's map. On the **Doune Cross** to **Dundee Law** PSA.
Dunburgidale NS 062660 *40300*	Remains of a galleried fort on Bute. "Dunburgidale fort is classified as a 'galleried dun' because of the chamber in the wall. If you stand on the moorland outside the fort you cannot see Holy Isle, but step up on the ramparts and away in the distance, the highest point of the isle comes into view." (LQ). The Dun is some distance off the alignment. The OS trig point 500m to the NE at NS 066664 gives a better fit. Another possible termination for the northern end of this alignment is **Hilton chambered cairn** overlooking Kames bay about 2.5km NNE, however Holy Island is not visible from this location.
Duncarnock NS 501559 *43882*	Mentioned in the text of *Glasgow's Secret* Geometry and appeared in the first edition on an alignment from **Walls Hill Fort** to **Craignethan Castle**. (GSG) Traces of rig-and-furrow cultivation are also visible on this knoll, while roughly in the centre of the fort there are the footings of a small rectangular building, with a second overlying the fort wall on the SE. In 1958 Frank Newall picked up a sherd of pottery and a fragment of worked shale near the NE end of the fort. (Canmore)
Duncolm NS 470774 *43238*	"Highest of the Kilpatrick Hills. The name means 'Fort of the Dove', or 'Fort of Columba'." (FF) "At first glance it looks like a Scots cousin of Ayers Rock. Its distinctive outline could have made it a useful landmark for prehistoric travellers..." (GSG) The remains of an enclosure were recorded in 1971, however, a subsequent examination of the hill by Royal Commission researchers in 1975 failed to reveal any trace of an enclosure. "Though only ten miles from Glasgow, it is surrounded by chambered tombs older than the pyramids. Some of the alignments passing through Glasgow originate here." *(Harry Bell, ACFA occasional paper)*
Duncryne NS 435859	"Unusual-shaped hill near the village of Gartocharn. Easy climb and a panoramic view of Loch Lomond. Witches were

89427

reputed to dance on the summit of Duncryne at Hallowe'en — could this be a folk-memory of the ancient Celtic festival of Samhain?" (FF)

Canmore records a possible beacon stance on the summit. Duncryne is fondly known as 'The Dumpling' for its shape. The 'cryne' element of the name comes from the Gaelic 'cruinn', so 'Duncryne may be translated as 'round or circular dun'.

Iain C Lees, *The Campsies and the Land of Lennox* (1933): "This conical hill, which is the outstanding landmark on the plain, was once the home of wizards. Farmers in the neighbourhood will tell you of meetings of the Devil and his minions round its base." (p. 108).

Dundee Law
NO 391313
31936

"Prehistoric earthwork surmounted by a war memorial. It commands an excellent view of Dundee and the River Tay." (FF)

Dun I
NM 284252
21613

Highest point on Iona at 101m (333 ft).

Close to the top of Dun I is an atmospheric rock pool named *Tobar na h-Aoise*, which translates as the Well of Age. Over time it became known to islanders and visitors as a 'Wishing Well' and was associated with the power to restore youth. Pilgrims often wash their faces in this pool, or sip from its waters, as a way of seeking new beginnings in their lives and world.

Dunning standing
stone
NO 018147
26715

Mentioned in the text of *Forgotten Footsteps* but not on the alignment.

The reputed burial place of Doncha, Abbot of Dunkeld, killed in AD 964 at the Battle of Duncrub.

Dunsapie Hillfort
NT 281731
52510

Hillfort on **Arthur's Seat**, Edinburgh. The midpoint of the Lothian Line.

This fort is situated on the broad summit of Dunsapie overlooking Dunsapie Loch, a location girt with cliffs and rocky escarpments around three sides and easily accessible only from the sloping E flank.

Dunstaffnage Castle
NM 882344
23036

"Like many more of Scotland's haunted castles, Dunstaffnage stands on a ley-line. In this instance, the ley-line runs to distant **Ben Cruachan**, passing through **Inverawe House** on the way." (HC)

Originally a stronghold of the MacDougalls, Dunstaffnage Castle came under the custodianship of the Campbells of Lorn in 1321 or 1322 following its capture by forces of Robert Bruce. Apart from a period in the late 14th and 15th centuries when it was held by Stewarts, it remained thereafter in the possession of the Campbells. (Canmore)

Dunwan hillfort NS 546489	"Traces of an Iron-Age hillfort were found here, a roughly triangular area 85m x 50m within a single rampart (D&E Scotland, 1958)." (GSG)
Eaglesham House (site) NS565538 *204397*	The site is now occupied by the factory of Linn Electronics. Located on the alignment from **Bonnyton Mound** to **Mains Castle**. Eaglesham House was built in 1859 for Allan Gilmour, timber importer and shipowner. The House cost £70,000 to build. Fire in the 1950s led to disuse and later demolition. (Canmore)
Eaglesham Moot Hill NS 571519 *43919*	"Possible site of the first wooden castle of the Montgomeries c. 12ᵗʰ century. Local tradition remembers it only as a venue for meetings and festivals." (GSG) Listed in the Gazetteer although not actually on any PSAs and only mentioned in the text as a location on the 'dowsing test day'. This motte is situated on the NW bank of the Eaglesham Burn and now forms a tree-covered feature in a public park in the centre of Eaglesham.
Easter Park/Fairy Knowe NS 528996 *167099*	Prehistoric settlement on Harry's hypothetical alignment from **Stirling Castle** to **Ben Lomond**. This site was found during harvesting operations in a forestry plantation. The homestead stands on a terrace overlooking the River Forth.
East Revoch cairn (rems.) aka Scott's Tourie NS 565504 *43943*	Seven cists, filled with calcined human bones and sticks, were found when this cairn was removed about 1836. The spot was pointed out by the farmer (J Scott, farmer — see **Scott's Tourie**) who made the discoveries.
Edinburgh Castle NT 251734 *52068*	"Beautifully situated, overlooking Princes Street in the middle of Edinburgh. First mentioned in a 6ᵗʰ century Old Welsh poem *The Gododdin of Aneurin*. The oldest part of the present castle is Queen Margaret's chapel, which dates back to the 11ᵗʰ century." (FF)
Edinburgh Labyrinth NT 258729	Chartres-replica labyrinth in George Square Gardens created in 2005 for EU Chaplaincy. Dowsed to be on this alignment by geomancer Grahame Gardner.
Elcho Castle NO 164210 *28197*	"Very clean and well-looked after 16ᵗʰ century castle 3.5 miles from Perth. It stands on the site of an earlier castle once used as a hideout by William Wallace." (FF) Also has a Wallace's Well! A canal or ditch formerly connected the castle with the River Tay, about 150 yards distant, and ended in a quarry.
Fairholm Cairn NS 754516	"...there appears to be another line half a degree off to the south. It leads from **Tinto** through the mound at

45724	**Craignethan** to a Bronze-Age monument known as Fairholm Cairn, and from there to the Iron Age fort at **Cadzow...**" (GSG)
Fairy Knowe NS 796981 *45986*	"A Bronze Age cairn on the Hill of Airthrey, 3 miles from Stirling. Excavation in 1868 uncovered a cist, a beaker and six arrowheads" (GSG) Connected to 'The Straight Road with No Path'; not marked on the map but mentioned in the gazetteer.
Finavon Castle NO 496564 *33673*	"One and a half miles north-east of **Glamis Castle** stands the famed **St Orland's Stone**, an eight-foot high monolith decorated by a cross on one side and mysterious Pictish symbols on the other. This stone is situated in direct alignment between Glamis Castle and a prehistoric earthwork 14 miles away at **Baldoukie**. Not far south of this alignment another ley runs straight from the castle to a group of standing stones at **Carse Gray**. From there it continues right on over the hill and through Finavon Castle..." (LQ)
Flint arrowhead (Stirling) NS 786927 *46278*	A leaf-shaped flint arrowhead approx. 2cm x 4cm was found in the garden of number 34 Park Place, Stirling. On the Stirling Castle - Old Sauchie alignment.
Gallowflat Mound NS 623615 *45075*	"Early Christian and Roman artefacts found here. Off East Main Street, Rutherglen. Ure (1973, p124), during the alterations to this site: '...a passage six feet broad and laid with unhewn stones was discovered, leading up to the top of the mound. Near to this passage was dug up two brass or copper vessels, shaped like a porringer...they had broad handles, about nine inches in length, having cut upon them the name CONGALLVS, or CONVALLVS.' These vessels possibly date from the early Christian period when St Conval is thought to have built a church in the Rutherglen area. The tumulus itself is surely earlier." (GSG) The mound once stood within the parklands of Gallowflat House. Its form, and records of many similar mounds in the area, long since removed, suggest that its origin is even earlier.
Gartur Crannog NS 571987 *44621*	On Harry's hypothetical **Stirling Castle** to **Ben Lomond** alignment but not mentioned by him. A small mound of earth, apparently artificial, in the midst of the marsh known as Black Loch. It is built round with stones and has on it a few plum trees. (Canmore)
Ghost's Knowe NS 747857	Not mentioned by Harry, but close to his **Stirling Castle** to **Drumduff Hill** PSA.

45953

A skeleton wrapped in decayed material was found, together with an unknown number of relics including a stone axe "of beautiful workmanship" and stone knife. Also found were a golden horn or cup and a gold ring. All the relics are now lost. (Canmore)

Glamis Castle
NO 386480
32055

"One and a half miles north-east of Glamis Castle stands the famed **St Orland's Stone**, an eight-foot-high monolith decorated by a cross on one side and mysterious Pictish symbols on the other. This stone is situated in direct alignment between Glamis Castle and a prehistoric earthwork 14 miles away at **Baldoukie**. Not far south of this alignment another ley runs straight from the castle to a group of standing stones at **Carse Grey**. From there it continues right on over the hill and through **Finavon Castle**..." (HC)

There was a castle on this site in 1376, when it was granted by Robert I to John Lyon, Lord **Glamis**, who reconstructed the castle about then. The L-plan tower, which is the earliest part of the present building, dates from this period (early 15th century).

Glasgow Cathedral
NS 602655
45002

"Glasgow Cathedral stands on one of the oldest Christian sites in Scotland. As Dr Joseph Robertson put it in his *Scottish Abbeys and Cathedrals*, 'Here the cross was planted and here was the ground blessed for Christian burial by a Christian bishop, while Iona was yet an unknown island among the western waves, while the promontory of St Andrews was the haunt of the wild boar and the sea mew, and only the smoke of a few heathen wigwams ascended from the Rock of Edinburgh'. The bishop referred to was St Ninian, who around 400 AD consecrated as a Christian burying place a small space of ground on the hill between the fort of Cathures (also Caer or Cathair) and the Moldendinar Burn." (GSG)

During the autumn and winter of 1992-3, extensive archaeological excavations were conducted in advance of the installation of a new heating and electrical system for the cathedral. In the Lower Church no features relating to the site of St Mungo's tomb were found and most of the burials date to the early 19th century.

Glassingal House
NN 795045
226838

Not mentioned in Harry's gazetteer but appears on the map. (FF)

Demolished 1966. Glassingal (aka Old Glassingall) was an 18th century former laird's house; however, the estate has a much older history and there may originally have been a castle here.

Glengarnock Castle
NS 310573
42179

"A ruined 15th century castle standing on a crag above the River Garnock, near Kilbirnie." (GSG)
The castle is in a good state of preservation. A tablet on the wall of the keep states that WC Patrick 'Strengthened the ruins of this ancient castle AD 1841'.

Gleniffer Braes
NS 453602
43151

Pair of standing stones. Not mentioned by Harry, but on his **Walls Hill** to **Necropolis** alignment.
On the other side of the road, a WW2 'Starfish' decoy site was deployed to divert enemy bombers away from Paisley. (Canmore): These two uninscribed standing stones are 1.2m in height; there is no local knowledge of their history.

Govan Old Parish Church
NS 553659
44077

Built on the site of a monastery. Inside is a collection of 26 stones of possible 10th or 11th century date. "Govan Old Parish Church is thought to occupy the site of St Constantine's monastery. Close to the Clyde, it stands only a street or two from Water Row where a ford with stepping stones existed in Roman times. The churchyard is almost circular, a shape often associated with pre-Christian burial grounds. As at **Rutherglen**, the level of the graveyard stands higher than that of the surrounding ground." (GSG)
The ford is also adjacent to the site of **Doomster Hill**, once a 45m diameter, 5m high stepped moot hill on Water Row, now buried under a new housing development.
A 2019 probe survey within the graveyard revealed three medieval gravestones previously thought to have been lost during demolition of the adjacent Harland and Wolff yard in 1973 along with some buried post-medieval gravestones. Further excavations in 2023 revealed foundations of a possible gatehouse in the corner nearest **Doomster Hill** and a stone fragment with what seems to be a Pictish-inspired carving of a warrior with shield.

Greenland cup marked stone
NS 449740
45383

A sandstone boulder with three cup marks lies on the slope of the Hill of Dun, about 100m N of Dunerbuck farmhouse was recorded by J Bruce in 1896 but subsequent surveys have been unable to locate it. Harry doesn't mention it, but the **Cathkin Braes** to **Bonhill** burial site PSA runs past the foot of the hill.

Halfway Well
NN 377001
128612

A natural hollow at SE-facing break of slope, containing 1m depth of water.
Harry shows this on a hand-drawn map in the galleys of *Glasgow's Secret Geometry*, but it didn't make it into the first edition.

Hamilton Motte NS 727566 *45683*	Near Hamilton Mausoleum. Said to be part of the ancient settlement of Netherton, the predecessor of Hamilton. "The motte at Hamilton is thought to have been part of the ancient settlement of Netherton, but for all anyone knows, the motte could have been built over a prehistoric cairn. It is situated about 200m north of Hamilton Mausoleum." (GSG) Canmore records that the motte is all that remains of an early fortified structure. and it can be presumed that the early settlement clustered around this site.
Harelaw Cairn (site) NS 612486 *44823*	"Remains of a late Bronze Age cairn, destroyed in 1808" (GSG) Many 'urns' and human bones are said to have been discovered, but nothing has survived.
High Cross Hill NS 610600 *45085*	An Early Bronze Age flat axe was found at High Crosshill (NS 617606) before 1888. Its present location is unknown. Not mentioned by Harry but on the **Necropolis** to **Harelaw Cairn** PSA.
Hill of Dun NS 447741 *43379*	Canmore records a possible dun site near this location. The area is called 'Hill of Dun' on the OS maps. "Vestiges of walling, which may have been used to adapt the natural rectangular hollow between two ridges of strata into a dun, were noted." Harry doesn't mention it, but the **Cathkin Braes** to **Bonhill** burial site PSA runs through this hill.
Hilton chambered cairn NS 066685 *40306*	Not mentioned by Harry, but this overgrown cairn overlooking Kames Bay is a possible fit for the northern termination of his *Leyline Quest* **Dunburgidale** to **Holy Island** PSA, although Holy Island is not visible from here.
Holy Island NS 063297	The summit of Mullach Mor on Holy Island is visible from Bute. "**Loch Quien crannog** on the Isle of Bute (is) aligned to Holy Isle off Arran 20 miles to the south, and **Loch Dhu crannog** and **Dunburgidale** fort to the north."(LQ)
Holyrood Palace NT 269739 *52380*	Located at the bottom of the Royal Mile in Edinburgh, at the opposite end to **Edinburgh Castle**, Holyrood Palace has served as the principal residence of the Kings and Queens of Scots since the 16th century and is a setting for state occasions and official entertaining.
Hopetoun House NT 088790 *49127*	"Scotland's greatest Adam mansion. Ancestral home of the Marquess of Linlithgow." (FF) The site of **Abercorn Castle** is located along the nature trail in the grounds.

Canmore says, "A truly princely mansion whose urn-capped balustrade, like a shimmering mirage, gradually rises from the landscape as you approach. As you reach the ha-ha and guardian sphinxes, carefully contrived to inculcate a sense of majesty, it reveals itself in its full splendour."

Houston Cross NS 405669 *43101*	"The shaft of this cross was set up by the knights of Huw's Town in the reign of King Malcolm IV." (FF) Harry's **Dechmont Hillfort** to **The Motte** alignment is supposed to run through Houston Cross, but it misses by several metres. The cross stands 3.6m high, and it is believed that the well-worn steps forming the plinth date from the 14th century. It formerly stood near Houston Parish Church and was moved to its present position when the new town was built. Its inclusion on the alignment seems nothing more than wishful thinking on Harry's part.
Houston South Mound NS 401664 *43100*	Excavations of this cairn uncovered several coffins of flag stones, set on edges, sides and ends, and covered with stones, in which were cremated human bones. In one was found many trinkets of a jet-black substance, probably a necklace. Excavation also revealed a series of Neolithic pits on the site.
Huly Hill NT 123726 *50795*	"Three upright stones surrounded by a wall near a busy traffic roundabout at Newbridge, Midlothian." (FF) Tumulus & standing stones, of which three remain. The outlying **Newbridge Standing Stone** across the motorway junction marks the alignment to **Edinburgh Castle**. The well-preserved remains of an Iron Age chariot burial were excavated near here during redevelopment of the motorway interchange. The site has been restored since Harry's visit.
Inch Castle (site) NS 513674 *44167*	"Six miles further on from **Capelrig**, still in alignment with the castle and tumulus, is the site of long-demolished Inch Castle built by old Palm-my-Arm on the lands he won in the wrestling match." (GSG) Mentioned in the text of *Glasgow's Secret Geometry*, but not in the gazetteer or map. In the latter half of the 15th century, Sir John Ross (died about 1474) was granted the lands of Inch with the ruins of this castle, upon which he built a three-storey castle known as the Inch Castle.

Iona Abbey
NM 286245
21664

Founded shortly before 1203 on the site of the Columban abbey, the Benedictine Abbey on Iona comprised a church dedicated to St Mary and a monastery dedicated to St Columba. In 1499 the church became the Cathedral of the Bishops of the Isles. Reportedly damaged by a reforming mob in 1561, by the end of the 17th century the abbey had fallen into ruins. Restoration work began at the end of the 19th century and, in 1938, the newly formed Iona Community took over the running of the abbey.

Inchinnan All
Hallows Church
NS 491680
43063

A Templar site thought to be the burial place of St Conval. Mentioned in the text by Harry, but not on his map, although it fits the **Camphill** to **Dumbarton Rock** PSA. "Other churches were subsequently built there, the last of the line being All Hallows Church which was demolished around 1969 during alterations to Glasgow Airport."(GSG)

Some Early Christian carved stones are now displayed in **Inchinnan New Parish church** at NS 479689. Inchinnan church (dedicated to St Conval) was given to the Knights Templar by David I (1124-53). It was demolished in 1828 and replaced by another which in turn was demolished and replaced in 1900 by All Hallows Church.

Inchinnan New
Parish church
NS 479689
195846

"When the airport was built, 13 sculptured stones from All Hallows' churchyard were taken to the new Inchinnan Parish Church, a modernistic structure on the Old Greenock Road." (GSG)

Inchinnan was probably an early Celtic foundation dedicated to St Conval, an Irish saint of the 5th or 6th century, and it served as the mother church for the area known later as Strathgryffe (the former county of Renfrew). The three earliest and most important stones have been placed beside the church porch.

Inverawe House
NN 022315
151295

Mentioned in *Haunted Castles* as being on a ley between **Dunstaffnage Castle** and **Ben Cruachan**. Has an interesting ghostly connection with Inverary Castle.

Jackschairs Wood
NO 072168
26551

Cairn and hill fort on the **Doune Cross** to **Dundee Law** alignment. Not mentioned in Harry's gazetteer but appears as 'Fort' on the map of *Forgotten Footsteps*.
The interior of the fort is dominated by a rocky knoll on the summit on which there are the remains of a small cairn. A 2007 excavation dated the fort to Early Iron Age.

John Knox House
NT 260737
52521

John Knox House, popularly known as 'John Knox's House', is a historic house in Edinburgh, Scotland, reputed to have been owned and lived in by Protestant reformer John Knox during the 16th century. Although his name became associated with the house, he appears to have lived in Warriston Close where a plaque indicates the approximate site of his actual residence.

Kilnside House
NS 489636
196408

"...to find any possible link with **Camphill** I had to resort to mapwork. The only possibility that presented itself was an alignment I discovered on a 1935 Glasgow Corporation Transport map: it ran from **Camphill** through **Ross Hall**, **Kilnside House** and **Auchentorlie House** to a spot in the vicinity of **Seedhill Craigs**, a waterfall some 200m south of the Abbey." (GSG)

Harry mentions this in the text of *Glasgow's Secret Geometry*, but says that he was unable to locate it. The site lies about 70m N of the **Seedhill** to **Camphill** PSA.

Kincardine Castle
NN 949114
36061

Not mentioned in Harry's gazetteer but plotted on the map on the **Doune Cross** to **Dundee Law** alignment in *Forgotten Footsteps*. Kincardine Castle is a 19th century manor house near Auchterarder in Perth and Kinross, Scotland. The Gothic house was constructed in 1801–1803 and is a category B listed building. The remains of an earlier 14th century keep were demolished in 1645. Little remains today beyond its rectangular foundations.

King's Park
NS 595605
44364

"In the open field, at the highest point of the park, near the Menock Road entrance is a roughly oval outline, 12m x 7m...(D&E Scotland 1977)." (GSG)

This entry was actually recorded by Harry himself!

Forgotten Footsteps says, "a site near Aikenhead House", although the alignment seems to run through the house itself.

King's Park (Stirling)
Cup and Ring Marks
NS 783930
46180

Marked on the map, but not otherwise mentioned by Harry in *Forgotten Footsteps*.

The panel is situated in woodland lying flat on level ground at the top of an escarpment that slopes steeply to the S. It is located 10m W of a memorial bench and 7m N of tarmac track which runs to the S of Kings Park Golf Course. This is a small sandstone boulder measuring 1m x 0.7m flush with the ground and with a flat upper surface. It features 1 cup with 2 rings, the outer ring being very faint, and 2 cups each with faint single rings barely discernible in the field but visible on 3D imagery. There is a depression in the panel between the eastern-most and central motifs which may be natural. (Canmore)

Knappers Farm
'Druid Temple'
NS 506712

Postulated Bronze Age henge reconstruction in 1937 by renegade Glasgow archaeologist Ludovic McLellan Mann, who theorised that it was constructed to commemorate a total solar eclipse, and that the site was linked to the **Cochno Stone** to the north. His interpretation of the site was not taken seriously by fellow archaeologists.

On an alignment between **Renfrew Parish Church** and the **Cochno Stone**.

Knappers Quarry
NS 507713
44524

Bronze Age burial ground excavated in 1937 by renegade Glasgow archaeologist Ludovic McLellan Mann, who called it a 'mortuary house'.

Strangely, given that he was familiar with Mann's work, Harry does not mention either site in *Glasgow's Secret Geometry*.

Canmore says, "In 1951, Mr Mann owned a number of items from this site, but after his death, his collection was given to Glasgow Art Gallery and Museum. He also constructed a bogus henge, W of the Great Western Road; not far from the Knappers Quarry. The catalogue of finds and re-assessment of site suggests the existence of a henge or a Bronze Age Barrow, pre-dating a Food Vessel cemetery."

Knightswood Cross
NS 537693

Not part of Harry's system and with no ancient connection, Knightswood Cross is an intersection containing four churches and is situated at the crossing point of two putative alignments.

A Roman bronze coin of the Byzantine Emperor Justin I (AD 518-527) was found by Mr Armstrong, 55 Pikeman Road in 1950 in his garden (centred NS 5350 6917).

Kylepark (site)
NS 688609
45043

Bronze Age funerary site. "In 1885, two cinerary urns were discovered, placed upside down over cremated bones." (GSG)

A food vessel, containing a cremation, which was an item in a cemetery of cinerary urns at Kyle Park, is in Glasgow Art Gallery and Museum.

Lady Isle
NS 275293
203606

Lady Isle off the coast of Troon once held a chapel dedicated to Mary and is 'The Secret' depicted in May Miles Thomas' blog *The Devil's Plantation*.

There is a freshwater spring in the centre of the island and a suggestion of a ruined building, presumably the chapel. Lady Isle was at one time connected with an ancient ecclesiastical establishment near Adamton, called Lady Kirk, situated about four miles north of Ayr. As stated, a chapel was built here, dedicated to the Virgin Mary and endowed by John Blair in 1446 with the common land of Adamton. John Adair's map indicates a religious building located in the centre of the island and Timothy Pont's 1608 map also indicates a structure of some sort. When the bird observatory and warden's post was being built, the architect noted that there were signs of some sort of ancient ecclesiastical building on the island. (Wikipedia)

Ladywell
NS 603653
45037

Also known as 'Our Lady's Well', Glasgow's Ladywell is an artesian spring noted on early city maps and can be reliably assumed to predate the city. It lay just outside the city wall and Drygate Port in medieval times and will have refreshed Romans travelling the old Carntyne Highway east-west between forts along the Antonine Wall. It was the last public well to be closed following the introduction of piped water from Loch Katrine to service the city in the 1860s, although the exact date of its capping is not known.

Laggen Hill
NS 486530
43047

Hut circles, a possible hillfort site.
Close to May Miles Thomas' 'The Secret' alignment.

Langside House
(cup & ring marked rock)
NS 572613
44291

"A boulder found in a former wood now covered with houses (overlooking the River Cart). May be seen in Glasgow Art Galleries and Museum." (GSG)
Mentioned in the site gazetteer, but it doesn't feature on Harry's map and is not on any alignment.
On its smooth but striated surface are: 2 cups-and-four-rings, 1 cup-and-three-rings and about 14 cups. (Canmore)

Lickprivick Castle
(site)
NS 616527
44978

The mansion house or castle of Lickprivick was built like the great feudal houses, with towers, battlements, etc. The whole was reduced to ruins about 1733 and all remains were completely gone by 1840.

Lickprivick Tumulus
NS 610519
44979

"A 220m high trig point on top of a possible tumulus in the Greenhills area of East Kilbride. The name Lickprivick is supposed to be derived from *llech* a flat stone, and *prifwig* a primeval forest." (GSG)
It is possibly an earlier site of the Lickprivick residence, occupying higher ground than the later castle, and thus is a possible motte.

Linlithgow Palace
NT 002773
49261

"Built on a mound above Linlithgow Loch on the site of an earlier building burned in 1424. Birthplace of Mary Queen of Scots." (FF)
The site was first occupied as far back as Roman times 2,000 years ago. There has been a royal residence here since at least the reign of David I (1124-53). He also founded the town that grew up around the royal residence. Even with bare walls and its ruinous state, the palace remains magnificent.

Loch Dhu Crannog
NS 066617
40380

In Leyline Quest, Harry claims that this is on an alignment between **Dunburgidale** and **Holy Island.** The remains of the crannog were completely submerged when the Dhu Loch was dammed to form a reservoir in the early 20th century.

Lochend Crannog
NS 706661
45769

Not mentioned by Harry, but as it is close to his **Woodend Loch** site, perhaps it's worthy of consideration.
The bones of two individuals were found, together with pottery fragments, animal bones, half of a jet bracelet and two quern stones. The pottery, some hazel-nut shells and animal bones are preserved in Airdrie Public Library, and fragments of crucibles are in Glasgow Art Gallery and Museum.

Loch Quien (North)
Crannog
NS 061592
42148

"Although they cannot be seen from **Dunburgidale**, the crannogs at **Loch Dhu** and Loch Quien are on the same alignment. An important point about this alignment is that the two crannogs on it are believed to date from the Iron Age. The idea of building crannogs (artificial islands) came late in prehistory … This shows that the custom of using alignments was part of a continuing tradition which does not necessarily date from Neolithic times as most people seem to think." (LQ)
There are two crannogs in Loch Quien. Although Harry's picture appears to show the South crannog, the North one seems to be the best alignment with **Loch Dhu Crannog** and **Holy Island**, although it misses **Dunburgidale** fort by around 500m.

Lochwinnoch Peel
NS 361587
42148

"Ruined keep, built 1547 at the south end of Castle Semple Loch, in an area now designated as a bird sanctuary." (GSG)
On early maps it is shown to have been on an island in Castle Semple Loch, but the remains are now on shore as the level of the loch has been lowered.

Mains Castle &
Motte
NS 627560
44900

"Privately-owned 15th century castle, a mile north of East Kilbride. The lands and castle of Mains were granted to join John Lindsay of Dunrode for assisting Robert the Bruce in the murder of the Red Comyn in Dumfries Kirk. Bronze-Age cairns, cists and urns have been discovered in the vicinity." (FF/GSG)
During digging operations around Mains Castle in 1976, several sherds of late green-glazed pottery were found.

Mearns Castle
NS 552553
43855

"This ancient site must still retain vibrations of sanctity; in the 1960s a peculiar piece of ley-line whimsy prompted the building of a modern church onto the derelict 15th century castle." (FF/GSG)

Harry says that this site is some 100m off the alignment. The castle's history dates from 1449 when King James II granted a licence to Lord Maxwell "to big a castle on ye Baronie of Mearnis in Renfrushir" and to surround it with walls and ditches, iron gates and warlike appliances. The church is built on an enclosure believed to be of an earlier date than the castle, which probably occupies the site of a fort.

Mearns Kirk NS 543550 *203874*	Religious settlement and site since at least 800 AD. The present church dates from 1813 and was extensively renovated in 1932. A phosphor-bronze weathercock weighing two and a half hundredweight atop the bell tower was erected in the late 1940s. The gate posts in the form of sentry boxes date from the era of the Resurrectionists. Mentioned by Harry in *Leyline Quest*.
Megginch Castle NO 241246 *30485*	"Private residence dating back to the 15th century." (FF) The north front still presents externally some striking features of the sixteenth century mansion-house. Over one of the windows is the inscription "Petrus Hay, Aedificium Exstruxit An: 1575".
Meikle Dripps NS 578553 *43848*	"A mound near the farm is described in a charter of 1371 (D&E 1983, p30). The footpath from Meikle Dripps to Thorntonhall passes this site." (GSG) The mound was to be retained by Lord Maxwell for holding courts, in a gift of the surrounding land to Nether Pollock. No trace remains. On the **Craw Stane** to **Woodend Loch** PSA.
Middleton (site) NS 562765 *44415*	Not mentioned by Harry but on his **Necropolis** to **Dumgoyne** PSA. A row of standing stones aligned NW-SE once stood here, the largest of which, at the NW end of the row, was called 'The Law Stone of Mugdock'. A number of "stone coffins" were discovered close by. No trace of the stones, or of the cists, can now be seen. This stone row possibly marked the alignment between **Camphill** and **Dumgoyne**.
Millhill fort NN 923100 *25903*	aka Loaninghead hillfort. On the **Doune Cross** to **Dundee Law** alignment. This fort occupies a low hillock within the W angle of the motorway interchange with the A823 public road to Gleneagles.

Mills Observatory (Balgay Hill) NO 377307 *233403*	"Public astronomical observatory built on the site of a vitrified fort atop the wooded summit of Balgay Hill, Dundee." (FF) The highest point of the hill is somewhat to the east of the observatory. The observatory contains a Victorian 10" refractor telescope by T Cooke, York, in a 1935 papier mâché dome by Grubb Parsons, Newcastle. The only comparable dome by that firm is in Toronto.
Milton sickle NS 589696 *44112*	A find on the **Necropolis** to **Dumgoyne** PSA, but not mentioned by Harry. Two barbed and tanged flint arrowheads and a crescentic flint sickle were found by boys of St Augustine's School at Milton, on waste land opposite the school, which is being prepared for housing development. Recent heavy work there and the churned-up nature of the deposit itself preclude any guess as to the original context of the flints, which were donated to the Hunterian Museum, Glasgow. (Canmore)
Muchalls Castle NO 891918 *37138*	Harry mentions a ley between Muchalls and **Crathes Castles**. (HC) Muchalls House is a well-preserved specimen of the Scottish mansion of the beginning of the 17th century. A vault, ruinous in 1864, probably the Donjon Keep or Prison, on the south side of the castle, is traditionally much older than the rest. (Canmore)
Mugdock Castle NS 550771 *44471*	"Once the second most important castle in Stirlingshire. Now in ruins amid woodlands in Mugdock Country Park." (FF) The fragmentary remains of Mugdock Castle occupy the summit of a plateau; enough remains to show that the site was extensively developed by a succession of buildings which suggest an almost constant occupation from the 14th to the beginning of the 20th century, the last phase being the construction of a mansion, with outhouses and gardens, in 1875.
Mumrills Roman Fort NS 920795 *47870*	"Site of Roman cavalry stronghold. No visible remains." (FF) On the **Cairnpapple Hill** to **Doune Cross** alignment. The largest fort on the Antonine Wall. Coins and a Roman altar were found here in 1937. There are no visible traces of the fort on the ground today, but subtle traces of the fort can still be seen in aerial photographs. Excavations have revealed that there were actually two separate forts

on the site, with the later fort using the earlier fort as an annex.

Inscribed stones found in the vicinity suggest that the fort was occupied on different occasions by both cavalry and infantry regiments, and further finds hint at a possibly earlier (1st century AD) Roman occupation of the site.

Myres Cairn
NS 573470
43726

Bronze Age cairn. Mentioned in the gazetteer of *Glasgow's Secret Geometry* and Harry mentions it in the text as a sighting point when he was trying to locate the sightline centre on **Drumduff Hill.**

The cairn, constructed of small stones as compared with the heavy scree boulders on the N face of the hill, has all the appearance of a Bronze Age burial mound.

Necropolis
NS 603654
45014

"A cemetery occupying the second highest hill in Glasgow. At **Barrack Street**, quarter of a mile away, a heavy deposit of oyster shells was found (Glasdig 2, 1982 p7). There is a possibility that this area was occupied in Mesolithic times." (GSG)

Glasgow Cathedral stands on one of the oldest Christian sites in Scotland, consecrated by St Ninian around AD400.

Hugh Mackintosh, in his *Origin and History of Glasgow Streets* (1902) writes, "…in ancient times, anterior to our ecclesiastical history, a Druidical place of worship stood on the site of the present Necropolis."

The Necropolis is laid out on similar lines to Pere LaChaise, Paris and was opened May 1833. 50,000 burials have taken place at the Necropolis and most of 3,500 tombs have been constructed up to 4.2m deep, with stone walls and brick partitions. On the top of the Necropolis, tombs were blasted out of the rock face.

Neil's Stone (site)
NS 478568
42978

On a postulated alignment between **Neilston Pad** and **Inchinnan All Hallows Church**.

A tradition exists of a combat between two chiefs named Arthur and Neil. Both died of their wounds, the former being buried at the site of the **Arthurlie Cross** while the latter was buried at Cross Stone Brae south of Neilston village, where a sepulchral cross is known to have been standing at the end of the 18th century.

There is another standing stone in a field some 215m to the northeast, but it is not thought to have any connection to this one.

Neilston Pad
NS 474551
42985

Prominent hill visible from many areas of north Glasgow and **Crookston Castle**, yet not mentioned at all by Harry.

A stone-faced bank, 2.5m to 4.0m broad, extends from crags on Neilston Pad at NS 474 552, and follows the 250m contour round the SW side of the hill, the only part not defined by crags. The bank is indistinct on the up-slope side, about 300m long, it ends just within the wood at NS 475 549. An area of about 26 acres is enclosed. (Canmore)

Netherholm cairn and hillfort
NO 071169
26551

Cairn and hillfort in **Jackschairs Wood**. Not mentioned in Harry's gazetteer but appears on the map of *Forgotten Footsteps*..

This fort is situated on a prominent hillock within mature woodland 220m ESE of Netherholm (formerly Jackschairs) farmsteading. The interior of the fort is dominated by a rocky knoll on the summit on which there are the remains of a small cairn. (Canmore)

Nether Pollok Castle (site)
NS 550616
44308

"A 13th century castle that stood on a rock now occupied by the stable block of **Pollok House**." (GSG)

The lands of Nether Pollok were the property of the Maxwell family from the 13th century. The original castle was built by Sir John Maxwell of Pollok, the second castle was inhabited until the mid-16th century, and the third was built in 1367.

Newbridge Standing Stone
NT 126726
50802

Mark stone, or outlier to **Huly Hill**, now gracing the entrance of a technology firm's offices. On the **Cairnpapple Hill - Edinburgh Castle** alignment.

Oakshaw Trinity Church
NS 479641
43169

Not mentioned at all by Harry, the present church was built in 1754-6 and is reputed to be haunted. "This is where a stone mason fell to his death while working on the top of the church and we believe he was called 'Wee Leitch'. There are tributes to him with his glasses and handkerchief chiselled into some work to mark the place where he fell." (Daily Record)

A fortified prehistoric hillfort existed at Oakshawhead and the hilltop is thought to have been occupied in Roman times, although physical evidence is lacking.

Ochiltree fort
NT 030740

aka Peace Knowe fort. This small fort is situated to the NW of Ochiltree Mill, occupying a hillock with a steep escarpment along its NNE flank. On the **Duncolm** to **Arthur's Seat** alignment in *Forgotten Footsteps*.

Old Kilpatrick Roman fort (site)
NS 459732
43327

"Once the terminal at the western end of the Antonine Wall, the site is now buried under the houses of Gavinburn Gardens, near the Forth & Clyde Canal. There is nothing to see there, but I liked the site, the view down the Clyde, and in fact, the whole area. Was it possible that a prehistoric site lay underneath?" (GSG)

Bronze Age cists (stone coffins) were found here in 1923 and 1924 (TGAS viii 1933, pp55-61).

Old Sauchie
NS 772881
45943

"A 16th century tower house beside the Sauchie Burn on the 'Straight Road with no Path'. The Rock of Stirling is visible from Old Sauchie, and an imaginary line drawn straight through these two points goes straight to the **Fairy Knowe** cairn." (GSG)

Mentioned in the gazetteer in *Glasgow's Secret Geometry*, although this extension of the 'Straight Road with No Path' is not mapped. Old Sauchie was the site of a battle in 1488 (Scottish Castles Association).

Our Lord's Cross
(site)
NS485632
43133

Canmore records a cross "near Saucel Hill" from WM Metcalf's *A History of Paisley*. On the postulated **Neilston Pad** – **Inchinnan All Hallows** alignment and also possibly Harry's **Castlehead Ringwork** – **Kylepark** PSA.

Paisley Abbey
NS 485639
43139

'In the 7th century, the Irish missionary St Mirin (or Meadhran) was buried in Paisley. His shrine became a place of pilgrimage and church was dedicated to him; Paisley Abbey is believed to have been built on the site of that church." (FF)

In *Glasgow's Secret Geometry*, Harry instead favours Seedhill Craigs as the node point: "I was disappointed that the line didn't go to the Abbey, but when I looked into the history of Paisley, I found to my amazement that the riverbank at **Seedhill Craigs** was the site of St Mirin's original settlement... Tradition has it that the site was also occupied in pre-Roman times." (GSG)

Peel of Drumry
(site)
NS 514711
44570

A square tower built around 1530. Possibly an earlier structure occupied the same site, because as far back as 1329 "ye ladye of Drumry" is mentioned in old records.

"The Peel of Drumry, another historic old Glasgow house, was demolished in 1959. The site... was in use for at least 600 years and is in perfect alignment between **Duncolm** and **Camphill**." (GSG)

An evaluation was undertaken in September 2004 in advance of the erection of a new primary school ... no remains of the tower house were present. (Canmore)

Plean Tower
NS 850869
46901

"A ruined rectangular tower house with parts of the building dating to the 15th century. It may also be the crossroads of an ancient **Ben Lomond** to **Arthur's Seat** ley (at present there is insufficient evidence for the **Ben Lomond** to **Bridgeness** section)." (FF)

Now restored as part of Plane Castle.

Pollock Castle (site)
NS 523568
43893

The start of Harry's Humbie Road ley, mentioned on *Leyline Quest* web pages. Pollock Castle, also known as Pollok Castle, was a tower house castle located to the west of modern Newton Mearns in East Renfrewshire, on the opposite side of the M77 motorway from the town. The first record of a castle is on Timothy Pont's map of c. 1596, the Baronee de Renfrew no. 33, where a castle named Pook is marked in the area of Over Pollok. It also appears on Blaeu's map of 1654.

Pollok Earthwork
NS 556626
44294

Not referred to by Harry and easily confused with his **'Burrell Ringwork'**, which is properly called 'Pollok Ringwork'.
Excavations carried out by Glasgow Archaeology Soc. in 1959-60 showed that a roughly circular house, 16' in internal diameter, with a well-made, central post socket had stood just S of the centre of the enclosure.

Pollok House
NS 548618
44390

Not mentioned in *Forgotten Footsteps*, but it is a close fit to Harry's **Dechmont Hill** to **The Motte** ley.
The original castle was built by Sir John Maxwell of Pollok, the second castle was inhabited until the mid-16th century, and the third was built in 1367. Sir John Maxwell, third baronet, started the present Mansion in 1747, completing it in 1752. In 1939 Sir John Stirling-Maxwell drew up a conservation agreement over the estate with the National Trust for Scotland, of which he was a founder member. His daughter gifted the house and estate to the City in 1966, with permission to build the Burrell Gallery in the grounds.

Provan Hall
NS 667663
44985

"A 15th century house, once a country mansion for the Laird of Provan, now in the care of the National Trust for Scotland, built about 100m above sea level on a fairly flat stretch of land, with a view of the Campsies in one direction and **Dechmont Hill fort** in the other. Dechmont and Provan Hall are in alignment with the Roman fort at **Auchendavy**." (GSG)
"As far back as 1120, a jury in Cumbria took oath that the lands of Provan belonged of old to the kirk of Glasgow." (FF)

Queen Mary's Well
NS 909584

Not on any alignment, but Harry mentions it in *Glasgow's Secret Geometry*. "**Cathkin Braes** was originally known as the Cathkin Hills and during the Iron Age a Celtic tribe known as the Damnonii lived here. There are records of many artefacts been found and several cairns still exist today. Queen Mary's seat is a large cairn in the park from where Mary Queen of Scots is reputed to have observed the defeat of her forces at the Battle of Langside on 13 May 1558. Queen Mary's Well is one of several locations where she is supposed to have watered her horse during her escape after the battle." (GSG)

Ramshorn Cemetery
NS 595652
245548

Not one of Harry's sites, but it sits well on the **Seedhill Craigs** to **Necropolis** alignment.
One of Glasgow's older burial grounds. It has had various names, both official and unofficial: North West Parish Kirkyard; St David's Kirkyard; and Ramshorn and Blackfriars. The latter name tells of its link to Blackfriars Church, linking in turn to the pre-Reformation connection to the Blackfriars Monastery in Glasgow.

Ramshorn Kirk
NS 595652
139311

The former church building sits within the **Ramshorn Cemetery**, one of Glasgow's oldest burial grounds. The Ramshorn was originally built as St David's Parish Church in 1824, replacing a church that had stood on the site since 1720. Not mentioned by Harry, it sits on his **Glengarnock Castle** to **Necropolis** PSA.

Renfrew Parish Church
NS 507675
44181

"Built on the site of an earlier church. There is a sculpted tomb inside and a 15th century effigy on the tower." (FF)
"Two earlier churches have occupied the same site as Renfrew Parish Church, and as far back as the reign of King David I (1084-1153) a parsonage stood here. The site is otherwise flat and has no known prehistoric connections. Nevertheless, because of its long history, I considered it a potential ley site." (GSG)
The first record of an existing church at Renfrew occurs in 1136, when it was given to **Glasgow Cathedral**.
The present church was built in 1861-2. A small bell, now in Renfrew Burgh Museum, was found when digging its foundations. Within it are the 14th-15th century tomb of John Ross and his wife, and the tomb of John Motherwell, attributed to the 15th century. The church boasted a dedicated pew where Queen Victoria used to worship on her visits to Renfrewshire to see Lord Blythswood.
The church was closed in 2013 due to rising costs and a dwindling congregation.

Robroyston
NS 634693
172805

"'Rabraeston it was near to the wayside and had one house where Wallace used to bide' wrote Blind Harry the minstrel. Close to the 'Straight Road with No Path', a modern Celtic cross marks the spot on which the house stood where Wallace was betrayed c. 1305." (FF)

The monument is a handsome tall pink granite Celtic cross on plinth, modelled after St Martin's cross on Iona.
William Wallace was reputedly captured here in 1305.

Roman coin found
NS 588612
44335

A worn bronze coin of Valentinian I (CE 364-75) was dug up in a garden in Norfield Drive, Mount Florida, on the **Cathkin Braes** to **Bonhill** PSA.

Roman coin found
NS 518629
44388

In 1950 a fairly well-worn bronze coin of Constantine I (c. 254), minted at Nicomedia, was dug up by Mr C Munro in his garden at 426 Crookston Road. It is still in his possession. On the PSA between **Crookston Castle** and **Paisley Abbey**.

Roman coin found
NS 535691
44227

Mentioned only because it is on a postulated alignment between **Stanlie Castle** and **Bardowie Castle**.
Canmore records that, "A Roman bronze coin of the Byzantine Emperor Justin I (A D 518-527) was found by Mr Armstrong, 55 Pikeman Road in 1950 in his garden (centred NS 5350 6917) and is now in his possession."

Roman coins found
NS 528692
44170 & 44177

Several Roman coins have been found on Knightswood Golf Course, on the alignment between **Camphill** and **Duncolm**.

Roseburn House
NT 227729
52697

"Private residence with 16th century origins. The ley site could be the mound next to a nearby bowling green." (FF)
Old traditions tell of visits by Queen Mary (in 1526) and Oliver Cromwell (in 1650).

Ross Hall
NS 522630

The grounds are now a public park. "...many years ago, the vestiges of an ancient British camp were found in the vicinity. (Brotchie 1923, p55)." (GSG)
Two PSAs cross here, but otherwise there is nothing of note and Harry is mistaken in noting this site. The "ancient British camp" Brotchie mentions is near **Rosshall Mains**, 1 mile away to the west and not on a PSA.

Rosshall Mains
NS 506631
44369

This is the site referred to by Brotchie as "ancient British Camp" that Harry refers to under **Ross Hall**. Described as "...an almost circular enclosure measuring about 250ft diameter" on Canmore. Crop marks, perhaps representing a native settlement, were observed here during air reconnaissance in 1957.

Rough Hill Motte
NS 607553
44902

Appears on the map for *Forgotten Footsteps*. On the alignment from **Bonnyton Mound** to **Mains Castle**.
Ruins of a building measuring 22m by 19m were recorded in 1935.
The mound is now completely overgrown.

**Rutherglen Old
Parish Church
NS 613617
*45079***

"An olde-worlde churchyard in Main Street, Rutherglen...the pre-Reformation tower of St Mary's Church has the gable of an even earlier Norman church attached to it on one side. This earlier church is believed to have replaced St Conval's wattled edifice, which survived till about the year 1100. The surface of the churchyard is about 1.5m above the level of the pavement outside. A large tumulus, said to have once stood here, is thought to have augmented the height of the churchyard when it was levelled off. (Ure 1973, p84)" (GSG)
The church belonged to **Paisley Abbey**. In 1791 the church was rebuilt all but the tower. This tower still stands, east of the present church along with the much older wall of the chancel against which it is built.

**St Enoch's
Sanctuary
NS 589649**

"Her sanctuary with its curative well was situated in the present day St Enoch Square, which has always been communal property. Through it ran the little stream called the Glasgow Burn..." (GSG)
See also **St Thenew's Well.**

**St Giles Cathedral
NT 257736
*52228***

"A Celtic parish church occupied this site in the 9th century. St Giles is a ley crossroads and appropriately enough, the Mercat Cross from which royal proclamations are read stands nearby on the site of an earlier cross. In Ian Nimmo's informative *Portrait of Edinburgh*, the legend is recalled of how a phantom voice naming those about to die rang out from the Mercat Cross the night before the Scots army marched to Flodden. Outside the cathedral, a heart set in the cobbles underfoot marks the site of the Old Tolbooth, the 'Heart of Midlothian'." (FF)
The Thistle Chapel contains a wealth of ornamental stonework and elaborate oak carvings which feature distinctively Scottish motifs such as bagpipe-playing angels.

**St John's Cross
NT 234737
*52301***

The burgh cross now stands in the south-east corner of Canongate Churchyard to the right-hand side of the entrance to **Canongate Kirk**. It used to stand farther to the west, and denoted the boundary between Edinburgh and the Canongate estate which in the Middle Ages was owned by the Knights of the Order of St John. The site is now marked by a Maltese cross in the road surface near the top of St John's Street. It was known as St John's Cross, because it stood on property belonging to the Knights of St John, and it marked the ancient boundary of Edinburgh which lay outwith the Netherbow Port.

*St Margaret's
Church
NS 536693
148507*

Built 1928-32, St Margaret's was Sir Robert Lorimer's very last church, completed posthumously by JF Matthew in Lorimer's Scottish style with Baltic-inspired profile. Hipped end roof and Arts & Crafts interior features.

St Michael's Church
NT 002772
49181

"Built next to **Linlithgow Palace** on the site of a chapel destroyed by fire in 1424, this church was the scene of another well-documented ley-line mystery. In 1513, as James IV knelt to pray in St Catherine's Aisle, a 'ghostly wight' appeared and warned him of his coming end at Flodden. In spite of Queen Margaret's pleas, the king ignored the warning and led his men to Flodden field where he was killed in battle." (FF)

Although it is undoubtedly of earlier origin the first mention of "the great church of Linlithgow" is in a charter of 1138 in which King David I gifted it "with all its chapels, lands and other rights" to the Cathedral of St Andrews.

Originally the tower had a stone 'crown' like **St Giles'** cathedral, but it was removed in 1821 as it was in danger of collapse. The striking and unique 'crown of thorns' spire was installed in 1964.

*St Mirren's Well
NS 724795
45896*

Not mentioned by Harry, but it is very close to the alignment to **Bar Hill**.

St Mirren's Well, a spring, is now enclosed within a modern building, and its water, which must originally have drained into the moss, is piped to Colzium. Beside the building is an unshaped stone, 1m x 0.7m x 0.25m, bearing near the top the date 1687 in large contemporary figures. The stone could not be raised for its other face to be examined.

*St Ninian's Chapel,
Redford
NO 415519
33869*

A private walled burial-ground on the SW side of the public road (A926) 130m SW of Redford stands upon the site of a church or chapel dedicated to St Ninian. (Canmore)

St Oran's Chapel
NM 285244
21617

Odhrán (St Oran in the anglicised form) was, according to legend, buried alive as a sacrifice to prevent the walls of the first church from falling down. Dedicated to his memory, the Reilig Odhráin is the cemetery adjacent to Iona Abbey. It was during the 9th-11th centuries that the cemetery became a royal burial ground. In 1549 an inventory of 48 Scottish, 8 Norwegian and 4 Irish kings was recorded. None of these graves are now identifiable (their inscriptions were reported to have worn away at the end of the 17th century) but it is undoubted that Iona is the burial ground for several Kings of Scotland, no matter how unsure the total number may be.

St Orland's Stone NO 400500 *33868*	"This stone is situated in direct alignment between **Glamis Castle** and a prehistoric earthwork 14 miles away at **Baldoukie**." (HC) A Class II upright cross-slab of Old Red Sandstone, nearly rectangular, 2.1m high, 0.7m wide at base, tapering slightly towards the top, and 10" thick. (Canmore)
St Serf's Kirk NO 019144 *26683*	"In the village of Dunning, St Serf's church is famed for its 13th century tower. North of the kirk, in a nearby field stands an ancient menhir. An interesting local legend has it that the tower of St Serf's lines up with two other church towers in the vicinity. There are many different versions of the story, but none of the churches mentioned are anywhere near alignment. Could some vague memory of ley-lines have been passed on for generations and somehow survived the centuries in an out-of-the way Perthshire village?" (FF) Legend attests that St Serf slew a mighty dragon here. The spectacular Dupplin Cross, housed inside the tower, has a dragon carving on one side.
St Thenew's Well NS 589649 *44288*	Andrew MacGeorge, in his *Old Glasgow* says — "It was shaded by an old tree, which drooped over it, and which remained till the end of the last century. On this tree the devotees who frequented the well were accustomed to nail as thanks-offerings small bits of tin-iron, probably manufactured for the purpose by a craftsman in the neighbourhood, representing the parts of the body supposed to have been cured by virtue of the blessed spring, a practice still common in Roman Catholic countries. The late Mr Robert Hart told me that he had been informed by an old man, a Mr Thomson, who had resided in the neighbourhood, that at the end of last century or the beginning of the present he had recollected this well being cleaned out, and of seeing picked out from the debris at the bottom several of those old votive offerings which had dropped from the tree, the stump of which at that time was still standing."
Scottish Parliament NT 267738 *159496*	In 1998 Holyrood was chosen as the location for the new Scottish Parliament building after consideration of a number of sites in Edinburgh. The parliament complex, comprising offices, administration centre, debating chamber and committee rooms, was designed by the Catalan architect Enric Miralles and incorporates the 17th century Queensberry House within the building complex.

Scott's Tourie (East Revoch Cairn) NS 567507 *43943*	"A Bronze Age burial cairn that got its name from a nearby farmer, John Scott of **East Revoch**, who destroyed it for use as building stone c. 1845. The residual mound is now 27m across and 1m high." Not mentioned in *Forgotten Footsteps* although it is sited on the **Drumduff Hill** to **Ben Lomond** PSA. When this tumulus was being removed, about 1836, several urns filled with calcined bones and sticks were found. The spot was pointed out by the farmer (J Scott, farmer) who made the discoveries.
Seedhill Craigs NS 486637	An old fording point of the river. Harry preferred this as the end of an alignment from **Camphill**; however, it is a rather poor ley with few sites. The other alignment through the **Necropolis** and **Provan Hall** is a slightly better match. "Prehistoric settlement site across the river from the Watermill Hotel, Paisley... I was disappointed that the line didn't go to the Abbey, but when I looked into the history of Paisley, I found to my amazement that the riverbank at Seedhill Craigs was the site of St Mirin's original settlement... Tradition has it that the site was also occupied in pre-Roman times." (GSG) Harry bases this claim on a statement in Margaret McCarthy's *A Social Geography of Paisley,* where she says that the site was believed to have been occupied in prehistoric times, long before the arrival of the saint.
Sheep Hill Fort NS 434744 *43388*	"A vitrified Iron Age fort excavated by Euan McKie in 1975. In the vicinity are two groups of rock carvings, the largest of which has 106 cup-marks, 22 sets of concentric rings and circles." (FF)
Sheils Farm (site) NS 525667 *44173 & 44189*	"Possible henge found in the vicinity." (GSG) This area seems to have been a large settlement with several features of interest. The henge site is beneath the Diageo warehouse to the W of IKEA. To the south a multi-vallate palisaded enclosure was found during construction of IKEA. This ditched enclosure, which has been interpreted as a possible henge (Burl 1969) was excavated by Scott in 1973-74. He revealed an enclosure, about 42m E-W by 36m, with a single entrance in the E. (Canmore)
Sheils of Gartlea Chambered Cairn NS 458807 and 'Lang Cairn'	A Neolithic cairn destroyed by quarrying during construction of a forestry road. Marked on the map with a speculative line to **Duncolm**, but otherwise not mentioned by Harry in the text of

NS 457814 *43454*	*Glasgow's Secret Geometry*. It's also in the gazetteer and map of his earlier book *Forgotten Footsteps*, where the alignment *is* extended to **Ben Lomond**. A recumbent slab, "probably a fallen standing stone" was recorded in 1972 about 10m W of the cairn but was destroyed during construction of the forestry road. The Shiels of Gartlea cairn is a Clyde-type cairn, which has been damaged by FCS plantation works to the NW of the structure. The cairn measures 10.3m along its ENE/WSW oriented axis and is 5.1m wide. It survives as an overgrown mound of dry stone rubble. Lang Cairn is a typical Neolithic Clyde-type long cairn with a grand facade composed of large orthostats and a long body of dry-stone rubble, now mostly overgrown with heather, grasses and small conifer trees. (Canmore)
Springhill Farm NS 679644 *45056*	Not mentioned by Harry, but right on his **Woodend Loch** to **Craw Stane** alignment. The partial remains of at least six undated inhumation burials were found in the vicinity. A blue glass bead, possible hammer-stones, fragments of steatite, and pits containing charcoal and iron slag were also recorded.
Stanelie Castle NS 463616 *43150*	"A 16th century tower house on an island in a Strathclyde Regional Council Water Department reservoir. A small medal of Roman date commemorating Titus' capture of Jerusalem was found here in 1829."(GSG)
Stirling Castle NS 789940 *46245*	"No traces of any early settlement remain, but the Castle Rock must have been a significant landmark in prehistoric times." (GSG) "Built on a volcanic plug. Remains of a vitrified hill fort occupy the north end of the outcrop. The present castle dates back to the 12th century and holds a prominent place in Scottish history." (FF) The castle is host to several ghosts, including a Green Lady, always associated with dire events; a Pink Lady, always seen leaving the castle and walking towards the neighbouring Church of the Holy Rude; and a phantom Highlander, who is often mistaken for a tour guide. Ghostly footsteps have also been heard pacing out a sentry beat on the battlements.
Stone axe (Port Glasgow) NS 340726 *75480*	The butt end of a mottled light-green axe was recovered by Mr T Hendry, while digging in his garden at 59 Slaemuir Avenue, Port Glasgow, at a depth of approx. 0.3m. It was retained by the finder.

The Hub
NT 255735
74032

Former Assembly of Church of Scotland, the spire of which is the highest point in central Edinburgh. The site was once called The Witches' Knowe.
Meeting place of the General Assembly of the Church of Scotland to 1929. Tallest spire in Edinburgh, at 73 metres.

The Motte
NS 358683
42228

"UFO-shaped mound off the B788, 3/4 mile from Kilmacolm. On private property but can be seen from the road." (FF)
aka Milton Bridge.
The remains of a motte associated with an Anglo-Norman timber castle... [and] visible as a substantial mound located in a prominent position overlooking the Gryfe Water. (Canmore)

Tinto Hill
NS 953343
47525

"Crowned by a massive Bronze Age cairn. Though 30 miles from Glasgow, this hill can be seen from the Necropolis on a clear day... At 2,300 feet Tinto Hill is prominent in the south-eastern skyline from many parts of Glasgow. Its summit is crowned by a huge 6m cairn dating back to the Bronze Age, and neolithic stone axes have been found there. The name Tinto signifies 'hill of fire', and old records state that its summit was once a place whereon the Druids lighted up their fires in heathen worship." (GSG)
The cairn on the summit of Tinto Hill is one of the largest bronze-age round cairns in Scotland, measuring 43m in diameter by almost 6m in height.

Torrance House
NS 654526
44967

"Built to replace an earlier structure burned to the ground in 1570, this tower house now serves as a museum for Calderglen Country Park. A possible rectangular motte was reported on a promontory beside the River Calder in the north angle of the park." (GSG)
In the tower is a wall-tablet with the inscription 'Built 1605 Restored 1875' and the arms of the Stuarts of Torrance. No trace of an earlier building. (Canmore)

Traprain Law
NT 580747
56374

One of the largest prehistoric forts in Scotland, home to the Gododdin, or Votadini as the Romans named them.
A large hoard of chopped-up Roman silver plate weighing over 563 lbs was excavated in 1919.

*Tron Kirk
(Edinburgh)*
NT 259738
52236

The Tron Kirk, Edinburgh's parish church, was started in 1637 but not completed until 1678 because of delays caused by the Wars of the Covenant after 1638. It was Edinburgh's first Presbyterian kirk, free of the taint of Catholicism attached to the history of Greyfriars and St

Giles. It takes its name from the 'tron', the weighing-machine that stood nearby to check that market traders were using genuine weights. The spire was rebuilt in 1828 following damage from a disastrous 1824 fire in adjacent Old Assembly Close.

Highly distinctive Dutch-influenced Classical-Gothic survival style square-plan church with octagonal steeple surmounting landmark clock tower. (Canmore)

Tumulus, Pollok Golf Course NS 545616 *44405*	"…as it was nearly 200m from the nearest PSA. I naturally did not include it in my maps." (GSG) An unglazed cinerary urn containing fragments of calcined bones was found in 1863. An amber bead was found near the urn (Canmore).
Underground cell NS 573622 *44295*	From Ludovic Mann's 1918 book *Mary Queen of Scots at Langside* "…situated precisely on a line leading from a prehistoric, circular, defensive earthwork in Queen's Park to a similar … earthwork in Pollok Wood". (Mann, p100) (Canmore) An underground galleried and alcoved house was brought to light at 36 Minard Road, Crossmyloof.
Viewpark (site) NS 708667 *45809*	An urn containing a cremation deposit was found about 120m SE of Viewpark, Uddingston, in about 1820. Not mentioned by Harry, but a good extension of his alignment through **Carmyle Fords**.
Wallace's Well NS 638696	Historic well where Wallace is said to have refreshed himself when visiting his friend in **Robroyston**.
Walls Hillfort NS 412588 *43011*	"Excavations have revealed traces of an early Iron Age occupation. The fort appears to have occupied an area of about seven hectares and is thought to have been an oppidum of the Damnoni tribe." (GSG) Exact location at OS trig point. One of the largest hillforts in Scotland. A struck flake of green flint was recovered from a runnel just outside the main entrance to the fort in 1970. In 1977, a rim fragment of a large cooking pot of coarse grey-black clay was found. (Canmore)
Wallstale Dun NS 774908 *46232*	Not mentioned in Harry's gazetteer but appears on the map of *Forgotten Footsteps* on the alignment from **Stirling Castle** to **Carron Fords**. A 1965 dig found fragments of both a saddle and a rotary quern, a piece of slag and a stone with a groove on it, possibly for sharpening needles.
Whitehill cup and ring marks NS 513739 *44538*	There are several examples of rock art in the immediate area. These are close to Harry's **Duncolm** to **Tinto Hill** alignment.

Wildshaw Burn
NS 881271
46425

Harry mentions this site in passing in an article for Northern Earth #79, autumn 1999.

This largely ruinous stone circle was 'rediscovered' in 1990 prior to road-building work to widen the M74 corridor. Equinox, midwinter and midsummer sunrise and sunset events have been observed over some of the stones in the circle by archaeologists from Biggar Museum .

Woodend Loch
NS 706669
45770

"A Mesolithic site in use before agriculture came to Scotland. Worked flint tools and waste flakes were recovered from the north shire ...unlike any other site mentioned so far, Woodend Loch dates from the Mesolithic or Middle Stone Age era. Some 60m from the water's edge there were two half-buried boulders that interested me...."(GSG)

DIRECTORY OF LEYS

LISTING OF ALIGNMENTS

Between *Forgotten Footsteps* and *Glasgow's Secret Geometry,* we can identify a total of 38 of Harry's PSAs. Adding material from *Haunted Castles* and *Leyline Quest* brings the total to 44. There may be more that he catalogued, for instance in Forgotten Footsteps he mentions "Ley 292, near Kilmacolm", or "Ley 698 in the King's Park, Stirling", but if so, that list has been lost. Most likely, he was simply adding these higher numbers for effect. We may never know. (Those numbers correspond to leys 11 and 9 respectively in the following directory.)

This listing contains all the alignments mentioned by Harry, with additional sites and alignments added from my own research and that of others. Sites that are not part of Harry's work are generally denoted by *italics*. Cross-references to the Gazetteer are marked in **bold**.

The Google Earth map showing all the sites and alignments can be found at:

glasgowsecretgeometry.uk/map.

Section 1 — Forgotten Footsteps

1. Dundee Law to Doune Cross (72.9km)

Dundee Law NO 391313	An Iron Age vitrified fort overlaid by a Medieval (c. 16th Century) fortification. The site was extensively damaged following WW2 by the addition of the war memorial.
Mills Observatory (Balgay Hill) NO 377307	The site of the fort is somewhat to the east of the observatory on the highest point of the hill. Built in 1935, Mills was the first purpose-built public astronomical observatory in the UK. The unusual papier-mâché dome contains a Victorian 10-inch refracting telescope.
Megginch Castle NO 241246	Over a thousand years ago, this was a monastic community of St Gilliemichael and All Saints, all that remains are four clumps of yew trees reputedly planted at the corners of the monastic gardens. The castle website records that *"the Ceinn Tour and fortalice of Megginch"* were already established by 1460. The Castle gardens are open once a year under Scotland's Gardens Scheme, but the castle itself is only open for special events such as weddings.
Elcho Castle NO 164210	One of Scotland's best-preserved 16th century tower houses, built by the family of Wemyss of that Ilk around 1560. It was closed the public in 2022 for repairs and conservation work. One of several Harry Bell sites associated with William Wallace.
Dunbarney House NO 110187	No mention of this in the text, but it appears on Harry's map. Built around 1697 or slightly later, the B-listed house is a private residence. The grounds contain an early 18th century vaulted tower mill that is a scheduled monument
Jackschairs Wood NO 072168	Cairn and hill fort. Not mentioned in Harry's gazetteer but marked on the map as 'Fort'. The interior is dominated by a rocky knoll and several platforms, of which three appear to be the remains of timber roundhouses.
St Serf's Kirk NO 019144	Legend attests that St Serf slew a mighty dragon here. An old quarry at a nearby hill is locally referred to as the Dragon's Lair. The church has a post-Reformation T-plan, and the tower contains the spectacular 3m high Dupplin Cross, a superb example of 9th century Pictish carving (including a dragon), that was relocated here from near Forteviot in 2002. (Historic Scotland – free entry)

Kincardine Castle NN 949114	Not mentioned in Harry's gazetteer, although it is plotted on his map. The old Kincardine Castle was built in the 13th century and was a classic quadrangle fortress without windows and surrounded by a moat. Pig bones found during a 2013 excavation were carbon dated to between 1040-1220 CE (95.4% probability). The later 19th century manor house on the site is a B-listed building.
Millhill fort NN 923100t	aka Loaninghead hillfort. A small wooded hillock next to the A823 Gleneagles junction.
Glassingal House (site) NN 795045	Plotted on the map but not mentioned in Harry's gazetteer. Demolished 1966.
Doune Cross NN 727015	Described in an Act of Parliament of 1696 as having been "recently erected".

2. Doune Cross to Cairnpapple Hill (39.8km)

Doune Cross NN 727015	A simpler cross originally stood at the site of the Kilmadock East Church in the Main Street. Doune obtained a Royal Charter from James VI in 1611, giving the Earl of Moray the right to hold markets.
Doune Castle NN 728010	A rather poor fit on this alignment. The site itself dates back at least to the 1st century CE when a Roman camp and hospital was established on Castlehill, now under the playing fields of the local school. This may be a better fit for the alignment.
Stirling Castle NS 789940	Stirling Castle was first mentioned in documents in 1110. This was when King Alexander I dedicated a chapel on top of the hill. From then on, the hill and the wooden fortress that was built on it became the primary Royal centre. The volcanic plug that it occupies has remains of a vitrified fort at the north end, so it was clearly occupied in prehistory.
Plean Tower NS 850869	Also known as 'Cock-a-Bendy' Castle. In January 1746 the castle was occupied by Jacobite troops while Bonnie Prince Charlie resided at the nearby Bannockburn House for a month. The tower is now restored as Plane Castle and is available for holiday accommodation sleeping six.
Mumrills Roman Fort NS 920795	Largest fort on the Antonine Wall. May have been the site of Wallace's defeat at the Battle of Falkirk. The farm at Mumrills was also used as an early site for the Falkirk Relief Church.

Cairnpapple Hill NS 987718	Undoubtedly the most important neolithic site in Central Scotland. The 'cairn' is actually a concrete dome erected to protect the cist burials inside. On a clear day, you can see from Goat Fell on Arran as far as Traprain Law in East Lothian.

3. Cairnpapple Hill to Bridgeness Roman Fort (10.2km)

Cairnpapple Hill NS 987718	In the care of Historic Scotland. The site is accessible all year round, but entrance to the main dome is only available April-September and a fee is payable. But, as Harry says, *"Don't miss this one!"*
St Michael's Church NT 002772	Canmore says this is "perhaps the finest parish church in Scotland." A great fire in 1424 caused great damage to the church and the neighbouring **Linlithgow Palace.**
Linlithgow Palace NT 002773	Linlithgow Palace stands on a low hill above a small inland loch. The name Linlithgow means 'the loch in the damp hollow'.
Bridgeness Roman Fort NT 014816	No visible remains, but a replica of the Distance Slab stands in Kinningars Park, close to where it was found.

4. Bridgeness to Arthur's Seat (96km/ 27.8km)

(Ben Lomond) NN 367028	Most southerly 'Munro' (mountain over 3,000ft./ 974m). Harry speculated about an alignment between here and **Bridgeness.**
(Plean Tower) NS 850869	Now also known as Plane Castle. The only site on the alignment between Ben Lomond and Bridgeness. The **Doune Cross** - **Cairnpapple** ley crosses here.
Bridgeness Roman Fort NT 014816	The precise location of this fort remains a mystery.
Blackness Castle NT 055802	*'The ship that never sailed'*, an epithet given to the castle from its prow-like end pointing into the Forth.
Abercorn Castle (site) NT 080792	Stage nine on the nature trail from Hopetoun House, all that remains is an uneven mound within a grassy area in the woods.
Hopetoun House NT 088790	Paid entry to grounds and the house. Used as a location in several episodes of the TV series 'Outlander'.
Dolphington House NT 158769	Appears on some maps as 'Dolphinton'. The house is some distance north of the alignment. However, a row of farm workers' cottages once stood about 7/8 mile to the SSW and was known as 'Standing Stane'.

| St Gile's Cathedral
NT 257736 | Situated on the crossing point with the **Royal Mile ley**. St Giles' was built on the very eastern edge of Edinburgh and pre-dates most of the Old Town. |
| Arthur's Seat
NT 276728 | In 1836 five boys hunting for rabbits found a set of 17 miniature coffins containing small wooden figures in a cave on the crags of Arthur's Seat. Their purpose has remained a mystery ever since. |

5. Arthur's Seat to Duncolm (81km)

Arthur's Seat NT 276728	Volcanic plug in the centre of Edinburgh, a popular climb offering great views over the city and beyond.
Edinburgh Labyrinth NT 258729	Chartres-replica labyrinth in George Square Gardens constructed by Edinburgh University Chaplaincy and dowsed to be on this alignment by Grahame Gardner. Open during daylight hours, free entry.
Beechmount House NT 212731	A questionable location, but two alignments cross between the house and the golf course on the south slope of Corstorphine Hill.
Ochiltree Fort NT 030740	A multivallate hillfort, called Peace Knowe on Canmore.
Cockleroy Fort NS 989745	One of the highest points in the Bathgate Hills, part of Beecraigs Country Park. Children use its easy slope for egg-rolling at Easter.
Bowdenhill Fort NS 977745	Hillfort overlooking the highest part of Bowden Hill. A substantial stone and earth rampart encloses an area approximately 250m x 100m.
Arns Tomb NS 805755	Thought to be the Melville family burial ground, probably 19th century in origin.
Cumbernauld House NS 770756	There is a group of stones on the hilltop near Castle Way, but they are some distance south of the alignment.
Bar Hill (Castle Hill) NS 709761	Castle hill is a prominent bump to the NE of the Roman fort, offering good views.
Mugdock Castle NS 550771	Built by the Graham family in the 14th century but now mostly in ruins apart from one restored tower of four stories containing a small museum. Situated in Mugdock Country Park.
Duncolm NS 470774	The largest of the Kilpatrick Hills, and a good walk in dry weather.

6.   Duncolm to Ben Lomond (27.5km) — 'Ley 374' in the text.

Duncolm NS 470774	"The name means 'Fort of the Dove', or 'Fort of Columba'."
Shiels of Gartlee Chambered Cairn (and Lang Cairn) NS 458807 NS 457814	A 'Clyde type' neolithic cairn, damaged by forestry workings on the NW. There used to be a recumbent stone about 10m west of the cairn, but it was destroyed during construction of the forestry road. Lang Cairn has a more imposing façade, although now much overgrown.
Duncryne NS 435859	Called locally 'The Dumpling' because of its shape. An easy walk to the summit offers spectacular views of Loch Lomond and 'The Lady of the Lake' (Inchcailloch island).
Craigie Fort NS 416909	Not much to see now, but a great viewpoint and part of the West Highland Way.
Arrochymore Dun NS 412919	Remains of a drystone fortification near Arrochymore Farmhouse. Not mentioned by Harry but clearly on the alignment.
Halfway Well NN 377001	Harry marked this on a hand-drawn map in the galleys of the first edition of *Glasgow's Secret Geometry* but did not include it in the final version.
Ben Lomond NN 367028	A fine walk in good weather, but don't take it for granted as the weather can change rapidly at 3,000ft.

7.   Cairnpapple Hill to Edinburgh Castle (26.5km)

Cairnpapple Hill NS 987718	Highest point in the Bathgate Hills with spectacular views. The original henge aligns to midwinter sunrise.
Huly Hill NT 123726	A now-restored tumulus with three surviving standing stones. A bronze dagger along with some animal charcoal and bones was found within.
Newbridge Stone NT 126726	An outlier across the busy motorway junction, now outside the entrance to a technology company's offices.
Beechmount House NT 212731	The mark point is where two alignments cross on the slopes of Corstorphine Hill.
Edinburgh Castle NT 251734	The most popular tourist attraction in Scotland, and probably also the most haunted.

8. Stirling Castle to Drumduff Hill (52km) — 'Ley 628' in the text.

Stirling Castle NS 789940	One of the largest and most historically significant castles in Scotland, and one of the most popular tourist attractions. Booking recommended.
King's Park Cup and Ring markings NS 783930	A small sandstone boulder 10m west of the memorial bench and 7m north of the track running round the south of the golf course. The markings are barely discernible now.
Wallstale Dun NS 774908	An almost circular dun or broch about 45ft. in diameter, situated on a rocky spur.
Ghost's Knowe NS 747857	About 250m west of the alignment, site of a large round cairn originally surrounded by 12 large stones. The cairn contained a burial with several artefacts including a stone axe and a golden horn, all now lost.
Carron Ford NS 743837	The old ford can be seen as some stepping stones just to the east of the huts.
St Mirin's Well NS 724795	Not mentioned by Harry, but tantalisingly close to this alignment between **Carron Fords** and **Bar Hill**.
Bar Hill (Castle Hill) NS 709761	This Roman fort and bathhouse is of interest as it is situated some 40m south of the Antonine Wall. **Castle Hill** is probably the site of the Druid sanctuary known to the Romans as *Medionemeton* (middle grove).
Provan Hall NS 667663	15th century house, although some parts may date back to the 12th century, making it a contender for being the oldest house in Glasgow. Recently restored (2023).
Carmyle Fords NS 646614	There used to be two fords here, about 300m apart, according to Harry. The riverside walkway is pleasant on a sunny day, but the site is otherwise unremarkable.
Mains Castle NS 627560	Motte and medieval tower house, now restored as a private residence.
Drumduff Hill NS 583462	Harry claimed to have found a turf-built enclosure on this alignment, about 50m southeast of the summit. The location is within the Whitelee wind farm.

9. Drumduff Hill to Duncolm (33.25km) — 'Ley 698' in the text.

Drumduff Hill NS 583462	Roughly in the centre of Whitelee wind farm.
Scott's Tourie NS 567507	Properly called **East Revoch Cairn**, this Bronze Age cairn was destroyed for use as building stone by the farmer John Scott around 1845.
Dei'ls Plantin NS 557535	Also known as **Bonnyton Mound**. The place where Harry began his explorations. The mound, identified as a tumulus, was roughly excavated by the landowner around 1900, but it is not known if anything was found.
Mearns Castle NS 552553	Harry notes that this is about 50m east of the alignment proper.
Crookston Castle NS 525627	A fortified castle was built here by Robert de Croc in the 12th century, but Harry thought the site could be prehistoric. Crookston Castle is the second-oldest building in Glasgow, after the Cathedral.
Renfrew Parish Church NS 507675	A church has stood on this site since at least the 12th century. Harry thought the site could be much older. Now closed.
Abbotsford Parish Church NS 498701	Now called Waterfront Church. Harry himself was dubious about this site, but thought it might be connected with a ancient ford over the Clyde near this point.
Cist, Duntocher NS 488726	A stone cist containing human remains was found here in 1817.
Duncolm NS 470774	It's a long walk in from Old Kilpatrick station or the car park just north of the Erskine Bridge, but the views over the Clyde are worth the climb.

*This alignment can be extended by following Ley number 6 to **Ben Lomond***

10. Dumgoyne to Craig of Todholes (29km)

Dumgoyne NS 541827	A very distinctive volcanic plug in the Campsie Hills. May have been used as a Roman signalling station.
Duncolm NS 470774	"At first glance it looks like a Scots cousin of Ayers Rock".
Sheep Hill Fort NS 434744	A vitrified Iron Age fort excavated by Euan McKie in 1975. Several large outcroppings of cup-and-ring markings were found.
The Motte NS 358683	A substantial mound, visible from the road, possibly a motte associated with a 15th century Anglo-Norman timber castle.

Duchal House NS 352679	The house dates from the mid-18th century, but the lands of Duchal were recorded as belonging to the Lyle family in the 13th century. Their stronghold was **Duchal Castle**. The house and gardens are occasionally opened to visitors.
Craig of Todholes NS 312647	Harry mentions "a site in this area", possibly referring to a ruined rectangular structure a little to the south. Canmore mentions some oval enclosures on the SW hilltop.

11. The Motte to Dechmont Hillfort (31.6km) — 'Ley 292' in the text.

The Motte NS 358683	Part of the Duchal estate, on private ground but can be seen from the road. A substantial mound located in a prominent position overlooking the Gryfe Water.
Houston Cross NS 405669	The cross used to stand outside the old Houston Parish Church before being moved to its present position. It is still some 160m north of Harry's alignment.
Paisley Abbey NS 485639	The alignment passes just to the north of the Abbey, but still within its grounds. It does, however, run through the site of the old Paisley Mercat Cross.
Crookston Castle NS 525627	Second-oldest building in Glasgow, open daily and well worth a visit. A Roman coin was dug up in a garden in Crookston Road, on this alignment.
Pollok House NS 548618	Not mentioned by Harry, but the alignment passes through the grounds of Pollok House, which dates back at least to the 13th century and is now managed by the National Trust for Scotland.
Aikenhead House NS 596602	Harry says in the text, "A site near Aikenhead House". In *Glasgow's Secret Geometry*, he mentions a different location in King's Park.
Dechmont Hillfort NS 656582	Little now visible of the fort that once stood here. Harry says that "Beltane fires were lit here until the beginning of the 19th century."

12. Duchal Castle to Crookston Castle (19.8km) — '*The Ghost Ley of Paisley*'.

Duchal Castle NS 334684	Stronghold of the Lyle family in the 13th century, little now remains other than some vegetation-covered ruins. The site of a series of hauntings by a ghostly monk from **Paisley Abbey**, described in the *Lanercost Chronicle*. Human bones were discovered in an upper room when the castle was dismantled in the 17th century to construct **Duchal House**.

Duchal House NS 352679	Private residence set within a late 17th / early 18th century designed formal landscape. Open for occasional open days. Also said to be haunted.
Houston South Mound NS 401664	A large cairn containing stone cists, or coffins, containing cremated human bones, a necklace, a flint knife and a Bronze Age food vessel.
Oakshaw Trinity Church NS 47964t	Formerly Paisley High Church. Haunted by the ghost of stonemason 'Wee Leitch' who fell to his death from the tower. The pavement outside has spectacles, a handkerchief and a heart worked into the cobbles to mark the spot where he fell. The hilltop of Oakshawhead was a defended hillfort in prehistory and is thought to have later been a major citadel during the Roman occupation, although little evidence has been found to support that assertion.
Paisley Town Hall NS 484369	A local ghost-hunting club reported ghostly goings-on in the basement during their visit.
Paisley Abbey NS 485639	The ghost of Duchal is said to be a monk from the Abbey, excommunicated for some undisclosed indiscretion, who appeared after his death and was banished from here by the other monks.
Crookston Castle NS 525627	In *Haunted Castles*, Harry reports a shadowy figure seen by RAF men occupying the site during WWII, and subsequently by some boy scouts camping on the hillside.

13. De'il's Plantin to Mains Castle (7.45km)

De'il's Plantin (Bonnyton Mound) NS 557535	"It was supposed to be haunted, if I remembered correctly." The site chosen by Harry to begin his research. Despite evidence of digging at the top, the rest of the mound remains largely undisturbed. Good views of **Duncolm** and **Ben Lomond** on a clear day.
Eaglesham House (site) NS 565538	19th century mansion designed by David Bryce in Scots baronial style; known locally as 'Eaglesham Castle'. Burnt down in 1954 and demolished in 1984 for the building of the Linn Products factory.
Rough Hill Motte NS 607553	Not mentioned by Harry but exactly on this alignment. There is evidence that a large structure, possibly a tower, once stood on the top,
Mains Castle & Motte NS 627560	15th century keep build on a large mound above a loch known as Crawford's Hole. Evidence of Bronze Age habitation has been found in the vicinity.

Section 2 – Glasgow's Secret Geometry

14. Fairy Knowe to Old Sauchie (9.9km)

Fairy Knowe NS 796981	A cist burial containing flint arrowheads, a beaker, and a stone spearhead was unearthed here. Local folklore tells of a drover/piper who encountered a fairy called 'Blue Jacket' who spirited him away into the mound. It is said that sometimes the sound of pipes can be heard within.
Stirling Castle NS 789940	Rather surprisingly, this is the only time that Stirling Castle features in *Glasgow's Secret Geometry*.
Flint arrowhead (Stirling) NS 786927	A leaf-shaped flint arrowhead was found in the garden of number 34 Park Place, Stirling.
Old Sauchie NS 772881	Site of a battle in 1488, this medieval tower house dates from the 16th century. The tower and associated buildings were restored and converted into dwellings c. 2000.

15. Old Sauchie to Camphill Ringwork (33km) – *'The Straight Road with No Path'*

Old Sauchie NS 772881	The start of Harry's *'Straight Road with No Path'* – although technically it should begin at **Carron Ford**, after St Kentigern has collected the body of Fergus the Holy Man.
Carron Ford NS 743837	The ford is visible just to the east of the huts. Stones can be seen protruding from the river when the water is low.
Balcastle Motte NS 701781	Almost completely surrounded by water courses, this 12th century motte was thought to be a possible Neolithic site by Harry. A polished stone axe was found nearby. On a clear day, the **Necropolis** is just visible to the southwest
Auchendavy Roman Fort NS 677749	No visible remains above ground. There is no suggestion of older occupation here, so why did Harry include it?
Robroyston NS 634693	A site with even less provenance than **Auchendavy**, the pink Iona granite Wallace monument marks the site of the house where William Wallace was betrayed to the English c. 1305.
Necropolis NS 603654	Once a 'Druidical place of worship' according to Hugh Mackintosh, and site of a prehistoric hillfort known as Dun Chattan according to Ludovic Mann.

Dovehill NS 599648	Not mentioned by Harry, this is where a mound was miraculously raised by St Kentigern so the crowd he was preaching to could better see him, according to legend.
Camphill Ringwork NS 577621	Much uncertainty still surrounds the origins of this site and the stones within, yet it can be a very atmospheric location to visit.

This alignment was extended by May Miles Thomas in her 'Devil's Plantation' iPhone app. See Ley number 51.

16. Camphill Ringwork to Dunwan hillfort (13.5km)

Camphill Ringwork NS 577621	One of the key points in Harry's 'Glasgow Triangle'. Thought to be prehistoric with later medieval use.
De'il's Plantin NS 557535	Still a very atmospheric location despite the traffic noise from the Southern Relief Road.
Dunwan hillfort NS 546489	Harry describes this in the text as his "early morning weather indicator". Easily accessible from Whitelees Windfarm.

17. Camphill Ringwork to Walls hillfort (17km)

Camphill Ringwork NS 577621	May have been used as an army camp by the army of Mary, Queen of Scots before the Battle of Langside.
Nether Pollok Castle (site) NS 550616	A 13th century castle once stood on the rock now occupied by the stable block of **Pollok House**.
Walls Hillfort NS 412588	Early Iron Age hillfort occupied by the Damnonii tribe. Harry lists three alignments from here, yet there are few sites on them.

18. Camphill Ringwork to Seedhill Craigs (9.3km)

Camphill Ringwork NS 577621	Marked as a 'Celtic Camp' on many old maps of the area.
Underground cell NS 573622	An underground "galleried and alcoved house" was excavated by Ludovic Mann, whose writings drew Harry's attention to this alignment
Ross Hall NS 522630	Harry is mistaken about this site. He refers to a "British Camp" mentioned by TCF Brotchie, but that is about 1.5km to the west at **Rosshall Mains**, and is not on the alignment.

| Auchentorlie House
NS 494635 | "According to Knox's plan of Paisley (1839 revised edition), Auchentorlie House was built on a knoll or mound. This structure, however, proved untraceable." |
| Seedhill Craigs
NS 486637 | An old fording point of the White Cart water, said to be the site of St Mirin's original settlement. |

19. Camphill Ringwork to Dumbarton Rock (21.7km)

Camphill Ringwork NS 577621	A peaceful and atmospheric location at any time of year.
Argyll Stane/ St Conval's Chariot NS 495678	A pair of stones behind railings in the car park of the Normandy Hotel. The Argyll Stane is supposed to have been a cross-base, but the hollow seems too small to have supported a cross shaft, so the two stones may be confused.
Inchinnan All Hallows Church NS 491680	Site thought to be the location of St Conval's first settlement. The site is managed by the Inchinnan Historical Society and is open on special occasions.
Inchinnan New Parish church NS 479689	Several Templar stones rescued from **All Hallows** church are displayed outside the church, including three intricately carved stones of the Govan School housed in the porch area. Also has a small grass labyrinth.
Dumbarton Rock NS 399745	*Alt Clut*, or *Dun Breatainn*, the Fort of the Britons, was the seat of power of the Brythonic kings of Strathclyde before falling to to Irish-based Vikings after a 4-month siege. The seat of power moved upriver to Govan and Partick.

20. Camphill Ringwork to Cochno Stone (13.9km)

Camphill Ringwork NS 577621	Harry used to play hide-and-seek here as a child, using the stones as the 'den'.
Govan Old Parish Church NS 553659	Thought to occupy the site of St Constantine's monastery. The church houses a fantastic collection of carved stones and Viking hogbacks dating from the 10th and 11th centuries. **Doomster Hill** stood nearby.
Cochno Stone NS 504738	Harry was unable to find the Cochno Stone as it was buried at the time. It was fully excavated in 2016 to allow a full LIDAR and photogrammetry scan before being reburied.

21. Viewpark to Castlehead Ringwork (23.5km)

Viewpark (site) NS 708667	An urn containing a Bronze Age cremation deposit was found about 120m SE of Viewpark, Uddingston, in about 1820. Not mentioned by Harry.
Kylepark (site) NS 688609	Another Bronze Age funerary site. One of the vessels found is in the Kelvingrove museum.
Carmyle Fords NS 646614	The easternmost point of Harry's 'Glasgow Triangle'. Harry mentions two fords, some 300m apart.
Gallowflat Mound NS 623615	A very large and impressive tumulus, once a garden feature of Gallowflat House, but now rather incongruously surrounded by social housing.
Rutherglen Old Parish Church NS 613617	Once the site of St Conval's wattle chapel. Another large tumulus is thought to have been levelled off to create the churchyard. William Wallace brokered a peace treaty with England here in 1297.
Camphill Ringwork NS 577621	There is a possible winter solstice sunrise alignment in the stones, and an equinox sunset alignment to the outlier down the slope.
Burrell Ringwork NS 555624	"There are two ringworks in Pollok Country Park, and this one, a semi-circular part-obliterated bank of earth, lies in the woods about 300m N of the Burrell Collection."
Crookston Castle NS 525627	The second-oldest building in Glasgow after the Cathedral. Free entry.
Our Lord's Cross (site)	Not mentioned by Harry. WM Metcalfe's A *History of Paisley* records a cross "near Saucel Hill".
Castlehead Ringwork NS 474633	Described as either "a Norman ringwork of earth and timber" or a site "of Iron Age provenance".

22. Necropolis to Hamilton Motte (15.2km)

Necropolis NS 603654	Ancient Druidic hillfort of Dun Chattan. The Necropolis was laid out by the city's guilds on similar lines to Pere LaChaise, Paris, and was opened May 1833.
Bothwell Castle NS 687593	Picturesque ruins of the 13th century castle that once enjoyed diplomatic links with the great courts of Europe.
Bothwell Bridge NS 710577	One of the few medieval ribbed-arch bridges remaining in Scotland, and site of an old fording point. Site of 1679 battle where the Duke of Monmouth defeated the Covenanters.
Hamilton Motte NS 727566	About 200m north of Hamilton Mausoleum, in the woodland next to Hamilton motorway services.

23. Necropolis to Harelaw Cairn (17km)

Necropolis NS 603654	Open daylight hours. The *Friends of Glasgow Necropolis* run excellent guided tours.
Ladywell NS 603653	The last public well to remain open in the city, now capped. Located at the foot of Ladywell Street, at the back of the Drygate Brewery.
Barrack Street NS 603651	Harry included this possibly Mesolithic site to fit his PSA from the **Cochno Stone** to **Tinto Hill**. A deposit of oyster shells was found during building work in 1962.
High Cross Hill NS 610600	Not mentioned by Harry. An Early Bronze Age axe was found here some time before 1888.
Lickprivick Tumulus NS 610519	Possibly a medieval motte associated with the former **Lickprivick Castle**, although Harry thought it more likely to be a prehistoric tumulus.
Harelaw Cairn (site) NS 612486	Site of a Bronze Age cairn, destroyed in 1808. Said to have contained urns with cremated human bones, but nothing has survived.

24. Necropolis to Glengarnock Castle (30.5km)

Necropolis NS 603654	From the top, **Tinto Hill** is visible on a clear day.
Ramshorn Kirk NS 595652	One of the oldest burial grounds in Glasgow. A church has stood here since at least 1720.
St Enoch's Sanctuary NS 589649	Site of a Holy Well dedicated to St Kentigern's mother, Thenew. St Enoch's Square is a corruption of her name, The section of Argyle Street leading here from Trongate used to be called St Thenew's Gait.
Ross Hall NS 522630	One of Harry's mistakes. The grounds are a public park and are nice to visit, but there is no ancient site here.
Stanelie Castle NS 463616	A 16th century tower house, now oddly marooned in the middle of a reservoir and not open to the public. A Roman medallion was found here in 1829.
Lochwinnoch Peel NS 361587	Remains of a keep on the southeastern shores of Castle Semple loch.
Glengarnock Castle NS 310573	A ruined castle on the banks of the River Garnock, near Kilbirnie. The ruins are in a good state of preservation.

25. Necropolis to Dumgoyne (18.5km)

Necropolis NS 603654	The main nexus of the PSAs is on the flatter area of the hilltop nearer the Monteath Mausoleum.
Milton sickle NS 589696	Not mentioned by Harry. Two flint arrowheads and a crescent-shaped flint sickle were found by boys of nearby St Augustine's school. There were donated to the Hunterian Museum.
Balmuildy Roman Fort NS 581717	Harry thought that this site pre-dated the building of the Antonine Wall and guarded a crossing point of the River Kelvin.
Middleton (site) NS 562765	Not mentioned by Harry, but a row of standing stones aligned NW-SE once stood here, possibly marking this alignment. The largest stone was called 'The Law Stone of Mugdock'.
Dumgoyne NS 541827	A prominent volcanic plug at the end of the Campsies, visible from many other sites in Glasgow. Harry thought there might be the remains of a prehistoric cairn on the top. A steep, but not too difficult, path leads from the Glengoyne Distillery at its foot.

26. Necropolis to Walls Hillfort (20.25km)

Necropolis NS 603654	As you cross the Bridge of Sighs, look down at the grassy bank on the right, where a metal drain cover marks the site of the Priest's Well.
St Thenew's Well NS 589649	Associated with **St Enoch's Sanctuary**, this well, sacred to St Kentigern's mother, is long lost to view, but is possibly culverted under a drain cover in Howard Street at the back of the St Enoch Centre.
Crookston Castle NS 525627	In 2008, a paranormal group claimed to have made contact with a "tetchy female ghost called Elspeth or Elspet".
Gleniffer Braes NS 453602	Two standing stones seem to mark this alignment, although they are not mentioned by Harry.
Walls Hillfort NS 774908	An early Iron Age hillfort. Some worked flakes of green flint and a fragment of a coarse clay cooking pot were found near the main entrance in 1977.

27. Tinto Hill to Auchenreoch Mains (69.5km)

Tinto Hill NS 953343	"30 miles from Glasgow, yet visible from the Necropolis on a clear day." A huge Bronze Age cairn crowns the summit.
Cadzow Castle NS 734537	Now a crumbling ruin overlooking the gorge of the Clyde. There is a nice circular walk from Chatelherault that passes this site.
Coatshill Cist (site) NS 683584	A Bronze Age cist containing a food vessel was found on this site in 1939.
Drumsargad Castle NS 666597	Some remains were extant about 1775, but no traces of the castle remain. (Canmore)
Carmyle Fords NS 646614	The 1st edition of the OS 25-inch map (Lanark 1864, Sheet XI.1) depicts a ferry crossing on the River Clyde at Carmyle. It is not shown on the 2nd edition of the map.
Bronze Age Burial Ground, Clyde Iron Works NS 638623	What appears to have been a Bronze Age burial ground was uncovered during the construction of the Clyde Iron Works. An 1836 excavation found "two cinerary urns filled with ashes, two bronze bridle-bits, and various other relics".
Necropolis NS 603654	Some 50,000 burials have taken place at the Necropolis and most of 3,500 tombs have been constructed up to 4.2m deep, with stone walls and brick partitions. On the top of the Necropolis, tombs were blasted out of the rock face.
Glasgow Cathedral NS 602655	Glasgow Cathedral stands on one of the oldest Christian sites in Scotland and is the oldest building in Glasgow.
Cairn Hill NS 543709	Harry writes, "I was unable to find information about any cairn that this hill could have been named after. At the time of my visit, Cairn Hill was a wasteland of thorny bushes that conspired to rip my casual attire..."
Castlehill Roman Fort NS 524727	"Pottery sherds have been found here in the roots of fallen trees, but little remains above ground to tell the story of the past... eighteen hundred years ago the 4th Cohort of Gauls guarded the Antonine Wall at this point."
Whitehill cup and ring marks NS 513739	There are several examples of rock art in the immediate area. These are close to Harry's **Duncolm** — **Tinto Hill** alignment.
Duncolm NS 470774	The remains of an enclosure were recorded in 1971, however, a subsequent examination of the hill by Royal Commission researchers in 1975 failed to reveal any trace of any structure.
Auchenreoch Mains NS 432803	Also called the Drover's Cairn, this was certainly visited by Harry, but is just marked as 'cairn' on the map of *Glasgow's Secret Geometry*. This is a Bronze Age burial cairn on the slopes of the 'Hill of Standing Stones'.

28. Tinto Hill to Cochno Stone (60km)

Very close to the previous alignment, but Harry records it as "half a degree to the left".

Tinto Hill NS 953343	The cairn on the summit of Tinto Hill (712m) is one of the largest bronze-age round cairns in Scotland, measuring 43m in diameter by almost 6m in height
Craignethan Castle NS 815463	A Bronze-Age flanged axe was found here. A nice walk leads from Crossford along the River Nethan.
Fairholm Cairn NS 754516	A cairn 15m in diameter and 1.5m in height. Stone cists were found nearby in the 19th century.
Cadzow Earthwork NS 734534	Iron Age promontory fort. In St Mungo's day there was a King of Cadzow known as Rhydderch Hael.
Carmyle Fords NS 646614	This alignment runs through the west, or King's Ford.
Barrack Street NS 603651	Harry favoured this site because a shell midden found in 1962 suggested Mesolithic occupation.
Cochno Stone NS 504738	Probably the finest examples of rock art in Scotland. Buried underground following 2016 excavation, awaiting funding to commission fabrication of a replica.

29. Drumduff Hill to Carron Ford (16.5km)

Drumduff Hill NS 583462	Harry claimed to have found a turf-built enclosure on this alignment, about 50m southeast of the summit. The location is within the Whitelee wind farm.
Carmyle Fords NS 646614	This alignment runs through the west, or King's Ford.
Provan Hall NS 667663	Harry claims that you can see the Campsie Hills and **Dechmont** hillfort from Provan Hall, but this is impossible nowadays with the surrounding tree cover.
Bar Hill Roman fort NS 707759	The highest fort on the Antonine Wall. Can be approached from Twechar or Croy.
Castle Hill (Bar Hill) NS 709761	Fortified hillfort site predating the Roman fort of **Bar Hill**. From its summit, the Rivers Forth and Clyde can be seen on a clear day.
St Mirren's Well NS 724795	Not mentioned by Harry, but close to the alignment to **Bar Hill**. The water is now piped to Colzium.
Carron Ford NS 743837	The ford lies a stone's through to the east of Carron Bridge and can be seen as a line of stones when the water is low.

In Forgotten Footsteps, *Ley number 8 extends this to **Stirling Castle**.*

30. Woodend Loch to Seedhill Craigs (22.4km)

Woodend Loch NS 706669	Evidence of a Mesolithic settlement on the north bank of the loch. Harry found "two half-buried boulders" of interest some 60m from the water's edge.
Provan Hall NS 667663	Recently refurbished in 2023 and well worth a visit.
Necropolis NS 603654	There are great views over the city from the highest point of the Necropolis by the John Knox statue. On a clear day you can see Tinto Hill, which is 30 miles away.
Ramshorn Cemetery NS 595652	One of Glasgow's oldest burial grounds, once linked to the Blackfriars monastery.
Seedhill Craigs NS 486637	Claimed by Harry to be the site of St Mirin's original settlement and traditionally thought to have been occupied in Roman times. Accessed from the car park of the Watermill Hotel.

31. Woodend Loch to Craw Stane (22km)

Woodend Loch NS 706669	Evidence of a Mesolithic settlement on the north bank of the loch. Harry says "two half-buried boulders" of interest some 60m from the water's edge.
Springhill Farm (site) NS 679644	Site of a Bronze Age burial ground. Not mentioned by Harry, although it is very close to the alignment.
Carmyle Fords NS 646614	"It looked like an excellent place for fording the river"
Cathkin Braes NS 614584	The trig point offers good views over the city. One of several spots where Queen Mary is alleged to have watched the Battle of Langside.
Devil's Plantation NS 557535	An atmospheric place to visit despite the noise from the Southern Relief Road. There is a parking area on the bend and you can access the field through a gate.
Craw Stane NS 545523	Probably a glacial erratic, but Harry thought it was a good sighting point for this PSA. Behind a fence just opposite a small parking area on the road.

32. Walls Hillfort to Craignethan Castle (42.3km)

Walls Hillfort NS 412588	Early Iron Age site, a hillfort of the Damnonii tribe. Not a very prominent site from the north of the city, yet Harry favoured it with three alignments.
Cowdon Hall (rems.) NS 466571	Site of a 17th century laird's house and farm steading. Recorded on Timothy Pont's 16th century map, so the site may be much older.
Neil's Stone (site) NS 478568	Tradition has it that this is the site of a combat between two local chiefs named Arthur and Neil. The OS Names Book repeats this tradition and says that the parish name derives from the stone.
Duncarnock NS 501559	The alignment grazes the north side of the hillfort. Harry had this PSA in the first edition of *Glasgow's Secret Geometry* but omitted it from later versions.
Lickprivick Tumulus NS 610519	Harry records this as "a possible tumulus" but it could also be a possible motte associated with nearby **Lickprivick Castle.**
Double Dykes NS 764479	Large fort occupying a promontory at the north end of Sodom Hill, between the Cander Water and Avon Water. Not recorded by Harry, but bang on the alignment
Craignethan Castle NS 815463	A large site overlooking the River Nethan. There is a nice walk from Crossford bridge that follows the line of the river to the castle.

33. Walls Hillfort to Drumduff Hill (21.3km)

Walls Hillfort NS 412588	Harry speculated about this alignment in the first edition of *Glasgow's Secret Geometry* but omitted it from later versions.
Dunwan Hillfort NS 546489	Only traces remain of an Iron Age hillfort. The site has been much disturbed by cultivation.
Myres Cairn NS 573470	Mentioned in the text of *GSG* when Harry was using it as a sighting point from Drumduff Hill when trying to locate this alignment.
Drumduff Hill NS 583462	Harry was trying to confirm a PSA from Carmyle Fords when he located this sightline centre by lining it up with Myres Cairn and Dunwan Hillfort.

34. Ardoch Rig to Pollock Castle 14.5km)

Ardoch Rig NS 627467	An unremarkable wooded hill inside Whitelee wind farm marks the start of this PSA. The visual alignment along the old Humbie Road is a classic Watkins ley.
Crosslees Cairn (site) NS 564529	Although destroyed, the cover of the cist is built into the wall of the farm on the north side of the road. A benchmark has been inscribed on it.
Devil's Plantation NS 557535	Before the Southern Relief Road was constructed, the Humbie Road used to divert around this mound.
Mearns Kirk NS 543550	A religious site since at least 800CE. The gateposts in the form of sentry boxes date from the era of the Resurrectionists (body snatchers).
Pollock Castle (site) NS 523568	Pollock Castle, also known as Pollok Castle, was a tower house castle located to the west of modern Newton Mearns in East Renfrewshire. A castle was recorded on this site in Timothy Pont's 16th century map.

35. Cathkin Braes to Crookston Castle (9.8km)

Cathkin Braes NS 614584	Cathkin Braes were used for mountain bike trials in the 2014 Commonwealth Games.
Cathcart Castle (rems.) NS 587600	A 15th century castle, demolished in 1980 following a partial collapse. There is a fallen Queen Mary's stone nearby, marking yet another location where she supposedly watched the Battle of Langside.
Nether Pollok Castle (site) NS 550616	A 13th century castle that stood on a rock now occupied by the stable block of Pollok House.
Crookston Castle NS 525627	Harry speculated that the site could be prehistoric, but no archaeological evidence has been found to support this theory.

36. Cathkin Braes to Bonhill Bronze Age burial site (30km)

Cathkin Braes NS 614584	There is a spring called **Queen Mary's Well** a short distance from the sighting centre, where the Queen is said to have watered her horse.
King's Park NS 595605	Harry recorded a "roughly oval outline, 12m x 7m" near the Menock Road entrance.
Roman coin found NS 588612	A worn bronze coin of Valentinian I (CE 364-75) was dug up in a garden in Norfield Drive, Mount Florida.
Camphill Ringwork NS 577621	There is a possible winter solstice sunrise alignment in the stones, and an equinox sunset alignment to the outlier down the slope.
Sheils Farm (site) NS 525667	There are several features of interest in this area of Braehead. Harry specifically mentions a henge site excavated in 1973-74.
Old Kilpatrick Roman fort (site) NS 459732	A large fort at the western terminus of the Antonine Wall, now buried under a housing estate. Some Bronze Age cists were excavated here in 1923 and 1924.
Greenland cup marked stone NS 449740	A sandstone boulder with three cup marks was recorded at this location on the slopes of Hill of Dun in 1896, but subsequent searches have failed to find it.
Bonhill Bronze Age cemetery NS 393793	Several cists of Early Bronze Age type containing human remains without urns have been found in Strathleven Sand and Gravel quarry. Harry mentions this site in the text of *Glasgow's Secret Geometry* but doesn't elaborate on the name or location.

37. Dechmont Hill to Auchendavy Roman fort (16.8km)

Dechmont Fort NS 656582	Harry says that "Beltane fires were lit here until the beginning of the 19th century." Little remains of the fort.
Provan Hall NS 667663	"As far back as 1120, a jury in Cumbria took oath that the lands of Provan belonged of old to the kirk of Glasgow."
Duntiblae Mound NS 675730	There is an intriguing tree-clad mound at this location that is reminiscent of the **De'il's Plantin** but is otherwise unrecorded. Yet it sits squarely on this alignment and I've added it to increase the site count on an otherwise poor 3-site ley. *(Reported by Louise Hamilton)*
Auchendavy Roman Fort NS 677749	Five roman altars were found here and can be seen in the Hunterian Museum, but the site has never been excavated. It is largely covered with buildings and there are no visible remains.

38. Torrance House to Duncolm (30.75km)

Torrance House NS 654526	"A possible rectangular motte was reported on a promontory beside the River Calder in the north angle of the park."
Mains Castle & Motte NS 627560	"Bronze-Age cairns, cists and urns have been discovered in the vicinity."
Carmunnock Ringwork NS 613577	"Circular ditch with slighted rampart on the 13th green of **Cathkin Braes** Golf Course."
Camphill Ringwork NS 577621	Some say that the stones at the top of the hill were a result of 18th century road clearance works.
Roman coins found NS 528692	Several Roman coins have been found on Knightswood Golf Course.
Peel of Drumry (site) NS 514711	A square tower built around 1530, demolished in 1959. Possibly an earlier structure occupied the same site, because as far back as 1329 "ye ladye of Drumry" is mentioned in old records.
Cleddans Roman Fortlet NS 508722	A Roman fortlet that predates the Antonine Wall which abuts it at the north-east corner at a sharp angle. Not mentioned by Harry.
Duncolm NS 470774	Highest of the Kilpatrick Hills and a stiff walk from the car park at Old Kilpatrick.

Other Harry Bell PSAs

39. Stirling to Dun I — 'The Old Straight Track to Iona' (153.7km)

Harry describes this as a flight of artistic fancy, saying that. "The Old Straight Track to Iona that filled a vacant space in the top left-hand corner is a piece of New Age nonsense inspired by the 'geomantic corridors' and long-distance ley-lines in vogue at the time. It was once said of it 'only a crow or a holy man with a paraglider could travel that way'."

Stirling Castle NS 789940	"Built on a volcanic plug. Remains of a vitrified hill fort occupy the north end of the outcrop. The present castle dates back to the 12th Century and holds a prominent place in Scottish history."
Ben Lomond NN 367028	"The cairn at the top doesn't look prehistoric, but who can say when the mountain was first climbed and for what reason?"
Dun I NM 284252	Highest point on Iona at 101m (333 ft).

40. Dunstaffnage Castle to Ben Cruachan (18.3km)

Dunstaffnage Castle NM 882344	"Like many more of Scotland's haunted castles, Dunstaffnage stands on a ley-line."
Inverawe House NN 022315	Mentioned in *Haunted Castles*. The ghost has an interesting connection with the Campbells of Inveraray.
Ben Cruachan NN 069304	Sacred mountain associated with the *Cailleach*. Cruachan Power Station is located deep within the mountain, like the lair of a Bond villain, and is well worth visiting.

41. Glamis Castle to Finavon Castle (14km)

Glamis Castle NO 386480	"Undoubtedly the most haunted house in Scotland..."
Berrymoss Wood NO 397489	A linear cropmark that is suggestive of a possible souterrain was recorded on aerial photography.
Carse Grey NO 462538	Three stones remain of a four-poster stone circle in the wood near to Carse Grey mansion house.
Finavon Castle NO 496564	Former seat of the Earls of Crawford that has stood in ruins for about 200 years.

42. Glamis Castle to Baldoukie (13.5km)

Glamis Castle NO 386480	Glamis' most famous ghost is probably the Grey Lady, who haunts the chapel and has been seen on several occasions.
St Orland's Stone NO 400500	Class II Pictish carved stone, eight feet high, still in its original position. It is carved with a cross on one side and several Pictish symbols on the other.
St Ninian's Chapel, Redford NO 415519	A private walled burial-ground on the SW side of the A926 stands on the site of a church or chapel dedicated to St Ninian.
Baldoukie NO 467588	The remains of a tumulus and souterrain, now much reduced by cultivation.

43. Muchalls Castle to Crathes Castle (16.5km)

Muchalls Castle NO 891918	Early 17th century mansion. A vault, ruinous in 1864, probably the Donjon Keep or Prison, on the south side of the castle, is traditionally much older than the rest.
Clune Wood NO 794949	Recumbent stone circle with ring cairn within the southern edge of Clune Wood.
Crathes Pit Alignment NO 737966	A series of five aligned pits were discovered in 2013. Analysis suggests that these comprise the world's oldest known lunar calendar dating from 8000 BCE to about 4000 BCE.
Crathes Castle NO 734968	Haunted by a ghost known as 'The Green Lady', who is seen with a child in her arms. In the 1800s, workmen discovered the skeletal remains of a woman and a child beneath the hearthstone of the fireplace.

44. Dunburgidale to Holy Island (From *Leyline Quest*) (39km)

Hilton chambered cairn NS 066685	This ruinous cairn above Kames Bay can be added to the alignment on the map, but Holy Island is not visible from this location.
Dunburgidale NS 062660	Harry suggests Dunburgidale fort as the terminus of this *Leyline Quest* ley, but it's some distance off the alignment. The OS trig point near Acholter (NS 066664) fits better.
Loch Dhu crannog NS 062613	Now submerged beneath the waters of Loch Dhu reservoir.
Loch Quien (north) crannog NS 061592	There are two crannogs in Loch Quien, this is the northern one. Harry's picture shows the south crannog, but it doesn't fit the alignment.
Ardnahoe fort NS 066574	Not mentioned by Harry, but neatly on the alignment to Holy Island.
Holy Island NS 063297	The summit of Mullach Mor is visible on this alignment. In *Leyline Quest*, Harry mentions this as one end of a ley running through Bute.

Additional leys by Grahame Gardner

Most of these alignments have been charted on the map but not checked 'in the field'. However, they all connect with one or more of Harry's sites and are included for that reason. Future investigation is encouraged.

45. Stanelie Castle to Bardowie Castle (16.7km)

Stanelie Castle NS 463616	A 16th century tower house bizarrely now located on an island in a reservoir. A Roman medal was found in 1829.
Paisley Abbey NS 485639	"Tradition has it that the site was also occupied in pre-Roman times."
Roman coin found NS 535691	"A Roman bronze coin of the Byzantine Emperor Justin I (AD 518-527) was found by Mr Armstrong, 55 Pikeman Road In 1950 in his garden."
Knightswood Cross NS 537693	No known ancient provenance, but Knightswood Cross is an intersection containing four churches and is situated at the crossing point of two putative alignments.
Boclair Roman Fortlet NS 568725	This is the expected location of a Roman interval fortlet; however, only the stone base of the Antonine Wall was found during a 1961 test trench excavation.
Bardowie Castle NS 578737	Dates from the 16th century with late 17th or early 18th century additions. Still inhabited as a modern mansion house.

46. Cochno Stone to Renfrew Parish Church (16.4km)

Only a three-point alignment, included because of its Ludovic Mann connection.

Cochno Stone NS 504738	Now buried once more following a 2016 excavation for LIDAR and photogrammetry scanning.
Knappers Farm 'Druid Temple' NS 506712	Postulated Bronze Age henge reconstruction in 1937 by renegade Glasgow archaeologist Ludovic McLellan Mann, who theorised that it was constructed to commemorate a total solar eclipse, and that the site was linked to the **Cochno Stone** to the north.
Renfrew Parish Church NS 507675	The first record of an existing church at Renfrew occurs in 1136, when it was given to **Glasgow Cathedral**, yet Harry thought this could be on a prehistoric site.

47. Neilston Pad to Inchinnan All Hallows Church (13.1km)

Neilston Pad NS 44551	Prominent hill visible from many areas of north Glasgow and **Crookston Castle**, yet not mentioned at all by Harry.
Neil's Stone (site) NS 478568	There is another standing stone in a field some 215m to the northeast, but it is not connected with this one.
Seedhill Craigs NS 486637	Old fording point of the river and the site of St Mirin's original settlement according to Harry.
Paisley Abbey NS 485639	Believed to be on the site of a shrine to St Mirin. The site is also supposed to have been occupied in pre-Roman times.
Inchinnan All Hallows Church NS 491680	A Templar site thought to be the burial place of St Conval. Harry mentions it in the text of *Glasgow's Secret Geometry*, but it is not recorded on his original map.

48. Neilston Pad to Balmuildy Roman Fort (19.7km)

Neilston Pad NS 44551	An earthwork bank on the summit encloses an area or about 26 acres, according to Canmore.
Arthurlie Cross NS 499585	The original site is believed to have been at NS 497581. Now protected by railings at the corner of Carnock Street and Springhill Road.
Crookston Castle NS 525627	The second oldest remaining building in Glasgow, after **Glasgow Cathedral.**
Balmuildy Roman Fort NS 581717	"Scarcely visible remains of a fort that guarded a crossing of the River Kelvin. This fort pre-dated the Antonine Wall, and it has been suggested that native traffic crossed the frontier at this point."

49. Dean Castle to The Bogle Stone (35.7km)

Dean Castle NS 436394	Harry mentions this site as they used to sell his *Forgotten Footsteps* book in the shop, until some local schoolchildren conducted a séance in the castle and claimed to have contacted a ghost called 'The Grey Lady'.
Cairn Duff NS 420451	Situated a little way off this alignment, Cairn Duff was almost entirely removed about 1810. It was a large mound of stones covered with grass and trees.
Clochoderick Stone NS 373612	Supposedly the burial place of King Rhyderrich Hael of Strathclyde. Often used by Harry and friends as a rendezvous point on cycling expeditions.
Duchal House NS 352679	Private residence, but the gardens are sometimes open to the public on special occasions.
Bronze axehead (Kilmacolm) NS 350689	Excavated by Ludovic McLellan Mann and now on display in the British Museum, according to Canmore.
Craigmarloch Wood NS 341723	Canmore records this as a turf and stone walled enclosure of uncertain date.
Stone axe (Port Glasgow) NS 340726	A fragment of a green stone axehead was found while digging in the garden of 59 Slaemuir Avenue, Port Glasgow. It was retained by the resident. (Canmore)
Bogle Stane NS 336736	This stone once stood 4m tall but the local minister had it blown up. It now has a maximum height of 1m and lies in several pieces. Folklore tells of a bogle who used to hide behind the stone and jump out to scare passers-by.

50. Devil's Head (Doune) to Duncryne (33km)

A possible extension of Harry's Dundee Law to Doune Cross PSA, although there are few sites along this section due to the marshy and inhospitable terrain.

Devil's Head or Fairy Stone NN 725018	Folklore records children dancing in a ring around this stone while chanting a rhyme to banish the Devil. Also called the Trysting Stone.
Boghall roundhouse NS 678992	A Late Prehistoric ring-ditch house was identified from crop markings.
Buchlyvie Fairy Knowe (Broch-rems) NS 585942	Excavation in 1976 discovered remains of a broch constructed over an earlier wooden roundhouse, possibly 1st century AD.
Drymen Parish Church NS 474880	The present church was built in 1771, but a number of earlier gravestones in the burial ground, one of which is dated 1618, suggest that this is a much older site.
Duncryne NS 435859	Folklore says that this was "once the home of wizards". Harry reports that witches were reputed to dance on its summit at Hallowe'en.

51. Stirling Castle to Dumyat (5.8km)

Stirling Castle NS 789940	One of Scotland's top tourist attractions and well worth a visit. The Royal Palace with its 'Stirling Heads' ceiling has been expertly restored to its former glory.
Abbey Craig NS 810957 74628	The construction of the Wallace Monument did immense damage to this (probably) prehistoric hillfort. William Wallace is said to have watched from the hillfort before the Battle of Stirling Bridge.
Blairlogie Castle NS 827969	A relatively modest tower house dating only from the 16th century, but it sits nicely on this alignment.
Castle Law (Dumyat) NS 832973	Early Iron Age fort, inhabited by the Pictish Meatae tribe.
Dumyat NS 835976	Several hut circles and enclosures around Dumyat suggest a long history of habitation. A polished greenstone axe was found near the summit in 1927.

Other alignments

52. Camphill to Lady Isle (44.6km)

This is May Miles Thomas' 'The Secret' alignment from her *Devil's Plantation* iPhone app and is an extension of 'The Straight Road with No Path'. Intermediate sites have been added by Grahame.

Camphill Ringwork NS 577621	This alignment is taken from the group of stones at the top end of the ringwork.
Black Law NS 464501	Described on Canmore as an Iron Age hillfort and galleried structure. Situated on a volcanic plug, the ridge closely follows the alignment.
Dod Hill NS 493532	'Dod' is often associated with leys, according to Alfred Watkins. There is a 19m diameter cairn on the hilltop.
Cairn Duff NS 420451	Cairn Duff was a large mound of stones covered with grass and trees. Three urns containing cremated human bones were found in it.
Lady Isle NS 275293	This small islet has a freshwater spring in the centre and once held a small chapel dedicated to Mary.

53. The Royal Mile Ley (1.8km)

Edinburgh Castle NT 251734	"First mentioned in a 6th century Old Welsh poem *'The Gododdin of Aneurin'*. The oldest part of the present castle is Queen Margaret's chapel, which dates back to the 11th Century." (FF)
The Hub NT 255735	Former Assembly of Church of Scotland, the spire of which is the highest point in central Edinburgh. The site was once called The Witches' Knowe.
St Giles Cathedral NT 257736	"A Celtic parish church occupied this site in the 9th Century. St Giles is a ley crossroads and appropriately enough, the Mercat Cross from which royal proclamations are read stands nearby on the site of an earlier cross."(FF)
Tron Kirk Edinburgh NT 259738	The Tron Kirk, Edinburgh's parish church, was started in 1637 but not completed until 1678 because of delays caused by the Wars of the Covenant after 1638. It was Edinburgh's first Presbyterian kirk, free of the taint of Catholicism attached to the history of Greyfriars and **St Giles.**
John Knox House NT 260737	Popularly known as 'John Knox's House', this historic house is reputed to have been owned and lived in by Protestant reformer John Knox during the 16th century.

St John's Cross NT 234737	This Maltese cross set in the road marks the site of the Burgh Cross, which now stands in the corner of Canongate kirkyard. It was known as St John's Cross, because it stood on property belonging to the Knights of St John, and it marked the ancient boundary of Edinburgh which lay outwith the Netherbow Port.
Canongate Kirk Edinburgh NT 265738	The kirk is the parish church for the **Palace of Holyroodhouse**, the official home of the Queen in Scotland. The churchyard contains the remains of many famous Scots, including economist Adam Smith, poet Robert Fergusson, and Mrs Agnes McLehose (Burns's Clarinda).
Scottish Parliament NT 267738	Built in 1998, the parliament complex was designed by the Catalan architect Enric Miralles and incorporates the 17th century Queensberry House within the building complex.
Holyrood Palace NT 269739	Holyrood Palace has served as the principal residence of the Kings and Queens of Scots since the 16th century, and is a setting for state occasions and official entertaining.

54. The Lothian Line (Philip Coppens) (60km)

Cairnpapple Hill NS 987718	Impressive Neolithic henge site in the Bathgate Hills. Probably the most important prehistoric site in Central Scotland.
Athur's Seat (Dunsapie Hillfort) NT 281731	This fort is situated on the broad summit of Dunsapie overlooking Dunsapie Loch, near the car park. The alignment passes just to the north of **Arthur's seat** summit.
Traprain Law NT 580747	One of the largest prehistoric forts in Scotland, home to the Gododdin, or Votadinii as the Romans named them. A cache of buried Roman silver was unearthed during excavations in 1919.

55. A Victorian Church Ley (Great Western Road) (9.75km)

The National Piping Centre NS 588660	Formerly Cowcaddens Free Church of Scotland, this building is now home to the National Piping Centre and includes a hotel and The Piper's Tryst restaurant. This is actually situated on Cowcaddens but is on the same alignment, which can even be extended to Harry's **Barrack Street** site at this end.

St Stephen's Free Church of Scotland (site) NS 582664	The 1892-1914 25-inch OS map records a Free Church on the corner of New City Road and Steven Street here. The site is now occupied by the Andalus Mosque.
St George's Cross NS 581665	Where Great Western Road takes over from New City Road. Once an important junction, recalled by the St George and the Dragon statue. Notable as the joining point of the two subterranean aqueducts bringing Glasgow's water supply from the Mugdock reservoirs. The access hatches are visible in the pavement. The alignment also passes through the St George's Cross Subway building.
Findlay Memorial Tabernacle NS 581666	An Independent Evangelical Church, hidden behind tenements about 80m north of St George's X. The church was founded by David Jack Findlay, who became a Christian in 1874 under the preaching of the American evangelist, DL Moody. Findlay started a kitchen meeting in a small tenement flat just north of the existing church, and very quickly became a popular preacher. In 1894, after several years of large tent missions in the St George's Cross area, the church was built, and was first known as the 'Tabernacle'. The hall is also used by the Chinese Christian Church.
Al-Furqan mosque NS 579666	Formerly Burnbank United Presbyterian Church, noted on the 1892-1914 25-inch OS map, the building is now the Al-Furqan mosque, situated about 30m south of the alignment in Carrington Street.
St Mary's Cathedral (Episcopal) NS 577668	This Category 'A' listed building was opened on 9 November 1871 as St Mary's Episcopal Church. The architect was Sir Gilbert Scott, although the spire was completed by his son J Oldrid Scott in 1893.
Woodside Parish Church (site) NS 576668	The former Woodside Parish Church, now demolished, stood on the corner of Montague Street. The site is now occupied by a Caffe Nero and a Tesco Express.
Webster's Theatre NS 575669	Formerly Lansdowne United Presbyterian Church, regarded as Glasgow's finest example of Gothic Revival architecture and claims to have the slenderest steeple in Europe. Designed by John Honeyman and completed in 1863. Category 'A' listed and on the Buildings at Risk register. Now run by the Four Acres Charitable Trust as Webster's Theatre, Bar and Playhouse.
Oran Mor NS 568673	Formerly Kelvinside Free Church, now houses bars, a restaurant, a theatre and wedding venue. Eight bells within the spire of the church are dedicated to the memory of local men lost in the First World War, and are still rung on the 11th November each year.

Struthers Memorial church NS 560677	Formerly Westbourne Free Church. Around 80m off the alignment, but worth visiting for its fine Italian Renaissance exterior.
Anniesland Halls NS 547686	Anniesland Mansions Hall was formerly used as a church — Anniesland Hall Church of Christian Brethren. It still sometimes hosts a gospel congregation.
Anniesland Cross NS 546688	Once considered the busiest junction in Britain, perhaps Anniesland Cross' most memorable feature is the former public toilets on the south side of Great Western Road, now marooned on an island. During the pandemic of 2020, work was started to convert them into a tapas bar. This is the termination of the straight section of Great Western Road, but the alignment continues through **Knightswood Cross.**
Knightswood Cross NS 537693	Not an ancient site by any standards, but this complex intersection houses four churches around it. A Roman coin was unearthed in a nearby garden.
St Margaret's Church NS 536693	Built 1928-32, St Margaret's was Sir Robert Lorimer's very last church, completed posthumously by JF Matthew in Lorimer's Scottish style with Baltic-inspired profile. Hipped end roof and Arts & Crafts interior features.
Knappers Farm NS 507713	Bronze Age burial ground excavated in 1937 by renegade Glasgow archaeologist Ludovic McLellan Mann, who called it a "mortuary house". Mann's theories were not popular with the rest of the archaeological establishment at the time. Strangely, given that he was familiar with Mann's work, Harry does not mention either site in *Glasgow's Secret Geometry.* The alignment can be extended in this direction as far as Ben More on Mull and marks the direction of the Beltane (1 May)/ Lughnasadh (1 August) sunset.

Selected Bibliography

Items marked with * are from the 1993 edition of *Glasgow's Secret Geometry*

Barr, William W	*Glaswegiana*, Vista, 1973
Bell, Harry	*Forgotten Footsteps*, Ley Line Publications, 1974 *Guide to the Haunted Castles of Scotland*, Ley Line Publications, 1981 *Glasgow's Secret Geometry*, Ley Line Publications, 1983 *Leyline Quest* (website), 2000
Biltcliffe, Gary & Hoare, Caroline	*The Holy Axis*, Sacred Lands Publishing, 2023
Brotchie, TCF	*Battlefields of Scotland*, TC & EC Jack, Edinburgh, 1913 *Glasgow Rivers and Streams*, James Maclehose & Sons, 1914 *Scottish Western Holiday Haunts*, John Menzies, 1914 *Some Sylvan Scenes Near Glasgow*, Aird & Coghill, 1921 *The Borderlands of Glasgow*, Glasgow Corporation, 1925
*Brown, Christina R	*Rural Eaglesham*, 1966
Daiches, David	*Glasgow*, Grafton Books, 1982
Forbes, Alexander Penrose (compiler)	*Lives of St Ninian and St Kentigern* in the series *The Historians of Scotland Vol. V*, Maclehose, 1874
Forman, Carol	*Hidden Glasgow* Birlion, 2008
Furlong, David	*Earth Energies*, Piatkus, 2003
James, Heather F	*Tracing the Past, excavations at All Hallows, Inchinnan 2017*, Inchinnan Historical Interest Group, 2018
Jocelyn of Furness	*Life of Kentigern*. Translated by Cynthis Whiddon Green, 1998. Referenced at: *sourcebooks.fordham.edu/basis/Jocelyn-LifeofKentigern.asp*
Knight, Peter and Perrott, Tony	*The Wessex Astrum*, Stone Seeker Publishing, 2008
Lees, Ian C	*The Campsies and the Lands of Lennox*, Blackie & Sons, 1933
Lockyer, Sir Norman	*Stonehenge and other British Stone Monuments Astronomically Considered*, Macmillan & Co., 1906. Referenced at: *archive.org/details/stonehengeandot00lockgoog*
Lugton, Thomas	*The Old Ludgings of Glasgow*, 1901
Macdonald, Hugh	*Rambles Round Glasgow*, Thomas Murray & Son, 1856. Referenced via Google Books

MacGeorge, Andrew   *Old Glasgow: The Place and the People*, Blackie and Son, 1880 p.136. Referenced at: *archive.org/details/oldglasgowfromr00macggoog*

Macintosh, Hugh   *The Origin and History of Glasgow Streets*, James Hedderwick, 1902

*McArthy, Mary   *A Social Geography of Paisley*, 1969

Mann, Ludovic   *Archaic Sculpturings in Dumfries and Galloway*, 1914. Referenced by Michael Behrend: *www.cantab.net/users/michael.behrend/repubs/mann_afr/pages/intro.html*
Earliest Glasgow, A Temple of the Moon, Mann Publishing, 1939
Mary, Queen of Scots at Langside, Mann Publishing 1918

Márkus, Gilbert   *Rock-Rider, Saint Conval and his church at Inchinnan*, Inchinnan Historical Interest Group, 2018

Metcalfe, WM   *A History of Paisley, 1840-1916*, Alexander Gardner, Paisley 1909

Michell, John   *The View Over Atlantis*, Abacus, 1969

Moffat, Alistair   *Scotland's Forgotten Past*, Thames & Hudson, 2023

*Morris, RBW   *The Prehistoric Rock Art of Southern Scotland*, 1981

Ritchie, Anna   *Govan and its Carved Stones*, Pinkfoot Press, 1999

Robb, Graham   *The Ancient Paths*, Picador, 2013

*Robertson, Anne S   *The Antonine Wall*, 4th edition, 1990

Screeton, Paul   *Quicksilver Heritage*, Abacus, 1977

SERF   *Strathearn Environs & Royal Forteviot Project Report 2006-2009*

*Shearer, WR   *Rutherglen Lore*, 1922

Simpson, Hubert L   *Saint Mungo (Kentigern)*, Gowans & Gray Ltd., Glasgow 1918

*Thomson, Rev TBS   *A Guide to Govan Old Parish Church*, 1963

*Ure, J   *History of Rutherglen and East Kilbride*, 1793

*Waddell, JJ   *Rambles Through Lanarkshire*, 1911

Watkins, Alfred   *The Old Straight Track*, Abacus, 1974
Early British Trackways, 1921. Source: Resurrection Press, 2004
www.ancient-wisdom.com/alfredwatkinslecture.pdf

Watson, David   *A Guide to Castlerigg Stone Circle*, 2015

*Welsh, Thomas C   *Eastwood District History and Heritage*, 1989

Hamlyn Encyclopedic World Dictionary   Accessed at: *archive.org/details/encyclopedicworl0000unse/mode/*

Index